MUSLIM CITIES IN THE LATER MIDDLE AGES

Published under the auspices of the Joint Center for Urban Studies of the Massachusetts Institute of Technology and Harvard University and the Center for Middle Eastern Studies, Harvard University.

MUSLIM CITIES IN THE LATER MIDDLE AGES

by Ira Marvin Lapidus

Harvard University Press, Cambridge, Massachusetts 1967

Distributed in Great Britain by Oxford University Press, London
Library of Congress Catalog Card Number 66-21339
Printed in the United States of America

TO MY MOTHER AND FATHER

PREFACE

This book is a study of the social structure and political processes of several Muslim cities in the late middle ages. Although its different perspectives are not always explicitly discussed, a number of problems in Islamic and medieval history and in the sociology of premodern cities lie behind the formulation of its hypotheses. From the point of view of Islamic history, this is an effort to examine the relationship between military regimes, composed of slave castes, and the local communities they ruled. This relationship is of utmost importance in understanding the nature of Islamic cities, and to our present appreciation of their structures this book seeks to add some consideration of the dynamic interactions between different classes and groups of the populations which created communal and political order.

Furthermore, in the context of medieval history, this book may also serve as a commentary on the problem of why European cities were organized as communes and why Asian cities in general, and Muslim cities in particular, were without autonomous self-governing associations. Behind these differences in political form lay social conditions and processes of a more general kind. By exploring these processes and attempting to see city life in terms of the actions and relationships between their various elites and groups of residents, rather than in terms of formal governmental or communal institutions, we may be able to transcend the dichotomies between European and Asian, between communal and noncommunal, between traditional and modern, and suggest other perspectives for the study of urban history. If I be not presumptuous, I think this approach more in accord with newly developing sociological conceptions and their stress on cities as process rather than cities as form.

However, I leave the full exploration of these possibilities to my readers, and confine myself in this book to a description of several Muslim cities. The book concentrates on Damascus and Aleppo in the period of the Mamluk Empire, 1250–1517, with supporting studies of the Mamluk capital of Cairo. Occasionally, when it seemed that the situations of all the cities must be similar, information based on the study of Cairo has been used to answer important questions for which data on the Syrian cities are lacking. Other cities in the Mamluk Empire, Alexandria, Beirut, Tripoli, and smaller towns, are also discussed.

The sources for a study of the social and political processes of these cities are many. They include chronicles, biographies, inscriptions, descriptions of towns, administrative manuals, travelers' reports, diplomatic correspondence, treaties, works of art, and archeological and artistic remains. Interpreting these materials poses many problems because they do not analyze the society out of which they came in terms which directly answer our present questions about historical reality. The information they give us about economic, social, and many political realities are but laconic references, abbreviations, clues which must have been meaningful to contemporaries but which are enigmatic for us. Any study of the period in which they were recorded requires gathering a multitude of tiny details, questioning their meaning, and using each one to cast light on the others until finally they begin to reveal the society which recorded them.

In preface to the study itself, however, a few paragraphs of explanation about the form of presentation which these innumerable details have required may be of help.

The argument of the book is presented in a manner which I hope will satisfy the interests of both the lay reader and the specialist in Islamic studies. An effort has been made to reduce Arabic terminology in the text to a minimum. Arabic words which have been accepted into standard English usage are presented as spelled in English, without transliteration or diacritical marks. Such words as Koran, sheikh, qadi, madrasa, ulama, Sufi, Shari'a, dirhem, and dinar are treated as English words. Many of these words, however, will nonetheless be unfamiliar to the lay reader and will be defined in a note. Arabic terms are also defined when they are used, but an effort has been made to substitute English equivalents wherever accurate translation is possible or approximate equivalents will suffice. English plural endings have been substituted for Arabic plurals. In the notes, however, all the technical terms are presented in precise transliterated form for the use of specialists. The transliteration system of the *Encyclopaedia of Islam* is used for Arabic words, except that the letters ḳ and d̲j̲ are rendered q and j.

Dates are generally given in both the Muslim and Christian eras in that order. The Muslim era dates will assist the specialist reader in referring to the sources. Centuries and occasionally regnal dates are quoted in Christian era only. In the notes Muslim era dates are used alone except when Christian sources are cited. Cities, villages, territories, and geographical features are located on the accompanying maps.

The system of notes requires a special explanation. Although the notes are basically intended to record references to the sources, a certain amount of supplementary substantive material is often included. Each note brings together all of the citations relevant to the topic of the paragraph or paragraphs to which it corresponds. It would have been impossible to number and record each bit of information separately. The interested reader will thus find it easy to explore all the materials on a topic, but awkward in some cases to identify the source of any particular assertion within a paragraph. Not *all* of the citations support each and every point in the text but notes which contain numerous citations are usually subdivided in order to facilitate search for a particular citation. Still it may be necessary to consult several citations before the correct one may be located.

The innumerable bits of evidence on which the study is constructed have also required special treatment of the form of the citations themselves. Limitations of space and cost make it impossible to cite each source of information in a fully explicit way. Instead, every work used in the preparation of this study has been assigned a number in the bibliography. Citations in the notes use these numbers in lieu of the name of the text to refer to the exact source. Commonly, but not always, they are prefaced by one word to indicate the author's name or a key word in the title of the work for readers who may not wish to examine the text itself, but would like to have a more convenient way of identifying the source. (Occasional books used only once or which came to the attention of the author after the completion of the manuscript are fully cited in the notes.) I apologize for the double task thus imposed, for the reader will have to look once to the notes and once again to the bibliography, but this has seemed the only feasible way of presenting the references at all. Even the usual method of abbreviated titles and authors' names would prove too lengthy and unsatisfactory in the many cases where the same work has been used in different manuscripts and printed editions. Volume and page numbers are cited immediately after the bibliography number. Manuscripts, however, pose special problems. In cases where the several volumes of a work have different library shelf marks, the notes will cite them as if they were volumes in sequence. For example, the manuscripts numbered Bodleian 803 and 812 in the bibliography will simply be cited as vol. I and II in the notes. References to manuscripts which have no pagination are made by the years in which the event in question occurred.

These cumbersome arrangements are entirely the work of the author but for important matters I am indebted and deeply grateful to the many people who have helped me prepare this book. Seemingly impersonal institutions have sustained this project. My thanks go to the Foreign Area Training Fellowship Program which supported much of my early training and gave me the opportunity to study essential manuscripts abroad, to the National Defense Foreign Language Training Program of the United States Government, and to the Joint Center for Urban Studies of the Massachusetts Institute of Technology and Harvard University which generously supported the completion of the book. I am particularly grateful to James Q. Wilson, formerly director of the Joint Center, and Derwood W. Lockard, associate director of the Harvard Center for Middle Eastern Studies, for their helpfulness and encouragement.

My thanks go also to Carol Cross, Janet Eckstein, and Brenda Sens, who have all labored through the preparation of successive manuscripts with cheerful patience and unfailing accuracy; to Barbara Larson who thoughtfully systematized the presentation of the bibliography; to Bruce G. Inksetter and Mustafa al-Musawi for assistance in compiling biographical data; to librarians everywhere for their courtesy and helpfulness, but especially to Dr. Azzat el-Hosn of the al-Ẓāhiriyya Library of Damascus and Mr. George Vajda of the Bibliothèque Nationale who called my attention to manuscripts which have proved very valuable.

I am especially grateful to Robert Bellah, Norton Long, and Charles Tilly, whose reflections about its sociological implications have illuminated this study, to Professor George Makdisi for his assistance with some of the Arabic problems of the research and his help in planning for study of manuscripts abroad, and to Professors Claude Cahen and Bernard Lewis, whose thoughtful criticisms and advice have been invaluable. William Brinner, Bernard Lewis, Stanford Shaw, Charles Tilly, and Avram Udovitch have read the final manuscript and made innumerable suggestions to improve and clarify the book. They have helped me beyond my ability to repay them. To Avram Udovitch whose careful reading of the manuscript and whose intimate knowledge of Islamic law has helped refine many of the findings I give special thanks.

What I owe to my wife Gail is best known to herself. Suffice it to say that she has many times read and considered this book, assisted with the details of its presentation, pondered it with me, foreseen its possibilities, and helped me think it through. To my teacher, Sir Hamilton Gibb, whose knowledge, wisdom, and grace of guiding have inspired this book, I owe not only the work in hand, but the better part of my education.

Berkeley, California
August 1966

I.M.L.

CONTENTS

INTRODUCTION 1

CHAPTER I · A HISTORY OF CITIES IN THE MAMLUK EMPIRE 9

The Pacification of Syria: 1260–1317
Prosperity and Security: The Fourteenth Century
The Time of Troubles: 1388–1422
The Fifteenth Century Restoration: 1422–1470
The Fall of the Mamluk Empire: 1470–1517

CHAPTER II · THE MAMLUK REGIME IN THE LIFE OF THE CITIES 44

The State and the Privatization of Power
The Economic Powers of the Mamluk Household
Controls over Property, Labor, and Materials
The Emirs in the Functioning of the Urban Community
Conclusion

CHAPTER III · THE URBAN SOCIETY 79

The Classes of the Population
The Organization of the Quarters
The Organization of Economic Life
Fraternal Associations on the Margin of Society
The Ulama and the Formation of an Urban Society
Conclusion

CHAPTER IV · THE POLITICAL SYSTEM: THE MAMLUK STATE AND THE URBAN NOTABLES 116

The Merchants
The Ulama
Conclusion

CHAPTER V · THE POLITICAL SYSTEM: THE COMMON PEOPLE BETWEEN VIOLENCE AND IMPOTENCE 143

Economic Grievances and the Protests of the Common People
The Roles of the Damascus *Zu'ar*
Mamluk Controls over Popular Military Actions
The Control of Lumpenproletarian Violence
Conclusion

CHAPTER VI · CONCLUSION: SOCIETY AND POLITY IN MEDIEVAL MUSLIM CITIES 185

APPENDIX A · WAQFS 195

APPENDIX B · INSTITUTIONAL CONSTRUCTIONS AND REPAIRS—DAMASCUS 199

APPENDIX C · INSTITUTIONAL CONSTRUCTIONS AND REPAIRS—ALEPPO 207

APPENDIX D · KĀRIMI (MERCHANTS IN THE SPICE TRADE) 211

APPENDIX E · TĀJIR-KHAWĀJĀ (MERCHANTS WITH OFFICIAL RANKING)

BIBLIOGRAPHY 217

NOTES 243

INDEX 295

MAPS

The Mamluk Empire 10
Aleppo at the Beginning of the Sixteenth Century 45
Damascus and Environs 47
Cairo 49

MUSLIM CITIES IN THE LATER MIDDLE AGES

INTRODUCTION

SELF-GOVERNING COMMUNE, bureaucratically administered city—this dichotomy has long dominated the study of medieval cities. The former term has come to describe European, the latter Asian cities, for communal associations have seemed crucial in accounting for differences in their experience. Our understanding of Asian, and of Muslim cities in particular, has suffered from this point of view. Idealizations of the European commune have so captured the imagination of historians that many have taken it to be the pure form of premodern city organization. The assembly of self-governing citizens or their chosen representatives has seemed to be the true, complete, and ideal fulfillment of city life. Communal associations enabled medieval European cities to overthrow imperial oppressors and other overlords, and to enjoy a vital and intense commercial life. Some of them sustained the crusades and the great adventures of European expansion, and formed within themselves the culture of the Renaissance.[1]

By contrast, many historians have imagined the Muslim world as governed by empires whose great bureaucracies snuffed out the independence of the towns. In Muslim cities the antique heritage of communal independence and voluntary association for public ends had been eliminated. Muslim cities are never regarded as communities but as collections of isolated internal groups unable to cooperate in any endeavor of the whole, with notables capable of common action only on an exceptional and ad hoc basis—as cities governed by fixed administrative arrangements imposed by imperial regimes, and by the ascription, through unchanging tradition, of certain essential tasks to different classes and bodies of the society. Rarely have they been understood as living and vital organisms. Observers have studied the development of towns as a consequence of the establishment of the Muslim empires, or of broad economic movements, or of the presumed requirements of the Islamic religion for urban settings, and the interior life of the cities has been discussed as if it were but a complex of religious and commercial facilities. Students have stressed the physical formlessness of Muslim towns as an expression of communal lifelessness and lack of public spirit. Who does not understand that the protean encroachment of home and shopowners on the public way, the twisting narrow streets of the quarters, and numerous blind alleys, cul-de-sacs, and blank walls connote that withdrawal from public concerns and public life which ultimately is said to distinguish cities in the oriental tradition from those in the classical?[2]

One of the central problems of medieval history has been to explain the freedom of the western towns and the subordination of the eastern; why it was that European cities came to be autonomous and self-governing while eastern cities were bereft of inner life; why out of the essentially uniform ecological situation of the Mediterranean region, and the common historical and political experience of the Roman Empire, such great differences in the experiences of cities should have come into being.

But this definition of the problem is now itself under attack. The classic outline for the investigation of the medieval city has begun to fade, for it is too little founded in a precise appreciation of the factors which shaped both eastern and western cities. More recent insights and discoveries suggest similarities behind the apparent differences between European and Muslim towns.[3] Contemporary sociologists insist on underlying uniformities in the social patterns of all preindustrial cities. Class and family structure, economic sophistication, technological competence, and forms of business enterprise express unities more profound than the apparent diversity of political forms. At the same time, historians of Muslim cities are beginning to discover elements of autonomy within the eastern towns. Far from being socially amorphous, Muslim cities spawned organized bodies demonstrating a solidarity and drive to independence from established imperial regimes similar to that found in the West. Civic spirit and the desire for autonomy were forces within the whole of the once-Roman world, and the forces which constituted a polity, formed a social order, and actually governed a population cannot be grasped in the simple dichotomy: commune-bureaucracy. Rarely in Europe did the commune become the universal expression of the needs, activities, and powers of the collectivity or the total context of urban experience. Rarely in the East did its absence actually entail a complete want of communal vitality.

Still, of these two recent lines of attack by sociologists and historians, the former overshoots the mark and the latter does not go far enough. The sociological approach stressing the similarities of premodern societies overlooks and cannot account for the evident differences, while the historical search for analogous communal forces mistakes the comparative problem by accepting one feature of the urban experience as essential before establishing the larger context of relationships. We must look more deeply into the urban constitution, behind static social and economic structures and beyond the formal political methods of organizing the city and the struggle for local autonomy, into the total configuration of relationships by which organized urban social life was carried on: the structure of the classes and internal collectivities, their public roles, the nature of their organization, and the forces which shaped their interaction; hence the principles by which individuals, classes, and groups of men were made into functioning communities. Only in this way can we arrive at some of the fundamentals of city life, and expose the social relationships by which order and community were created.

To find our way from these general considerations to a more precise formulation of the problems involved in a study of the social and political characteristics of Muslim cities and their differences from European cities, we must return to the prior history of the Middle Eastern and Mediterranean worlds in which these cities had common roots. This history shows the dichotomy commune-bureaucracy to be an inadequate analytical formulation. The Greco-Roman experience suggests that social factors lying behind the forms of city political organization were crucial. Both communal and bureaucratically administered cities had common roots in the Greco-Roman urban heritage. While the forms of Greco-Roman city life were communal, in reality bitter struggles between the aristocracies and the populace shaped the history of the towns. Eventually the Roman Empire gave effective preponderance to artistocrats who, behind democratic and communal forms, came to select councillors and magistrates without regard for the popular assembly.* Aristocratic domination became the basis for the transformation of the free ancient communes into administered cities, for as the towns grew less and less able to manage and finance their own affairs, Rome compelled local aristocrats to take up essential administrative burdens as a class responsibility. Local administration was preserved but not local

* The situation is reminiscent of the way in which the medieval communes were not assemblies of the whole, but unions of the most wealthy and powerful members of the community, towns which experienced similar bitter struggles between their patricians and plebeians, the merchants and artisans.

autonomy. The municipality became a cog in the machine of the Roman state, and its leading citizens functionaries in the Roman bureaucracy. In one uninterrupted movement, without interregnum and without revolution, the Greco-Roman city evolved from one to the other of the city forms which we find in the later middle ages. While formal institutions changed, inner mechanisms of rule remained the same. The cities were not intrinsically different in political character, but varied along a continuum of possibilities created by common underlying factors.[4]

The first of these was the role of the notables. No city, whatever the form of its assemblies, was entirely democratic; and no city, however developed the bureaucratic apparatus of the world in which it found itself, was entirely governed from without. The cooperation of people who were familiar with the populace and its legal and financial affairs was essential for effective local administration. The urban polity was neither administered nor communal as such, but was defined by the roles of regimes externally based and notables rooted within the town, by the way in which influence was divided between them, and by the degree of their cooperation or antagonism. The place of the urban polity on the continuum of forms from pure communal democracy to pure oppression and tyranny was basically defined by the actions of these notables.

A second factor was the roles of the common people and the relations between the notables and the masses. The common people were not an inert and thoroughly malleable mass, but on the contrary, because of their organization into families, quarters, guilds, or other associations, and because of their numbers and capacity for violence, played a decisive part in the actual politics of the cities if not in their formal councils. The government of any city depended on the actions and reactions of the populations, patricians and plebeians both, be they formally empowered to govern, be they organized into communes, or not.

Thus, the ancient heritage of medieval cities suggests that the two poles of notables and masses, and the fields of force created between them in which social, economic, and political considerations were inexorably intertwined, are central to our study. But in the Islamic world and in the cities of Egypt and Syria in the Mamluk period, the problem of notables and masses appears in a form complicated by a long and specifically Islamic development. To understand the immediate form of the political and social problems of Muslim cities in the Mamluk period, we must digress briefly to examine the fundamental legacy of the Arab-

Islamic empires and the evolution of the Muslim community life up to the Mamluk period.

The Islamic political heritage was shaped by the solutions adopted by the Arab Caliphates to rule the territories and peoples they had conquered. The essential political problem of both the Umayyad and Abbasid Caliphates was to unify the incredibly diverse provinces of their empire. The peoples of the western provinces were mainly Christians and Jews and spoke various Semitic and Berber languages. In the eastern provinces, Zoroastrianism and other Iranian religions and Persian languages prevailed. The diversity of these populations can scarcely be evoked, for the provinces were themselves subdivided into innumerable tiny communities, villages, town quarters, and nomadic tribes and clans each of which bore its own variation of the greater regional culture. The task of the empires, especially under the Abbasid dynasty, was to create one system of rule and to convert these peoples to a single religious culture.

Their solution, in a word, was bureaucracy—a hierarchy designed to connect each of the tiny communities of the Middle East to some provincial, regional, and ultimately imperial center. To create this organization the Caliphs did not impose their own cadres, but cooperated with the existing order by drawing the socially powerful and technically skilled families of the realm—the landowning families, the secretarial and administrative dynasties of both the Byzantine and Sassanian ancestor empires, Arab tribal chieftains, and Muslim religious leaders—into the hierarchy which they commanded and at whose summit they stood. A common cultural idiom, a common style of life, and conformity in religious convictions welded a coherent governing elite out of these disparate elements. This elite governed with the cooperation of the classes of provincial notables and officials from which it had come. Without the loyalty of village headmen, elders, landowners, and divines the system could not have been formed. The bureaucracy then served to organize the cooperation of men of prominence throughout the empire on behalf of a single Middle Eastern polity.

Metaphorically, we can describe Abbasid society as vertically organized. Its communities had no ties to each other, but were bound directly to some higher center of coordination. Authority and privilege of office were conferred by the Caliph and could not in theory be assumed without express delegation. In principle, controls over financial and military resources were also vested in the Caliph or his designated substitutes. Privilege in landowning, taxation, or class status was similarly ratified by association with the state.

The idea of a unified polity, exclusive in political authority and centralized in this way, gave shape to statecraft in the Middle East long after Abbasid power was shattered. Even though the empire was fragmented, characteristic relations within the official classes and their relations to the rest of the population did not basically change. Though power was no longer centralized in Bagdad, at whatever level it was held it was exercised in much the same way.

Nonetheless, radical transformations in political life took place. The breakdown of the empire in the tenth century permitted the heartlands of West Asia to be invaded by Turkish nomads from Central Asia. For over two and a half centuries repeated infiltrations and invasions shattered efforts to restore a Middle-Eastern-wide empire. Turkish chieftains supplanted the old Arab-Persian bureaucratic elites, evolved a new military and landholding system, and gradually worked out a fresh accommodation with the conquered peoples.

From our present point of view, the crucial development of this period was the almost universal extension of the Mamluk military system. To sustain the new principalities, slaves, imported as youths from peripheral regions, were trained at the court of their masters to be a fighting and administrative elite loyal to them alone and to their comrades in arms. This Mamluk system had its origins in the reigns of the Abbasid Caliphs, but became a general practice only in the eleventh and twelfth centuries. Almost universally in West Asia the ruling military elites were minorities alien in race, language, ethos, and duties from the Arab and Persian populations whom they ruled. These superbly organized Turkish armies mastered the resources and people of the area and towered over the subject societies in power and wealth.

In the same period, the communities of the area evolved a stable social and religious life which preserved their integrity in the face of Mamluk military regimes. The practices and beliefs which may be called Islamic had been developing for centuries, and though the consolidation of the faith owed much to the patronage of the state and its protection, never were the religious communities entirely subordinate to its claims. Muslim religious leaders had rejected the efforts of the state to define orthodox religious beliefs and to subordinate the administration of judicial and ritual affairs entirely to the interests of the state. They remained free to mold the life of the community as conscience, circumstance, and, above all, revelation required.

By the eleventh century, Islam had achieved a full sense of its inner character. Its basic idea was that the righteous life was embodied in a fundamental law, the Shari'a, whose principles—applying to all matters of religious, administrative, educational, commercial, social, and family life—were revealed to Muhammad in the Koran, clarified by the sayings and examples of the prophet, and elaborated by the efforts of the scholars and schools of law. The Shari'a was a complete vision of the good life. No distinction was made between church and society. The church was coterminous with the whole body of believers whose learned members took responsibility for the study of the Shari'a and Muslim traditions, for their application in everyday affairs, and for the organization of ritual worship. Scholars of the Koran, traditions, and legal sciences, who held the key to the divine intention elaborated the network of educational and religious institutions which consolidated the teachings of Islam down to the present time. Against the powerful and now alien state the communities of West Asia had developed an integrated, relatively little differentiated religious-social-political form which was their triumph, dignity, and bulwark in time of troubles.

The emergent strength of Islam was reflected in the social order of the cities. The ulama, or religious leaders, had emerged as the effective spokesmen and representatives of urban communities. The development of fraternal movements among the common people and the proliferation of convents and monasteries for Muslim mystics or Sufis also lent the cities a cohesiveness, not equal to the alien political regimes, but not a wholly ineffectual counterpoise. The Mamluk period represented the culmination of a centuries long evolutionary process by which this social form had been worked out.

Thus in Islamic society the problems of urban social and political organization were complicated by the ascendancy of an alien military elite, and the partial insulation of local urban society from the interventions of the rulers. The classic question of the relations between notables and masses must then be rephrased in terms of a triple interaction between alien military elites, local notables, and urban commoners. In Muslim cities both state or bureaucratic and local communal elements shaped a more complex urban configuration than historians have hitherto imagined. To analyze this pattern, this study will first present a brief history of cities in the Mamluk Empire focusing on

Aleppo and Damascus to describe the political and economic environment of Muslim urban life in this period. Then, in subsequent chapters, the roles of the Mamluk elite, the structures of the Muslim urban community, and the manner in which its various elements interacted with each other and with the Mamluks will be analyzed. In conclusion an effort will be made to suggest a new view of Muslim cities and some of the reasons for the apparent contrasts with medieval European cities.

CHAPTER I · A HISTORY OF CITIES IN THE MAMLUK EMPIRE

IN 1250 A PALACE COUP snuffed out the Ayyūbid house which had ruled Egypt since the time of Saladin (1169–1193), and brought to the throne of the Sultans the chiefs of Mamluk regiments who were already the effective if not the recognized masters of the state. The moment was surely unpropitious for the establishment of a new regime, and not without enormous effort was its survival secured. Threatened by both Mongol invasions and Christian crusades and weakened internally because of their tainted possession of power, the Mamluks waged relentless wars against both the Mongols and the crusader principalities for over fifty years. By 1312 the greatest danger had passed on both fronts and the Mamluk Empire entered a period of stable prosperity which was to last almost until the end of the century. A peaceful and prosperous period, brilliant in cultural as well as economic attainments, succeeded the hardships of the first half century. This most splendid era in turn came to an end about 1388, when the ambitions of ruthless Mamluk factions plunged the empire into a quarter century of unrelieved civil wars. The weakness of the state encouraged bedouin and nomadic rebellions and Tatar and Christian assaults. In 1400 Tamerlane devastated Aleppo and Damascus while Christian pirates ceaselessly plagued Muslim shipping and coastal regions. Only from 1422, after the advent of Sultan Barsbāy, was order finally restored. The time of troubles cost heavily in permanent losses to both agricultural and urban productive capacity and in the vitality of civic and religious institutions, but from 1422 until about 1468 a period of partial recovery and reconstruction allowed the Mamluk domains to regain some of their former glory. From 1468, however, until the Mamluk Empire's absorption into the Ottoman Empire in 1517, forces beyond its control robbed the empire of even the shadow of its former security and prosperity. Northern wars against the Ottoman Empire or its satellites, and naval efforts to protect Muslim commerce and coasts from Christian pirates in the Mediterranean and later from the Portuguese in the Red Sea and the Indian Ocean, exhausted the re-

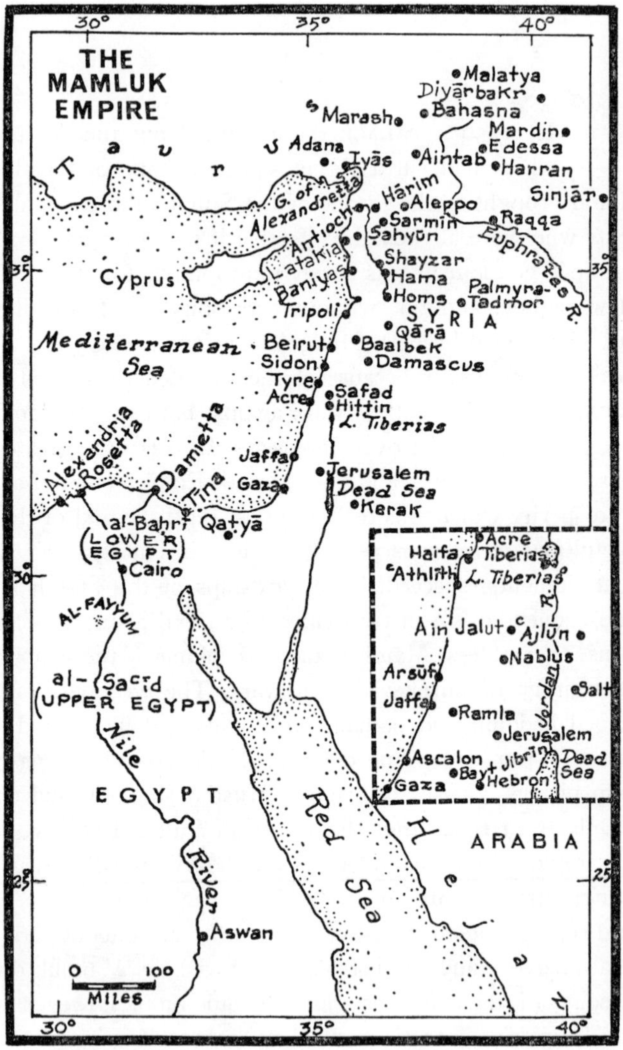
THE
MAMLUK
EMPIRE
30°
35°
40°
Taurus
Malatya
Diyārbakr
Bahasna
Marash
Mardin
Adana
Edessa
Iyās
Aintab
Harran
Sinjār
G. of Alexandretta
Hārim
Aleppo
Antioch
Sarmin
Raqqa
Latakia
Sahyūn
Euphrates R.
Shayzar
Cyprus
Baniyas
Hama
Homs
Palmyra-Tadmor
Tripoli
SYRIA
Qārā
Mediterranean Sea
Beirut
Baalbek
Sidon
Damascus
Tyre
Safad
Acre
Hittin
L. Tiberias
Alexandria
Rosetta
Damietta
Jaffa
Jerusalem
Tina
Gaza
Dead Sea
Kerak
al-Bahrī
Qatyā
(LOWER EGYPT)
Cairo
AL-FAYYUM
al-Sacīd
(UPPER EGYPT)
Nile
EGYPT
Red Sea
Hejaz
ARABIA
River
Aswan
0 100
Miles
Acre
Haifa
Tiberias
cAthlīth
L. Tiberias
Ain Jalut
cAjlūn
Nablus
Arsūf
Jordan R.
Salt
Jaffa
Ramla
Jerusalem
Ascalon
Bayt Jibrīn
Dead Sea
Gaza
Hebron
25°
30°
35°

sources of the state. The result was economic collapse, intensified exploitation of an ever poorer population, and social unrest and rebellion until finally in 1517 the Ottoman Empire relieved Egypt and Syria of burdens they could not shoulder.

The life of the cities was intimately linked to the fortunes of the empire. Each successive phase of Mamluk history had a special impact on the quality of urban life, and in the succeeding sections we shall trace the varying rhythms of political security, social stability, activity in trade and production, and internal physical development, and set these movements into the context of Mamluk imperial history. By tracing the history of the Syrian cities, in particular, we shall try to assess the general importance of the Mamluk state in shaping their experiences. In the subsequent chapter we shall try to penetrate the more intricate mechanisms by which this influence was exerted.

THE PACIFICATION OF SYRIA: 1260–1317

In the first decades of Mamluk rule, the Mamluk strategy of consolidation called for the expansion of the Egyptian state into Syria, Cilician Armenia, and Anatolia. These buffers protected the Mamluks from military dangers and symbolized service to Islam by victories over pagans and infidels. In 1260, at Ain Jalut, the Mamluks won the first Muslim victory over the hitherto invincible Mongols. Each successive Mongol invasion was resisted by Mamluk armies in Syria and by Mamluk counterattacks in Armenia and Anatolia. At the same time the Mamluks expelled the remaining crusader principalities. After a long truce the work of Saladin was resumed and concluded in 1291 with the destruction of Acre, the last crusader stronghold on the mainland. The victory was a signal accomplishment, fulfilling centuries old ambitions for the reconquest of Muslim lands. Emboldened by the victory at Acre the Mamluks defeated the Mongols and in 1317 won a definitive peace. Within Syria, minor Muslim potentates readily collapsed into the empire. The remaining Ayyūbid families were dispossessed. Mountain peoples were subjected to Mamluk suzerainty, and rebellious emirs seeking to restore the city-based principalities of the previous century were quickly routed.[1]

These victories helped win recognition as well as power for the new regime. The Mamluks had saved Syria from pagan Mongols and infidel Christians. They had rescued an Islamic land from dismemberment and Muslim peoples from slavery and humiliation. The Mamluks were quick to reinforce the good impression made by their victories with generous support for the religious classes and their educational and religious institutions, and with careful observance of the gestures appropriate to Muslim rulers.

The incorporation of Syria into an Egyptian empire was a tour de force. Never in her history was Syria so long and firmly dominated by Egypt, and rarely have the two regions been so well protected against external forces. Damascus served as an advance position for the defense of Egypt. Aleppo defended the Syrian heartlands and Cilician Armenia covered Aleppo. To protect the interior from attack by Europeans, coastal fortresses were razed, the remaining towns garrisoned, and the coastal plains settled by warlike Kurdish and Turkoman peoples. Syria was closed to the outside world, and the political and religious order imposed by the Mamluks fixed her historical situation for two and a half centuries until the Ottoman conquests and thus governed the experience of the Syrian cities.

Damascus, taken by the Mamluks in 1260, became a second capital of the empire and administrative center for Syria. Formerly distinct districts such as Homs, Gaza, and the rest of Palestine were made administratively subordinate to her. Here Mamluk armies were organized for campaigns against the crusader principalities and Mongol states. Damascus also became the nodal point of Mamluk communications in Syria from which postal routes ran north to Homs and Aleppo, west to the coastal towns of Beirut, Sidon, and Tripoli, to al-Raḥba on the eastern desert frontier, and to Safad in Palestine and Kerak. In 714/1314–15, all the Syrian governors were ordered to communicate with Egypt through Damascus.[2]

For Damascus, these were heady times. An intense public life of parade, pageant, and celebration quickened the city. Visiting Sultans and armies required military reviews, sports displays, collective prayers, and official receptions for rewarding officials, arbitrating disputes, and hearing pleas. Battle days or celebration of victories brought masses of Sufis, jurists, students, and commoners into the streets and public places for candlelit processions and all-night prayers and revels.[3] Inspired by the spirit of holy war, jubilant over the renewed glory of the true faith, Damascenes even volunteered to defend the city against the Mongols and enlisted in campaigns against the Franks and Armenians. The passion for holy war spilled over into intense impatience with Muslim heretics. Damascenes volunteered with special fervor to war against the infidels within. The Shi'ite minorities in Syria were ravaged, and the mountain regions subjected to stricter orthodox control. The Muslim community triumphant brooked no defiance.[4]

Expansive and vital as was the mood of the city, the political situation also had its costs. Hardships were created by contention among the leading emirs for control of the Sultanate.[5] More important, Damascus, as the key to Syria, was the object of Mongol assaults. Twice occupied to the terror of its inhabitants, Damascus suffered whenever Mamluk defenses failed. In 658/1260, the city escaped severe damage though the walls and towers of the citadel were ruined in the fighting. Some further losses were occasioned by the unearthing of foundation stones and water courses to provide the Mongols with shot.[6]

In 699/1299–1300, however, the Mongols devastated most of the city. Virtually the whole of al-Ṣāliḥiyya suburb to the north was pillaged and burned. Many important buildings were destroyed and the population was plundered and murdered. The Mongol Sultan Ghāzān was later persuaded by the protests of the ulama, the religious leaders, to deprive the guilty Mongols of their booty, but the hospital and many mosques and madrasas (colleges) were lost. Inside the city the area around the citadel was severely damaged, and important schools were burned. The outlying villages of al-Mizza, Dārayyā, and 'Uqayba suffered too. Besides the physical damage, Ghāzān extorted 3,600,000 dirhems for himself by taxing the markets and wealthy individuals, and his officials are said to have taken a like amount. Horses and animals were confiscated, and the possessions of absent notables were plundered. A good deal of grain, cloth, woodwork, and furnishings were removed.[7]

Even when spared civil strife and foreign attack, Damascus was heavily burdened to pay the costs of defense. Aside from innumerable regular dues, special taxes often aggregating a million dirhems were periodically laid on the gardens and villages of the area to pay for extraordinary needs. Sultan Baybars (1260–1277) was notorious for these heavy levies, but other Sultans, though not unwilling to relax the duties in quiet times, were also quick to impose them in case of need. Only in 714/1314–15 with the definitive completion of the Mongol and crusader wars were many of the usual taxes allowed to lapse.[8]

On balance, however, the city was favored by absorption into the Mamluk Empire, and resumed in spite of constant warfare the sustained and intense growth begun in Ayyūbid times. The Mamluks made Damascus a refuge for the beleaguered populations of Iraq,

Mesopotamia, Anatolia, and northern Syria. Immigrants brought invaluable administrative and commercial experience and technical and craft skills, and included a complement of scholars and divines who helped inaugurate a century of distinguished Muslim learning in Damascus.[9]

Above all, the very presence of the Mamluk forces favored the economic life of the city. The large garrison and the constant passage of Egyptian troops stimulated a lively trade. The city grew as markets serving the soldiers migrated from the center to the northwest sector outside the walls. Military spending for food supplies, armor and weapons, clothing, recreation, saddle and bridle equipment, and animals gave employment and a living to countless craftsmen and traders. Moreover, Damascus, famous for the skill of its crafts, won the patronage of the Sultan and great emirs for her luxury products. Inlaid copper and brassware, fine cloth, silks, saddles, and gilded glass were among the distinguished products of the city.[10]

The prosperity of the city was also enhanced by the construction and endowment of new religious, educational, and philanthropic institutions. The surplus wealth of the regime spilled over into the construction of new mosques, schools, and convents which not only gave work to builders and furnishers, but permanent employment and endowments to the religious classes. In the period between 658/1260 and 710/1311–12 some forty-three institutions are known to have been founded or restored, including the famous al-Ẓāhiriyya Madrasa, the tomb of Sultan Baybars. The pre-eminence of Damascene scholarship in Syria was thus assured. Still, the prosecution of the wars interfered with a full flowering of such endowments and confined them to peaceful interludes. A truly great period of building and expansion awaited the quieter prosperity of succeeding decades.[11]

By contrast, in this first half century of Mamluk rule, the situation of Aleppo was desperate. Directly exposed to the eastern and northern frontiers and thrice occupied by the Mongols, Aleppo was reduced to destitution. In 658/1260 the citadel, the walls, the grand mosque, and some surrounding structures were destroyed. According to some accounts part of the population was systematically slaughtered when the Mongols called the permanent residents and the strangers to form two groups, and then murdered the strangers including many Aleppins who believed it would be safer to conceal their identity. On the other hand, a large part of the population was guaranteed safety by the sale of immunities to several notables who opened their houses and quarters to as much of the populace as they could hold. Fifty thousand people are said to have been saved in this way. In 679/1280, mosques, madrasas, the houses of emirs, and the Sultan's palace were pillaged and burned. In 699/1300, and in the following year as well, the Mongols besieged the city, but no specific damage is indicated.[12]

For this situation, Mamluk policy was directly at fault. The Mamluks virtually abandoned Aleppo to its fate. The walls and citadel, severely damaged in 658/1260, were not fully repaired until the end of the following century.[13] Nor were Mongol incursions met to the north of Aleppo, but instead the Aleppo garrison was actually withdrawn to reinforce the main armies making their stand between Homs and Hama, north of Damascus. Even the Mongols ceased to regard the city as an important objective, and were content either to bypass or occupy it as part of their mopping up operations in northern Syria. Once in 670/1271–72 the Sultan brought his armies up to Aleppo after its garrison had retreated to join the main force near Hama. Twenty-eight years later, the Hama garrison was sent forward to back up Aleppo at word of a Mongol attack, but when the main blow fell in 699/1300 Aleppo was deserted and the Mamluks chose to make their stand near Homs. Again in the following year the Aleppo garrison deserted the city, though in 712/1312 Hama forces were first sent to Aleppo before falling back to Homs. Only slowly, as the Mongol menace receded, did the Mamluks revise their defensive strategy in favor of Aleppo, but never so much as to guarantee the security of the city and thus assure the fundamental condition of its redevelopment.[14]

Aleppo remained without the stimulus of investment, construction, or trade and production which eased the hardships of the age for Damascus. Her real recovery waited for the reversal of the tides of warfare in northern Syria. When Mamluk counterattacks regularly carried into Armenia, Aleppo again became an important military base, absorbed as Damascus had been in the prosecution of victorious wars, and thus enjoying similar benefits. In 700/1301 the first new school and convent was endowed, though not until 717/1317–18 was an institution of monumental importance constructed. In 713/1313 a new aqueduct and canal were begun to improve the city's water supply.[15] Until then, without assurance of the most elementary protection, Aleppo could not even begin to recover though Damascus was already on the verge of a splendid epoch.

Similarly, the history of the Syrian coastal towns reflected the preeminent importance of Mamluk policies. Passionately determined to expel the crusaders and prevent the Europeans from ever again obtaining a foothold on the coast, the Mamluks destroyed the fortifications of Caesarea, Ascalon, Jaffa, Arsūf, ʻAthlīth, Tyre, Sidon, Haifa, Acre, and Tripoli.[16] Tripoli, however, was completely rebuilt, this time inland, to serve as a garrison town. Endowed with new mosques, schools, markets, baths, mills, residences, and canals, it became an important center for the pacification of the Lebanon and the suppression of heretical sects. Beirut, on the other hand, the only functioning port in Syria, was left to languish, her trade cut off and her defense entrusted to the Emirs of the Gharb, mountain chieftains whose main interests lay elsewhere.[17] For the towns of Syria, no factor was more important than the policies of the Mamluk regime.

PROSPERITY AND SECURITY: THE FOURTEENTH CENTURY

The pacification of Syria in the first decades of the fourteenth century inaugurated a brilliant period in Mamluk history. Until the last decade of the century Egypt and Syria generally enjoyed great prosperity and security. The Mamluks initiated the fourteenth century prosperity by reorganizing state finances. Between 1313 and 1324 the Mamluk system of military payments was put on a regular basis as rural revenues were divided between the Sultan and the Mamluk emirs. The numbers of required troops were specified and the salaries for all ranks fixed. The reorganization served to concentrate control of the armies and the tax revenues in the hands of the Sultan, but was even more important for its contribution to the general economy. The tax revenues of the state were an immense component of the total wealth of the region, and the stabilization of the salaries of emirs and the duties of the taxpayers thus set the basis for a stable economy.[18]

Fiscal stability contributed to exceptional monetary stability. Long-term constancy in the value of gold and silver and in the prices of basic food products—wheat, barley, and beans—also helped secure the general prosperity. Gold and silver coin held throughout the period at around twenty dirhems to the gold dinar and the secular price of wheat was about fifteen to twenty dirhems per *irdabb** in Cairo, de-

* *Irdabb*—a measure of capacity. In Egypt, about five bushels. (**425**, XVI, 38.) Also: Walther Hinz, *Islamische Masse und Gewichte,* vol. I, Handbuch der Orientalistik (Leiden, 1955), pp. 39–40.

pending on the season. Barley and beans were worth about two-thirds as much as wheat.[19]

These average prices, however, although a good index of the long-term standard of living, cannot be taken to imply uninterrupted stability. In medieval economies long-term tendencies cannot be equated with freedom from fluctuations which in the short run, especially for the poorer classes, were of the utmost consequence. Beneath century-long trends of agricultural output, population, and demand, uncertainties introduced by weather conditions, political disturbances, delays in shipment and distribution, and above all by hoarding and speculation, prevented prices from resting at their secular averages or from changing in any predictable manner. In addition, the use of copper coin for small everyday transactions was another important source of erratic fluctuations. Whereas gold and silver held a fairly constant ratio, the most commonly used coins were likely to vary considerably in worth. Copper was sometimes in too short supply for everyday needs, sometimes so abundant as to be worthless. Copper was subject to rapid debasement, and the instability of this coin seemed beyond remedy despite the constant attention of the regime. Its fluctuations, quite apart from the real market situation, were frequently the cause of market disturbances resulting in consumer demonstrations, somewhat arbitrary government efforts to maintain the value of the coin, and consequent sellers' strikes.[20] Mamluk prosperity entailed circumstances now regarded as evidence of severe hardship.

Mamluk policy was also a crucial factor in shaping the patterns of trade and production. Regional trade was basically oriented to the two capital cities, Damascus and Cairo, while other towns played but a subordinate role. Damascus, for example, imported her needs from all of Syria. Fruits came from the immediate district in which the city was situated, and grain from the Hauran to the south. Specialty products from further away also flowed to their largest market. Rice from the Ḥūla area, oil from Nablus, milk from Baalbek, figs and pistachios from Aleppo, and soap from Sarmīn all came to Damascus. Other intra-regional trades were no doubt lively since Aleppo, Jerusalem, and other big towns reached out for the products of their hinterlands, but the demands of Damascus were the most extensive in the region.[21]

Syrian products also went to Cairo. Syria exported oil, soap, candles, fruits, sheep, horses, iron, and wood. From Damascus itself came ceramics, glass, metal, and luxury cloth goods. Proceeding both by sea from the coastal ports of Syria, Sidon and Beirut, and overland through the customs stations at Qaṭyā on the Syrian-Egyptian frontier, merchants carried on regular exchanges. On the basis of an ad-valorum tax of five to ten per cent, the revenues of Qaṭyā were reported to have been a thousand dinars a day. Bazaars were maintained in Cairo for Syrian merchants and products,[22] and throughout the late thirteenth and fourteenth centuries, the regime assisted this traffic by building and maintaining bridges and caravansaries as resting places for commercial caravans.[23]

However, there is little evidence that these imports were purchased by a compensating outflow of urban manufactured goods. Some Damascus silks seem to have been exported to the hinterland, and no doubt peasants purchased urban goods in exchange for their produce. Grain growing peasants came, for example, from the Hauran to Damascus and villagers from Qārā to Aleppo to raise cash and satisfy needs which only the cities could serve. The value of this trade cannot be assessed, but it seems likely that it was slight. The surplus of the peasantry and its purchasing power were probably not substantial. Moreover, the peasants who shipped their products from the further hinterlands of Syria to Damascus would not usually make purchases there. In general, Damascene manufactures went to Cairo rather than to the provinces which supplied her needs. Similarly, although cloth exports are indicated, the basic Egyptian compensations for Syrian products were occasional grain shipments to relieve hardship in Syria or more commonly to supply the Sultan's armies without making any further demands on Syria's scant resources. The trading system was organized around the concentration of rural products in the major cities, a certain amount of exchange of manufactured goods between Damascus and Cairo, and no equivalent trade between the giants and the rest of the region.[24]

The reason no compensating trade was required was that much of the raw material imports were the tax revenues of the Mamluks or the waqf* revenues of religious institutions. The apparatus of both the state and religion in Cairo and Damascus were supported by grants of land in far off localities, for whose political payments no exchange was necessary.[25]

Aside from the intra-Syrian and Syrian-Egyptian trades the most

* Waqf—a foundation; an endowment of funds in perpetuity for a religious, educational, or philanthropic purpose.

important routes were between Cairo and Damascus on the one hand, and Bagdad and Persia in the east or Anatolia and Black Sea ports in the north, on the other. Sporadic notices about the major Bagdad-Damascus route indicate that until the middle of the fourteenth century a lively trade was carried on, but from then until 789/1387, when there is mention of a merchant coming from Bagdad, we have no information about the use of this route. Quite probably, Damascus received spices, silks, dyes, and drugs from Bagdad until the revival of other international routes depressed this transit.[26]

The second orientation, to Armenia, Anatolia, and the Black Sea, was motivated by other needs. Trading caravans were active even during the counter-crusading wars, for this northern traffic was of great strategic value. Precious slave manpower, horses, and metals were brought into Syria from the north, and though a certain amount of Syrian oil and soap is known to have been exported, it seems likely that these expensive imports were paid for in specie.[27] Here too factors extraneous to a local urban exchange economy were crucial. Either strategic needs or external demand for nonindigenous products were more important than activity generated by the commercial life of the towns.

Urban production was similarly closely tied to political considerations. While all towns produced such common goods as cloth, leather, pottery, and occasional soap or building materials, only a few produced specialties of luxury quality. Aleppo had notable achievements, according to the judgment of her historians, in wood and marble working, textiles, soap, perfume, and weapons. Baalbek was noted for a very fine cotton cloth, widely used in Cairo. Tripoli, which had been famous in earlier centuries for silks and textiles, had lost the industry, but was an important sugar-growing region and may have had a large refining industry. Only in Damascus and Cairo, however, did the patronage of the Mamluks sustain a full range of luxury outputs. Damascus, for example, produced fine household decorations, utensils, and jewelry in gold, silver, brass, and copper. She was also famous for silks, cottons, linens, decorative brocades and embroidered garments, tents, horse-trappings, and robes made for the Mamluk elites. The city's craftsmen also turned their skills to weapons and precision instruments such as quadrants and astrolabes. High quality building crafts flourished. Even Cairo made use of her plasterers, masons, marble workers, and brick manufacturies. Damascus had an active glass industry, noted for gilded lamps, vases, ewers, and bowls. Nor were iron, ceramics, leather, paper, and the manufacture of fine confections neglected. Damascus was of singular importance as a producer of luxury goods which were exported throughout the empire and abroad. In these crafts the fourteenth was a splendid century.[28]

Equally formative of urban economies was the Mamluk contribution to the maintenance of the urban physical plant. The reorganization of finances by Sultan Nāṣir Muḥammad (d. 741/1341) and decades of peace brought forth surplus wealth for investment in street and road repairs, water works, and new buildings and the endowment of religious institutions on a scale unmatched since Ayyūbid days. Notably, however, the pace of activity had different rhythms in different cities in ways which corresponded closely to Mamluk political policy.

In the fourteenth century a basic trend of this policy was the transfer of active military responsibilities from Damascus to Aleppo. With the passing of the Mongol menace and the expulsion of the crusaders, Damascus was no longer an active center for the prosecution of the wars. After the last important campaign in 722/1322, Aleppo became the staging point for the raiding expeditions which forced Armenia to pay tribute to the Mamluk state, cede fortress after fortress, and eventually capitulate to incorporation in the Mamluk Empire. Between 735/1334–35 and 748/1347–48, eight successful campaigns were waged from Aleppo, only one with assistance from the Damascus and Egyptian armies, until the *coup de grâce* was given in 776/1374-75 to a virtually absorbed Armenia.[29] With these victories came increased administrative responsibilities and larger revenues in the form of grants of land awarded to Aleppo emirs from the conquered territories. Military success increased the surplus wealth available for investment in Aleppo, and possibly expanded local commercial opportunities as Muslim-Mamluk domains in that region were extended.[30]

A second political development which enhanced the status of Aleppo was the weakening of the Mamluk state organization. The death of Sultan Nāṣir Muḥammad in 1341 left the Mamluk regime in constant tension. While the Sultanate remained in his dynasty, the price of continuity was ever-renewed civil war for control of the state. Cairo in particular was beset by frequent street battles between cliques of soldiers and their followers among the common people. The swaggering of the troops, violence of the mobs, greed of officials, and popular uneasiness disorganized Cairo. In both a military and social sense this contributed to weakening her stature in the empire.[31]

These political storms tempted both Damascus and Aleppo Mamluks to seek control of the regime. Civil wars in Syria were virtually continuous between 741/1340–41 and 753/1352 and flared up several times again in the ensuing decade. Sometimes in support of the Cairo factions, but in addition and more ominously in support of Syrian pretensions to the Sultanate, the risings were most often provoked by the Damascus emirs. Nonetheless, events reflected a drift of political importance toward Aleppo's governors and forces. Ambitious and aggressive, Aleppo emirs for the first time in 752/1351 initiated their own rising, using their expanded military capabilities to contest control of the whole empire. Hitherto only Damascus and Cairo emirs had sustained such attempts. Thus the civil wars even had a tonic effect on Aleppo, giving her forces further opportunity to demonstrate their strength and importance.[32]

In yet another way the difficulties of the regime enhanced the importance of Aleppo. The weakening of the state permitted and even fostered the outbreak of bedouin violence in both Syria and Egypt. The preoccupation of the Mamluks gave bedouin chieftains an opportunity to press their own ambitions, and rebellious emirs often even induced the bedouins into joining the struggles by giving them free scope for their depredations. Bedouin attacks began in the 730's/1330's and then rose in intensity. At the same time the crystallization of new Turkoman principalities in Anatolia, first the Dulghādir state and later Ramaḍān,* posed an even more formidable threat to the security of Syria. Not only internal barbarians but nomads from across the frontiers threatened to uproot the economy of the Mamluk domains. Nomad attacks, whether in upper Egypt, Syria, Palestine, the eastern desert, or on the northern frontiers, were extremely costly. Raids on caravans interrupted lucrative long distance and international trading. Rural food surpluses intended for urban consumption were endangered. Raids on villages often destroyed the crops at their source, and prolonged bedouin pressure on marginal villages could mean permanent loss of cultivation,

* Dulghādir—a Turkoman principality founded in the middle of the fourteenth century in Anatolia at Albistān, to the west of the Euphrates River. Ramaḍān—another Turkoman principality founded at the end of the fourteenth century at Adana, north of the Gulf of Alexandretta.

the loss of the sown to the desert, of the civilized to the void. Taking over responsibility both for curbing the Arab bedouins and for checking the expanding and aggressive Turkoman principalities in the north, Aleppo gained further in both military importance and political status.[33]

These political circumstances governed the inner growth of the cities. Damascus, enjoying the fruits of earlier victories, entered early in the century, under Governor Tankiz (1312–1340), a period of three decades of unequaled splendor and expansion. Tankiz undertook to repair the major canal systems on which the water supply of the city depended. Street works spread over almost a decade helped to rationalize chaotic expansion, especially on the northern and western flanks, and to reintroduce the necessary streets, bridges, and spaces to assure communications within the busy district. Having brought the economic infrastructures up to date, Tankiz endowed new schools, mosques, and other institutions and helped stimulate other constructions and endowments. During his tenure almost forty institutions were newly built or repaired and other important emirs, judges, and rich merchants joined in endowing the city.[34]

By contrast, the decades of greatest expansion in Damascus were an epoch of but modest construction and repairs for Aleppo. But as the pace of construction gradually subsided by mid-century in Damascus, Aleppo began to overtake her. From the death of Tankiz in 741/1340 until about 770/1368–69 we know of twenty-three construction and repair projects in Damascus and thirteen in Aleppo. From that point on, the relative decline of Damascus became precipitous. Between 767/1365–66 and the invasions of Tamerlane in 803/1400 we know of only eight projects in Damascus while in Aleppo no less than twenty-two works were undertaken. From slow and halting beginnings, Aleppo overtook Damascus in the intensity of endowment and construction, in the splendor of the monuments built, and in the consequent attractiveness of the city as a center of religion and learning. New schools, mosques, and convents were not the only works, for Aleppo was also endowed with a hospital in 755/1354. Aleppo, moreover, began to expand beyond her old boundaries in the late fourteenth century, pushing new quarters out to the south and east of the old city.[35] Aleppo owed this burst of activity to her enhanced military importance and wealth.

Although the fiscal and economic situation of Egypt and Syria, and the patterns of trade, production, and urban physical development were influenced by the behavior of the Mamluks, one economic variable, the international spice trade, was governed by other forces. The Mamluk Empire stood athwart the great trade routes which led to Europe from India, China, and Southeast Asia. The Arabs, as is well known, were the world's middlemen, but the routes across Egypt and Syria were not always employed, and the fluctuations in their use enable us to assess the relative influence of local or international factors, and of political as compared with commercial forces in the economies of the major towns.

In the centuries immediately prior to the Mamluk period the crusades had given an extraordinary impetus to international trade. Not only did spices, dyes, and drugs from the Far East make their way to Italy via the emporia of the Middle East, but regional goods were exported to the West and local manufactures encouraged. By the middle of the thirteenth century, however, two developments conspired to deprive Alexandria and the smaller Syrian ports of these beneficial activities. One, of course, was the hostility of the Mamluk regime to the presence of westerners. Not that it opposed trade, for a lively commerce was carried on with and through the crusader towns, but the strain of systematic warfare could not but have a deleterious effect. In the latter half of the century trading between the Europeans and the Mamluks became sporadic and much reduced in volume.

The second factor was of greater long-term importance for it vitiated what efforts the Mamluks could make to keep the international trade alive. World trade routes between the orient and occident underwent a major reorientation in the thirteenth century. The establishment of Mongol empires in Central Asia facilitated an overland traffic which bypassed the high costs, political difficulties, and other uncertainties of the Yemen-Egypt route, and debouched spices either at Armenian or Black Sea ports.

Despite these difficulties Mamluk Egypt struggled to keep open the trade between Alexandria and the West. It was vital for the importation of metals, timber, and other war materials of which Egypt was in short supply. Despite the opposition of the papacy and its sanction for pirate assaults on contraband goods, Alexandria continued to receive the attention of European merchants. Catalans, Venetians, Genoese, and others visited there, and treaties were concluded with their home cities. Slaves and war materials came into Egypt and a trickle of Levantine goods made their way west through her major port. Between 1290 and 1345 the trade remained of interest, but only of secondary importance. It served local needs and some of the commercial desires of the Europeans, but could not replace the richness of the international transfer trade in spices, silks, dyes, and drugs.

Syria languished even more, for she was quickly superseded by Armenia and Cyprus as outlets for eastern goods. Only rarely did western ships call directly at Beirut. Instead, Venice promptly made trade treaties with Armenia. What contact Syria did keep with Europe was mostly through the mediation of Cypriot vessels, which seem to have carried on a brisk traffic with Syrian ports.

Before mid-century, however, a major reversal of this pattern was underway. In 1345 Venice concluded a treaty with the Mamluks by which, for the first time, she established a regular annual service with Alexandria. Renewed Venetian interest was spurred by difficulties with the overland Central Asian routes. Her Black Sea outlets were attacked by the Mongols. Armenia was under pressure from the Mamluks themselves, and as early as 1322 the port of Iyās fell into Muslim hands.

Two decades later, new developments reopened the international trade through Syria. In 1365, Peter I of Cyprus waged a latter day crusade against Alexandria and the Syrian coastal towns. Venice, shocked by what seemed to her an anachronistic policy, sought to prevent the disruption of her eastern Mediterranean trade by making peace between Peter and the Mamluks. At the same time she took advantage of the dispute to send her first expedition to Beirut. Venetian and Catalan ships came to trade there in 1366, for Peter's aggression had cut off the intermediary Cypriote-Syrian trade. Yet the time was not quite ripe for a complete revival. Another decade had to pass before Venice established an annual service with Beirut on the same basis as Alexandria. For by 1375 the Mamluks completed their conquest of Armenia, and Genoa took control of Famagusta, which meant the exclusion of Venetians from the island's traffic. At the same time the inner Asian routes collapsed completely. After a lapse of about a century, the world spice trade came back to Egypt and Syria. Venetian, Catalan, French, and Genoese traffic again came to Alexandria, Beirut, and other Syrian ports. Not only the port cities, but Cairo, Damascus, and other Syrian towns were visited by western merchants and pilgrims.[36]

Surprisingly, despite the wealth of this trade, it seems to have had no visible effect on the towns themselves. Alexandria, which had been sacked in 1365, remained a city in ruins. Many of the smaller trading places in Syria such as Jaffa and Acre remained simple way stations, and did not receive sufficient stimulus to be rebuilt and repopulated. A few defensive military constructions were all that Beirut could show for its revival though it was the major Syrian beneficiary of the trade. Tripoli, whose prosperity was founded on agriculture and military and administrative functions as well as a trickle of commerce, continued to be the more important town. New mosques and madrasas were built throughout the century and fortifications were repaired. Damascus, through which caravan traffic from Arabia and the East was directed on its way to the sea, also failed to manifest any advantages. There is nothing to indicate that she ceased to decline with respect to Aleppo, though the latter participated but little in the commerce. International trade does not seem to have had an impact comparable to the policies of the state on the prosperity of the cities. International trade would continue uninterrupted, profitable, and lively for well over a century while the conditions of town life in the region varied with internal changes.[37]

The fundamental reason for the superficial impact of the international trade was that in the Muslim world this was a transfer trade in which goods coming from the orient were resold to Europeans. Despite some internal consumption of eastern luxuries, there were no secondary repercussions. Only a thin stratum of officials, merchants, boatmen, porters, translators, and so on profited from the commerce. In Europe, by contrast, shipbuilding, mining, manufacturing, and banking were encouraged in order to pay for spices. The whole populations of towns were involved in seafaring, manufacturing, distribution of goods to diverse markets, banking, insurance, and administration. Economically independent European bourgeoisies were able to win political independence and to govern themselves. For the Mamluk Empire, the revival of the international spice trade was an important bonus of income, but for the society as a whole and its economy and civil organization, the international trade had none of the profound implications it had in the West. It could not outweigh the force of political factors in the experience of the towns.

THE TIME OF TROUBLES: 1388–1422

General prosperity continued until the last decade of the fourteenth century. True, there were disturbing signs. Mamluk civil wars and bedouin or Turkoman uprisings disturbed the peace and were costly to trade and agriculture. In the countryside there were signs of fiscal exploitation and agricultural recession. Public investments in Damascus were also in decline. Yet not before 1388 did these inner weaknesses combine to plunge the Mamluk Empire into a crisis of such magnitude that it would never fully recover. The society entered a time of troubles which lasted from about 790/1388 to 825/1422 before they subsided or were finally suppressed in all their dimensions.

The immediate cause of the difficulties was the seizure of the Sultanate in 784/1382 by the Circassian Mamluk factions. Imperfectly disciplined, inordinately ambitious, and heedless of consequences, these Mamluks battled each other almost continuously for control of the state. Sultan Barqūq came to power in 784/1382 as the victor of the first round of Circassian battles, but in 789–90/1387–88 fighting resumed in earnest. In the next three years the Sultanate changed hands twice. Cairo and Damascus alternated in the possession of the major contestants, and pitched battles were fought at Aleppo as well. Another rebellion and civil war in Syria occurred in 802/1399. Then, from 806/1403 to 815/1412 Mamluk factions waged continuous warfare in Egypt and Syria. Each faction, refusing to allow any other to consolidate, deserted victorious allies for defeated enemies to keep the balance of power. Not until Sultan al-Mu'ayyad Sheikh (1412–1421) could a stable governing coalition be formed. Even so, ambitious emirs fought again in 824–25/1421–22 over his succession.[38]

Disunited, the Mamluk Empire faced again those dangers which more than a century before had threatened to extinguish Muslim urban civilization in Syria. From the north came Mongol and Turkoman invasions; from the sea, renewed danger of Christian crusades in the guise of piracy.

The threat of Tatar invasion was over a decade in materializing. Tamerlane, in ever widening spheres of assault, finally struck Syria in 1400. Aleppo, though defended, was overwhelmed by the invader who scattered the garrison and an unruly mob of auxiliary infantry. Damascus, after a pitched but indecisive battle, was abandoned to the Mongols. Sultan Faraj, fearing plots against his throne in Egypt, withdrew in unconscionable neglect of his responsibility for the defense of the region. Damascus held out for two days and then surrendered to the inevitable. The city was systematically taxed, and every person was obliged to contribute. Rents of houses and revenues of waqfs were taken, and some four million dinars were thus raised to satisfy the conqueror. In addition, all animals, weapons, and other valuables, including the property of people who had fled the city, were confiscated. The city was then combed over for opportunities to extort still more money and pillaged by the troops, district by district. The damage was incalculable, and the immediate costs were horribly compounded by the forced transfer of thousands of prisoners, young boys and girls, skilled workmen and scholars, to Samarkand. The Tatars are also said to have burned the city, but, except for important blazes in the area of the Umayyad Mosque and the citadel, these accounts are exaggerated.[39]

Moreover, though Tamerlane retired and died soon afterwards, his invasions bolstered the Turkoman principalities of Anatolia and northwestern Iran, and kept alive the menace of other Turkoman incursions from the north. In particular, the warring confederations of the Ak Koyunlu and the Kara Koyunlu threatened another barbarian flood while lesser Turkoman principalities scrambled to snatch gains in northern Syria from the prostrate Mamluk state.[40] Syria's renewed vulnerability was manifest.

At the same time, beginning with the crusade of Peter I of Cyprus in 1365 Christian piracy in the eastern Mediterranean intensified. Genoese and Catalan parasites on the revived Venetian commerce with Beirut and Alexandria were perhaps inevitable, but based on Cyprus, Rhodes, and other Aegean islands, they appeared to the Muslims as renewed crusading enterprises. Sporadically, in the 1370's, 80's, and 90's, the Tripoli region and other parts of the Syrian and Egyptian coasts were subject to pirate landings while the extensive raids of Boucicaut in 806/1403 and his avowed intentions compounded fears that piracy, like the Turkoman menace, was no longer to be suppressed. Preying on Muslim traffic on the high seas, the emboldened pirates began to attack in the very confines of Alexandria and Damietta. Mamluk complaints to Cyprus were of no avail.[41]

The damage done by these civil wars and invasions was considerable. In the cities, severe battles fought without restraint or respect for the limiting needs of a complex environment caused great physical losses. Gates and walls were demolished, whole quarters were fired and plundered, and suburban districts especially suffered. Even water canals, the precious lifelines of urban life, were cut. For example, the damage to Damascus in 791/1389 was widespread and exceeded even the much overestimated effect of Tamerlane's occupation. Whereas Tamerlane severely damaged the citadel and the grand mosque, in 791/1389 not only the quarters around the citadel and the Umayyad Mosque, but the areas of Bāb al-Jābiya, Bāb al-Salāma, Bāb al-Shāghūr, Qaṣr al-Hajjāj, al-Muṣallā, al-Qubaybāt, and the markets of the smiths, merchants, and hatmakers among others were burned in heedless Mamluk fighting. Further damage was done in later years by warfare and by a series of conflagrations. Equally senseless was the harm done by the Mamluks in their hasty efforts to repair ruined fortifications. At both Aleppo and Damascus valuable buildings were demolished and the materials removed for fortifications. The loss of mosques, schools, and houses probably caused as much hardship as did the direct damage of war.[42]

The civil wars also did great harm to the fabric of organized urban social life. Seeking support, the Mamluks enlisted the urban masses in their struggles, and tore apart the major towns by internal dissension, rioting, and pillage. The common people of Damascus in 791–93/1389–91, 804/1401–02, and 812/1409–10 gave themselves to one or another faction. Aleppo divided into two parties whose hostilities reverberated throughout the rest of the Mamluk period while Cairo became the scene of unruly mob fighting and plunder.[43]

Economically disastrous was the destruction of productive agricultural areas. Bedouin unrest and fiscal exploitation had already precipitated rural decline. Now, in addition, marching and plundering armies, bedouins from whom all restraints had been removed by the diversions of the regime, and Turkomans infiltrating the empire did untold damage to agricultural production, the fundamental source of wealth. Scarcely contained in Upper Egypt and al-Fayyūm, the bedouins attacked villages, interfered with communications and the transport of merchandise, and cut off grain shipments to Cairo. In Syria employment of the bedouins as auxiliary forces gave scope for raids on the villages around Damascus and Aleppo. Similarly involved, Turkomans of northern Syria and Anatolia not only plundered agricultural settlements, but in 806/1403–04 actually extended their domains into the administrative territory of Aleppo. Not until 814/1411–12 were such important districts as Antioch, Sarmīn, Ṣahyūn, Quṣayr, Ḥārim, and Diyār Kush returned with their revenues to the control of Aleppo and the Mamluk state.

The Mamluks did no less to foster the ruin of the countryside. Oppression forced peasants to flee the villages. Greed meant neglect of irrigation and investments in agricultural production. The results cannot be immediately measured, but it seems that the enormous losses in revenue reported for the end of the fifteenth century and the beginning of the sixteenth originated in this time of troubles.[44]

These losses made themselves felt throughout the economy. Losses in total income and the inordinate expenditure of resources for military purposes meant that the surpluses available for investment in urban structures and for the patronage of the fine crafts were dissipated. The diversion was immediately reflected in the declining number of endowments and constructions of new public works. Public projects in Damascus came to a virtual standstill after 790/1388, and only as the civil wars abated did they resume with modest vigor after 811/1408–09. Even so, most projects were repairs and minor constructions rather than rivals of the expensive structures of the previous century. Sporadic replacement of damaged structures or quarters was not even adequate to keep up with losses from fighting and devastating fires of uncertain origin. A decade after the restoration of order, Bertrandon de la Broquière remarked that sections of Damascus were in decay. Similarly, although Aleppo carried the momentum of previous growth throughout the 790's, construction of religious and educational institutions came to a virtual standstill between 800/1397 and 824/1421. Damascus suffered from neglect and lack of adequate funds, but some of Aleppo's rural revenues had fallen into Turkoman hands. Only when the administrative district was reconstituted could the endowment of new institutions resume and needed repairs be taken up.[45]

Urban manufactures suffered equally from the regression of the Mamluk economy. So large was the part of the Mamluk garrisons in the consumption of craft output and the employment of urban workers that the decline of their incomes had widespread repercussions. Luxury craft work collapsed from lack of patronage. Fine inlaid brassware which had been the staple household utensil and decorative furnishing ceased to command a clientele. High quality glass, pottery, and cloth also ceased to be produced in Syria and Egypt as both the Mamluk and wealthy civilian classes found themselves without adequate funds to sustain the appointments which had been part of the splendors of the fourteenth century.[46]

Other factors help account for the decline of the luxury crafts, but do not so fully explain it as the decline of patronage. The depression of building activity must have had considerable impact on associated crafts. Relentless taxation could not have alleviated the difficulties, nor could arbitrary confiscation and plunder have promoted commerce.[47]

The evident damage done by Tamerlane to the fine crafts of Damascus by the forced removal of skilled workers is also rightly taken to be an important cause of the ruin of Damascus, but wrongly to be the source of the general weakness of fine crafts in the fifteenth century.[48] If Tamerlane's seizure of the skilled workers of Damascus were the only cause of the regression of the fine crafts in the fifteenth century, how can the simultaneous decline of Cairo as well as of other Syrian towns as artistic centers be explained? Agricultural decline was the ultimate source of urban economic difficulties, for the reduction of Mamluk incomes entailed a corresponding withdrawal of patronage from luxury crafts.

With craft production and agriculture failing, internal trade followed suit. The important Egyptian-Syrian trade did not completely cease, but sporadic evidence indicates that it was in serious straits. Unprotected from harassment by bedouins and errant soldiers the routes were unsafe. The state's courier and postal communications system collapsed and the way-stations on which caravans depended fell into disrepair. Bazaars selling Syrian goods in Cairo closed down for lack of commerce, though certain foodstuffs and related products continued to come through. The customs of Qaṭyā, once reported to be a thousand dinars (or about 20,000 dirhems) a day fell to about 130,000 or 150,000 dirhems a month by 798/1395–96.[49] Only the international spice trade continued to flourish. Confined basically to the coastal towns, the few necessary interior caravans were secured, and the trade remained lively in spite of events in the hinterland. Nothing better demonstrates the superficial relation of the international trade to the rest of the regional economy than its continued prosperity in the face of general decline.

The most arresting aspect of the economic crisis was the breakdown of the monetary system and the inflation of prices. From about 781/1379–80 excessive monetization of copper provoked an inflation of prices quoted in its terms. Increasing amounts of copper forced silver out of circulation, and by about 1400 silver ceased to be used and copper coin reckoned in dirhems of account became the common medium of exchange. Copper vis-à-vis gold quickly depreciated and reached its depths in 808/1405–06. The crisis was aggravated, if not precipitated, by international metal movements which brought heavy quantities of copper into Egypt and probably drew out silver. These arbitrage movements reflected an Italian, indeed, a world-wide monetary disturbance. In Egypt prices rose precipitously and fluctuated madly. Total confusion reigned in all markets. Yet basically the worst was over by 808/1405–06. Copper then stabilized and in 815/1412 actually rose slightly in value. At that time a new silver coin of extremely good quality was introduced and prices resumed a steady course.[50]

This crisis, though exceedingly brief and disturbing in the short run, must itself be ruled out as a cause of the long-term economic difficulties which had their roots in this period. Though it has often been treated, both by contemporaries such as al-Maqrīzī and later by western scholars, as the cause of the economic hardships, long-term price changes cannot be correlated with the monetary inflation. Grain prices showed a slight secular rise in terms of gold, though not so severe as the monetary inflation, while manufactured goods rose enormously in value, totally out of proportion to the inflation.[51] Obviously real factors in food supply and demand, raw materials, and wages were more important than the coinage difficulties themselves.

These decades of tumult were a severe hardship for all classes of the population. Although it is likely that some holders of goods, soldiers, officials, or peasants may have prospered from inflation, or certain artisans such as millers and bakers from a precipitous rise of wages, most people suffered. Famines and shortages became frequent. Egypt underwent major crises in 796/1394 and 798/1396 and again between 805–08/1402–05. 813/1410 and 818/1416 were also harsh years. Moreover, apart from particularly severe crises, the general price level of grain rose in this period about twenty per cent in constant gold terms, and probably vastly more in terms of the copper money available to most of the people.[52]

The middle classes were also hard hit by the rising cost of cloth and other manufactured goods. Cotton, wool, and linen cloth rose from three to ten times their original price. Middle-class merchants and ulama suffered because clothing, drapes, rugs, pillows, blankets, and the like were the most important forms of bourgeois wealth. Cloth played the same part that automobiles and durable mechanical goods play today in the American middle-class standard of living. The drastic rise of cloth prices made it impossible for middle income families ever again to enjoy the prosperity of earlier times.[53] With the religious classes impoverished by stipends which lagged behind the inflation, the men of state by declining tax revenues, the merchants by falling trade, and the common people by high food prices, all Mamluk society suffered.

THE FIFTEENTH CENTURY RESTORATION: 1422–1470

Yet beginning with the reign of Sultan al-Mu'ayyad Sheikh (1412–1421) and his successor Sultan Barsbāy (1422–1438) a partial restoration of the fortunes of the empire was achieved. Deliberately they set about to restore its glory as it had been in the time of Baybars (1260–1277). Al-Mu'ayyad Sheikh put an end to internal wars. Mamluk rebellions were snuffed out. Bedouin anarchy, though never entirely quelled, was reduced to exceptional and sporadic circumstances.

Above all, al-Mu'ayyad Sheikh and Barsbāy re-established the security of the empire. In a series of vigorous campaigns between 817/1414 and 838/1434–35 the Turkoman states were pushed out of northern Syria, and Mamluk supremacy in the upper Euphrates region was restored. The Turkomans of Dulghādir, Ramaḍān, and Karamān* were chastised. Albistān, Tarsus, and Adana were again incorporated into the empire. In 842/1439 new annexations in Diyārbakr brought the empire to its furthest limits. The threats of the Ak Koyunlu and Kara Koyunlu confederations were also warded off. Though the region of Aleppo was attacked and Aintab burned in 821/1418, the Mamluks managed in 836/1433 to extract a favorable peace from the Ak Koyunlu.[54]

Resistance to Christian piracy was equally vigorous. A series of raids against Cyprus mushroomed in 829/1426 into the complete conquest of the island, the first Muslim victory at sea in centuries. The attacks on Cyprus were followed in 843/1439, 846/1442, and 848/1444 by similar, though indecisive, raids on Rhodes.[55]

Al-Mu'ayyad Sheikh and Barsbāy also succeeded in re-establishing the domestic economy. Under al-Mu'ayyad Sheikh the monetary situation was stabilized. Silver dirhems of high quality were again minted in abundance for the first time since before the turn of the century. Barsbāy followed by issuing the Ashrāfī dinar as the standard gold coin of the empire, to compete with the commonly circulated Venetian ducat. With coinage stabilized, prices inflated by the monetary disturbances assumed more normal levels. Incomplete figures indicate that at least until the middle of the century food prices compared favorably with fourteenth century norms. A partial restoration of the popular standard of living seems indicated.[56]

The restoration made itself felt throughout the economy. For most

* Karamān—a Turkoman principality founded in the thirteenth century to the north and west of Syria.

of the remainder of the fifteenth century some agricultural improvements were made, and urban production and trade resumed something of their old vigor. Production of goods for mass consumption carried on as usual. Damascus continued to be a manufacturing and craft center of all-round importance. Silk, cotton, linen textiles and embroideries, felt, and carpets were manufactured. Military supplies, weapons, knives, bows, lances and equestrian equipment, saddles, and horse covers supplied the Mamluk forces. Iron, copper, ceramic, wood, leather, and straw utensils and household goods were also fashioned. Building materials and builders' skills were available. Carpenters, masons, and lime and brick makers are mentioned in the sources.[57]

Though not so well rounded as Damascus, other important towns carried on a wide range of activities. At Aleppo, tanning, cotton carding, spinning, bleaching, dyeing, and weaving were important industries. There too copper, iron, ceramics, paper, glass, saddles, and weapons were produced. Soap, however, was Aleppo's specialty. It was manufactured in the city itself, and also collected from surrounding regions to be marketed in Anatolia, Diyārbakr, Iraq, Syria, and Egypt. Jerusalem and Tripoli made silks, and almost all of the smaller cities and towns produced cotton goods. Oil, hides, soap, glass, and minerals were processed in the lesser towns.[58]

By contrast, the manufacture of luxury goods remained in evident decline. Inlaid brass and copper ware and gilded glass continued to be manufactured, but the evidence of surviving pieces shows that output was much reduced and of inferior quality. Jewelry continued to be made and gold was imported from Genoa to be worked in Damascus and then re-exported. Both Arabic and European sources also report that fine silks, brocades, velvets, satins, and other specialty textiles were still woven in Damascus, though the spectacular cloths and furnishings fashioned in the fourteenth century are no longer mentioned. In other towns, at Aleppo, Tripoli, and Jerusalem, some silk, gold, and copper wares continued to be produced. High quality ceramics, however, disappeared completely. Other specialized skills were lost. Skilled builders such as lead roofers, for example, had to be imported from Anatolia to repair the ravages of a fire of 884/1479–80 in the Umayyad Mosque of Damascus, and even then did allegedly inferior work.[59]

The reasons for the failure of the luxury trades to revive are various. The most important general factor was the slackening of Mamluk patronage discussed above, but perhaps equally important in certain instances was international competition. Craft work is necessarily specialty work, and the novelty and variety of foreign goods are always tempting. In this particular case, the competition of Italy's acquired capacity to produce imitations of Syrian brocades, damask, and gilded glass, and the competition of Florentine woolen garments cost local initiative heavily. Al-Maqrīzī complained of disastrous imports of Italian cloth and the universal preference for the high quality, low cost goods coming from Europe. From the other side of the world, the competition of Chinese ceramics also took a heavy toll. Deprived of an important part of their patronage, artistic abilities in Syria and Egypt were declining in the fifteenth century.[60]

For the history of internal trade, most of our information about the Syrian-Egyptian traffic comes from the middle of the century or later, but it points clearly to a steady flow though under increasingly precarious circumstances. Egypt continued to import Syrian agricultural products such as sheep, fruits, rose water, dates, rice, and shrubs. Cloth including Baalbek cotton, brocades from Damascus, and silks from Hama, Damascus, and Baalbek also found markets in Cairo. Paper and marble are mentioned. The only known Egyptian export was grain. Other routes also remained active. Damascus continued to find her needs throughout the Syrian hinterlands, and Aleppo imported food stuffs, salt, and cloth from different parts of Syria. In Palestine a local trade in fruit, grain, animals, and cotton went on as usual.[61]

These economic successes were nonetheless burdened by unremitting military pressures, and as the burdens became greater, the available resources of the state declined. First among the hardships was the effort to maintain the northern frontiers. By contrast with Mamluk experience in the fourteenth century, victories and annexations did not once and forever dispel the Tatar and Turkoman pressures. The Ak Koyunlu raised new fears of attack on Aleppo. More menacing still was the growing strength of the already colossal Ottoman Empire. The pressures of its expansion on Dulghādir and Karamān forced these lesser principalities into frequent clashes with the Mamluks as they struggled to hold their balance in the kaleidoscopic turmoil of Anatolian politics. Until 870/1465–66, however, the situation remained under Mamluk control.[62]

At the same time, pirate attacks on Muslim shipping and shores proved another costly danger. Neither the conquest of Cyprus in 829/1426, nor the attacks on Rhodes, nor the massive intervention of the Mamluks to preserve their suzerainty on Cyprus in the decade of the 860's/1456–66 relieved the pressure. Nor did passive defenses avail. Efforts to reinforce coastal defenses, especially between 843/1439–40 and 857/1453, with new fortresses, watch towers, better roads, and fresh garrisons did little to protect Beirut, Tripoli, Alexandria, Rosetta, Ṭīna, Damietta, or lesser places on the coasts of Syria, Palestine, and Egypt.

Thus the Mamluks were obliged to take up the inordinate burdens of defense at sea. Though lacking in materials and skilled manpower, ship construction was nonetheless intensified. Materials when not available from Europe were in desperation acquired by escorted expeditions to the Anatolian coasts. The costs of this effort are beyond calculation and contributed as much as any other factor to the bankruptcy of the Mamluk system. Only in 1480 did constant pirate pressure slacken and even cease for almost three decades. Yet this remission was itself an ominous sign. Decades of Mamluk effort had not succeeded in repressing piracy. Rather the establishment of Ottoman hegemony in the Aegean and eastern Mediterranean accomplished what the Mamluks could not do for themselves. Egypt and Syria were already becoming dependent on the Ottoman Empire.[63]

The high costs of these military efforts, of maintaining a navy, and of importing slaves to fill ranks decimated by plague and wars required increased revenues precisely at a moment when the resources of Syria and Egypt were reduced. The result was intensified taxation of the subject population. New taxes were levied on almost all goods in common use. Fruits, vegetables, and grain brought into towns were subject to sales and market taxes. Craftsmen engaged in blacksmithing, cloth dyeing, carding, spinning, weaving, tanning, and other industries were now subjected to new taxation. Unprecedented and arbitrary levies were introduced, and no matter what efforts were made abuse could never be rooted out. Each particular instance might be appealed, but no matter how many times the Sultan was induced to abolish a particular tax, or remove a corrupt official, taxes of a similar kind were later reintroduced or permitted elsewhere. Endless variation in the products taxed, rates of taxation, manner of assessment, regions of application, methods of collection, and agencies of administration made the tax system a hydra. Besides direct taxation of sales or output by tax farmers and officials, the *muḥtasib,* or market inspector, collected a monthly tax from all trades. Taxes were also levied indirectly through the fees of brokers or witnesses who turned over part of their commissions to the regime.[64]

Not content with this, the Sultan and the more important emirs sought to seize a larger share of the fruits of commerce by direct intervention in trade. One Mamluk response to the shortage of funds was to monopolize parts of the normal merchant economy. The first monopoly was established in the spice trade by Sultan Barsbāy (1422–1438), but other trades were at least temporarily made into state monopolies. To supplement monopoly profits, Barsbāy also had recourse to forced purchases in which merchants or the public in general were obliged to buy fixed quantities of goods at given prices from the Sultan or his agents.[65] By and large, however, such complex commercial exploitations proved difficult to maintain and after Barsbāy's reign were abandoned until the third quarter of the century when these supplementary devices were resurrected and new ones introduced.

This exploitation did not serve to personally enrich the Mamluks. On the contrary, the incomes and wealth of high ranking officers declined in the fifteenth century. Evidence from the size of gifts exchanged, salary levels, and the treasures of Sultans and emirs points to a catastrophic reduction in Mamluk incomes. At times, it was even impossible to distribute wages and rations to the troops. Far from being enriched by heavy taxation, the Mamluks struggled merely to preserve vestiges of their style of life, support at least the semblance of full military contingents, and meet the costs of exceptionally heavy warfare.[66] Exploitation was a sign of the impoverishment of Syria and Egypt and their inability to sustain the costs of defense.

With the empire but partially restored, the welfare of the towns was only partially assured. Aleppo remained exposed to the menace of Turkoman and Ak Koyunlu attack, but seems to have suffered no deleterious effects on this account. Damascus was more secure, sheltered by Aleppo and the coastal towns from both northern and western pressures. Within Syria, at least until the third quarter of the century, bedouin raiding, intervillage warfare, and banditry remained within control although sporadic difficulties especially in southern Syria and along the pilgrimage route are noted. The towns, moreover, were by and large spared the bickering of the Mamluks. Only in 842/1438–39 and 866/1461–62 were there rebellions in Damascus and Aleppo and fighting among the troops.[67]

On the other hand, the internal stability of the towns was progressively more disturbed by economic decline and fiscal exploitation. Violent demonstrations, assaults against officials, and public protests became more frequent as popular exasperation with abusive taxation overwhelmed patience with the usual methods of petition and negotiation. In Cairo, moreover, the Mamluks themselves became a threat to internal security. Imperfectly assimilated forces eager to avoid the hardships of war and enjoy the fruits of power plagued the city with riots and indiscriminate pillage and fighting. Succession struggles and food and pay riots spilled over at the expense of the populace as a whole. Stealing from merchants and artisans, molesting and abducting women, assaulting citizens who annoyed or offended them, looting and burning on the flimsiest pretexts, the defense forces of the empire made life in Cairo more precarious than any threat of foreign invasion or bedouin attack. Other cities whose garrisons did not include the unruly recruits were spared such troubles save when the Cairo armies appeared on expedition.[68]

Equally symptomatic of decline was the falling off of investment in maintenance of the urban physical plant. Construction and public works languished, for the great surplus revenues which had created the splendors of earlier centuries were simply no longer available. Street works and canalizations were for the most part unknown. Only in the reign of Barsbāy when replacements for old losses were imperative, and in a curious Indian summer of construction in the final decades of the Mamluk period, did Damascus show any vigor in the endowment of communal facilities. Aleppo, on the other hand, was neglected throughout. In both cases, emphasis shifted from the endowment and construction of great monuments to the founding of small schools and convents which often required no more than the house of the founder for capital. These smaller foundations represented the efforts of the ulama to sustain communal and religious life in the face of growing neglect by the Mamluk regime. Without a fresh stimulus and investment of funds from without, the ulama had to resort to their own efforts. In Damascus, for example, whereas only about a fifth of the new endowments up to 820/1417 were financed by the ulama, about a third of the works in the subsequent century were at the expense of qadis (judges) and sheikhs. Merchants and merchant-officials similarly accounted for about one-sixth of the fifteenth and early sixteenth century projects, whereas they were responsible for only a tenth of earlier works. In Aleppo, the situation was even more extreme. Local qadis, ulama, and merchants were responsible for fully two-thirds of the known projects. Thus major investments of rural incomes were replaced by the transfer of smaller urban-created reserves to local communal uses.

On the other hand, it seems that Aleppo did continue to grow in size and possibly in population. New quarters on the south and east of the city were included within the new fortifications constructed in the twenties and thirties of the fifteenth century, and about the turn of the sixteenth century new water canals and fountains were installed in quarters to the north and south of the old city. At the same time numerous khans and other commercial buildings were constructed as well. In Damascus, however, parts of the old city were in ruins, and suburban areas had long since lost their facilities and attractions.[69] These differences may be due to the fact that Damascus carried on the remnants of a better founded religious tradition and thus lent her remaining energy and wealth to mosques and schools, while Aleppo better responded to economic influences emanating largely from the expansion of the Ottoman Empire in the north.

THE FALL OF THE MAMLUK EMPIRE: 1470–1517

Withal, the empire and the major towns held their own through the middle decades of the century. But from about 1470 fresh and cumulative strains pushed Mamluk Syria and Egypt into the vortex of complete economic, political, and social collapse from which they would ultimately be rescued only by incorporation into the Ottoman Empire.

The immediate cause of this new time of troubles was the resumption of war in Anatolia. From 870/1465–66 to 877/1472–73, the Mamluks fought to protect their sphere of influence from Ottoman-supported factions. In the struggle between the Dulghādir princes, the Mamluks backed Shāh Buḍa' against Ottoman-supported Shāh Suwār, and almost lost control of Adana and Tarsus. Northern Syria was actually occupied by Shāh Suwār, Aintab burned, and Aleppo again endangered. Mamluk defenses were severely tested even though the Ottomans did not intervene directly in the fighting. Then, from 889/1484 to 895/1490 the two empires confronted each other directly in Adana and Tarsus. The Mamluks retained the provinces, but the Ottomans won a symbolic victory, obliging the Mamluks to divert the revenues of the districts solely to the support of Medina and Mecca. The outcome was not too unfavorable, but what for the Mamluks had taken on the aspect of a war for survival had been for the Ottomans but a frontier skirmish.[70]

An important internal correlative of these discouraging wars was the resumption of intensive bedouin marauding throughout Mamluk domains. In the 870's/1460's–70's bedouins in Upper Egypt and the delta destroyed villages and interfered with grain supplies for Cairo. Bedouin risings in Syria devastated the Hauran south of Damascus and areas around Aleppo and Tripoli. In the ensuing decades, bedouins further destroyed the Hama region and parts of Palestine. Ramla was reported in ruins, and the Nablus region the scene of fighting between Mamluk forces and local tribes. From about the turn of the century, the situation took a drastic turn for the worse. Bedouin raiding in Upper Egypt intensified. In Syria Damascus became the scene of constant inter-village and inter-tribal warfare as well as rebellions against the regime. The Ghūṭa, the Hauran, and al-Biqāʿ were devastated, the former reduced from some three hundred to forty-two surviving villages. In one episode alone, bedouins burned two hundred villages and taxed countless others. Elsewhere the damage was comparable. When in 926/1520 the Ottomans made their first survey of Tripoli, they found only eight hundred out of three thousand villages still productive.

This cumulative destruction, heaped on a century of neglect and abuse, proved ruinous. In their first census of Egypt the Ottomans found total revenue reduced from 9.5 million in the fourteenth century to no more than 1.8 million dinars. The economy of Egypt mocked its former potential.[71]

Simultaneously, overland trade between Syria and Egypt was severely inhibited. At least from 875/1470–71, merchants had to cross the desert from Cairo to Gaza in caravans with military escort. At least two hundred camels were needed for safety, and a month usually passed between journeys. The Gaza-Damascus section of the route remained relatively safe, but was so ill provided for that travelers had to provision themselves for a ten day journey. The waqfs which had once supported communications had fallen into disrepair. Trade declined, and the tolls at Qaṭyā, our only index of the relative volume of trade, which a century earlier had been 150,000 dirhems (about 8,000 dinars at an average of twenty to one) a month, fell to 8,000 dinars a year. Other routes in Syria were equally depressed. So unsafe had the pilgrimage become that between 900/1494–95 and 918/1513 scarcely a year passed in which the pilgrimage was neither attacked by bedouins nor abandoned in advance as hopelessly dangerous.[72]

Mamluk efforts to stave off economic collapse only precipitated further hardships. The burdens of illegal taxation were immeasurably increased. Thefts and extortions became more frequent, and from about the third quarter of the century such special devices as the forced purchase came into common use. Once reserved for the needs of the Sultan, the forced purchase became an instrument of emirs, provincial governors, and officials for the consolidation of private fortunes. It was at this time, though with precedent, that emirs in Jerusalem, Damascus, Tripoli, and Aleppo obliged, not only merchants, but urban populations as a whole to make purchases. For example, from about 890/1485, Jerusalem and surrounding towns were regularly required to buy fixed quantities of oil at outrageous prices.

At the same time, the market inspector's taxes reached unprecedented levels in Cairo and Damascus. In addition, property taxes and fixed fees were levied on a community wide basis. The quarters of Damascus were directly assessed to pay for infantry support for military expeditions against the Ottomans and the bedouins. Waqfs and endowments were no more respected than other forms of wealth. Waqf inspectors seized institutional revenues, and then levied supplementary taxes on the revenue-producing properties to the detriment of their ability to support the religious institutions. Capital slowly accumulated for community use was diverted and destroyed. Illegal taxation reached the economic breaking point and endangered the whole fabric of urban social life.[73]

Economic distress made itself felt in the common standard of living. The second half of the fifteenth century seems to have been a period of unusually high prices in which both shortages of agricultural commodities and the burdens of taxation played their part. In the last decade of the century debasement of the copper coinage once more added to popular hardships. Moreover, from 889/1484 the big cities, notably Cairo, began to suffer dislocations in marketing organization. Not only were grain prices high or irregular, but there were unexpected shortages of meat, at one time, or rice, cheese, and cotton at others. Information on the situation in the Syrian towns is lacking, but it seems clear that at least from 906/1500–01 Damascus too began to suffer irregular shortages and high prices.[74]

The crowning blow to the Mamluk economy was the disruption of the established Mediterranean trading patterns. The Portuguese discoveries were a decisive moment, but internal forces in the Mediterranean had for some decades already sapped the value of the traffic. Throughout the early part of the fifteenth century, Syria and Egypt remained in contact with Italian, Spanish, French, and Balkan towns. Traffic from Venice made its way to Egypt and Syria via the Peloponnesus while Genoese tramps sailed the North African coast to Alexandria and often touched at Beirut on the return voyage. Provençals, Catalans, Ragusans, and others were also active. Despite Egyptian monopolies, taxes, confiscations, arrests, and disputes of all sorts, the profitable Levant trade continued in the face of all difficulties. Temporary suspensions were common as part of the war of nerves over the division of advantages, but did little harm to the trade in which the Europeans hauled spices, sugar, dyes, silks, and cotton westward and brought wood, metals, and cloth to the East.

From about 1460, however, the definitive consolidation of the Ottoman Empire in the eastern Mediterranean changed the intensities of these patterns. The Ottomans excluded the Italians from their Aegean and Black Sea possessions, and, especially Genoa, from the eastern traffic. Most of her interests had been in what were already Ottoman territories, and to obtain dyes, silks, spices, alum, and sugar Genoa turned her attention westward with a vigor which was to bear the most astonishing economic consequences. Venice, on the other hand, maintained her traffic with Syria and Egypt and inherited the Genoese North African trade, but found herself under considerable pressure. The Ottomans were developing Bursa and Istanbul as centers for the distribution of spices in the Balkans and in northern and eastern Europe. In 1468 Venice was obliged to reduce her activity in Syria. Having once called at Latakia, Jaffa, and Acre as well, the Venetians confined themselves henceforth to Beirut and Tripoli. The Ottomans did not destroy the spice routes, but they did quash the eastern intra-Mediterranean traffic.

In response, however, there seems to have been an expansion of the overland Syrian-Anatolian trade. With the emergence of Bursa as a redistributing center for oriental goods on their way to eastern Europe, Turkish merchants came to Damascus to buy spices, and Ottoman records reveal Syrians from Aleppo and Damascus selling spices, dyes, and silks in Bursa. Adding fresh impetus to the older traffic in slaves from the Caucasus and in local specialties such as Aleppo soap, the new spice interests gave valuable support to an otherwise declining economy. Overland commerce flourished again, and auxiliary routes were encouraged. Annual pilgrimage caravans from Mecca made Bursa their new terminus. Persian merchants appeared in Damascus, Cairo, and Aleppo, and Syrian merchants went to Hormuz. Alexandria too kept up contacts with Anatolia by sea and Turkish merchants maintained a *funduq** there.[75] The reorientation of the trade routes was not without benefit to the economy of the provinces, but it was nonetheless at the expense of what were probably more lucrative routes.

Portuguese discoveries, however, further reduced the Egyptian and Syrian share of the international spice trade. By the beginning of the sixteenth century, the Venetians could no longer find adequate supplies of spices in Egypt, and would not import valuable metals and cloth. As trade dwindled, the Mamluk state was deprived of crucial revenues and strategic goods. The slackening of the trade by no means destroyed the economy, but it removed what had been for well over a century one of its most reliable and useful props.[76]

Indeed, Portuguese interference with Muslim shipping in the Indian Ocean not only reduced revenues but required further heavy investments to protect the commerce. At the same time that the Mamluks sought to put new fleets into eastern waters, piracy in the Mediterranean jeopardized the lifeline of supplies from the Ottoman Empire. Ottoman shipments of timber, iron, naval stores, and cannon were seized by pirates while the Mamluks exhausted themselves throwing good money after bad in vain efforts to protect the trade.[77]

Defeated on land and sea, and economically exhausted, the authority of the Mamluk regime began to collapse. Mamluk rebellions became common in Syria as well as Egypt. Fighting at Damascus and Aleppo in 903/1497–98, 905/1499–1500, and again in 910/1504–05 again involved the populace of the towns in Mamluk battles. The state became the prey of its own elite while the urban populaces divided in support of different Mamluk factions. Worse still, having abused and neglected both town and countryside to the limit, the Mamluks found they could no longer command obedience. Riots, attacks on abusive officials, and mass protests by the end of the century turned into movements of organized resistance. In Damascus after 890/1485 bands of young men called *zuʿar* fought the Mamluks, resisted their demands, and virtually required the Mamluk regime to govern by negotiation with the urban masses. Order in the Syrian countryside was equally precarious and

* *Funduq*—an inn, warehouse, and marketplace for foreign merchants.

was kept only by constant raiding and counter-raiding as the Mamluks sought to govern by intimidation. With the authority and even the power of the state broken, communal feuds in Syria also came to the fore. Villages, tribes, and organized factions of urban quarters fought each other in rounds of vicious bickering. Armed gangs preyed on the rich, extorting money from shopkeepers, pillaging the rich quarters, and assaulting likely victims in the streets. The collapse of internal order brought the Mamluk regime to its term. When it was defeated in 1517 by the Ottomans the populations of Syria and later of Egypt welcomed the victor.[78]

In strength and in weakness, in clear form and confusion, the Mamluk system had persisted for over two and a half centuries and dominated the historical and economic experiences of the cities. However, to understand how this influence was exerted, we shall have to make explicit the precise means by which Mamluk power permeated city life.

CHAPTER II · THE MAMLUK REGIME IN THE LIFE OF THE CITIES

THE STATE AND THE PRIVATIZATION OF POWER

No FORCE in the life of the cities of Syria and Egypt was of greater importance than the Mamluk state, for organized urban life depended on the intimate participation of the Mamluks in many important aspects of urban affairs. This participation, however, was complicated by the fact that the Mamluk regime was a government of slave soldiers, mostly Turks and Circassians, who not only differed racially but in origin, language, ethos, and privilege from the largely Arabic speaking peoples of Egypt and Syria over whom they ruled. The Mamluks were recruited as slaves in the Caucasus and the Russian steppes while still young, and though converted to Islam, remained isolated from their subjects by a system of upbringing which confined them to barracks and won their sole allegiance to the emirs who trained them and to their brothers in arms. No study of Mamluk "court culture" has yet been made, save of the taste for military sports and games, but we know well enough of the lack of mutual comprehension between the populace and the foreigners, who cannot have been better loved for their monopoly of military skill and for the dependence of the rest of the society upon them.[1] A wide gulf separated the rulers and the ruled who could never aspire to military positions and, thus, to an important place in the state.

The essential concerns of this military elite were the organization of the army and the exploitation of the subject population. The military was organized into regiments of men who were the personal slaves of their officers. The Sultans' royal Mamluks were the core of the state's armies and were garrisoned in Cairo, while each of the high ranking emirs similarly maintained forces appropriate to his rank and supervised the training, discipline, and deployment of the troops. In addition, the Sultan maintained a large court to which he appointed leading officers to manage his military affairs, private revenues, and a host of court functions. This state sustained itself by taxing both rural and urban trade and production and it employed a large bureaucracy,

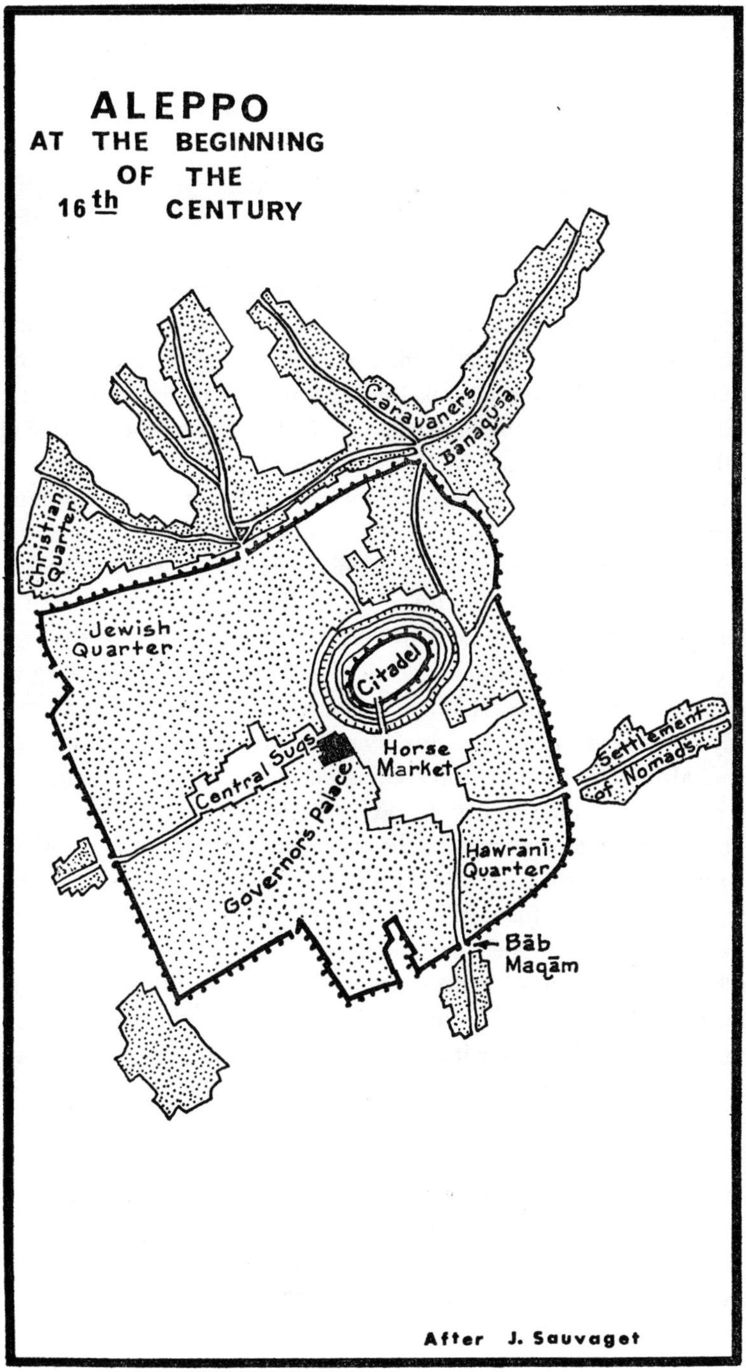
ALEPPO
AT THE BEGINNING
OF THE
16th CENTURY
Caravaners
Bānaqūsā
Christian Quarter
Jewish Quarter
Citadel
Central Suqs
Horse Market
Governors Palace
Settlement of Nomads
Hawrānī Quarter
Bāb Maqām
After J. Sauvaget

staffed by Muslim, Christian, and Jewish scribes, accountants, and tax agents. Despite a great array of titles and functions, the bureaucracy was basically organized into three types of bureaus—for correspondence and record keeping, for tax collection, and for the administration of the troops. Special commissioners for construction, granaries, hospitals, presses, the mint, and so on, were assigned management of the Sultan's properties while the religious leaders of the Muslim community were appointed to be judges, supervisors of the public treasury, and market inspectors. Despite basic division of civil and military functions, the offices of the Sultan's court tended to encroach on their civil counterparts, and Mamluk emirs took leading positions in the other service.[2]

Most important of the bureaucracy's functions was the management of the land revenues set aside to support the army. The army was garrisoned in the major towns and land was assigned to pay annual taxes to the officers in accord with their rank and the numbers of soldiers they maintained, but the soldiers did not have direct access to the land and depended on the civil services for its administration.[3] Thus, the bureaucracy served to curb the independence of the troops vis-à-vis their masters and above all vis-à-vis the Sultan. As long as it controlled access to the land it protected the ruler against the frittering away of his resources and ultimately of his disciplinary powers over the army. More important, by intervening between the soldiery, ignorant of the character of the population and of the requirements of productivity in agriculture and the crafts, and the subject peoples of the empire, the bureaucracy served to defend the long-term interests of both populace and regime against the unthinking rapacity of aliens who lacked commitments to mitigate their demands upon the society they ruled. Nonetheless, over-all control and direction of the apparatus lay in Mamluk hands and insofar as a distinction is to be made in actual operations between civil and military it can be only at lower levels of action rather than in the policy and objectives of the whole. The bureaucracy was an instrument of Mamluk government, a subordinate part of the Mamluk state.

Basically this bureaucracy existed to serve the needs of the Sultan and to control the administration of rural revenues. Apart from the central government and armies, however, administrative functions were parceled out to the leading emirs who were allowed to act in a quasi-independent manner. Each city was assigned a governor and other Mamluk officials to take charge of both the army and the collection of

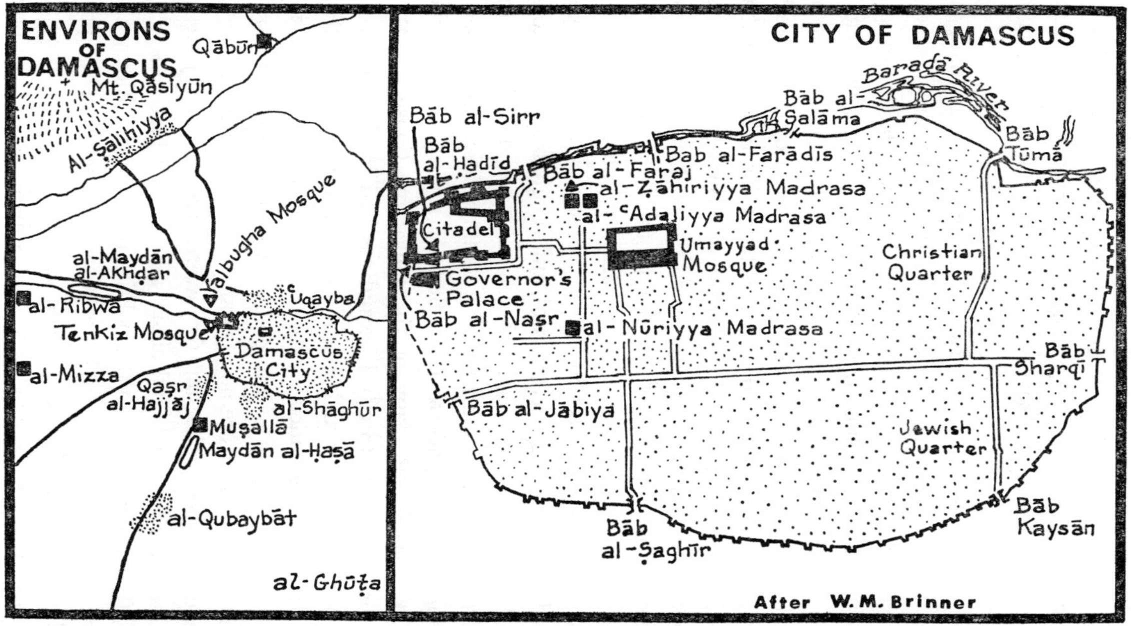
ENVIRONS OF DAMASCUS
Qābūn
Mt. Qāsiyūn
Al-Ṣāliḥiyya
Yalbugha Mosque
al-Maydān al-Akhḍar
al-Ribwa
ʿUqayba
Tenkiz Mosque
Damascus City
al-Mizza
Qaṣr al-Ḥajjāj
al-Shāghūr
Muṣallā
Maydān al-Ḥaṣā
al-Qubaybāt
al-Ghūṭa
CITY OF DAMASCUS
Baradā River
Bāb al-Salāma
Bāb Tūmā
Bāb al-Sirr
Bāb al-Ḥadīd
Bab al-Farādīs
Bāb al-Faraj
al-Ẓāhiriyya Madrasa
al-ʿAdaliyya Madrasa
Citadel
Umayyad Mosque
Christian Quarter
Governor's Palace
Bāb al-Naṣr
al-Nūriyya Madrasa
Bāb Sharqī
Bāb al-Jābiya
Jewish Quarter
Bāb Kaysān
Bāb al-Ṣaghīr
After W. M. Brinner

some of the urban taxes essential to their own salaries and the maintenance of the military establishment. The governor was the commander in chief and the leading administrator, but other emirs, coordinate in authority, were assigned their duties independently in order to check his powers and preserve the influence of the Sultan. Local administration was built around these governors and high ranking emirs who carried out their duties by organizing extensive households around themselves. The military retinues of Mamluks and auxiliary retainers made up the core of these households, but the emirs also employed scribes, accountants, lawyers, merchants, and tax collectors to administer their wealth and provision the troops. The military household thus became a center of local administration analogous to the state bureaus, but based on the personal dependents and clients of the emirs.[4]

These households had a larger importance for urban life than their strict military and fiscal duties would imply. Since the central government took no responsibility for the usual needs of urban administration, responsibility for public services fell to the Mamluk governors and emirs as an indirect consequence of their military and fiscal duties. There were no state services, budgets, procedures, or special personnel concerned with the economic, cultural, and religious needs of townsmen, but the Mamluks were considered generally responsible for the well-being of the towns and for whatever administrative works seemed essential for internal peace and the flow of revenues. Thus the emirs personally carried out many of the police functions, sanitation, and public works essential to city life, and assisted in the endowment and management of religious and educational institutions.[5] Since these were not strictly speaking official duties, they were left to the initiative, discretion, and interests of the emirs. Authority was decentralized to the point where there were no assignments of or sanctions for the nonperformance of these roles, but they were accepted or rejected for important social, traditional, and above all personal motives.

Thus, the crucial factor in the politics of Mamluk cities was not the structure of the regime or the bureaucracy as such, but the position in which the powers and facilities which accrued to its individual members placed them in the society at large. The substitution of the households of the leading Mamluk officials for bureaucratic machinery was of the greatest importance because the households were not merely branches of the state, but potential sources of private power and influence which could be used for independent ends. The Mamluk house-

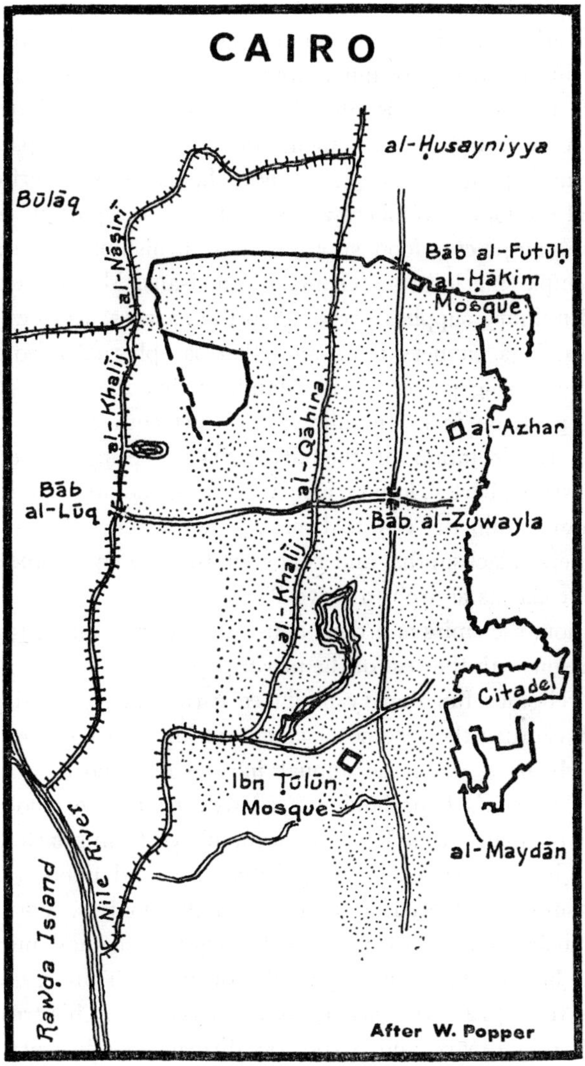
CAIRO
al-Ḥusayniyya
Būlāq
al-Nāṣirī
Bāb al-Futūḥ
al-Ḥākim
Mosque
al-Khalīj
al-Qāhira
al-Azhar
Bāb
al-Lūq
Bāb al-Zuwayla
al-Khalīj
Citadel
Ibn Ṭūlūn
Mosque
al-Maydān
Nile River
Rawḍa Island
After W. Popper

hold was a means of transforming public into private powers and state authority into personal superiority.[6]

THE ECONOMIC POWERS OF THE MAMLUK HOUSEHOLD

The privatization of power and the dominance of the Mamluks in the larger urban society resulted from the central role of the Mamluk households in the economic life of the towns. Composed of soldiers, servants, scribes, and officials, their families, and the people allied to them by marriage or clientage, these households were powerful patrons of the local economy. Numbers alone made them important consumers of military equipment, food supplies, and furnishing and services of all sorts, employing local merchants and artisans. Mamluk expeditions demanded military supplies prepared in the bazaars. Reviews required new clothes, flags, banners, tents, and other paraphernalia. So important was the purchasing power of the Mamluks that the expansion of the Damascus garrison in the middle of the thirteenth century induced a prodigious reorientation of the city markets. Suppliers of saddles, harnesses, straw, barley, knives, armor, leather, and other military needs moved from within the city to beneath the citadel. They were joined by carpenters, blacksmiths, and coppersmiths and by brothels, restaurants, and cabarets as well to serve the troops.[7]

In addition, the emirs and their households were enormously wealthy in comparison with the rest of the urban population. Whereas a worker or minor religious functionary might earn two dirhems a day,[8] in the fourteenth century the income of emirs ran up to a half million and a million dirhems a year, the annual income of almost two thousand workers. An emir's household was as wealthy as the whole working population of small towns. Reserves accumulated from salaries, exploitation, and gifts created enormous fortunes revealed upon confiscations or in treasures discovered at the death of the holders. Vast stocks of grain, animals, clothes, weapons, stable equipment, and utensils then came to light. When, for example, the fortune of Tankiz, governor of Damascus from 712/1312–741/1340, was confiscated, his treasury contained 360,000 dinars and 1,500,000 dirhems, cloth worth 640,000 dinars, and 4,200 animals. Besides land and villages, he owned palaces, khans, baths, and markets in Damascus worth about 2,600,000 dirhems, and over 900,000 dirhems worth of property in Beirut, Homs, and other smaller towns. Tankiz was exceptionally rich in real estate holdings, but similar fortunes appeared for other emirs. Gifts exchanged between the Sultan and emirs also revealed treasures of cloth, gold, slaves, furs, jeweled weapons, silks, and even food delicacies. Fifteenth century fortunes were not as grand as those of the fourteenth, but in relation to the income of the common people were still exceedingly large.[9] The livelihood of everyone was attuned to the Mamluks, and in addition the emirs were patrons of the local quality crafts which only they and the small class of their economic peers could afford.

Even more important for the power of the Mamluk households over urban economies was the structure of the tax system devised to support the armies. The Mamluks were paid part of their salaries in kind. Grain payments were intended to meet their household needs, but it gave the Mamluks a vital part in the intra-urban economies. To convert their incomes to cash the emirs sold surplus grain on the urban markets. They became the towns most important suppliers of foodstuffs, and in consequence equally important as consumers of urban products and services. The Mamluks thus disrupted the normal pattern of urban-rural exchange of manufactured for unprocessed goods, collected surplus rural produce without paying any direct compensation, and sold those goods for the balance of urban output which now went to supply the consuming classes supported by official revenues. The towns were made economically dependent on the regime which controlled the land and in particular on the policy of emirs who individually were able to dispose of surplus produce as they wished.[10]

This vital power over the urban livelihood resulted from the massive size of Mamluk grain holdings. The Sultan held great supplies, and emirs with high salaries and large households also had substantial stocks. The chronicles describe huge amounts of grain confiscated from emirs or revealed when they died. For example, the emir Sayf al-dīn Sallār left a fortune of 300,000 *irdabbs* (circa 1,500,000 bushels) of wheat, barley, and beans aside from treasures of gold, silver, precious cloths, weapons, animals, and other property. Such supplies were of course exceptional but they help to indicate the potential magnitudes involved.[11] Moreover, not only emirs but other officials were also paid in kind. Legal scholars complained about falling food prices because their incomes depended on disposal of grain in a favorable market. Qadis and market inspectors also speculated in grain and were subjected to confiscation of their stores.[12]

Emirs and officials thus became the grain dealers par excellence of the medieval Muslim city. To sell supplies in excess of household needs, functionaries were employed to manage their warehouses and grain brokers (*al-simsār;* plural *al-samāsira*) to dispose of the produce. Officials not only sold their own stocks but helped to organize more extensive markets by speculations. For example, in 751/1351 a vizier purchased grain from minor officials who received it as part of their salaries for some six or seven dirhems per *irdabb,* and amassed about 12,000 *irdabbs.* A market existed in which the small supplies given to minor salary holders might be turned into cash by selling, evidently below value, to other officials who thus accumulated the larger holdings necessary for serious speculations.[13] In addition, emirs were active in the interregional grain and livestock trade between Syria and Egypt. Syria was a net importer of grain and in time of hardship Egypt usually helped make up her needs. In 724/1323 emirs and merchants each sent 20,000 *irdabbs* of grain to Tripoli and Beirut to relieve a crisis in Syria. In another transaction, the governor of Cairo sent wheat to Beirut where it was purchased by the ruling emir. In return Syria supplied Egypt with meat. For example, in a mid-fifteenth-century transaction, both official and private means were combined. While the tax officer of Damascus took 16,000 sheep from the Turkomans, the governor purchased some 20,000 more for shipment to Egypt. Such transactions were often arranged by order of the Sultan and cooperation of the emirs rather than through a market mechanism, but important private opportunities inhered in these official powers over produce.[14] Payments in kind to the emirs were not only a fiscal convenience, but a means of arranging complex market operations for which neither adequate capital nor organization was otherwise available.

The emirs and even the Sultan himself, however, were rarely content to let their revenues depend on the conditions of local supply and demand, but rather sought to control and exploit the grain market for the sake of further profits. Efforts were made to corner supplies, but this proved to be rather difficult. Requiring extensive capital or great political power, monopolies ran a strong risk of failure and complete loss. Even Sultans did not always succeed. In 832/1429 Sultan Barsbāy made heavy speculative grain purchases, and ordered all grain to be sold only to his warehouses. To make good his monopoly, the market inspector then forbade wheat imports, and millers were obliged to buy exclusively from the Sultan. In the following year Barsbāy sold his grain for a profit of 300,000 dinars. Nonetheless, when he tried again in 835/1432 to purchase all grain in the villages, the net effect was to precipitate general hoarding and price rises. It proved beyond the power of this Sultan famous for monopolies to corner Cairo's food supplies.

Still, other emirs and officials occasionally tried to do it, but no pattern emerges. In 799/1397, Damascus crowds murdered Ibn al-Nashū, a grain broker, for hoarding in time of famine. He was widely hated for previous speculations, but it is doubtful that he was the sole culprit or that his efforts constituted a monopoly in the strict sense. At another time in Damascus, an emir attached to the governor tried to monopolize the meat supply by purchasing all available sheep. His efforts forced the price of meat up from two and a half to eight dirhems per *raṭl** but he was soon arrested. Different circumstances tempted an inspector for Upper Egypt to try to monopolize grain supplies at their source and by preventing their export to Cairo to dispose of his goods at a great profit.[15]

More commonly, Sultans and emirs sought to exploit their grain holdings by forcing grain merchants, millers, and sometimes even their own subordinates or townsmen in general to buy grain above the market price. In the Mamluk period the Sultan and his controller of the privy purse were the first to force merchants to buy food supplies. In 737/1336–37 they were obliged to buy sheep and cattle at twice their value, and in the following year wheat, beans, and clover were sold at excessively high prices. Such sales were repeated in 787/1385 and 788/1386, and the crisis of the 1390's increased their frequency. In 791/1389 the Cairo market inspector caused bread prices to rise while grain prices were falling by forcing people to buy grain at high prices. On the other hand, in the Cairo famine of 798/1395 the inspector resigned because more powerful Mamluk officials forced him against his will to compel millers to buy wheat at higher and higher prices. The Sultan intervened and decided, presumably to the satisfaction of both sides, to continue the forced purchases but to lower prices. Several months later, even though imports tended to depress prices, they were still held at artificially high levels by forced purchases. Abuses of this kind at Tripoli continued until 817/1414 where the governor had been purchasing food from the cultivators and reselling it at exorbitant prices, and occurred sporadically at other times in the century.[16]

The most common sort of speculation was to withhold supplies from

* *Raṭl*—approximately one pound in Cairo and 4.2 pounds in Damascus. (**425**, XVI, 40.)

the market in expectation of rising prices. Any threat of famine, any rumors of water shortages or crop failures could create a crisis out of a normal situation and a disaster out of a crisis. Prediction of rising prices was a self-fulfilling prophecy. Typically in such secondary crises the Sultan and the market inspector, eager to break the hold of the grain owners on the market, would turn their pressure on the largest grain holders, the emirs, forcing them to open their storehouses and sell grain either at the usual market price or one fixed by decree. To combat famine in 682/1283, Sultan Qalāūn forced the emirs to sell in Cairo at a fixed price of twenty-five dirhems per *irdabb,* ten dirhems below the market price. Again in 720/1320, with trade halted because of confusion over the copper coinage, the Sultan turned on the emirs, and rebuked them for not selling grain to mills and wholesalers for redistribution to the people.

Another struggle over the distribution of food in Cairo in 736/1336 best reveals the structure of the market. According to al-Maqrīzī, as wheat prices began to rise the emirs ceased to sell, hoping for greater future profits. While the market inspector sought to alleviate the growing hardship by punishing millers and bakers, and the Sultan ordered imports from Syria and Upper Egypt, an official tariff for wheat was fixed at thirty dirhems per *irdabb,* somewhat above the secularly normal price of twenty. Nonetheless, the emirs would sell only at sixty to seventy dirhems. Appointing a new market inspector with full powers, the Sultan had him put seals on the storehouses of the emirs and take inventories of the available stocks, including estimates of the amounts necessary for the emirs' households until the following harvest. Other large grain holders and brokers were similarly registered. The inspector then required that grain be sold only by his orders, and gradually placed food on the market until the price fell to the desired thirty dirhems per *irdabb.* Fearing the wrath of the determined Sultan, no one dared sell without permission. When new shipments began to enter Cairo, the shortage was overcome.

Similarly bold efforts were made in 796/1394. To cope with excessively high prices the market inspector of Cairo ordered that storehouses either be opened for sales or subjected to plunder. According to one account food became abundant, and anyone who wanted an *irdabb* of grain could get five, while another source reports no spectacular success, but a reduction of prices sufficient to calm the populace. Throughout the fifteenth century, efforts continued to be made to mitigate the severity of food crises by forcing the responsible emirs to open their storehouses and sell grain at reasonable prices. Sometimes to supplement direct regulations, the Sultan might sell grain from his own stores, directly reducing prices and stimulating further declines as the appearance of food on the market induced speculators to sell immediately rather than risk still lower prices. Just as rising prices induced further rises, falling prices led to further falls, unless speculators were prepared to hold out indefinitely.[17]

Occasionally, emirs and officials were made to supply the needs of the populace by feeding the poor, each in proportion to his wealth or to the number of Mamluks he was obliged to keep. Sultan Baybars was the first to assign poor beggars and Sufis to emirs, officials, and rich merchants for feeding, and similar measures were taken by his successors in 694/1295, 749/1348, 798/1395–96, and 808/1405. In the fifteenth century, however, the Sultans were no longer strong enough to compel the emirs to aid the poor, even though in principle such measures had recognized the responsibility of the Sultan and the emirs for provisioning the towns—the duty of those who controlled the urban livelihood to succor the needy.[18]

Unfortunately, such efforts by the Sultans and inspectors to protect the populace were often replaced by less effective measures. In general, they usually dared go no further than to announce price ceilings, arrange for further imports, and abuse the more defenseless of the grain millers and traders[19] even though the success of the measures of 736/1336 should have demonstrated once and for all that the only effective control of the market situation was to control supplies or at least to survey existing stocks so that a fair market price could be determined and made known. Wheat speculation continued but to the greater advantage of the emirs. The safety of city food supplies was left to the uncertain determination of the Sultans in resisting the greed of the emirs.

Other Mamluk fiscal prerogatives also conduced to a general control over the urban economy and the exploitation of public duties for private gains. Since the salaries of officials as well as the revenues demanded by the Sultan or the state were often collected directly from the subjects, collectors had both incentive to extort money from the taxpayers, and if necessary, legal means to conceal their exactions from superiors and give them the semblance of legitimacy. The Mamluks, entrusted with tax collection in the towns, often abused the resources and people made available to them by outright seizures, confiscations, forced purchases, illegal and arbitrary taxes, and demands for fees and bribes.[20]

Of these abuses, forced purchases, though not the most common, were characteristic of the relationships between the subjects and their Mamluk masters. A forced purchase, called *rimāya* or *ṭarḥ,* was the sale of goods by the Sultan, emirs, or other officials to merchants or others at a price in excess of the market value and contrary to the wishes of the purchaser. It was in effect a partial confiscation of capital, and a way of legitimizing while finding an excuse for confiscations. Forced purchases might be fortified by a monopoly which made it easier to fix an abnormally high price. In the fifteenth century they became a tax. Instead of sporadic extortions at the expense of occasional merchants and officials, wealthy notables and the populace as a whole were compelled to buy fixed quantities of goods year after year at fixed prices. They became a tax like the *gabelles* in France under the *ancien régime* in which the whole population was obliged to buy a fixed quantity of salt from the General Farm at a price far in excess of its commercial value in regions where *gabelles* were not in force. This fiscal power enabled the Mamluks to acquire personal control over the general economy and to put each and every citizen at the mercy of their demands. Every property owner, merchant, or artisan had personally to come to terms with the governors, emirs, and officials. Not the office but the man himself became the power to be reckoned with for there could be no appeal to justice, but only to mercy and countervailing influences and to protection no less costly than previous exactions.

The earliest instance of forced purchase in the Mamluk period goes back to a Damascus episode of 688/1289. An emir was found hoarding wood, sugar, and other goods, planning to force the people to buy them at twice their value. Six years later merchants were twice forced to buy goods at exorbitant prices and ultimately forced purchases became part of the Sultan's fiscal policy. From 733/1333 to 738/1338, when al-Nashū served the Sultan as controller of the privy purse, forced purchases of cloth, wood, furs, iron, cotton, oil, tar, and colocasia were required. His successors continued the practice until it was abolished in 741/1341. For the remainder of the century the device remained in abeyance save for an incident in 778/1376, but it was revived in the civil war period of 790/1388 to 825/1422. In both Cairo and Damascus, merchants and ulama were at times obliged to purchase sugar and other unwanted goods at great personal loss.[21]

In the reign of Barsbāy (1422–1438) forced purchases again became part of the economic policy of the Sultan. His so-called sugar monopoly was more properly a system of forced purchases in the form of a *gabelle*. In 826/1423, 832/1428–29, and 837/1433–34 merchants and the public as a whole were obliged to buy specified amounts of sugar at the government's price. Barsbāy's policy is reminiscent of the systematic exploitation of Nāṣir Muḥammad's reign (d. 1341) save that it came not at a peak of prosperity, but at the end of an exhausting period of civil wars, to compensate the state for a tremendous decline in agricultural revenues. The passing of the reign, however, and the failure of the monopolies led to a temporary abandonment of forced purchases. Only in 859/1454–55 and 865/1460–61 did they recur. In the latter case, however, the Sultan intervened to stop the maneuver, preferring an interest-free loan to the forced purchase of his spices.

From the third quarter of the century the forced purchase, until then largely a measure of the Sultan and his officials, was taken up by emirs, provincial governors, and officials in general for the sake of consolidating private fortunes. At this time, though precedented earlier, the forced purchase regularly became a *gabelle* laid on some large part of a town community, rather than a transfer of goods to merchants. In 876/1471–72, for example, the ulama, cotton dealers, and the people of Jerusalem, Nablus, and Hebron were taxed in this way. At Aleppo the soap market was monopolized by an emir who forced all manufacturers to sell to him alone, and resold and exported the product on his own terms. Sultan Qāyitbāy abolished this abuse on his visit to Aleppo in 882/1477, but his decree had no general force, and insofar as each forced purchase was a local matter the practice had to be condemned again and again to no avail at Jabala, a town on the Syrian coast, Tripoli, and Damascus. Nor was the ingenuity of self-seeking emirs limited to these commonplace measures. A traveler to Egypt in 886/1481 reports that for transportation up the Nile to Cairo, emirs forced passengers to accept their own price.[22]

The most famed of these measures were the forced purchases of oil at Nablus, Jerusalem, and Hebron. From about 890/1485, local officials were cornering the olive oil production of Nablus. In 896/1491, Jerusalem was hard hit. The governor made lists of the populace and obliged everyone to buy a *qinṭār** of oil at fifteen dinars. The oil was

* *Qinṭār*—one hundred *raṭl,* or about one hundred pounds in Cairo and four hundred and twenty in Damascus. (425, XVI, 39-40.)

worth only about 250 dirhems on resale, or about five dinar at the current price of the local dirhem, and the emirs made a profit of some 20,000 dinars. Many of the notables were beaten and forced to sell their possessions to raise the money.

Two years later soap merchants and Christians and Jews were forced to buy olive oil, though the common people were excused. Hebron was forced to buy 160 *qinṭārs,* Jerusalem 1,340, Gaza 1,000, and Ramla an unspecified amount. At fifteen dinars per *qinṭār* this represented a sale of 12,500 dinars worth of goods for 37,500 dinars. 900/1495 brought renewal of the forced purchase of Nablus oil on Ramla, Gaza, and Jerusalem. Hebron and Jerusalem were obliged to take nine hundred *qinṭārs* and Ramla two hundred. Later an additional burden of three hundred *qinṭārs* was added to the lot of Jerusalem merchants. The oil was again sold at fifteen dinars with a supplement of a dinar, probably a fee for the officials, though the oil was worth only nine dinars at that time.

In the final decades of Mamluk rule all the major towns were sorely pressed by forced purchases. In 886/1481 the governor of Damascus obliged brokers and others to buy sugar from his refinery at prices varying from a premium of three dirhems per *raṭl* to a charge of twenty-eight or thirty dirhems, twice the normal price. The protests of the subjects induced the Sultan to order that this abuse be stopped, and the governor's price then fell to eleven dirhems. Forced purchases of soap and animals plundered from the bedouins by the army are also occasionally mentioned in the chronicles. Not only Damascus, but Tripoli and Cairo were also subjected to them. In 917/1511 the Sultan tried to force Cairo butchers to buy work cattle at forty dinars per head, but they went on strike and meat disappeared from the markets. At the same time he obliged other merchants to buy cloth, wool, veils, oil, honey, and raisins. At the very end of the Mamluk period the Sultan forced merchants and officials to buy his household furnishings at twice their value in a last desperate effort to raise cash.[23]

These purchases were important not only as means of exploitation, but because the materials involved and the modes of their acquisition and distribution enabled the Sultan and the emirs to intervene in almost every aspect of the urban economies. Sometimes, as in the case of wood and iron, the products were semi-monopolies of the state, or like sugar, products which the Sultan, emirs, and officials manufactured in their own factories and sold in any case to the public at large. Sometimes, as in the case of grain and animals, they were products derived from the tax revenues. Other goods such as cloth, oil, grapes, and honey may simply have been purchased at one time or another for use by the household of the emir involved, or as a speculation, or may even have been confiscated or requisitioned with the intent of making a profit on both the acquisition and the disposal of the goods by extralegal means. Along with the purchasing power of the Mamluk households and their influence over the grain markets, forced purchases gave them a decisive hand in the urban economy.

CONTROLS OVER PROPERTY, LABOR, AND MATERIALS

Other powers reinforced the dominant position of the emirs in the economic life of the cities. Not only did their fiscal powers give them a vast generalized capacity to control the towns, but by virtue of their special abilities to dispose of real estate, to organize labor, and to control the flow of scarce materials the Mamluks occupied a strategic position in the maintenance of urban communal life. No large or expensive public project could be undertaken without Mamluk cooperation.

Control of property was perhaps the most important of these powers. By investing part of their rural incomes the emirs became owners of baths, markets, khans, and *qayṣariyyas* (bazaars). Their residential palaces were the largest and most valued in the cities. The extensive properties of Tankiz have already been mentioned, but indications from the records of waqf donations make clear how widespread were the holdings of emirs. Of the seventy-eight records known to us which indicate both the donor and the gift, no less than forty-eight were grants of houses, shops, mills, *qayṣariyyas,* ovens, baths, khans, stables, storerooms, granaries, residences, markets, and factories owned by emirs. Nine other foundations were due to the Sultan himself, and only about a quarter came from merchants, qadis, ulama, and civil officials. The amounts and the proportions of the properties involved make qualitatively clear the dominance of the emirs in the urban property landscape.[24]

In fact the emirs were not only owners of existing property but virtually monopolized new investments. In Damascus, for example, out of forty-one commercial construction projects, whose builders are known, twenty-eight were carried out by emirs and five by the Sultan. The emirs built twelve of fifteen baths, six of nine *qayṣariyyas,* seven of twelve markets, and three of five khans. Merchants built but two khans and a market, and the only other named investor of importance was the waqf of the Umayyad Mosque which financed a *qayṣariyya,* shops, and a bath. For Aleppo we know of nine khans, four baths, and a market built by emirs in the Mamluk period, but only two baths, a market, and a khan were built by named merchants.[25]

The special power of the emirs made such investments particularly secure. To guarantee returns, emirs often transferred lucrative crafts or trades to their own markets or *qayṣariyyas* or otherwise established monopolies to assure high revenues. In Damascus in 691/1292, an emir purchased the cotton *qayṣariyya* from the public treasury, and induced the Sultan to permit him to move all silk merchants from their own location to his *qayṣariyya.* The old market was left empty for two years before the silk merchants returned. In 726/1326 cloth merchants were transferred out of a *qayṣariyya* belonging to the waqf of the Umayyad Mosque, while in 829/1426 chance alone intervened to save the Umayyad Mosque a loss of 60,000 dirhems a year. The Sultan ordered the transfer of the Suq of Merchants back to an older location, though the governor wished to transfer it to one of his markets to increase its income. However, the Mamluk who was bringing the Sultan's instructions was seized en route by the bedouins, and the order was never delivered. In the confusion, the governor gave up his plans, and the mosque was spared a large loss.[26]

Moreover, the powers of the emirs were compounded by the ability to dispose of properties which they did not own in the first instance. Since the Sultan and emirs in general were property owners, parcels desired for endowments or public works could be purchased from other emirs[27] or obtained by negotiation with the public treasury. For example, in Cairo in 744/1343–44, an emir purchased the *khizānat al-bunūd,** and "redeveloped" the area, tearing down the old structure and renting the land for the construction of new houses and mills.[28]

Emirs were also in a favored position to obtain the judicial consent necessary for buying waqf properties. A qadi could authorize the sale of waqfs in his charge after witnesses specialized in real estate assessments had certified their worth. Some such means of overcoming restricting immobility was essential because waqf properties made up a very large part of the cities' resources. Understandably, however, the

* The *khizānat al-bunūd* was a prison notorious as a center of debauchery. Religious pressures finally brought about its condemnation and destruction despite the profits of the Sultan from taxes on wine and prostitution.

ulama were reluctant to surrender such property for both practical and moral reasons, and when thwarted, emirs sometimes abused the judicial process. Witnesses might be found to certify false values or qadis to authorize financially disadvantageous sales. In 730/1330 Emir Qawsūn, eager to obtain a bath immobilized in a waqf, had adjacent properties destroyed and then brought professional witnesses, who were his accomplices, to testify that the bath was of no value, and that the ruins were furthermore dangerous to the neighborhood and should be removed. Armed with this testimony, legal authorization for the sale of the waqf property was then obtained. Sultans could of course similarly obtain rulings which enabled them to acquire desirable waqfs. In 814/1411 qadis under the influence of Sultan al-Mu'ayyad Sheikh abolished older waqfs and transferred a school to the Sultan which he tore down to enlarge the area around the Cairo citadel. When access to property depended only in part on the ability to pay for it, and largely on personal influence in obtaining its sale, the high ranking officials were in a favored position.[29]

The authority of the emirs also enabled them to carry out desired projects by instructing their subordinates. After the invasions, wars, and fires of the first decade of the fifteenth century in Damascus, the governor compelled *al-nās,* probably emirs and officials over whose incomes he had direct authority, to rebuild houses, waqfs, and schools. In other circumstances, the disgrace of emirs or defeat of rebels led to confiscation of property for the use of their successors.[30]

Aside from ownership general control over property rights was derived from the responsibility of the regime to protect the public spaces from encroachments by private owners. In the flimsily built Muslim city of medieval days, shops and houses quickly grew over all available public spaces—squares, streets, mosque and school facades, walls, and bridges. Governors sporadically exercised a right of eminent domain, seizing properties which encroached on public spaces, removing nuisances and dangers, and widening the streets. People could be forcibly moved from their homes and shops. No compensation was paid private owners, although actual demolitions and improvements were made at the governors' expense. Such measures, despite the presumed ultimate rights of the community as a whole, were unjust from the point of view of property owners who may not themselves have built on the common way, but purchased property long ago erected in this fashion. Occasionally, special interests were protected, and waqfs in particular were likely to be compensated for their losses. Tankiz paid for a khan belonging to the waqfs of al-Ẓāhiriyya Madrasa and replaced shops belonging to the Umayyad Mosque, and at other times property owners and managers of waqfs were consulted about street widening projects, and compensation was agreed upon. More commonly to legitimize confiscations without payments authorization was sought from the qadis. To condemn baths and latrines polluting the Baradā River in Damascus, the governor called on judges and jurists to validate the proceedings and in other instances permission was given to tear down shops and houses.[31]

It was also in the power of the regime to seize private properties in order to further works of interest to the state such as fortifications or hippodromes. In 690/1291, in order to extend al-Maydān al-Akhḍar (The Green Hippodrome) of Damascus, buildings along the Bāniyās River were torn down at the expense of private owners. In other cases property owners were compensated, as in 725/1324–25 when some of the people injured by Cairo canal works were reimbursed. Existing structures might also be torn down solely to obtain materials. Houses were seized in Aleppo to provide stone and make way for the reconstruction of the citadel and walls in the early decades of the fifteenth century.[32] Confiscations, partial confiscations, and forced sales were even used to assemble property for new religious and educational institutions. The ancient Muslim debate over the legitimacy of accepting tainted money for religious purposes had reason to continue.[33] Naturally such vast powers could be used to increase the personal fortunes of emirs as well as the common good. Property was taken simply to enable some powerful emir or governor to enlarge his palace or to obtain valuable materials.[34] Here too public powers were turned to private advantage.

Religious and judicial opinion was fundamentally opposed to confiscations without the agreement of the owners and appropriate compensations. Some ulama even opposed eminent domain, though it could be used to favor the expansion or construction of religious institutions. Qadis debated the difficulties of acquiring property for the expansion of a mosque in terms of the absolute right of property ownership versus the right of eminent domain with compensation. In one instance, the Mālikī jurists were willing to admit that the state had the power to oblige owners when compensated to sell property for the purpose of improving a mosque, but the Shāfi'ī held the opposite point of view:

that an unwilling owner could not be forced to yield his property on any terms. The ulama generally held it illegal to take houses against the wishes of their owners or waqfs without proper proceedings.[35] The reasons for this strict view are not stated in the chronicles though three might be adduced. The judges may have been opposed in principle to the use of illegally acquired properties and revenues for religious purposes. They also may have been opposed to procedures endangering the waqfs of existing institutions and other interests which they represented; but their resistance probably stemmed ultimately from an unwillingness to give rein to illegal procedures in a society already overburdened with arbitrary oppression.

On the other hand, other notions of property and legality conflicted with this tendency. From the point of view of Muslim law it was the responsibility of the state or the market inspector to protect and recover public lands. This tradition could be easily reconciled with concern for the safety of private property, but a more dangerous alternative was the notion that all land in principle belonged to the Sultan. In 735/1335 in order to obtain land for a mosque, house owners were offered half the value of their property on the grounds that only the buildings belonged to private owners while the land belonged to the Sultan.[36] Indeed, the separation of land and building ownership was founded in Islamic tax and renting practices. Ground and building rents were separate components of property.[37] Emirs as the agents of the Sultan may have thought it within their rights to seize lands and buildings for public purposes or even for private ones insofar as they embodied the state. While the qadis debated whether they could acquire property at all, with or without compensation, the impatient officers seized necessary parcels without either compensation or further ado. The conflict between the religious and the Mamluk points of view was not settled by adjudication, but by the power of the emirs.

Control over property was only one of the powers which enabled the emirs to carry out public works. They were also in a favored position to command the necessary manpower. For major construction projects in which masses of unskilled labor were needed, the soldiers formed a standing army of laborers. Sections of canals, bridges, fortifications, or street repairs were often assigned to emirs who were required to carry out construction projects with their troops. When Ghāzī rebuilt the walls of Aleppo at the end of the twelfth century he assigned the construction of each tower to an emir, and inscribed the name of the responsible officer onto the tower he built. The precedent was extended to other construction projects to which the emirs not only brought their troops, but if necessary the whole of their extensive clienteles: servants, grooms, messengers, secretaries, employees, and even the religious personnel of institutions they had endowed. Nor would neighbors be able to escape their demands.[38] In case of disaster the troops also formed a ready body of fire fighters although they sometimes rewarded themselves by plundering panic stricken neighborhoods. Occasionally, skilled stoneworkers and carpenters were also called upon to help tear down structures in the path of a conflagration, but unskilled manpower was hard to raise because these workers more easily fled impressment. The Mamluks were virtually the only organized manpower available on a stand-by basis, and completely subject to the orders of their officers.[39]

The regime did, however, requisition supplementary manpower from the urban populations for public works. Corvées were used for canal works, and sometimes beggars, prisoners, and the dregs of the populace were impressed and even seized in the mosques. At other times, a small wage was paid workers. In one instance some 30,000 dinars were spent on wages, and in another workers were paid one and a half dirhems a day plus three loaves of bread. The distribution of rations in these cases has the aura of ancient Egypt with thousands of workers and soldiers laboring while the ruler's scribes kept lists and distributed grain. Yet another technique for raising manpower was the registration of booths in the market and the systematic enrollment of officials, shopkeepers, Sufis, and soldiers by classes. This was extremely uncommon, for the Mamluk regime rarely rose to such feats of organization.[40]

Corvées were also used for construction of fortifications. In 658/1260 even women were put to work with the soldiers to rebuild the citadel of Damascus, and in 792/1390 most of the people of Aleppo volunteered or were made to volunteer their labor for the reconstruction of the walls. Again after the devastations of Tamerlane, the common people of Damascus worked on the reconstruction of the governor's headquarters and the citadel. Urban workers were also taken to fortification projects outside their cities. In 735–36/1335–36 some 20,000 workmen including half the laboring population of the villages, craftsmen from Aleppo and Damascus, and the army were taken to build Ja'bar in the Aleppo region.[41]

The recruitment of skilled labor posed special problems. Skilled manpower could be hired in Cairo and Damascus but in addition the Sultan maintained a regular work force, including prisoners, for his own use and for the projects of favored emirs. In a sense, just as property was available to the emirs from the public treasury, so too was labor available from the Sultan's work shops. In the fourteenth century the Sultan had workers constantly in his employ. In 730/1330 he lent an emir the services of prisoners to move stones, and in 738/1338, "various types of workers attached to the Sultan" worked on the house of an emir without pay. Two years later "workers of the Sultan" were obliged to work one day in seven without pay to build a mosque, a bath, markets, and a fountain. Travelers who visited Syria in the middle of the fourteenth century reported that the Sultan used Christian prisoners as slave labor. Templars made prisoner at the fall of Acre were said to be wood-cutters in the hills near Jericho, although after sixty years this seems unlikely. Another contemporary traveler noted that Christian carpenters, masons, and other craftsmen who were slaves of the Sultan were fairly well off and decently treated. They had been gathered in a Cairo barracks to do construction work, and later to sell wine at no inconsiderable profit to the Sultan. In the fifteenth century too the Sultan carried on a wide variety of economic activities, and employed different specialists for his purposes. Arsenals, shipyards, and foundries were large employers though their employees were not available for public works.[42]

Craftsmen were both employed for projects within the major cities and were dispatched by the Sultan and emirs to provincial towns too small to maintain an adequately specialized labor force. Smaller towns were necessarily dependent on the regime for the workers, tools, and materials essential for public improvements. The first few decades of the Mamluk regime in Syria were marked by intense construction activity, and the Sultan and emirs used Damascus as a labor pool for works at Jerusalem, Kerak, and other places. Men were taken to repair mosques and fortifications and to build bridges. Masons, carpenters, sawyers, and stoneworkers were also sent with tools and materials from Cairo to Mecca and Medina to repair the sanctuaries. Mamluk support for smaller towns of religious or military importance continued in the fifteenth century as well. To what extent the workers forced to leave home were regular employees of the Sultan, prisoners, or hired laborers is impossible to say, but it is probable, since most of the works requiring the organization and dispatch of large numbers of skilled men occurred in reigns otherwise noted for extensive construction activities, that these were, in larger measure than is apparent, the regular workers of the Sultan. In other cases it would seem likely that skilled workers were paid for their services, although occasional warnings by qadis about injustices indicate a temptation to cut costs.[43]

Workers and craftsmen also accompanied the armies on campaign to serve the troops and to assist in siege operations. It was normal for armies to travel with food vendors, shoemakers, and tailors as well as carpenters and stoneworkers.[44]

The Mamluks could also indirectly requisition manpower by imposing the performance of tasks in the public interest as a liturgy on private individuals. The shopkeepers of the city, for example, were obliged to sweep and wet down the streets and even to clean and repair the part of the public way which passed their property. They met this burden by hiring workers or by paying the costs directly to the state. Canal projects were similarly carried out by assigning shares of the work to riparian owners. Householders were asked to build barriers and dig and clear the canals. As in the case of major street repairs they had to hire workers to do the job, and many even had their property confiscated to meet the costs of carting off the earth removed by deepening of the canals. The principle of public works had not been fully established and it remained part of the police powers of the regime to require such contributions. Instead of distributing the tax on the city as a whole, the people most directly concerned were held responsible.

Other tasks equally important in maintaining public life were also assigned the shopkeepers. They were occasionally made responsible for sanitary measures such as removing stray dogs. Shopkeepers also were obliged to hang out lanterns at night and to prepare water buckets as a precaution against fire. One final responsibility was to beautify the city. Shopkeepers and houseowners were sometimes ordered to whitewash their properties and even to decorate them with specified designs. As in ancient times, the domains of public and private responsibilities were not clearly distinguished.[45]

Finally, the importance of the emirs in urban communal life established by their firm control of property and their ability to command and organize mass labor was confirmed by their powers over the distribution of strategic and scarce building materials. For this reason alone their importance for public works and religious endowments would have been assured. Wood was regarded as a strategic material, and in wood-scarce Egypt and Syria the reasons for this are obvious. It was essential both to the economy and defense, and the Mamluk regime carefully controlled the available reserves. Forests in the Damascus region and the Lebanese mountains were the property of the Sultan, and strategically valuable trees, whether owned by the state or not, were subject to control in emergencies. Nonetheless, with available supplies dwindling and inadequate in quality, commercial imports from Europe, though meager in volume, were essential. Imported timbers were deemed war materials to be purchased by the state, and were either monopolized by the royal magazines or subject to licensing for sale to individuals. In addition the Mamluks organized military expeditions to the Gulf of Alexandretta to bring lumber down from the afforested regions of northern Syria and maritime Anatolia. By treaty arrangement Istanbul sent naval supplies at the very end of the Mamluk era.

The internal allocation of wood supplies was closely controlled by the regime. The Sultan allocated wood as well as manpower for citadel and mosque constructions and repairs in the Hejaz. Other important wood supplies were available to the Sultan and emirs in the existing buildings which they owned, and old edifices were frequently torn down to provide materials for new ones. The cities pillaged themselves, transferring existing stocks from one building to another as priorities and demands changed.[46]

Egypt and Syria were also dependent on imports for their supply of metals, and so metals too were subject to monopoly or control by the state. The Sultans maintained their own weapons and armor shops and cannon foundries and supplied lead and iron for construction projects. Commercially available metals also came from the surplus of the Sultan's holdings.[47]

Stone, though of local provenance, was for different reasons in the hands of the regime. Quarries, so far as we can tell from uncertain evidence, were owned by the state and emirs, and so too were the most important sources of all—existing buildings which were pillaged to provide materials for new structures. The Mamluks had important advantages in this Darwinian struggle. Monuments, ruined or not, yielded good quality stone for fortifications, and favored mosques and schools rose up at the expense of older buildings. A madrasa built in Damascus at the end of the Mamluk period used so much stone from other mosques that it was called the "reunion of mosques," a pun on the Arabic word *jama'a*—to gather, and therefore the root of the word for mosque (*jāmiʿ*). Marble was especially valued in Mamluk decoration, and no fine mosque or palace could do without marble mosaic inlays and facings. However, there is no information on sources of new marble, save for one indication that it came from Baʿādhīn near Aleppo, and it would seem that the existing stock was transferred from one use to another. Most of it was owned by emirs and the Sultan, who made it available for new mosques and schools, sometimes confiscating it from the houses of other emirs.[48]

THE EMIRS IN THE FUNCTIONING OF THE URBAN COMMUNITY

These extraordinary powers enabled the leading Mamluk emirs to play vital roles in the communal and religious life of the towns. The specific obligations of their office required only that they fight and defend the cities, and extract from them the costs of their maintenance; but because the Mamluks depended on the tax revenues of the communities they ruled they were obliged to sustain the ongoing social and economic life of the people on whose subordination their powers were based. The massive investments required for irrigation, water works, roads and streets, fortifications, and for religious and educational institutions had to be contributed by the Mamluks for they were essential to the stability and productivity of the society. Because they controlled the wealth of the society they had to take the part of patrons and seigneurs.

The motives which led the Mamluks to undertake such extensive responsibilities did not automatically follow need or power. A preliminary indoctrination of the alien soldiery was necessary so that they would understand what was required of them. For the Mamluks to accept these duties, conversion to the faith of their subjects and instruction in Islam was essential. In a culture which drew little distinction between religious conviction and social behavior, "conversion" to Islam was a way of introducing foreigners to the habits and expectations of the people over whom they ruled, a way of fostering conformity to the ways of Islamic societies. Their education in Islam served as an initiation to the roles of local notables in carrying on public affairs for which no regular governmental provision had been made. Conversely, al-Maqrīzī, in an observation more acute than he himself may have realized, ascribed the chaos of the early fifteenth century not just to factionalism among the troops, but to failure to educate the new soldiers in Islam. When they failed to be imbued with respect for the elders of the community and with desire for the approval of the religious authorities, the cause of the community was ill served.[49]

Self-interested considerations also motivated Mamluk concern for the welfare of the cities. The Mamluks, though alien in origin, were not totally isolated from their subjects. In the fourteenth century, concern for the public weal was at a peak because long tenures in office offered opportunities for personal enrichment and for the growth of political and family ties with the indigenous populations. Involvement in local affairs led necessarily to dependence on local notables for legitimation and for political and administrative assistance. Similarly, marriages between Mamluks and urban notable families brought the Mamluks into more intimate contact with the needs of their subjects. Moreover, the children of Mamluks, the *awlād al-nās,* excluded from important positions in the state, often became scholars or Sufis and merged into the general urban society. To a degree, ties of generations mitigated the isolation of the Mamluks from their subjects.

In the fifteenth century, however, self-interested involvement in local affairs waned as the soldiers, absorbed in ceaseless factional struggles, could not occupy posts long enough to develop local ties, accumulate large fortunes, or even live long enough to found a family and consider long-term investments. They had less interest in maintaining the towns and more in exploiting them. In the turbulent fifteenth century public works and endowments of religious institutions did not come to a halt, but they nonetheless slowed considerably. In principle, however, performance of services for the community remained a way of winning its approval, support, and cooperation. To build great public edifices—symbols of grandeur—and to do charitable works served to expiate the inevitable sins of public life, win the accolades of men, and ensure the prayers of the pious after one's death.

The activities actually undertaken, however, varied with circumstances and the interplay of interests. Some public works, such as maintenance of adequate water supplies, were never neglected by the regime and the Mamluks. Water works were beneficial to all concerned, and unlike street and building projects affected no one's interests adversely. Moreover, they were of supreme importance. Without an abundant supply of water, neither the necessities nor the amenities of civilization could exist. Syrian towns, often at the center of oases, depended on irrigation for the cultivation of the land and for their food supplies. Without water the fruit gardens, which in the Arab consciousness are the gardens of paradise, could not survive. The quality of beverages depended on the purity of water. Without water, paper, leather, soap, and dyed cloth could not be produced. Nor in Islam could proper worship be carried on. Water was brought to schools and mosques for ablutions, and thence to the surrounding quarters, baths, and fountains. With water, streets could be wet down, the dust settled, the heat eased, and the air freshened. Water brought calm, music, and blossom. Urbanity depended upon it.[50] In the chronicles, governors who provided water were always well remembered. They were the eternal benefactors of the settlement who assured its viability, prosperity, and civilization. What more could be said for the glory of a reign!

Of the Syrian cities, Damascus was most favored with an extensive and complete water system. The rivers Baradā, Qanawāt, and Bāniyās supplied the city through two sets of underground canals, one for fresh water and the other for drainage, which brought water to mosques, schools, baths, public fountains, and private homes. In the time of Tankiz (1312–1340) this system was cleaned, repaired, and overhauled to assure the distribution of water in the center of the city. The project cost the governor 300,000 dirhems, but aside from this, no major water works were carried out in Damascus in the Mamluk period. Canals were brought into new quarters in 902/1497, and other repairs and improvements were made at about that time. Otherwise only occasional public fountains to embellish the city were built or restored by emirs and officials.[51]

In Aleppo the pattern of investments in water was very different. Unlike Damascus, Aleppo had suffered greatly from the Mongol attacks in the latter half of the thirteenth century, and only after 712/1312 when the danger had passed were water works begun to recreate the city's former greatness and sustain larger garrisons and a restored or even growing population. A fountain was built by the governor of Aleppo in 703/1303–04, but a more important project was soon to follow. Between 713/1313 and 731/1331 Governor Sayf al-dīn Arghūn, completed work on a canal from the River Sājūr, 40,000 cubits long, costing, according to most estimates, about 300,000 dirhems, but possibly as much as 800,000. Half of the expense was borne by the governor and the other half by the Sultan. This canal was intended for the city alone, and villages along its course were forbidden to make use of the waters. Aleppo was henceforth well endowed, but this great aqueduct was vulnerable to destruction, and reserves had to be kept in cisterns and in a great reservoir built in the grand mosque.

This basic investment was followed in the next half century by the construction of fountains throughout the city and branch canals to feed them. Most of these fountains were built by emirs and governors but local notables—officials and prominent merchant and ulama families—also contributed. Even in the dark days of the fifteenth century new and growing southern and eastern quarters of Aleppo continued to be supplied with water. Some canalizations were begun before Tamerlane, but his invasion interrupted the projects. The governor of the citadel in 833/1429–30 finally brought water down to the Maqām Gate from the main canals, and Ibn al-Shiḥna, the historian of Aleppo, says that he himself arranged to conduct it to a mausoleum in the area. A reservoir was built in the city at about mid-century, and other canals and fountains were added. Another period of major construction began in the 890's/1485–95. Emirs, and in particular one Bardbak, a slave dealer in the service of the Sultan, built a series of canals and fountains. Even at the end of our period, when the Mamluks had reached a peak of rapacity and a nadir of concern for the communities they ruled, these important and vital works continued to be carried out at Mamluk initiative and expense.[52]

Other Syrian towns were less well endowed, but nonetheless, the Sultan, emirs, and governors took charge of providing water to places large or small. Sultan Baybars and his successors improved the water supply of Hebron, Safad, and the village of Balaṭūnūs. Emirs, and especially the emirs of the Gharb, mountain chiefs of the Lebanon, repaired water canals in Beirut and built aqueducts, and other Syrian towns were similarly assisted. The only known Syrian project not carried out by an emir was the construction of a canal in Hebron in 801/1398 by a civil official.

Water for the holy places of Jerusalem and Hebron was also the responsibility of the Sultan and the emirs he appointed as administrators. For over a decade and a half between 713/1313 and 728/1328 a major canal and cistern project was carried out to supply Jerusalem with water. Further repairs were made at the expense of Sultan Barqūq in 785/1384, and a century later Sultan Qāyitbāy restored the aqueducts at the request of qadis, sheikhs, and other notables of the city. Canals and a fountain were also built for the sanctuary of Hebron between 857/1453 and 865/1461.[53] Though emirs paid for most of the water projects, waqfs were often left for the maintenance of the canals. General supervision probably lay with the governors of the cities, but the market inspectors and royal commissioners also had some responsibilities.[54]

Other public works, such as street widening and provision for adequate communications within the city, less compelling and never prized in the *urbanisme* of the time, were much more sporadically attended. In Muslim towns without a highly developed sense of the importance of public spaces and ways, shopkeepers constantly encroached on the streets, occupying strategic positions closer and closer to the center as they pushed out their wares to catch the attention of the passersby, and crowded bridges and gates just at the points of highest density of circulation. Yet, despite the obvious importance of disengaging the streets and squares, and the recognized authority of the emirs to protect the public, only in times of great prosperity, and when long tenure of office made governors both responsive to popular needs and sufficiently powerful to override special interests, were such projects actually carried out. For example, in Damascus during the long tenure of Tankiz (1312–1340), a great effort was made to provide adequate streets in new parts of the city. Shops were knocked down and benches removed to widen the way. The interior of the city, long established, was not touched or improved, but Tankiz tried to rationalize the expansion around the citadel on the city's northern and western boundaries. Once this urgent need was satisfied, only minor projects were carried out. In all of two and a half centuries there was but the faintest echo of these efforts in other cities.[55]

In this case reliance on the whims of notables rather than on bureaucratic or communal means was costly. The governors and emirs may have had an interest in easy communications for military reasons, but otherwise the words of the pious texts enjoining their responsibilities fell on deaf ears. They did not have the high priority of water works. They had to be paid for by the emir or governor himself and earned him no reward save the approval of the ulama who cited his good deeds in chronicles which might scarcely be read, and the resentment of those who found that the confusion and financial harm inflicted outweighed the benefits of ease of circulation. Equally uncommon was attention to public sanitation. Only Tankiz, who took the interest of a sovereign prince in the glory of his capital, tried to free Damascus of the nuisance of stray dogs. His war on the animals became a passion. Soldiers, the nightwatch, door boys, sheikhs of the quarters and chiefs of the markets, and even the shopkeepers in general were at one time or another made responsible for removing the pests when the nuisance they caused outweighed their value as scavengers.[56]

Occasionally, however, emirs did undertake the development of whole quarters or even of small towns. Between 700 and 709/1300–1310, Emir Asandamūr governor of the newly rebuilt city of Tripoli, himself endowed it with mosques, schools, baths, khans, and markets. In 711/1311, Emir Sinjar al-Jāwalī built a palace, a bath, a school, a khan, a hospital, and a mosque, the basic elements of a complete city, at Kerak. In 824/1421 Tyre was rebuilt by an emir who constructed new fortifications and markets, and emirs also created quarters in Beirut and Cairo by building palaces and providing for water supply and drainage.[57]

On the other hand, the emirs took so large a part in the construction and endowment of religious institutions that a special explanation is required. In the Mamluk period there were in Damascus one hundred and seventy-one foundings, reconstructions, or repairs of mosques, schools, colleges, and convents for Sufis for which the donors are known. Many other projects, of course, have escaped the attention of the chroniclers, but these perforce must have been smaller and more obscure. Of these one hundred and seventy-one, eighty-two were gifts of emirs. Ten were financed by the Sultan. Merchants and people who were both merchants and officials initiated twenty-five, officials eleven, qadis thirteen, and other ulama thirty. Thus almost half of the projects were undertaken by emirs, especially governors and tax officials, while the ulama in their own domain were responsible for but a quarter of the works.[58]

The emirs were even more important than the raw figures would imply. The donations of ulama and merchants were concentrated on small mosques, schools, and convents. *Zāwiyas* (Sufi convents) in particular, which accounted for more than half of the foundations by ulama, required very little capital, and were often no longer lived than the personal appeal of the sheikh who initiated the cell. Thus, whereas only half of the total activity is attributed to emirs the actual importance of these projects was much greater. Almost two-thirds of endowments of property in perpetuity came from emirs,[59] and the institutions which received them were likely to represent a still greater proportion of the scholarly and religious activity of the community.

Furthermore, the regime was the ultimate source of funds for many of the donations by people who were not Mamluks. Apart from the eleven officials and thirteen qadis, six of the twenty-five merchants held official positions. Strictly private donors accounted for but twenty-seven per cent of these investments. The situation at Aleppo was much the same.[60] The greater part of the religious, educational, and philanthropic life of urban communities was endowed by the emirs and the regime.

In these cases family self-interest guided the Mamluks. The donation of a religious institution and of waqf properties was a way of providing for the future of their families. The Mamluk system was predicated on the isolation of the soldiers from the rest of the society they ruled, and thus the exclusion of their children from high positions in the army and the state. Fathers could not pass on their status to sons, and were thus compelled to make a place for them in the larger society. Waqfs enabled them to designate their heirs as administrators in perpetuity with a fixed income.[61] This generosity may also have won the gratitude of the ulama and an influential place in the community for Mamluk families. Waqfs in any case spared the emirs confiscation of their properties by the regime, and preserved at least part of their fortunes for both charitable or religious and family purposes. Especially when given late in an emir's life or at his death, it was a gift which cost him nothing.

Mamluk concern further expressed itself in the large part they took in the management of the institutions. If the ulama failed to successfully manage their own affairs or when external circumstances made the financial condition of the religious and educational institutions precarious, the governors intervened to protect the long-term interests of the Islamic community. They helped discipline the functionaries, saw to the proper performance of duties, and suppressed corruption and abuses. For example in 904/1498–99 the governor of Damascus required all the officers of the Umayyad Mosque to fulfill their duties in person and not delegate their responsibilities to others. Governors also arbitrated disputes among the ulama over the management or control of waqf properties, arranged for minor repairs, or used connections in Cairo to obtain skilled workers.[62]

Most important, they regulated the finances of the institutions to protect their long-term viability against the depredations of the current stipendiaries. Annual salaries were reduced or beneficiaries not authorized in the original terms of the grant dismissed, either for the sake of a general improvement in the finances of an institution or to raise capital for repairs. In Damascus in 687/1288 the governor intervened in the management of the Umayyad Mosque to raise funds for repairs by suspending payment of salaries and again in 710/1311–12 assembled the administrators, and decided to reduce salaries by two and three months to improve finances. Under Tankiz, in 727/1327, the Sultan ordered a general review of the waqfs of the city to see that they were managed in conformity with the intentions of the original endowments. Necessary repairs were to be made, salaries reduced and superfluous stipendiaries dropped. Tankiz gathered qadis, jurists, professors, Sufis, and other notables to read and discuss the stipulations of the waqfs. Several Damascus madrasas were found to be well ordered, but others were not. Al-ʿĀdaliyya and al-Ghazāliyya were in good condition, but al-Shāmiyya al-Juwāniyya had no fewer than one hundred and ninety instead of the prescribed twenty jurists. After much discussion, pleas, and protests, the governor and the ulama leaders decided to cut out one hundred and thirty of the stipendiaries and leave sixty. Other institutions were similarly compelled to eliminate large numbers of teachers, repeaters, prayer leaders, and jurists. Tankiz next turned his attention from expenditures to the use of properties. Finding people living illegally on the premises of madrasas and using the space for private storehouses, he expelled and obliged them to pay rent for past occupancy. Savings of this kind enabled the Umayyad Mosque to pay for repairs and redecoration. Improved management even led after two years to a 70,000 dirhem surplus which Tankiz, after consultation with the qadis and administrators, ordered to be spent for marble and further repairs. At Hama, the governor forbade freeloaders to live off the waqf of the hospital, denied increases in salaries, and ordered the proper distributions of food to the poor.[63]

The period of civil wars and Tatar invasions around the turn of the fifteenth century again threw the religious institutions into disarray. In 815/1412 the Sultan, visiting Damascus, ordered that several walls of the Umayyad Mosque be decorated with marble and that a minaret be repaired. To pay for this the salaries of professors were reduced by the equivalent of three months' wages. In 819/1416, however, the governor and the qadis turned to more fundamental problems in the administration of the mosque. To reduce excessive expenditures, the salaries of professors were reduced by half and in 820/1417 to a third. Still, an operating deficit of 40,000 dirhems remained, and in the following year two months' pay was deducted from the stipends of qadis, administrators, and preachers, and one month from muezzins and professors. Moreover, the governor visited the mosque and in the presence of qadis, scholars, and Koran readers had the names of the professors read to him, dismissed a number who had no right to the position, and reorganized payments to the others. Two years later lack of funds and excessive staffs bloated by over a century of neglect forced a still more drastic reorganization. Again the governor gathered the leading qadis and jurists and reviewed the lists of stipendiaries. First, a number of functionaries were removed, and the salary of the administrator was cut by six hundred dirhems a month. The saving from reducing the administrative staffs alone came to some 35,000 dirhems which in the opinion of the governor sufficed for repairs. Construction workers were dismissed at a saving to the mosque of 10,000 dirhems and the administrator was advised to use a laborer who earned two dirhems a day when needed. More professors were dismissed but by this time the saving was small. Fourteen muezzins for whom there were no minarets were also dismissed. The salaries of Koran readers were cut by a third, the total bill falling from 18,000 to 12,000 dirhems. Proceeding further, the governor turned the fate of the recitors of tradition over to the chief qadi, but then dismissed six of the eight supervisors and a number of servants as well. Having relieved the institution of its excess functionaries, he promised to restore to the remaining professors and muezzins the quarter of their salaries deducted for the year. This promise was never fulfilled, for the money saved was absorbed by the cost of repairs.[64]

Similar restorations of waqf finances took place throughout the empire. In Mecca, Medina, Cairo, and Aleppo inspections were carried out by order of the Sultan. At Aleppo, functionaries employed in violation of the original conditions of the hospital's waqf were dismissed. In Jerusalem, the governor restored the waqfs and created a surplus to be placed in a permanent treasury for the sanctuary.[65] Governors and the Sultan took this interest in the management of waqfs for mixed personal and public motives. By making the institutions better able to weather demands for investment and repairs, and less encumbered with useless functionaries who drained energy and funds from educational, religious, or philanthropic tasks, the governors simultaneously performed a public service and spared themselves expenses, shifting the burden to the ulama and stipendiaries of the waqfs.

Unfortunately, the Mamluks used their supervisory authority to abuse the religious institutions as well as to assist them. The deepening economic decline in the fifteenth century spurred the hungry regime to take money from waqfs. Inspectors demanded illegal fees. Emirs seized or purchased properties set aside as endowments, and conspired with qadis and witnesses to divert them from their rightful uses. Corruption became so widespread that the ulama administrators themselves stole or diverted waqf revenues. Most commonly, the emirs levied illegal supplementary taxes on properties assigned to religious and charitable purposes, reducing their capacity to sustain communal needs. Taxes of this sort are noted for the late fourteenth century, but with the period of civil wars illegal demands on waqf properties became more common. In the chaotic circumstances of the last quarter of the fifteenth century, despite a flood of decrees forbidding the practice, such taxes became impossible to check. However often local ulama might obtain relief the tide of exploitation could not be stemmed.[66]

In either supporting or abusing communal institutions, the behavior of the Mamluks reflected their personal concerns and interests and not the policies of the Sultan. The governors' own funds, their willingness to help finance adjustments, and the intimacy of their relations with the ulama were crucial individual factors in the management of public affairs. Emirs, who were not duty or legally bound to act in these matters save as interests and the play of pressures and influences prescribed, nonetheless took an intimate part in city life as foci of wealth, power, protection, or abuse.

CONCLUSION

In the political processes of Muslim cities, the Mamluk regime as such did not behave as an alien military establishment, but penetrated the wider urban society through the powers which accrued to its members. Masters of large mounted military forces owing allegiance only to themselves, heads of vast households, and thus powerful patrons of local crafts and trades, controllers by their grain revenues of the very livelihood of the cities, despots by their powers of taxation over all incomes, owners of vast properties, bearers of access to strategic building materials, labor, and property rights—the emirs, and in particular the governors, by these extraordinary personal powers dominated all urban affairs. In a situation where responsibility for communal needs was not entrusted to regular governmental or communal agencies, public needs were left to the self-interest of the Mamluks, their sense of duty, and their desire for legitimation in the eyes of the ulama and the populace. By assuming responsibility for public works and the support of the religious and educational community the emirs, although totally alien in race, origin, and function became seigneurs, patrons, and notables of the local society. The regime did not govern from without, but merged political control with economic and social roles. Regime and society did not confront each other, reacting only on the interface between them; rather they permeated each other, the stronger pressing its way through the structure of the latter, and the subject society resisting, bending, accommodating, assimilating, taking cognizance of Mamluk powers and actions in ways which created an over-all political and social pattern which we shall examine in the subsequent chapters.

CHAPTER III · THE URBAN SOCIETY

MAMLUK INFLUENCE on the cities of Egypt and Syria derived from the immense economic and political powers of the Mamluk governors and other emirs. The exercise of these powers contributed to forming the relationships between the Mamluks and the rest of the urban populations, but to understand the import of these relationships for the political organization of the cities it is essential to consider first the organization of urban community life.

Aleppo, Cairo, and Damascus were socially complex and large for premodern times. Visitors to Damascus in the late fourteenth and early fifteenth centuries commonly estimated its population to be about 100,000, and agreed that Cairo was much larger. More accurate statistics from Ottoman censuses taken a century later, between 1520 and 1530, put the population of Damascus at about 57,000, and the population of Aleppo at about 67,000 in 1520 and 57,000 a decade later. For Cairo there are no known statistics.[1]

Ancient walls divided these cities into two major sectors, within and outside the fortifications. In addition, at Damascus there were major suburbs such as al-Ṣāliḥiyya, at a short distance from the main city, and large villages in the surrounding fruit-growing oasis called the Ghūṭa which impinged on the city itself and might also be considered part of a "metropolitan" conglomeration. These villages, though primarily agricultural, were not strictly peasant communities, but were sophisticated and urbane communities. Al-Mizza and Dārayyā, for example, were sites of mosques and schools. There too notable Damascene ulama, merchant, and landowning families made their residences.[2]

THE CLASSES OF THE POPULATION

Contemporary Muslim writers were well aware of the complexity of the cities and saw them as divided into four broad levels—the ruling elite, the notables, the common people, and the lumpenproletarians. The study of these classes, however, is complicated by the uncertainties of Arabic terminology. Arabic terms often had multiple referents or inconclusive connotations while time itself, in over two and a half centuries, also caused the meaning of terms to vary. Yet the situation is not entirely hopeless for the historian. In some instances context reveals the precise meaning of words, and often shows that even terms with broad ranges of meanings had a hard core of usage from which they diffused. This central meaning can be ferreted out, and even though the periphery is blurred, understanding how words diffuse is itself a key to the logic of Muslim views.

The most important of the classes was the Mamluk elite which we have discussed. The ruling elite was called *al-khāṣṣa* as opposed to *al-ʿāmma,* the common mass of people. *Al-khāṣṣa* proper were the Sultan and his retinue, the highest ranking Mamluk emirs, and officials, and the term distinguished this commanding elite from the broader class of functionaries and soldiers who were of subordinate importance in the state apparatus and were sometimes even called *al-ʿāmma.* For example, the expression *jamīʿ al-nās al-khāṣṣ wal-ʿāmm arbāb al-suyūf wal-qalam*—all of the people, elite and commoners, masters of the sword and the pen—treats soldiers and bureaucrats as no better than commoners. The term *al-khāṣṣa,* however, was used more broadly in some contexts to mean not only the very highest ranking emirs, but other important officials, judges, and religious leaders albeit of secondary rank. When *al-khāṣṣa* was used in this way, *al-ʿāmma* then referred to the subject masses, sometimes called *al-raʿiyya,* who were the workers and peasants.[3]

A second social level noted by Muslim writers was a stratum between *al-khāṣṣa* and *al-ʿāmma* called *al-aʿyān.* The word is usually translated "notables." Generally it applied to the most prominent and respected leaders of groups or classes of people. Thus we have *al-aʿyān* of the Mamluks, *al-aʿyān* of the ulama, *al-aʿyān* of the merchants, and *al-aʿyān* of *al-nās* (people). The term *al-aʿyān,* however, also had a more precise denotation. It referred in particular to the leading ulama —religious leaders, the scholars, teachers, judges, sheikhs, and preachers who were the most respected members of the community.[4]

Al-khāṣṣa thus referred to the imperial elite. Holders of the highest offices in the state administration, *al-khāṣṣa* embodied the directing interest of the empire. Their status reflected the power and wealth of the state itself. *Al-aʿyān,* lower in rank, privilege, and power, were rather the leading members of smaller communities. Their sphere of influence was the locality in which they were known and respected. Their status derived from respect for the religion they represented, and from deference to their technical qualifications and contribution to the maintenance of community life. Whereas *al-khāṣṣa* governed, *al-aʿyān* were intermediaries between them and the masses over whom they ruled.

While *al-aʿyān* referred to the religious notables, the term *al-nās* defined notability more broadly to include rich merchants. The term, however, was used in a variety of ways. In its most general sense it simply meant "people" or "populace" without reference to any particular class. When used in opposition to *al-ʿāmma* as in *al-nās wal-ʿāmma,* notables and commoners, the word *al-nās* had more specific denotations. In some contexts it applied to the Mamluks, in others to *al-aʿyān*—to bureaucrats and ulama. But men of low rank in the institutions of state and religion, people of great skill, specialists in medicine, architecture, and accounting, distinguished families, and merchants who had at least a more than average fortune were also *al-nās.* International traders, merchants of the *qayṣariyyas,* wholesalers, brokers, dealers in luxuries, property owners, and other large taxpayers were called *al-aʿyān* or *al-kabīr* (dignitaries) of the merchant class. The leading merchants were among the richest men of their times, often the equal of emirs. They received many official honors, were entitled to attend official ceremonies, and could be represented at official discussions. Rich merchants with the appropriate style of life were included among the notables of the city, for in Islamic society trade was not considered ignoble or derogating, nor were rents, pensions, and taxes regarded as the only worthy forms of income.[5] Social position was thus defined in terms of three values. Awe of political power ultimately made all statuses a function of proximity to the state. At every level of society, state office or influence with the Mamluk regime was a component of notability, while conversely, social distinction on other grounds tended to confer a measure of political power. Religious dignity, however, was an independent basis of social esteem. Scholars, teachers, and divines who embodied the ideals of the community earned its respect. Finally, wealth, family, and style of life were also recognized bases of high rank. They were of derivative importance, but tended to entail political or religious influence. However, the different criteria in use introduced an ambiguity into status rankings. Political power, at least from one point of view, might be decisive, but from the religious point of view it was also corrupting. Similarly, wealth might bring high status but however lucrative, certain trades were still regarded as tainted.

Deprived of all advantages were the common people, the respectable working classes who fitted into the communal, kinship, and religious structures but occupied no distinguished place within them. *Al-ʿāmma* possessed neither office, learning, nor wealth. To *al-khāṣṣa* they were the taxpayers. To *al-nās* they were often simply the *canaille.*[6]

Al-ʿāmma proper, sometimes called *al-ʿāmmat al-nās* (common members of the *nās*), as if to emphasize a degree of respectability, were the trading and working people of the cities. They were the shopkeepers, retailers and artisans, taxpayers, men known and accessible, the honest toilers. Some were of recognized social importance. Middle-class retailers were made responsible for fiscal and monetary measures taken by the regime. Skilled craftsmen such as carpenters, masons, and marble workers were awarded the prized Sultan's robes of honor on the completion of important projects. Other commoners variously called *bāʿa, sūqa, mutaʿayyishūn,* or *mutasabbibūn,* who were food dealers, artisans, workers, and peddlers made up the remainder of this working population.[7]

Yet included in the meaning of the word *al-ʿāmma* was a still lower class of the population, in the eyes of the middle classes a morally and socially despised mass, possessing little or none of the Muslim attributes in family life, occupation, or religious behavior, and often holding heretical religious beliefs. Though the boundaries between the respectable and the disreputable masses were not clearly set, a virtual caste apart from the rest of the common people was an important element in urban social life.

Muslim literary sources from various periods describe a theoretical distinction between the respectable and the disreputable on religious grounds. First among the disreputable were the usurers, or all those who profited from chicanery or transactions forbidden by Muslim law —brokers, criers, money changers, slave dealers, and people who sold forbidden objects. In a second category fell people of questionable morality—male or female prostitutes, wine sellers, cock fighters, professional mourners, dancers, and other entertainers. Thirdly, people defiled by dead beasts or animal wastes were included among the impure. Barbers and surgeons were valued on other grounds, but butchers, tanners, donkey and dog handlers, hunters, and waste scavengers were despised.[8]

Similar views pervaded the Mamluk period. The market inspector's manual of Ibn ʿAbd al-Hādī repeats much the same moral and aesthetic preferences. Following the views of the prophet Muḥammad and his companions perfume and milk were thought of as excellent trades, and the carpenter was valued because Zachariah was said to have been one, and tailors because Mary, it was believed, would intercede for them. On the other hand, the usurious trades of silver, gold, and silks were not highly regarded, and of course dealing in wine and pork and selling weapons to the enemy was strictly forbidden. The various cooking trades could be either good or evil. In general, bakers, furriers, carpenters, tailors, and perfumers were among the finer tradesmen, while silk weavers, wooden clog makers, goldsmiths, porters, wood gatherers, and water pourers belonged to subordinate occupations. The socially rejected tradesmen were weighers, camel and donkey drivers, changers, falconers, cuppers, leather workers and tanners, geomancers, jugglers, and barbers.[9]

In these somewhat theoretical views, people otherwise of high status such as money changers and silk dealers are put together with menials for religious reasons. Notices scattered throughout the chronicles, however, bring the despised underworld or lumpenproletarian elements proper more clearly into view. This outcast body was generally referred to as the *arādhil al-ʿāmma* (lowest of the common people), *awbāsh al-ʿāmma* (riff-raff of the common people), and *ghawghāʾ* (troublemakers), the mob of the city streets. The menials included were scavengers, entertainers, funeral workers, and refuse collectors. Wrestlers, clowns, players, story tellers, and singing women who amused the common people in the streets and around the citadels were part of this low class, irregularly employed, knocking about for a living, associated with vice and begging.[10]

The menials shaded over into a second category of despised persons, thieves and common criminals, prostitutes, and gamblers. The menial and the criminal seem to have been closely related. For example, *al-mashāʿiliyya,* the nightwatchmen and torch bearers who cleaned the latrines, removed refuse from the streets, and carried off the bodies of dead animals served as police, guards, executioners, and public criers, and paraded people condemned to public disgrace whose shame may have consisted in part in being handled by such men. At the same time *al-mashāʿiliyya* made use of their intimacy with nightlife to become involved in gambling, theft, and dealing in hashish and wine. Similarly, *al-ḥurrās* and *al-khufarāʾ,* other auxiliary nightwatchmen and police, shared in the same distasteful tasks. They removed dogs from the city and may also have been, as was the Cairo night watch, *aṣḥāb al-arbāʿ,*

in touch with the drinking places, in that ambiguous relationship which seems to be typical of police everywhere.

The slaves and servants of the Sultan and the emirs formed another group which did not share in the producing and trading activities of the city or in its normal family and district life. Standing outside the social structure of artisan, quarter, and religious life was an undisciplined and turbulent mass of kitchen helpers, stable hands, dog handlers, falconers, and huntsmen. They, too, were often associated with criminals and with traders in wine and hashish.[11]

Apart from the menials, criminals, and slaves there were the homeless and poverty stricken. The large towns attracted a floating population of immigrants. Many were wealthy, learned, or had come to make their fortune and soon found a place in society, but the towns also harbored rootless foreigners. These included transient merchants, pilgrims or traveling scholars, and sheikhs who had accommodations, friends, and contacts, but poor peasants and bedouins fleeing rural hardship fell into the nameless and faceless mass. These bedouins and peasants were unruly, often threatened pillage, and along with criminals and political prisoners made up the population of the jails. Strangers were the cause of anxiety and hardship. They were feared as pillagers, assassins, spies, and saboteurs. Other rootless people, without family or friends, were called *ṭarḥī* or *khasharī* in the chronicles. These were the unclaimed dead or people without heirs for whose burial special charities were founded. Masses of poverty stricken Sufi beggars peopled the towns, and sick, infirm, and crippled people lived in the streets and mosques.[12]

Certain circumstances temporarily swelled the population of the towns with homeless refugees. Fugitives from Aleppo, Hama, and Homs sought safety in Damascus and Baalbek from the thirteenth century Mongol invasions. Refugees from Syria often went to Egypt. So, too, the people of surrounding villages sought safety in walled towns, staying with friends if they were fortunate, but most often living and sleeping in the streets with their families. Refugees caused local prices to rise and spread the hardships of their flight inside the walls.[13]

Thus, outside the established kinship, occupational, and religious nexus was a body of the unemployed, menials, slaves and servants, unassimilated immigrants, drifters, criminals, and violent elements representing a social and cultural world far removed from the rest of the society. Below the productive *al-ʿāmma* of the medieval towns we find a lumpenproletariat gravitating into the interstices of cohesive city life, forming an underworld of social and moral life.[14]

Muslim cities were divided into these classes, but their relationships to each other formed cohesive patterns of public life. Strong solidarities based on the residential quarters of the cities, an attenuated form of professional and guild associations in the market districts, active lumpenproletarian gangs, and overarching religious affiliations cut across class divisions to create a more broadly based communal life.

THE ORGANIZATION OF THE QUARTERS

The cities were divided into districts called *ḥārāt, maḥallāt,* or *akhṭāṭ*. These were residential quarters with small local markets and perhaps workshops, especially for weaving, but characteristically isolated from the bustle of the main central city bazaars. In Damascus and Aleppo the quarters were about the size of small villages. Lists compiled before the middle of the sixteenth century assign about seventy quarters to Damascus proper and about thirty to the large suburb of al-Ṣāliḥiyya, indicating an average size of about five or six hundred people in a city of some 50,000. Late fifteenth century sources report some fifty odd quarters in Aleppo, indicating an average size of about a thousand or twelve hundred people, well within the limits of face to face intimacy for all the residents. Cairo, by contrast, a much larger city than either Damascus or Aleppo, had fewer *ḥārāt,* only thirty-seven according to the reckoning of al-Maqrīzī at the beginning of the fifteenth century, but in addition many *akhṭāṭ* and streets, lanes and alleys which may also have been vital units of social life are also listed. The quarters were thus small neighborhoods within the urban whole, but the lists do not necessarily imply that every one was a real unit of social organization. In some cases, as is probable for al-Ṣāliḥiyya in Damascus and Bānaqūsā in Aleppo, a larger area containing many quarters was the unit of effective social action. In Jerusalem there were forty in all, but only nine of consequence.[15]

Many of the quarters, though not every one need have been a solidarity, were closely knit and homogeneous communities. The tendency of different groups to seek the comfort and protection of their own members was very strong in a world where no man was truly safe except among his kin. The solidarity of some districts was based on religious identity. In Cairo each Christian and Jewish sect had its own street. There were Jewish quarters attested in Damascus; at Aleppo,

Armenians and Maronites occupied quarters in the northwest part of the city. Jewish and Christian quarters were found in Jerusalem. Though it has been asserted that the evidence of quarrels over neighboring synagogues and mosques, or over the height of houses, shows that the Jewish and Christian minorities were dispersed in the population, it would be more correct to say that they lived in separate districts but adjacent to Muslim streets. There was some separation of persons by community but no ghetto-like isolation of communities in the whole.[16]

Among the Muslims, different ethnic or racial groups lived apart. Aleppo had quarters of Turkomans outside the walls, a Kurdish quarter, and a street of Persians. Many of the smaller towns also had quarters of Kurds, Turks, bedouins in process of sedentarization, or small communities of refugees from abroad.[17]

For the dominant Arab-Muslim population, common village origin unified some urban districts. Villagers gathered with their cousins, retained contacts with people at home, and recreated the old life within the walls. Migrants from Harran kept their identity in Damascus and their own street in Aleppo. Jerusalem had several quarters of people from different villages and tribal groups. Moreover, expanding cities sometimes englobed villages lying just outside the old city into a continuous urban agglomeration. Al-Qubaybāt quarter, outside Damascus in the thirteenth century and still a village in 721/1321 when endowed with a new mosque and canals, was gradually absorbed by the growth of the city. Such districts retained a special character throughout the period.[18]

The solidarity of some Muslim quarters depended on sectarian religious affiliations. For example, al-Ṣāliḥiyya in Damascus was affiliated with the Ḥanbalī law school while most of the rest of the city was Shāfiʿī. No prior unity of race, origin, or family, but unity grown out of the leadership of the sheikhs and the eventual association of the whole quarter with the school created a strong focus of feeling.[19]

There were also economic bases for the homogeneity of particular quarters. Some were named after a market or craft. A common occupation often gave these quarters their special character. Mills, lime works, brick kilns, dye works, and tanneries drew workers into separate districts at Aleppo. They needed water and space, and the rest of the townsmen needed protection from noxious wastes, noises, and smells. Quarters on the main roads specialized in caravaning, transport, and animal and grain marketing, and dealt in goods and services for bedouins and peasants. The quarters south of Damascus grew along the main road to the grain growing areas, and al-Fusqār quarter was a center of trade with peasants. At Aleppo too, bedouin encampments grew into permanent districts for the caravan trades.[20]

There is no evidence, however, that homogeneity of social classes was a basis of solidarity. Certain neighborhoods were favored by the wealthy because of their salubrity, or proximity to the citadel and public affairs, and gave these districts an "upper" class character, but no class came to dominate a district. Though the emirs tended to concentrate near the citadel and in central quarters, these were also centers for markets and religious institutions. They had mixed populations of ulama, merchants, craftsmen, and functionaries. At most, the central quarters tended to be wealthier while the quarters outside the walls of Damascus, Aleppo, or Cairo were more likely to retain the qualities of the villages or other settlements around which they were built, and to concentrate the more turbulent and least well integrated elements of the city populace. They were not, however, without resident notables. Economic, religious, and social life were not so differentiated from each other as to create the basis for any radical separation of classes by quarter. Quarters were communities of both rich and poor.[21]

In certain districts, solidarity engendered fierce hostilities between quarters which came to the fore whenever the Mamluk government was weak. In the Palestinian towns, the quarrels of Kurdish, Turkoman, or Arab bedouin clans having kinship ties and alliances with outside villagers and bedouins were a cause of internal warfare. For example, at Hebron in 878/1473–74, parties of Kurds and people called Dāriya fought each other while tribesmen from the surrounding countryside poured in to aid their brethren. Fighting in Jerusalem broke out in 885/1480 because the governor executed some of the Banū Zayd. Their allies or kin from outside the city attacked the town, raided the markets and mosques, and set free prisoners. A few years later in Ramla (889/1484) quarters of Turkomans and Bashkir fought each other as a result of such quarrels.[22]

Damascus suffered from similar strife for similar reasons. Here quarters outside the walls whose populations were, in part, of rural origin were the source of violent feuds. Al-Qubaybāt had been a village until the fifteenth century, and it is probable that other peasant migrants to Damascus made suburban districts their first stopping place. In the civil wars of 791/1389, which we shall discuss later, the city divided in support of Sultan Barqūq and the rebel Emir Minṭāsh along lines reminiscent of rural disputes. Quarters of the city called the Ḥārāt al-Kilāb supported the Sultan while the defenders of Minṭāsh were called Qays, names going back to the ancient struggles of Arabian bedouin confederations which had plagued the Umayyad dynasty in the first century of the Arab conquests and disrupted the history of Syria ever since.* In the struggle between the quarters in the late fifteenth century the same outside districts were involved. In 885/1480 al-Qubaybāt and Maydān al-Ḥaṣā were at loggerheads attributed by Ibn Ṭūlūn to the ancient Qays-Yemen bedouin rivalries. In 890/1485, a roundhouse of battles shook Damascus. Al-Qubaybāt and al-Maydān al-Akhḍar fought bitterly until finally pacified by the sheikhs. To take revenge after a quarrel, the people of al-Shāghūr quarter attacked the bowmakers market and were driven off by Mamluks who invaded their home district while the populace blocked the streets, cut bridges, and stoned the troops. Later in the year al-Shāghūr fought al-Maydān al-Akhḍar and al-Qubaybāt. Three years after, the *zu'ar* (young toughs) of that district attacked the *zu'ar* of al-Mazābil quarter, and were subsequently involved in disputes with the Maydān al-Ḥaṣā. Subsequent quarrels involved al-Qubaybāt in 895/1490, and in 902/1496–97 after a battle between Maydān al-Ḥaṣā and al-Shāghūr, emirs and qadis pacified the quarters by arranging that no retaliation be sought for the dead. At this time, one important factor in the eruption of these deep-rooted enmities was civil war among the Mamluks. In 903/1497–98, the city was polarized into factions favoring each of two fighting Mamluk parties. Al-Qubaybāt quarter supported the rebel Emir Aqbirdī and was attacked, pillaged, and burned by his enemies, while a similar fate was meted out to al-Ṣāliḥiyya which supported the government.[23]

Aleppo was also plagued by sporadic battles between two factions which had a very long and intense but elusive history. Aleppo was divided between the Bānaqūsā district lying outside the walls and the

* The Qays were a confederation of tribes presumably originating in northern Arabia while the Yemen group came from southern Arabia. The Yemeni tribes were settled in Syria and Iraq before the Arab conquests in the seventh century brought a heavy influx of northerners into the region. Their conflicts may reflect genealogical and tribal or political antagonisms, or they may represent an unconscious solution to the problem of security by the formation of ever larger confederations out of the smaller clans which were the normal social units.

populace within, or at least into fighting cliques recruited in each of the two major zones. The geographer, al-Qazwīnī, writing in the middle of the thirteenth century, reported a custom of Aleppo called the *shalāq* in which the populace divided annually into two factions to fight each other. Presumably these were games, but in the civil war of 791/1389 fighting broke out in earnest when Bānaqūsā supported the rebel Minṭāsh, while the rest of Aleppo favored Sultan Barqūq.

In 853/1449 or 855/1451, two parties, called the Banāqisa and al-Ḥawrānī, came into conflict. The Banāqisa wanted to parade in the pilgrimage procession, armed as was their custom, because one of their people had been made an official of the celebration. The governor opposed the parade for fear of a clash, but relented when reassured by leading merchants from Bānaqūsā. The procession soon realized his worst expectations. By the time the troops had restored order, many people, both fighters and bystanders, had been killed. The fight was attributed to the struggle of Qays and Yemen, and indeed according to one account, the signal that touched it off was the shout "Qays." The factions also had their origin in bedouin settlements, but in fact commercial and cultural differences must have whetted hostilities between the populations.

Al-Ḥawrānī of this battle appear for the first time and are only a little less mysterious than the Banāqisa. The name implies origins in the grain growing region south of Damascus, but they were identified as a group from the southern quarters of Aleppo near the Maqām Gate, and were called *qassābīn* (butchers) which implies either craft affiliation, presumed unity of descent, or common relationship to some patron saint. Apart from their enmity to the Banāqisa, al-Ḥawrānī were alienated from the state, ever ready to fight and resist the government. In 884/1479, they attacked the governor's agents, presumably because of fiscal oppression. Several were seized, and the qadis, without sympathy, sentenced them to death.

At the very end of the Mamluk period, in 923/1517, we again hear about hostile moieties. This time they were called the Ḥaww and the Ḥās, but were considered to belong to Qays and Yemen, or in the local variant, Qays and Janab. We know nothing about them save that they were a menace to the Jews of Aleppo. A food shopkeeper converted from Judaism to Islam used to protect his former co-religionists by barring entry to the Jewish quarter to any drunken members of either faction. At best, the report suggests the same sorts of lumpenproletarian solidarities, hostile to the regime, hostile to enemy factions, and dangerous to the populace at large as do the other accounts.[24]

Thus the localization of these struggles in quarters outside the old city walls, and the involvement of people of rural origins and their identification with Qays-Yemen disputes point to the survival within the city of a system of conflicts more usually encountered in rural life.* Inter-communal warfare was associated primarily with bedouins and patterns of organization which seem rooted in their way of life. Kinship solidarities served them well in fierce competitions over grazing lands and livestock, and competition encouraged clans to agglomerate into large tribal alliances which eventually divided the bedouins into hostile confederations. In the fourteenth century, such tribes threw all of Syria into turmoil. Fighting between hostile tribes around Gaza, Tripoli, Baalbek, and Nablus and between Arabs and Kurds near Shayzar caused great hardship. In the fifteenth century as well there are scattered instances of bedouin warfare around Kerak, Nablus, and Gaza.[25]

Villagers or groups of villagers similarly fought their neighbors. The motives for this hostility are obscure. Conceivably, the tendency was spread to villagers by the bedouins. The villages, though differing in economic civilization, were often social analogues of bedouin tribes, which were kinship solidarities and were instinctively self-protective, though much of their unity must itself have been derived from the fact of rivalries. Many villages were semi-sedentarized settlements continuing old habits and maintaining old ties to the bedouins. Factionalism also spread among villagers as a consequence of alliances with the bedouins on the basis of real or presumed kinship ties. The existence of the unchecked free-roaming bedouin compromised the security of the villages and preserved habits of social organization more appropriate to the nomadic than the sedentary way of life.

Thus villages in the Hauran were divided into factions identified after the ancient tribal struggles as the Qays and Yemen. In 709/1310–11 serious fighting took the lives of a thousand people, after which some of the defeated party took refuge in Damascus while the victors fled the wrath of the state. Villages and cultivation were abandoned, and part

* There is a tendency to exaggerate the religious, cultural, economic, and even racial differences between urban and rural areas in Syria. Writers are even sometimes inclined to speak of Islam as an urban civilization, but the evidence of rural migrations to cities should prevent us from embracing this view without reservations. (Cf. **530**.)

of the area was left desolate. In 759/1358 and 762/1361, Hauran peasants battled and forces were sent from Damascus to pacify them. Later, at the beginning of the sixteenth century, the weakening of the state permitted latent hostility to come to the fore, and the Qays-Yemen struggles resumed in the Ghūṭa of Damascus. The village of Dārayyā fought several others, and the government may even have encouraged the hostilities just as it encouraged the common people of the cities to take sides in disputes between the emirs. In 920/1514, a leading Damascus emir induced the villages of Ashrafiyya and Ṣaḥnāyā to join in the plunder of Dārayyā Kubrā. Two years later Dārayyā and al-Mizza came to blows until parted by people from al-Ṣāliḥiyya. Dārayyā itself, to complicate these struggles, was divided into a northern and a southern quarter. In 921/1515, the southerners attacked the Banū Bābiyya clan living in the northern quarter and killed two brothers.[26]

Unfortunately, apart from their over-all character, very little is known about the inner organization of quarters. They were evidently built around families or clans, and from the law codes we can see that the Muslim family was not the nuclear unit of parents and children with which we are now most familiar, but an agnatic clan extending over generations under the leadership of its eldest members. Giving intimate support, the family was a primary locus of allegiance and responsibility. It was the basic agency for mutual aid and protection, the teaching of religion to the young, the management of private property, and the regulation of social intercourse in the community. In Islamic society, men did not exist alone, but only as validated and inspired by their clans.[27]

How such families were related and unified into quarters remains a mystery. We may speculate that extended kinship ties, real or presumed as evidenced in the Qays-Yemen identifications, were one means. Clienteles were probably another. Quarters may have been organized with the household of some important family surrounded by the residences of cadet branches and the families of retainers, servants, employees, disciples, and so on. For example, in the Mongol assault on Aleppo in 658/1260 the merchant, Ibn Naḥḥās, saved countless Aleppins by purchasing a patent of security from Hūlūgū, not for himself alone, but for his whole quarter, which promptly filled with refugees. In the Cairo riots of 791/1389, the house of a qadi was attacked by pillagers and defended by his family, slaves and servants, and the people of his quarter. Also in Cairo, al-Ḥusayniyya quarter was under the protection of an emir who had been born there of a common family. He sought to protect the district against minor taxes, and this proved to be his undoing.[28] No doubt, however, many quarters which are known by name were lacking in internal cohesion while quarters in areas outside the city walls seemed strongest in this respect.

In any case, the solidarity of the quarters was reinforced by the important social and administrative responsibilities which devolved upon it. One of the leading notables, called the sheikh or *'arīf* of the *ḥāra,* was the chief spokesman and administrator of the district, but he was selected (with how much freedom of choice is uncertain) by the governor of the city and was subject to removal by him. The sheikhs were entitled to places of honor in public gatherings, and received governors, ambassadors, and other visiting dignitaries. In consultation with other notables, ulama, merchants, and officials they carried on the life of the district. For example, they saw to small endowments for communal purposes and took the lead in maintenance and repairs.[29]

Their essential administrative duty, however, was to mediate between the fiscal requirements of the Mamluk regime and the resources of the people. They were the government's agents for apportioning and collecting taxes, especially for extraordinary taxes, not levied on a regular basis which the sheikhs tried by negotiation to fend off or reduce. The Mamluks had to persuade them to yield the funds and prevent them from using their influence within the regime itself to protect their clients. The sheikhs stood in a key position, essential to the regime for collection, essential to the people for evasion, linking government and subjects, belonging to both and to neither.

Most of our information about the quarters as fiscal collectivities comes from the history of Damascus and Aleppo after 890/1485. At the end of the thirteenth century market taxes were levied in Damascus by quarter, and in the later period market or excise taxes were assessed on particular crafts or trades, but collected by quarter. After 890/1485, however, the severity of wars against the Dulghādir Turkomans and the Ottoman Empire, and the intensity of bedouin and village violence all over Syria, which required frequent punitive expeditions, caused the Mamluks for the first time to levy global fees on the population of entire quarters. Sometimes these fees are called *rimāya* which may imply a forced purchase. These taxes were in addition to an already burdensome taxation but may have suggested themselves because the

Mamluks, faced with intensified resistance from the city masses, could directly rely on the assistance of the notables. For example, in 890/1485, the governor of Damascus was advised to have some person well known for learning and piety authorize a tax so that all doubts about its legality would be removed. Sheikh Taqy al-dīn ibn Qāḍī Ajlūn was willing to persuade the sheikhs of the quarters who in turn persuaded the populace at large to accept the levies. Ibn Ṭūlūn, who reported the episode, accused the sheikhs of ignoring the well known and detailed provisions of the law. While the governor and the sheikhs of the quarters and tax collectors profited, the poor, widows, orphans, students, and waqfs were made to pay. Three years later taxes were again levied to pay for new troops. They were raised from the markets and landed estates, but also from al-Ṣāliḥiyya, al-Qābūn, al-Qubaybāt, and al-Shāghūr quarters. These may have been punitive taxes applied specifically to the quarters most frequently resisting the regime. Al-Shāghūr and al-Ṣāliḥiyya were again taxed in 901/1495–96, and other quarters were assessed *rimāya* in 905/1499–1500 and 907/1501–02. In Damascus in 907/1501–02 serious fighting broke out when 100,000 dinars was demanded, and even though agreement was reached by the sheikhs on 20,000, the common people refused to pay at all. In successive years the quarters paid new taxes to protect the pilgrimage and to pay for infantry to curb the bedouins and assure the flow of food supplies into Damascus. The aggressiveness of Shāh Ismā'īl, the Safavid ruler of Persia, caused still more taxes to be collected. Sometimes the expenses were very great. For example, in 920/1514, the quarters were assessed for 4,000 troops at twenty-five dinars each, a total of 100,000 dinars. Most of this money was wasted, and neither the bedouin unrest nor the threats of would-be conquerors were stilled. At Aleppo as well, in 910/1504–05, the governor wished to have the populace pay for new troops, but only some of the sheikhs would agree to collect the money.[30]

Administrative responsibilities extended to police functions as well. Mamluk governors required the sheikhs of the quarters to enforce special ordinances, assist in the suppression of wine drinking, restrict circulation at night, regulate the opening and closing of shops, and enforce sanitary rules.[31] They were also held responsible for the prevention of crime, return of fugitives, and apprehension of criminals or payment of indemnities in unsolved cases.

In these matters a collective responsibility akin to that which bound the closest of all Middle Eastern solidarities, the bedouin tribe, was imposed on the quarters. Long-standing Islamic law and practice treated quarters as responsible for the payment of blood money. The indemnities forced them to discipline themselves in inner recesses of community life which no outsider could effectively reach. The quarters, however, appealed against collective responsibility, and affirmed the liability of each man and him alone for his offenses. Collective responsibility was an extension of the police duties of the quarters, but the objections were not unjust, because fines were often arbitrarily imposed. So far as we know they were not applied in the Mamluk period before being conceived as a device for turning the insecurity of the towns to the profit of the governors. In Damascus at the beginning of the sixteenth century indemnities were frequently levied to protect oppressive tax officials from assault. Vigorous protests resulted in 906/1500–01 in the abolition of such taxes, and an inscription was carved to remind posterity of the event. Nonetheless, in 911/1505–06 remission had to be granted again, and all persons arrested for nonpayment of the taxes were released. Of course, this was not the last heard of these penalties.[32]

Social and administrative cohesiveness naturally extended to communal defense. In insecure times, when thieves, bandits, civil war, or invasion threatened, the quarters barricaded themselves behind great doors, closed off the thoroughfares to the rest of the city, and hid themselves from attack. In the Cairo civil war of 791/1389, the exits of the quarters were guarded, and armed people, led by the chiefs of the *ḥārāt,* patrolled the city to prevent looting.

Yet, in Mamluk times at least, the quarters of Syrian and Egyptian towns should not be imagined as armed fortresses. Permanent defenses had not yet been built into the *ḥārāt,* and the defensive aspect of Muslim urban quarters which was characteristic of later Ottoman times, when heavy doors barred unauthorized entry, had not fully evolved. Gates had to be erected or repaired afresh for every crisis. For example, gates were not in regular use at the end of the thirteenth century in Damascus, for after a shocking series of murders of nightwatchmen in 695/1296, Damascus had first to restore internal barriers and begin to illuminate the streets at night. Even Cairo, though very much more plagued by insecurity than Damascus, seems to have found no permanent need for defensive walls. Once in 728/1328 the quarters rebuilt their gates because of difficulties caused by rapacious officials, and only in the fifteenth century, when plunder by slaves, Mamluks, or gangs of bandits was an everpresent likelihood, did the *ḥārāt* again become units of defense. For example, in 860/1456 the people of Bāb al-Lūk fought and routed plundering slaves. In 864/1460 gates with locks were newly built on the streets of Cairo and were closed at night. For security against hoodlums, bandits, and Mamluks, women were forbidden to go out, and people did not visit outlying shrines and tombs. Decades later, in 902/1496–97, barricades and palisades were once more erected around markets and quarters to protect them from gangs of thieves. When barricades were restored in 922/1516 taxes were levied to pay for communal and market fortifications. These taxes were forcibly collected by the nightwatchmen and police and were regarded as an abuse. In fact, defense by quarter may not have had strong natural foundations in Cairo, and had to be imposed from without by the regime.[33] Barricades were not a permanent feature of the Mamluk urban scene, and however cohesive within, the quarters were not isolated ghettos, but adjacent streets and districts within the cities. Not in their daily lives, but only in time of troubles did they seal themselves off from each other.

Thus many urban quarters were small, integrated communities. By quasi-physical isolation, close family ties, ethnic or religious homogeneity, strong group solidarity, economic and administrative unity, and spokesmen elites, they were analogues of village communities inside the urban agglomeration.

THE ORGANIZATION OF ECONOMIC LIFE

However intense the society of the quarters they did not wholly absorb the social existence of their members. The bazaars in which the economic life of the cities as opposed to the communal and family life of the *ḥārāt* was focused formed another arena of social life. The central business districts were mainly composed of rows of shops and workshops, khans, and *qayṣariyyas* for wholesaling and manufacturing, but schools, mosques, "monasteries," baths, and other public facilities were all found in the market district. There too scribes, official witnesses, tax collectors, and judges had their booths. Adjacent to the markets were the citadel and the residences of the leading Mamluk emirs. In other nearby houses, officials and leading religious and merchant families made their homes. Here the concerns of the whole city were carried on by the people of the quarters who came, separated from their families, differentiated from their communal roles.

The population of the markets, however, was very imperfectly organized by comparison with the quarters. Professional, merchant, and artisan guilds were virtually nonexistent, and what rudimentary forms did exist were created by the state for its own purposes rather than by the solidarity and self-interest of the members. The so-called corporations of physicians, surgeons, and oculists are so designated only because chiefs called *ra'īses* were appointed by the state to maintain standards of teaching, practice, and discipline in the professions. There is no indication that these functionaries represented guild solidarities.[34]

Neither were merchants organized into guilds. In the fourteenth century the *kārimī* merchants in the spice trade between Egypt and India were supervised by a *ra'īs,* selected from their number, but appointed by the Sultan to act as a liason for the organization of their banking, diplomatic, and fiscal duties to the state. As in the case of the *ra'īses* of the medical professions, the evidence does not point to merchant guilds, but only to state efforts to utilize the wealth and influence of a leading merchant for its own purposes. Aside from the *kārimī* chiefs, there are only five examples of *ra'īses* of merchants. In the three cases for which there is further information, circumstances indicate that the title was an official post rather than the leadership of a guild association. Three of the *ra'īses* were state officials, and two of them were involved in the orient spice trade. The merchant, al-Ṭībī, who traveled between China and Hormuz in the fourteenth century, was called *ra'īs al-tujjār* (chief of the merchants). Another *ra'īs al-tujjār,* al-Ṭanbudī, had a part in the sugar monopolies of Sultan Barsbāy. The third was *ra'īs* of the merchants of Mecca.[35]

Similarly, local merchants in the markets of important towns were supervised by sheikhs of the markets. We usually know them only by their titles: a sheikh of the Damascus gold suq, a merchant who was sheikh of a *qayṣariyya,* a pharmacist sheikh of his suq, and others. These sheikhs were appointed by the governor of the city from among the notable merchants, but they were not chiefs of merchant corporations. Indeed in one case a merchant wished to refuse the post and was beaten into accepting it. The sheikhs were responsible for discipline, prevention of fraud, and collection of taxes. In the fifteenth century, a sheikh levied an inspection tax on the millers of Aleppo, and the sheikh of a Damascus market belonging to the waqf of the hospital was concerned with the misappropriation of its revenues by the administrators of the hospital.[36]

Other official sounding titles might seem to imply merchant organizations. The terms *kabīr al-tujjār* (head of the merchants), *tājir kabīr* (merchant head), or *al-aʿyān* (notables) are occasionally used. But in only one instance do they actually indicate an official position. In the mid-fifteenth century, Badr al-dīn Ḥasan, who had been a commissioner in Jidda and supervisor of the sanctuaries of Mecca, became *kabīr* of the merchants. *Al-aʿyān,* however, is occasionally used in a context which implies the role of a spokesman. For example, *al-aʿyān* appeared before the Sultan to hear new fiscal or monetary regulations. In one episode, in 892/1487 the market inspector of Cairo gathered the merchant notables and imposed a tax of 40,000 dinars, of which they agreed to pay 12,000. No evidence suggests, however, that *al-aʿyān* meant anything but, "most prominent, richest" from whom the Sultan wanted money.[37]

The same pattern of close supervision without evident corporate structure also prevailed among the artisanate. A good deal of scholarly controversy surrounds the question of whether or not there were guilds in Muslim towns, but much of the confusion stems from uncertainty about the meaning of the word "guild."[38] First of all, guilds must be distinguished from the more inclusive category of fraternal societies. Only associations which restricted their membership to a single or allied crafts and trades and existed to serve the economic as well as the social interests of their members were, properly speaking, guilds. The term, however, poses further problems, for in the contemporary Mediterranean world guild referred to two very different types of craft corporations.

The guilds of western Europe were, characteristically, voluntary and self-governing associations. Founded as religious fraternities, they later became associations for economic defense or aggrandizement, seeking to protect themselves against coercion either by obtaining legal recognition of their interests or by waging economic and political warfare to assure de-facto acceptance of their claims. As corporations, guilds were responsible in their spheres of activity, and could choose their members, select their leaders, and dispose of resources considered as belonging not to any one member but to the group as a whole. Guilds were more or less autonomous, more or less organized, more or less well founded in the adherence and loyalty of their members, but none of the variations in principle affected their essential quality as voluntary associations whose members were responsible in common.

The guilds of the Byzantine Empire differed from those of western Europe. Byzantine corporations were organized by the police powers of the state, not by the voluntary adhesion of the members. Created to fulfill economic functions, they were granted monopolies in their spheres. Nonetheless they were never autonomous and possessed neither treasuries nor officers elected at the pleasure of the memberships. Rules for their functioning were drafted and enforced from without. Though this did not preclude solidarity within the corporations, it removed control over economic affairs from the artisans and tradesmen.[39]

Strictly speaking, neither the European nor the Byzantine type of guild was to be found in the bazaars of the Muslim city. In the Mamluk period, trades and crafts were subject, like the Byzantine guilds, to rigorous external controls intended to keep worker activities within certain political, economic, fiscal, and moral bounds. But supervision did not entail incorporation. In Muslim towns, basic control of trades and crafts was delegated to the *muḥtasibs* or market inspectors. Their supervisory functions were conceived as part of a general communal obligation to promote good and restrain evil, and their economic duties were an extension of the desire for moral communal life. The market inspectors were responsible for upholding fair and honest business practices. They supervised the quality of manufactures, eliminating frauds and unfair competition, regulated the grain markets, and were vested with authority to control prices and coinage values in times of crisis. Moreover, they had an important part in the collection of market taxes.[40]

The *muḥtasibs* thus embodied both the ulama concern for moral order, and the fiscal interests of the state. They were chosen from among the ulama, merchants, and officials, but the fiscal importance of the office often prevailed in the fifteenth century and the post occasionally went to Mamluks.[41]

To assist the *muḥtasibs,* each craft or trade had an *ʿarīf* appointed as its overseer. These were selected from among the craftsmen, but appointed by the *muḥtasibs* to be their agents and agents of the state authority. No doubt, their intermediary position caused them to become *porte-parole* for the pleas of the craftsmen and possibly protectors as well, but they were not the spokesmen of independent interests and represented no internal solidarity save as the workers were obliged by outside controls to act in common. The duties of the *'arīfs* were to advise the *muḥtasibs* about the practices of the trade, and the general condition of the market. They were generally responsible for the execution of whatever duties were assigned the craftsmen. They assisted in the organization of the markets for auxiliary military service, and when ordered by the government brought out the workers for ceremonial occasions such as meeting returning Sultans or armies in candlelit processions. Most probably they were also in charge of the decoration of the markets when royal or gubernatorial decrees required the shopkeepers to celebrate military victories, visits of important dignitaries, and other public events. Once promulgated by the criers these decrees were laws, and the Mamluks threatened to confiscate the goods of shopkeepers who failed to obey. At times, the shopkeepers were also obliged to keep their shops open and lit all night despite the hardship, the cold, and the danger of theft. In addition, when liturgical services were assigned the market people, the *'arīfs* were assembled to hear the governor's instructions. In return for these services they might be exempted from taxation. In general, they were the counterpart of the sheikhs of the merchant bazaars.[42]

The most important duty of the *muḥtasibs* and the *'arīfs* was the taxation of the markets. From the middle of the fourteenth century the market inspectors grew in importance as intermediaries in the tax process. The first indication we have of such responsibilities is contained in a decree of the year 762/1360–61, in which a fee taken from the *muḥtasib* and evidently collected by him in turn from the markets, was abolished. By the beginning of the fifteenth century it was already a normal, though extra-legal, practice of the market inspector to levy a monthly tax on trades and crafts. Despite an endless series of cancellations, the practice was permanently enshrined because the government collected a share of these revenues. Relief could be obtained in special circumstances although the tax was never abolished in principle. It was canceled in Beirut in 806/1403, and then sporadically throughout the century in Jerusalem, Baalbek, Damascus, and Cairo. But however often abolished, the tax came back to plague the markets. At the beginning of the sixteenth century in both Damascus and Cairo it yielded about 2,000 dinars a month. The Damascus farm was so valuable that the office of *muḥtasib*'s assistant was purchased for 16,000 dinars. When finally abolished in Cairo in 922/1516 the monthly taxes were still worth about 2,000 dinars, but the total of weekly and monthly taxes raised by the market inspector was 76,000 dinars a year. These heavy duties raised prices so much that even the Mamluks complained about the high cost of food.[43]

In addition, trade and production were subject to a battery of other supervisory arrangements, mostly to facilitate taxation. To prevent evasion and assure the Mamluk regime a more effective exploitation of the markets, traders were often required to gather in one place. The practice, called *taḥkīr,* was especially useful to prevent tax evasion in the food trades where many of the suppliers were peddlers, peasants, and bedouins gathered on market days to sell their produce. Thus Aleppo in the middle of the fifteenth century had an egg khan while at Damascus all the confectioners were grouped together. The most extensive *taḥkīr* recorded was in Damascus where a myriad of foodstuffs had to be assembled in one place. Sale of oil, butter, flour, dates, figs, lemons, cucumbers, straw, charcoal, colocasia, sugar, eggplants, and fish were until 882/1477–78 restricted in this way. Indeed not until the middle of the sixteenth century did the Ottomans abolish the monopoly of certain khans on the sale of charcoal and raisins. *Taḥkīr* controls extended to crafts as well. At Baalbek, for example, cotton was required to be sold in only one suq. The practice benefited the emirs as property owners as well as tax collectors, for by this requirement the ability to raise rents to the highest possible levels was assured.

Although originally conceived as tax measures, the importance of these controls transcended their fiscal intention. First, the characteristic spatial quality of the Muslim bazaar in which all the sellers or craftsmen in a particular trade are gathered together in one location was reinforced. Moreover, by forcing all potential buyers and sellers together, true markets were created in which a fair and competitive price could be determined.[44]

Fiscal supervision overburdened the markets with tax collectors and tax farmers (*ḍāmin*). Once, when the Sultan abolished certain levies, he "sent off the scribes from the places where they used to sit in order to take the market taxes." Indirectly professional witnesses, brokers, and criers were also enlisted in the tax collecting machine. Brokers paid half their fees as a tax, and thus indirectly levied a sales tax in the guise of their commissions.[45]

In no case, however, despite the elaboration of the tax collecting machinery, were worker collectivities required. Taxes were assessed on each transaction or on the value of goods, but with only an occasional exception known to us, never as a global fee levied by craft. For example, when the *zakāt* tax was levied in 791/1389, merchants declared their worth individually to the qadis and paid the assessed rates.[46] Thus, a degree of market control sufficient for the purposes of taxation, the inhibition of frauds, and the enforcement of general regulations was adopted; but a regime so thoroughgoing as to create any profound unities in the markets was avoided. It accorded better with the inclinations of the Mamluks to permit each emir to exploit the tax revenues as he wished rather than to create a statewide management. So, too, the *muḥtasibs* eschewed controls over prices, wages, or numbers of craftsmen which would have required the assistance of corporations. The Muslim market place was less highly organized than markets in the other contemporary Mediterranean civilizations.[47]

Considered from the point of view of political organization, economic regulation, or even corporate fraternal life, there were no guilds in Muslim cities in this period in any usual sense of the term. Still, workmen must have had a more highly organized social life than our sources reveal. Apprenticeship arrangements for the perpetuation of craft skills and long training under the close personal supervision of master-workers must have been necessary. Nonetheless, there is no evidence that the terms of apprenticeship were organized on a craft-wide basis. Informal traditions must have created uniform employment conditions.[48]

Moreover, it seems probable in some cases that solidarity of workers in a particular craft or trade was based on the broader social life of the quarters. Some quarters, as we have seen, were economically specialized and in these cases workers' solidarities may have been due to communal as well as occupational bonds. One episode suggests such a relationship. In 913/1507–08, a group of Jawābir and a group of Nafar in Būlāk (Cairo) fought each other. The Jawābir were boatmen, and the Nafar attacked their grain boats, pillaged them, stole turbans from the inhabitants of the district, and broke into the shops. The Jawābir joined by sailors of Būlāk took their revenge on the Nafar and fighting went on for several days until the groups applied to emirs who were their protectors and the Sultan settled the disputes. Not only workers, but the quarters of Būlāk, their ulama, and their markets were involved in this dispute, and it seems probable that in the riverain quarters, whose men were involved in the boating trades, occupation and residence coalesced to form the basis of solidarity. We cannot yet, however, speak of guilds or corporations. Guilds are not any social solidarity, but a special sort of economic association.[49]

Though there were no guilds there seems to have been one religious fraternity based on craft affiliation and thus capable of acting on behalf of the economic interests of its members. This was a Sufi fraternity of silk workers in Damascus. Most of our information comes from biographies of people named *ḥarīrī* (silk merchant or weaver), but the name itself was very common and does not necessarily indicate that the bearer was actually in the silk trade. At least a few contexts, however, plainly identify silk weavers who were also Sufis. For instance, a Sheikh Muḥammad who taught tradition in Damascus and died in 683/1284 was called *faqīr min al-ḥarīriyya* (Sufi of the silk workers). Another sheikh was called *faqīr al-ḥarīriyya* (silk worker Sufi). Sheikh 'Alī al-Ḥarīrī, a Sufi, was employed as a silk worker until he became a jurist. These Sufi silk workers formed fraternities, for we hear of *ṭā'ifa* (groups) of *ḥarīriyya*. Some silk workers were called sheikhs of the *ṭā'ifa*, sheikhs of the *ḥarīriyya*, or sheikhs of the *faqīr al-ḥarīriyya*. These groups probably had some distinctive costume, for one sheikh, 'Abd-allāh, is said to have dressed in the fashion of the *ḥarīriyya*.[50]

In one isolated episode, the silk workers acted as a group to defend their economic interests. In 897/1492, according to one account, the Damascus silk workers gathered in the Umayyad Mosque to protest a tax of two hundred dinars. This tax was the fee of the messenger announcing the abolition of other taxes levied on silks. A more complete and probable account is given by Ibn Ṭūlūn who reports that the silk workers coming from all the quarters of the city with the (tax?) notifications posted in the mosques demonstrated in front of the governor's palace against a tax on looms amounting to a total of 15,000 dirhems. This tax was assessed by quarter. The governor refused to receive the workers, and the outcome of the episode is not stated. It seems likely that the workers received no redress. Unfortunately, the role of their fraternities is not in evidence, and the episode implies that the quarters may have been the effective organizing force. But so unique is this instance of self-defense by one particular trade rather than by the community or the markets as a whole that it may well imply the covert activities of the Sufi fraternity.[51] Aside from the silk workers, there is no evidence to my knowledge of any other craft-based religious fraternity.

Still, less formal solidarities must have been known among the common people. Those who shared a common station in life, daily experience, and business or class interests could not wholly be without uniting bonds. The organization of the markets which kept merchants and artisans of each trade together surely created informal ties, even though the forms of cohesion remained extremely circumscribed. Another basis for solidarity existed in the attachment of workers to particular local mosques. The myriad hundreds of small places of worship scattered throughout the quarters and markets made them vital centers of social and religious life. Many mosques bore the name of the trade of their market. Some were endowed by artisans. But there were limits to the depths of solidarity which could develop around these mosques, for the working population itself does not seem to have been passionately rigorous in the performance of religious duties. Efforts were often made by the ulama to raise the level of religious performance in the markets. Sheikhs were assigned to teach the people to pray and indeed to oblige them to do so. In 660/1262, the governor, the supervisor of the Umayyad Mosque, and the sheikhs of Damascus teamed up to require regular prayer. Again in 744/1343–44 prayer leaders were assigned to the markets, and the people ordered to imitate them when the muezzin called. In 790/1388 the market inspector ordered the jurists to teach the common shopkeepers the introduction to the Koran and how to pray. In this case, a small fee of a few coppers was levied on each of the shopkeepers for the support of the poor scholars.[52]

In general, the prevailing religious and social attitudes of Mamluk society were opposed to independent associations of artisans and workmen, and strongly inclined to suppress such tendencies if any existed. Social leadership and political affairs were so closely integrated that any association, whatever its original purpose, was parapolitical, capable of being turned to political action and resistance in the interests of its members. It was a natural tendency of empires to inhibit the development of foci of resistance especially among the working populace whose taxes were essential, whose masses were powerful and capable of violent outbursts, and with whom communication and consultation were otherwise at a minimum. Even the medieval cities of the West, so accustomed to voluntary societies, opposed them in the hands of journeymen free from master-artisans' control.

In religious terms, objection was made to entities which subdivided the community and compromised the wider unity of the Muslim peoples. The ulama were opposed to associations as sources of conflict, injustice, and party strife. The memory of the damage done to the early Islamic community by bedouin feuds was carried over and generalized to all other groups. Moreover, groups which compromised the larger unity of Islam were also likely to create implicit opposition to ulama teaching and authority. The ulama had even waged a centuries old rearguard action against the Sufi movement and its cells of devotees, trying to assimilate it to Islamic norms and tendencies.

In addition, associations among workers were feared as sources of heresy, and there were ample grounds for fear of mass heterodoxy in the Mamluk period. The historical, eschatological, and religious views of the masses differed greatly from the approved high religion, and popular sheikhs and preachers of doubtful orthodoxy and respectability had large followings. Whether they were religiously correct or not, women and the common people in general revered and loved their holy men while the ulama feared popular cults and the anamistic, magical, and pagan tendencies which could become open competitors with orthodox Islam.

Sometimes tendencies of religious feeling among the masses were orthodox, but out of the control of the authorities, and dangerous because of strong feelings which could be turned against ulama who were compromised by association with the state. In 878/1473–74, for example, a Sufi accused the Mālikī qadi of Aleppo of being an infidel. The charge was doubly dangerous because the "close ties of the masses to the sheikh were known." The only way found to spare the qadi the wrath of the mobs was to have him beaten and paraded in disgrace.[53]

Thus resistance to association was a struggle to prevent the whole of political, social, economic, and religious life from falling into the hands of the lower classes. When al-Nuwayrī and Ibn Taymiyya instructed the market inspectors to suppress worker associations they spoke for both the state and the ulama.[54] Of course, vigilance and repression alone were too crude to inhibit the formation of such associations. The supervisory roles of the state and its attitude toward economic management had an important part to play. So, too, did profoundly ingrained

Islamic values and norms. Above all, the reorganization of society into schools and clienteles based on religious leadership, and the creation of loyalties which cut across class lines served to unite the whole community and discourage special interests or particularistic and corporate ties.

FRATERNAL ASSOCIATIONS ON THE MARGIN OF SOCIETY

On the other hand, outside the contexts of quarters and market economic life, there were pronounced tendencies toward the formation of organized groups. In social and political realms remote from the values of the ulama and the integrating pressures of the rest of the society, group solidarities could become particularly powerful. Thus, occasionally we find associations of rebellious emirs, bursting all prior obligations to their masters and comrades, swearing life and property to their cause by solemn oath, one of the rare instances of the *conjuratio* in Islamic society.[55] Other associations were created in the lumpen-proletarian class of society. Large and apparently well organized criminal gangs operated in Cairo and Damascus, and similarly gangs of black slaves created their own social organizations.[56]

More important among the common people were the development of young men's associations. Young men's gangs in Damascus called the *zuʿar* played a profound role in the life of the city and similar groups seem to have existed in Aleppo and Cairo.[57] Possibly allied to these clubs were the Sufi or dervish fraternities. The solidarity of the Sufis, their impassioning impact on the common people, and their deep penetration to all levels of society made them a potent organizing force in Mamluk cities.

Sufism had been the mystical expression of the Islamic religion for centuries, but by the thirteenth century had taken on the form of congregational life. Small bands of devotees took up life in common around the sheikhs and teachers whom they revered. Muslim cities harbored many groups of these Sufis who lived according to the disciplined "way" of their master in convents called *zāwiyas, khānaqās,* and *ribāṭs,* supported by endowments or the charity of the community. On the basis of a common rite or discipline or acceptance of the teachings of a common founding sheikh these Sufi convents were affiliated into orders with branches throughout the Muslim world. In Egypt and Syria an official called the *shaykh al-shuyūkh,* or chief sheikh, was responsible for the over-all administration and discipline of the Sufis and for their liason with the Sultan. Such closely knit bodies were important foci of communal aggregation, but the nature of their ties with the population at large remains obscure.[58]

At one level of society the Sufis seem to have been well integrated into the social and religious world of the ulama. Sufis took a part in the political life of the towns, sharing in official receptions, marching under the banners of their orders to express political preferences, and defending the rights of their sheikhs and associates.

Yet other Sufis belonged to the low life of the cities, and inspired divergent and "unIslamic" religious views among the common people. Some of them represented the passionately puritanical strand of Islamic religious feeling and their personal wars on vice were an embarrassment to the more patient ulama. Sufi sheikhs and their followers often attacked the wine shops to spill out the forbidden beverages, and equally vigorously condemned the use of hashish. Emirs were not exempt from such assaults. These raids sometimes led to a good deal of trouble as people defended their activities and popular factions supporting and opposing the Sufis came to blows. In 758/1357 a group of Sufis broke up the wine and hashish parlors in Damascus, but the falconers and dog handlers who profited from the business fought them, counter-attacked their mosque, seized some of the Sufis, and paraded their prisoners about in the city for interfering with their business. Respectable opinion put a stop to this, but similar episodes often recurred. Sometimes the Sufis were arrested, and the incidents became local *cause célèbre* as the Sufis demonstrated in support of their incarcerated sheikhs, and delegations of favorable ulama and Mamluks intervened to secure their release. In one incident in Damascus in 899/1493–94 a Negro beggar, a Sufi sheikh named Mubārak, took up the Muslim injunction to "command good and forbid evil" and attacked wine drinkers. The governor arrested him, but a qadi arranged to have him freed. A second arrest, however, resulted in fighting which took thirty lives before the incident was closed. Strong emotions and parties were involved in these events.[59]

Perhaps more unusual than this irregular assumption of responsibility for mores by Sufi divines were the Sufis who belonged to the lumpenproletarian classes of menials. Sufis called *ḥarāfīsh* were a rabble of vagabonds who scandalized the towns by their barbarous dress and rites. The *ḥarāfīsh* were equally a riotous and dangerous part of the population, as we shall see.[60]

Apart from the Sufis, these lower class gangs were powerful, but remained by and large at a rudimentary organizational level. Their forms of association were borrowed from Islamic high society which itself was singularly lacking in collective experience, and the paucity of social models in the high culture was matched by a lack of creativity in the alienated minority. Only the state, Mamluk households, or the close community life of clans or quarters were available as models, and in general, the lumpenproletarians fell back on patronage relationships between chiefs and their followers. This fell short of a truly collective life in which all the members had obligations to each other, and not just to the chief alone. Independent groups belonged to the margin of society, on the brink of alienation, heresy, and rebellion. They continued to have a powerful impact on the society, but fundamentally intra-urban organization was not in their hands.

THE ULAMA AND THE FORMATION OF AN URBAN SOCIETY

These internal divisions pose an important problem. Composed of small communities, how could the larger city achieve a sufficient cohesiveness to maintain itself as an entity and fulfill the needs of the whole? What provision could be made for public order and discipline, defense, education, commerce, public works, charity, and welfare on a scale beyond the means of any of the smaller quarters, beyond the organizational possibilities of the crafts but essential for the civilized life of the whole? In Mamluk cities no central agency for coordination or administration of the affairs of the whole existed. There were no municipalities, nor communes, nor state bureaucracies for urban affairs. Rather the cohesion of the city depended not on any particular institutions but on patterns of social activity and organization which served to create a more broadly based community, and this community was built around the religious elites.

The ulama were that part of the Muslim community learned in the literature, laws, and doctrines of Islam. They were judges, jurists, prayer-leaders, scholars, teachers, readers of Koran, reciters of traditions, Sufis, functionaries of mosques, and so on. Their essential duty was to preserve the knowledge of the divine will, and to sustain the community as an Islamic community and give it religious and moral guidance. They carried on the teaching of Islam, enforced its morals, upheld its laws, proclaimed its doctrines, suppressed corruption and vice; in Muslim terms: promoted good and condemned evil.[61]

The ulama, however, were an administrative and social as well as a religious elite. In Islam, religion manifests itself not only in theology, but in a divinely inspired law by which all civil affairs are ordered. Because of the extension of Muslim religious law to familial, commercial, educational, and administrative concerns, the ulama carried on the organizational as well as the spiritual tasks of Muslim communal life. As administrators of the religious law, marriage, divorce, and guardianship were under their jurisdiction. Inheritances, wills, and creations of religious or charitable foundations were regulated by the qadis. To be legally valid, marriages, commercial transactions, and property transfers had to be witnessed by people authorized by a qadi as trustworthy and competent in Islamic law. Both the state bureaucracy and the religious institutions employed witnesses authorized by the qadis as competent in Islamic law to certify their dealings. Business practices, criteria of honesty in weights and measures, quality, and prices also came under Islamic norms, and for the sake of fair and orderly markets were regulated by the market inspectors. The ulama also controlled the business as well as the cultic aspects of the communities' institutions. They were the managers, scribes, and accountants for the administration of mosques, schools, philanthropies, and their properties in trust. Thus, the ulama were judges, lawyers, professional witnesses, and servants attached to the legal profession; and functionaries of the state bureaucracy, market inspectors, supervisors of waqfs, and treasury officers. They were the literate and professional elite of the cities. All realms of public affairs were an intrinsic part of the duties of this multicompetent, undifferentiated, and unspecialized communal elite.[62]

Moreover, the ulama were not a distinct class, but a category of persons overlapping other classes and social divisions, permeating the whole of society. So diverse were their contacts that they played a crucial role in the processes by which social communication was carried on and thus in the integration of the society into a working whole.

At one end of the social scale, the ulama were closely intermeshed with the bureaucratic class. Many, as we shall see, were appointed by the state. Many ulama also made careers in the nonreligious, financial, and secretarial services just as professional scribes and accountants qualified as members of the ulama by knowledge of tradition or law and sometimes by part-time teaching.[63]

The ties between the ulama and the merchant class were also exceedingly close. Many ulama were part-time merchants and earned part of their living from trade while many merchants were part-time scholars and teachers. Traveling merchants combined commerce with pilgrimage and study with famous scholars, returning to their home cities to teach traditions learned abroad to other scholars starved to hear those precious recollections of the words of the prophet Muḥammad from sources which they could otherwise not reach. An example of the extent to which merchants embraced the functions of the ulama may be found in a sample of some six hundred merchants. Of these, two hundred and twenty-five were ulama—not merely educated in traditions, but practicing teachers, sheikhs, members of law schools, prayer leaders, and preachers; and on the more administrative and managerial side, judges, market inspectors, professional witnesses, and administrators of waqfs. There were eighty-four teachers of traditions, fifty-six sheikhs, sixty other members of law schools, and twenty-seven Koran readers, preachers, prayer leaders, and Sufis. There were twenty-one witnesses, fifteen judges, six administrators, and six market inspectors. The most common combination was merchant-teacher, where the demands of the two professions seem most compatible. The sample is no doubt disproportionately laden with biographies of ulama due to the interests of the biographers, but the absolute numbers involved show that the overlap must in any case have been substantial. Instead of two distinct classes, one broad ulama-merchant body was formed.[64]

Similarly, the status of being one of the ulama was available to workers and craftsmen, and a similar sharing of educational achievement and part-time multiple employment bridged barriers between ulama and craft statuses. Biographies indicate that many masons, stoneworkers, carpenters, coppersmiths, soap makers, and especially pharmacists were ulama. So too were saddlers, bow makers, weavers, blacksmiths, ropemakers, bakers, tailors, butchers, wool dealers, and small traders and producers of all sorts, learned in the traditions of the prophet and the laws of Islam, vested with membership in the schools of law, and employed as religious functionaries and even as judges and administrators.[65]

Even the Mamluks and the lumpenproletarians were not entirely out of touch with the ulama stratum. Separated from the rest of society by specialized military function, race, language, and privilege, the Mamluks were nonetheless converted to Islam. Many married into ulama families to acquire some place in the society over which they stood guard but in which they were basically foreigners. Many a son of a Mamluk automatically excluded from a military career found a place in the community and a worthwhile status in succession to a high ranking father through scholarship.[66] Similarly, the lumpenproletarians had points of contact with elements of the ulama. Begging dervishes or Sufis, popular preachers, and half-Muslim, half-heretical, half-secular entertainers mediated between the respectable ulama and the despised masses.[67]

Reinforcing the close relationships between the body of the ulama and the various classes of the society was a strong current of social mobility. In the biographical records there appear numerous examples of sons of ulama who became officials, and sons of officials, who were ulama. The intergenerational movement between ulama and merchant occupations was also intense. In families involved in the spice trade, fathers, sons, uncles, nephews, brothers, and cousins were likely to be either merchants or religious leaders. So, too, the great ulama clans, like the Ibn Taymiyya, had merchant members. Even craftsmen shared in the social movement for their sons, too, could and did become ulama.[68]

Mobility and entry into the body of the ulama was favored by the values implicit in Muslim notions of status. Wealth was respectable, learning and piety were highly regarded, and these were universally, or almost universally, available without barriers of caste or corporation. Even the established families did not constitute, at least before the Ottoman Empire, a strong barrier to mobility. Of course, they were favored in the perpetuation of control over wealth, offices, knowledge, and prestige, but many factors militated against family monopolies of such opportunities. High infant mortality and decimation by plague and famine raised biological barriers to family longevity. Formidable political and economic uncertainties, changes of government, and strong currents of migration of skilled personnel from lands overrun by the Mongols also restricted dynastic success. No statistical analyses are possible, but the qualitative evidence points to long-term family weakness. A few spectacularly long-lived dynasties are known, but they are uncommon and their continued prominence in fact was probably much exaggerated by the biographers. Any number of ulama families may have had great temporary success in passing their positions to their heirs, but three or four generations was most unusual. Persistance in a post or status does not on balance seem to have been a long-term barrier to the ambitions of new blood.

By this interpenetration with all levels of the society, the ulama mitigated the importance of communal and status divisions, and provided the framework of a common social and normative order. This basis for a larger community was reinforced by the crystallization of associational life around the ulama. Through the ulama wider unities than those based on the quarters were offered to the society at large. The importance of this function can scarcely be overestimated, for in these cities, associational bonds apart from religious life or under other than ulama auspices were singularly underdeveloped.

The bases of ulama society were study groups formed around distinguished sheikhs and teachers which radiated outward into the urban community. Scholars famous for their learning and piety became authoritative spokesmen on legal, social, and theological matters for other ulama, students, and lay admirers. Eventually patrons and perhaps a respectful following of the common people who lived in the district around the mosque or school which was the center of their activity formed a clique (*jamāʿa*) around these teachers.[69] Sufi sheikhs were particularly potent in gathering bands of devoted disciples.

Ulama in administrative positions as well as learned sheikhs and pious Sufis also created clienteles. The qadis because of their important judicial and administrative duties gathered bodies of subordinates, employees, students, and dependents around themselves. Qadis appointed sub-delegated judges and executive and clerical deputies, authorized professional witnesses, and employed court attendants and strong-arm men in their service.[70] Similarly, the *naqīb al-ashrāf,* the syndic of the descendants of the prophet Muḥammad, who managed financial, pension, and endowment interests and adjudicated disputes within the group was the chief of another kind of ulama association. In large institutions, religious functionaries such as the muezzins or Koran readers had a *ra'īs* (chief) or sheikh who saw to their training and discipline and the proper performance of their duties. In each mosque or madrasa the members of a law school also had their *imām* or prayer leader. Conceivably other people described as *naqīb* or *ra'īs* for the men of learning were sufficiently influential to form clienteles though many may have been minor honorific functionaries such as roll-keepers or ushers for groups of notables.[71]

The most comprehensive of these ulama groupings were the schools of law. They were associations of scholars, judges, and students who elaborated the legal and ritual practices of Islam according to four variant traditions of equally authoritative and orthodox versions of the Shari'a. Each of the schools, the Shāfi'ī, Ḥanafī, Mālikī, and Ḥanbalī, named after their founders, differed in detailed matters of practice, but by and large held to similar Islamic beliefs and principles. All of the ulama belonged to one or another of these schools. Even the Sufis were often, if not always, affiliated with them. In Damascus the Shāfi'ī and Ḥanafī schools were the most prominent although the Ḥanbalī was well established, especially in al-Ṣāliḥiyya. The Damascus Ḥanbalīs had been strongly fortified in the thirteenth century by the forced migration of scholars from Harran in Mesopotamia, who fleeing the Mongols, came to Damascus for their safety. At Aleppo and in Egypt the Shāfi'īs and the Ḥanafīs were the most prominent schools.[72]

Very little is known about the internal organization of the schools. They were sometimes called *ṭā'ifa* meaning communal groups, a term usually reserved for Sufi fraternities or Mamluk corps. One may surmise that the circles formed by leading sheikhs and teachers were the components of the schools, and that around them, led by their *imāms,* informal "memberships" were formed in the mosques and madrasas. The schools of law in each major city or perhaps in each region of the empire were headed by a man called the *ra'īs,* sheikh, or *imām* of the school. It is not clear whether these titles signified an administrative rank rather than an honorific distinction, but in any case the chief qadis, of whom there was one for each school in the major cities, were responsible for administration and sometimes bore these titles. The chief qadis were responsible for appointments to positions within each school, for the maintenance of discipline and religious standards, and for the management of properties and endowments.[73]

Though primarily organized for the study of Islamic law, the schools were foci of mass affiliation. Everyone was considered to be a member of one or another of the schools, and as is normally the case in religious matters, membership in the schools was inherited or followed the practice of one's village, quarter, or region. The schools were authoritative interpreters of Islamic law to the people who practiced Islam according to the rules of the school and who looked to its scholars for guidance on proper Muslim conduct, to its witnesses for the registration of contracts and marriages, and to its judges for the mediation of disputes.

Thus merchants, officials, and Mamluks were associated with the schools as patrons, and the common people regarding themselves as their members looked to the ulama for advice, representation, and leadership. These were informal ties and the leadership of the ulama was by no means institutionalized for political purposes. The schools served rather as channels for the spread of their influence, the communication of their views, and the persuasion of the populace. The schools of law were the most comprehensive intra-urban communities, but it is important to note that they did not necessarily encompass the whole population. There were no city-wide organizations of any kind in Mamluk Muslim towns.

Scattered but numerous episodes in the chronicles reveal the solidarity of the common people with their ulama. Renowned divines inspired deeply felt religious passions in the populace at large, but more to the point, mass demonstrations and fighting on behalf of their sheikhs and qadis exposed the depths of these loyalties. For example, the decades' long quarrels of Ibn Taymiyya with his theological and political opponents awoke a massive popular response. When he was arrested in 693/1294, the common people stoned the governor, and serious fighting followed. Some years later Damascus craftsmen and merchants joined the sheikhs of the *khānaqās* and some five hundred Sufis to petition the governor of Damascus. Other illustrations abound. In 743/1342, there were demonstrations in the Umayyad Mosque on behalf of a preacher removed from his post. The common people refused to hear the new appointee and forced the return of their favorite. In 822/1419, in a dispute among Cairo qadis, mobs of commoners supported the claims of one man to be market inspector. In Jerusalem, in 874/1469–70, a dispute among the ulama resulted in the plunder of a qadi's house by the supporters of his opponents. In Damascus a few years later, the common people protected a qadi from arrest and attacked and stoned his enemy's house.[74]

Thus in the absence of other strong and comprehensive associational ties, the ulama had a central position in sustaining the normative and social life of the cities. With the quarters too parochial, the crafts too little organized, and other fraternal associations too much on the periphery of society, the ulama created what loose forms of cohesion were found in the Mamluk cities.

CONCLUSION

Muslim urban society was divided into numerous small communities, and what held them together were the ulama and their ties across divisive family and community lines. Their competences, their judicial, managerial, legal, educational, secretarial, financial, commercial, and familial authority grounded in the multiple dimensions of Muslim law brought them into contact with every concern of the city. We may imagine the coordination of all public affairs as an intrinsic part of the multiple roles of an unspecialized elite in which each man in his capacity as teacher, merchant, administrator, judge, and so on represented in himself or in the circle of his associates all of the "interests" of the city. The ulama were part of all economic, political, and social interests inasmuch as they belonged themselves to different classes. Moreover, what organized means there were for handling the community's affairs were informal circles and clienteles, and the schools of law built around the ulama. No special interests within the city were so well organized as to stand apart from these wider relationships or fail to be represented in them. Nor were there special agencies to deal with the affairs of the city as a whole. There were no municipalities, and as we have seen, no regular bureaucracy to deal with city-wide concerns. For these reasons the ulama had a unique social role to play. As an undifferentiated elite their roles, their ramified ties, and the pattern of their social interaction held Muslim cities together without recourse to more formal institutions of representation or control.

From this perspective, we can understand the shapelessness, the apparently fluid, twisting, and amorphous structure of the markets. The *ḥārāt* may have lacked, as many writers have suggested, defined physical form because of the need for privacy, isolation, and protection, and because of the lack of concern for public as opposed to family life. But in the markets, in the public part of the city, amorphous form resulted from the absorption of physical features by the style of social life. All institutions, shops, mosques, schools, and administrative offices were thoroughly intermingled to accommodate the demand for easy access and constant change of activities, from trade to prayer to teaching and so on. Only in societies where functions and personnel are more clearly separated will there be a consequent differentiation of physical entities to accommodate the separate functions. Cities need boulevards when people must travel a great deal for their affairs. Factories and churches and homes and schools will be apart when life itself is more compartmentalized. The Muslim city had the physical form of the bazaar because it was appropriate to the fluid pattern of social interchange and of daily living.

This was the internal social organization of Mamluk Muslim cities, but not the whole of the urban order. There were limits on the capacity of a social system of this sort. Ease of communication and discussion, and the capacity to choose objectives and coordinate efforts on a city-wide basis, were severely limited by the lack of central institutions. Adequate to form a social whole, these institutions were too little differentiated, too little organized, and too weak to cope with all urban concerns.

Two vital realms of city life escaped the powers of the ulama. As we have seen, the first was the defense of the cities and the suppression of internal violence for which they lacked adequate military force. The second was the control of the rural resources essential for the sustenance of the towns and for the generation of capital for expensive investments in social facilities which the urban economies were themselves too poor to manage. In both the military and the economic spheres the intervention of the Mamluk regime was essential. To complement their own roles in the cities the notables had to cooperate with the Mamluk masters of the state. The relationship of the local notability to the state is the first element in the dynamics of relationships which made up the political system of the cities, and which we shall consider in the following chapters.

CHAPTER IV · THE POLITICAL SYSTEM: THE MAMLUK STATE AND THE URBAN NOTABLES

THE STRUCTURE of urban society, and the preponderance of the Mamluk regime in the economic and social life of the cities, created the configuration of political actions by which the cities were ruled. Urban societies, dependent as they were on the Mamluk elites for the defense of the cities, food supply, investments in communal institutions, and maintenance of the urban physical infrastructure, operated within the context created by Mamluk behavior. In response to these powers, the notables were drawn into a governing condominium with the Mamluks, a shared control over the society. While the Mamluks took up the massive economic and military responsibilities, the notables lent their intimate grasp of local affairs to the service of the state and coordinated the government of the society at more intricate levels. Their original social importance made them indispensable auxiliaries of the Mamluk state apparatus, and in turn their partial assimilation to the regime served to validate their local status and to assure their success in communal roles. In this chapter we shall discuss the special case of the merchant notables and the politically more crucial relationship of the ulama notability to the Mamluk regime.

Two other components of the civilian notability do not seem to have had a comparable importance in mediating between the regime and the populace. The *awlād al-nās,* the sons of Mamluks, who might be thought to have an important position of this sort were largely employed in an auxiliary military force, the *ḥalqa,* created expressly for the purpose of finding a socially and financially suitable employment for the sons of former officers. Many sons of emirs in fact even became emirs through promotion in the *ḥalqa* auxiliary corps, but they were otherwise not likely to have a prominent role in the government. The whole Mamluk system was predicated on the importation of new men in each generation to take the highest positions of the state, and the old Mamluk families, though given a relatively privileged position, were basically deprived of influence. There was no reason for the *awlād al-nās* to have any greater degree of access to influence in the state than other notables.

Furthermore, we may also infer that the families of Mamluks were not, as a group, of particular prominence in the rest of urban society. There is reason to believe that the Mamluks were biologically unsuccessful in Egypt and Syria and that they failed to establish large or long lived families. The third generation of a Mamluk family is scarcely found in the biographical records. The biographical dictionaries report few examples of the sons of Mamluks, and though there are cases of sons of Mamluks who were jurists, qadis, and Sufis, and a few cases of sons of emirs who married into the families of ulama notables, any part they played in mediating between the Mamluks and the masses was not distinct from that of the general body of the ulama.

Nor would it seem that civilian scribes and officials had any mediating role of importance. Many were simply employed as technicians in the bureaus of the Sultans or in the service of the emirs to whose clienteles they belonged. No doubt the employment of local families as officials of the Mamluk government moderated the impact of the Mamluks on the general society and afforded a measure of political stability and continuity, but insofar as many scribes came from families which had for generations been employed in the government service, or from families many of whose members were simultaneously employed in the government, no mediating function seems likely.

Other scribal families, however, were tied to merchant and to ulama elements of the society. Many scribes were educated in Muslim traditions and were part-time teachers or members of the law schools. Many also found employment as functionaries for the management of communal religious affairs as well as in the service of the Sultans and the emirs. Others were tied to the religious community at least by friendly social relationships and some gave grants for waqfs. Still others were the sons of ulama or the fathers of ulama, and some part of the scribal class was tied to the body of the rest of the community by family ties bridging the gap between the two branches of the notability. However, for our purposes, we shall consider such people part of the ulama, for the officials as such did not play the same intermediary roles as did merchants and ulama, except insofar as they merged with the families of the other notables.

THE MERCHANTS

The merchant notables in Islamic cities were, as we have seen, a rich, powerful, and socially honored class. They were the wholesalers, brokers, international traders, and dealers in luxury goods. The patrician merchants were among the richest men of their times, occasionally even the equal of emirs. Some enjoyed a fabulous standard of living. Palatial residences were not uncommon. 'Abd al-Raḥmān, a grain broker, spent 5,000 dinars to buy a house and furnished it with splendid woodwork and marbles. Burhān al-dīn al-Maḥallī (d. 806/1403), the chief of the *kārimī* merchants, owned a palace worth 50,000 dinars. Save for the palaces of Tankiz, governor of Damascus from 1312 to 1340, few Mamluk properties are known to have been worth more than that. Like the Mamluks, wealthy merchants patronized the luxury crafts and enjoyed silver and copper utensils, precious woods, paper, and fine cloth.[1]

Direct estimates of merchant fortunes are somewhat unreliable. Occasional biographies indicate fortunes between 100,000 and 400,000 dinars plus other goods, and vast fortunes are also suggested by reports of confiscations amounting to several hundred thousand dinars. These were truly princely estates. A European visitor in Cairo, Thenaud, at the very end of the Mamluk period was told that two hundred merchants had fortunes of a million gold seraphs, and that 2,000 more were worth 100,000 gold seraphs. The figures so far exceed the fortunes of emirs in the fifteenth century that they are quite improbable. Indeed Thenaud was cautioned not to believe his eyes in the matter. Such fortunes, he was told, would not be in evidence because the merchants feared confiscations. Arnold von Harff, visiting shortly before this, was perhaps better informed when told that merchants commonly had fortunes of 30,000 to 40,000 ducats, and that some even had 200,000. Fines and confiscations of merchant wealth in the fourteenth century, however, imply, though no reliable conclusions may be drawn, that prominent merchants often had still smaller fortunes. We cannot tell what proportion of their total worth these fines represented, but even if the percentages were small, merchants' wealth was not so very great. A forced purchase in Cairo in 737/1337 brought in 50,000 dinars, and merchants were required to take goods valued at between one and three thousand dinars. Only between seventeen and fifty merchants could have been involved. Fines at Alexandria in the following year cost three merchants 10,000 dinars, but 5,000 was taken from the market inspector alone. In other cases a fine of 10,000 dinars was considered appropriate for a group of merchants.[2]

Merchant fortunes were also held in properties which gave them considerable social power. Many owned land, especially vineyards, orchards, and gardens as seen in waqf records, even though Mamluk control of the land placed severe limitations on their opportunities. In the Damascus region many rich merchants lived in villages close to the city. Merchants were more commonly owners of urban property, especially of houses, and occasionally of markets, *qayṣariyyas,* shops, presses, baths, and khans. Smaller properties were so widely owned that there could be a regular market for them with specialist brokers and witnesses to assist in arranging transactions.[3]

Merchant wealth also converted itself into social power through the ownership of slaves. Some were domestics, but others were used as business agents especially in the spice trade. Slave traders often kept slaves in their personal service before selling them to emirs. (Ibn Baṭṭūṭa gives an interesting example of the potential scale of great merchant households in describing Ibn Rawāḥa, an Alexandrian merchant, who kept a hundred to two hundred armed retainers, and even had the audacity to volunteer to keep order in the city on behalf of the Sultan.)[4]

Apart from their wealth, the patrician merchants drew their preeminence from the vital role they played in integrating the economic life of the towns. Merchants mediated some of the exchanges of materials between the household economy of the state and the urban economy at large. They also managed the distribution of grain between country and city, dealing in free grain, or acting as brokers for the sale of emirs' grains. Traveling merchants exchanged goods between towns and provinces and in foreign trade mediated the movement of goods between the Mamluk Empire and Southeast Asia, Turkey, Iran, and Europe.[5]

In all these activities merchants found themselves intimately linked to the Mamluk state. The state's economic importance necessarily drew them into dealing with the regime. Because so much land, urban property, grain, and raw materials were in the hands of the emirs and the Sultans, and so much of the purchasing power in the towns was generated by vast Mamluk households which consumed luxury products, food, cloth, animals, military equipment, and the array of trifles which filled the lives of the rich—utensils, decorations, furniture, and so forth—a good part of the business done by merchants was done with the Sultan and the Mamluks. As purveyors of staples and luxury goods they regularly served Mamluk households. The services of butchers, for example, so closely tied them to the households of Sultans that they actually became functionaries incorporated into the palace staffs whose continuing duty it was to purchase and distribute meat supplies. On the other hand, merchants purchased excess supplies for resale on the urban markets, standing ready to buy grain, other raw materials, utensils, or jewels for cash. Though a certain scepticism is warranted in view of the frequency of forced purchases, most of these transactions appear to have been honest exchanges.[6]

The Mamluks were not only consumers but investors in commerce, and thus employed or created partnerships with merchants to trade on their behalf. Emirs provided working capital for spice trading expeditions to the orient. One emir invested 100,000 dinars in an expedition to Yemen which was lost at sea. Emirs also invested in a wide range of routine commercial activities, possibly taking advantage of their status to avoid market taxes or cover illegal affairs. They were known to sell wine and hogs to European traders, violating religious prohibitions. In the fifteenth century, however, there are surprisingly few instances of emirs in business except in the sale of cotton to the Venetians. This may be due to a chance of reporting, but it may reflect a turn to less legitimate means of profiting financially from political strength.[7]

Moreover, the scale of the state economy required merchants to act as bankers for the regime. So far as we can tell from the chronicles, compared with contemporary European practices, banking institutions were only developed to a rudimentary level. Nonetheless, the complexity of the economy required a fair amount of banking activity in some form or other. Deposit banking was known, and the important distinction between deposits made for safe-keeping and those for investment was made. For safe-keeping, ulama rather than merchants seemed the more usual bankers, and in fact the only known instance of a merchant holding deposits proves to be that of a merchant-sheikh. Certain forms of state or tax banking were also used. Money changers called *ṣayrafis* assisted in collecting revenues and keeping financial records, sometimes acting as paymasters for the government bureaus. The changers also played a crucial part in the implementation of Mamluk monetary policy. Responsibility for supporting monetary price ratios and the smooth distribution and collection of new and old monies depended on them. Cooperation with the regime had its rewards, for the *ṣayrafis* were entitled to a three per cent commission on tax transactions, and the close involvement of money changing with the state promoted the entry of changers into the bureaucratic service. The case of Tāj al-dīn al-Arminī, who became governor of Qaṭyā, the Egyptian customs station on the Syrian frontier, is the most dramatic. His father was an Armenian Christian who was converted to Islam in Cairo and became a changer at Qaṭyā. Tāj al-dīn carried on this work as a functionary. He later rose through various offices until he finally became the governor. His son succeeded him in turn.[8]

The most important of banking functions, money lending, was largely in the hands of the *kārimī* spice merchants. Their unusual wealth and organization enabled them to make large loans, not as individuals, but most probably as consortia represented by a few of their leading members. They raised cash for the Sultan and assisted officials and visiting dignitaries who could not safely bring sufficient amounts of gold with them. Much of this lending activity involved them closely in state affairs. For example, in 687/1288, they were asked to put up the fines of Damascus officials who had been called to Cairo but had no ready cash. The vizier, fearing they would evade his demands if he permitted their return before receiving the money, had the *kārimī* advance the funds. It is not unlikely that their trading and official connections made it easy for them to collect. An analogous arrangement was made by *kārimī* merchants in 711/1311. Sultan Nāṣir Muḥammad owed 16,000 dinars to several European merchants, and settled it by canceling the Europeans' debt to the *kārimī* in the same amount while the *kārimī* accepted the Sultan's obligations.[9] The *kārimī* also lent the Sultans money to finance important military expeditions. In the 790's/1390's when Sultan Barqūq was hard pressed for money, extremely large loans were taken from the great *kārimī* chiefs. Al-Maḥallī, al-Kharrūbī, and Ibn Musallam lent the Sultan 100,000 dinars. The *kārimī* also lent money to foreign princes. The Sultan of Mali borrowed money from Ibn Kuwayk on a visit to Cairo, and the ruler of Yemen also had need of *kārimī* help. In 751/1350 he borrowed 400,000 dinars to pay his ransom to the Sultan, and an additional 100,000 for the costs of his journey home. His mother had pressed the *kārimī* to make these loans by threatening to confiscate their goods in Aden. They were repaid in 753/1352, for though vulnerable their continuing activities in Yemen were extremely valuable.

The *kārimī* were not alone in lending money to the state. Other merchants and money changers made heavy loans to the Sultan and emirs. Some of these "loans," however, were in fact extortions or forced loans, and it is doubtful that they were ever paid back. For example, *kārimī* goods were seized under the pretext of a loan in 737/1337, and in the following year, loans were made in Alexandria in the midst of other extortions, a circumstance which casts suspicion on the intentions of the regime. Similarly in 803/1400 the Sultan forced merchants to "lend" him half their goods. If a man were not present in his shop, everything was taken. Even when loans were repaid the Sultans may have had no scruples about shortchanging the merchants. Sultan Nāṣir Muḥammad repaid his debts in 740/1340 in silver after revaluing it by decree in his favor. A loan at the behest of a supremely more powerful borrower in great need was a poor risk, and the merchant who offered it probably used it as a bribe to avoid more decisive extortions. The merchant class was treated as a repository of funds which the regime could tap on need. Merchants, like officials, were permitted to become wealthy as an incentive for their efforts, but were obliged to share their wealth with the state which created or permitted the opportunities out of which it was amassed.[10]

In addition to these interchanges, the state and the Sultan's households gave direct employment to merchants because of their extensive manufacturing and trading activities. The private treasury of the Sultan included his *matjars* or trading bureaus in Cairo and Alexandria which stockpiled, managed, and sold household or strategic supplies. The managers of these bureaus were often emirs or professional functionaries, but merchants sometimes held the post of merchant of the Sultan. Another position held by merchants was merchant of the Sultan's privy purse, a post once held by Ismā'īl ibn Muḥammad, who was a straw merchant connected to Arghūn Shāh, one-time governor of Damascus. Ismā'īl later entered the Sultan's service and reached the rank of *khawājā,* a distinction often applied to merchants in official service. The great *kārimī* merchant chief, Burhān al-dīn al-Maḥallī, was a merchant of the Sultan and merchant of the noble privy purse. Other commercial offices in the service of the Sultan were called merchant and controller of the trading bureaus. The post of *wakīl al-khāṣṣ,* agent of the privy purse, was also sometimes held by merchants because it may have involved commerce.[11]

Merchants were also employed in the slave trade and in this case too merchant activities tended to merge into bureaucratic posts. The trading connections to the Crimea, the Russian steppes, and the Caucasian highlands were lifelines of the state and slave trading was of great political and diplomatic consequence. To bring in adequate numbers of slaves the Sultan commissioned merchants, provided cash in advance, and often entrusted diplomatic relations with the Tatar khanates to them. Merchants familiar with the northern lands were ambassadors and even agents for creating parties favorable to the Sultan in the Tatar and Turkoman kingdoms. Many slave merchants held the rank of *khawājā,* and became important figures in Mamluk circles. Their influence was reinforced by the bonds between owner and slave, which were very close in Islamic law and Mamluk practice. Slave dealers often held positions of considerable influence because Mamluks respected the merchants who brought them to Egypt almost as they did the emirs who raised them afterwards.[12]

Even in the realm of thoroughly private trading activity merchants were in many ways dependent on the protection or assistance of the regime. International trade was contingent on good political relations and was often guaranteed by formal treaties. To keep open the slave routes to the Crimea, treaties with the Byzantine Empire reciprocally guaranteed merchants and their possessions in the territories of either signatory, and similar treaties with Armenia, Tyre, and Acre were made in the late thirteenth century. Most important were the treaties which guaranteed personal safety and consular protection to European merchants coming to buy spices in the Mamluk Empire. Arrangements were made for living quarters, and rules for taxation, customs fees, terms of trade, and business practices were all specified.[13]

Short of formal treaties, good political relations and the exchange of friendly embassies served to guarantee the safety of merchants. The Mamluks, for example, offered general protection in a circular letter issued in 687/1288 for distribution in India, China, and Yemen. This was the necessary eastern counterpart of the formal treaties with the Europeans. Foreign governments in turn sought to cultivate good relations with the Mamluks. From the East, in 682/1283-84 the rulers of Ceylon sent gifts and called for direct trade between themselves and the Mamluks. Indian states also sent gifts and ambassadors to promote good relations and encourage trade. The first known delegation in Mamluk times came in 730/1330, but was seized and murdered in Yemen. The next one got through in the following year and others followed. In the fifteenth century Indian states placed themselves under Mamluk suzerainty, and again sent ambassadors to encourage religious and commercial ties.[14]

A more active diplomatic and military protection was extended to merchants in special need. Mamluk efforts to protect Muslims against European pirates were the most common of all. Europeans and their goods inside the Mamluk Empire were seized, and Christian holy places and clerics threatened in retaliation for pirate outrages, while protests were sent to the European cities and diplomatic efforts made to encourage the European states interested in the Levant trade to make war on pirate bases. Eventually the Mamluks themselves had to go to war at sea. In Yemen, where Mamluk power could make itself better felt, the country was reduced to vassalage in order to protect the spice trade. On their land frontiers the Mamluks raided towns and villages which interfered with traffic, and sent ambassadors to protest Anatolian or Nubian interferences with caravans. They once even refused to begin negotiations to end a war with the Ottomans until merchants in Ottoman hands were set free.[15]

Even within the Mamluk Empire the protection afforded commercial activity and the intimate dependence of merchants on the policies of the state was marked. Though it was part of general Mamluk objectives to assure the pacification of the empire, special attention had to be paid to the needs of trade. The roads had to be kept free of bedouins and highwaymen. Bedouins had to be enrolled to protect caravans across the desert and to police the postal, pilgrimage, and trade routes. For these services they received tributes from merchants or stipends from the state, but punitive expeditions were often needed to make clear to the bedouins the superior virtue of accepting what money was offered.[16]

Not only protection, but important assistance was given merchants by the official postal service and relays of caravansaries along the main roads supported either by the state or waqfs. Merchants could find shelter and supplies, and so highly valued was the service and so costly that the Sultan decided in 740/1340 to require merchants to apply to him for special permission for future use. However, with the weakening of the state bedouin violence increased, and conseqeuntly the postal system and the assistance it could give to traveling merchants declined. By the beginning of the fifteenth century the network of caravansaries was in disarray and communications were severely hampered.[17]

While it was in the general interest to protect trade against the bedouins, state protection against the rapacity of the Mamluks themselves was uncertain. Fiscal abuses were so common as to be a natural way of life in Mamluk Egypt and Syria, and what protection merchants could obtain depended on patronage, appeals to higher officials against the abuses of lesser ones, the intercession of the religious notables, and above all on bribery and compromise.[18]

The situation of the *kārimī* spice merchants epitomized this whole pattern of relations between the merchants and the state in the fourteenth century. The *kārimī* operated in the Red Sea and Indian Ocean, bringing spices to Egypt for resale to Italian and other Mediterranean merchants. This most lucrative trade made them the elite of the patrician merchant class and the darlings of the state. Taxation of the spice transactions not only brought an immense revenue to the state, but many Mamluks placed lucrative investments in *kārimī* hands. They were also, of course, purveyors of spices to the Sultan and the Mamluk elites. Perhaps still more important were the other uses of their wealth and the seemingly inexhaustible productivity of the spice trade. They were important bankers, as we have seen. They also assisted the regime by purchasing surplus government stocks. The *kārimī* purchased food and other goods in large volumes when the state was eager to raise cash, even though these transactions were often forced purchases and partial confiscations. They served the state as ambassadors, mostly in the diplomatic niceties of the Yemen trade. Finally, they were slave traders as well.

This exceptional economic importance explains the lengths to which the Mamluk regime was willing to go in the thirteenth and fourteenth centuries to assure the success of the trade. Of all commercial activities, it was the most highly organized and protected. The state lent its diplomatic efforts to defend the trade, convoyed valuable cargoes, and protected them from pirates and petty potentates along the Indian Ocean and the Red Sea coasts. At the same time the royal bureaus were authorized to give the *kārimī* a free hand, and did not compete with them in the fourteenth and early years of the fifteenth centuries. However, to prevent anarchy in the trade and evasion of taxes special supervisors were assigned to Red Sea ports and to *kārimī* warehouses in Cairo, Alexandria, and Damascus. These officials were called *nāẓir al-kārim* (controllers of the spices). The merchants themselves were headed by *ra'īses* who were a liaison between them and the state for discipline, and diplomatic, banking, and other services. Though selected from among the *kārimī,* they brought the authority of the regime to whatever controls were introduced into the spice trade. Their relation to the state was thus closer than that of other merchants, and many *ra'īses* and other *kārimī* served in official capacities.

However, the factors which made the *kārimī* an organized group—the bases for admission, the financial arrangements among the participants, the existence of corporate property or jurisdictions, the organization of expeditions—elude us. The trade was not a monopoly, and it would seem probable that individuals were allowed to participate on application. Other merchants did operate in the China, India, and Yemen trades, and brought spices in the pilgrimage caravans from Mecca to Damascus. Possibly there was no fixed membership, but a hard core of participants who organized the trade and set terms for the entry of new members.[19]

The *kārimī* disappeared in the first decades of the fifteenth century, and their fate marked a turning point in the relations of the merchant class as a whole to the state. The *kārimī* heritage of state protection, fiscal supervision, close banking and merchandising relations, and a degree of official employment was transformed so greatly in degree as to create a radically new situation. In the fifteenth century giant steps were taken toward the fuller assimilation of the merchants into the state and the reduction of the independent merchant class.

These changes stemmed from the marked transformation in the social organization of the economy which followed on the civil war period of 790/1388 to 825/1422. As a result of tremendous losses in productivity and the severe drains of incessant warfare, the Mamluks resorted to intensified exploitation of the subject population to meet their needs. Apart from the usual devices, they sought to increase their relative share of the existing wealth by controlling, absorbing, and monopolizing larger parts of what had been the private economy. Sultan Barsbāy first established a Sultan's monopoly in the spice trade in 832/1428. He obliged the Europeans to buy fixed amounts of spice at fixed prices from his own agents. Muslim merchants were forbidden to trade privately until the Sultan had completed his transactions, and sometimes they were altogether excluded. The result was that a state monopoly replaced the *kārimī* traders and their methods for regulating competition and protecting the trade so as to maximize the advantages of the Muslims vis-à-vis their European customers. Their successors were merchants who enrolled in the new organization as merchants of the Sultan.

In the earliest stages of the monopoly the Sultan commissioned merchants to purchase spices for him. One of these agents, ʿAlī al-Kīlānī, sent with 5,000 dinars to buy spices, turned a profit of 12,000 dinars for the Sultan as well as a share for himself. He died in 848/1444. Apparently, the Sultan invested his funds with the merchant and was entitled to a proportion of the profits while the merchant retained the rest for his work. Thus the traditional Mediterranean form of trading investment, the *commenda,* was used on behalf of the Sultan's monopoly. Later in the fifteenth century, however, the spice trade seems to have been routinized. Traders became regular officials, and an officer called the *mālik al-tujjār* (king of the merchants), supervised the eastern section of the spice routes in India, Aden, and Mecca. In Alexandria the spice traffic was handled on behalf of the Sultan by his merchants and the office of the trading service in Alexandria.[20]

While the spice trade was the most valuable and permanent of the state acquisitions because it was easiest to control, other trades were at least temporarily made into state monopolies. The growing, manufacture, and sale of sugar was made a monopoly in Barsbāy's reign, but it was dropped in 836/1433 even though the Sultan and many emirs continued to own sugar factories and act as important suppliers. Other goods were from time to time subjected to temporary monopolies. Cotton, an important export, was so treated. Natron for cloth dying was held as a state monopoly. Bureaucratic controls on wood and metal imports, ownership of forests and quarries, quasi-monopolies in the form of forced sales, and monopolistic practices in grain trading are further examples of state intervention in the economy.[21]

In the fifteenth century the slave trade was similarly organized as an agency of the government. The Sultans continued to commission factors to buy slaves, and even employed Genoese merchants who had the necessary contacts in Kaffa. By and large, however, the trade was entrusted to merchant-officials called *khawājās* or sometimes styled the Sultan's merchants for Mamluks who were supervised by an emir called the *muʿallim tujjār al-mamālīk* (supervisor of the slave merchants). Many of the slave merchants were no longer merchants in the professional sense, but emirs or men closely related to the families of emirs. To the degree that the activity was organized by the bureaucracy, it was more and more carried on by officials.[22]

Thus, the outcome of this intensified state participation in the economy was an increase in the number of merchants serving as agents and regular employees of the Sultan, and a proliferation of state offices and functionaries for trading. The offices of the Sultan's merchants became more common.[23] Above all, the title of *khawājā* became more and more common in the fifteenth century in both Egypt and Syria, and its spread marked the assimilation of important elements of the patrician merchant class to the state. *Khawājā* was an official rank, and to it were attached the same distinctions of position in the Sultan's council as were applied to other officials. The rank was one of the lowest in the system of chancery honors, being the seventh of eight grades. Most of the slave traders were *khawājās,* and many of the merchant-*khawājās* were in the spice trade. Some of them were merchants of the Sultan.[24]

This growing association of merchants with the state had as a further consequence the employment of merchants in other administrative positions and a growing tendency for merchant and official careers to merge. Throughout the Mamluk period merchants held posts in the bureaucracy, or were identified by titles which imply bureaucratic rank. Some were even market inspectors and judges. The *kārimī* merchants in particular became officials because of their close association with the government. Merchants evidently moved from private status, through association or employ in government trading activities, to full-blown official careers. Of the *khawājās* in the state service employed in commercial capacities, about one-quarter held other official positions. Conversely, it seems probable that many officials holding the rank of *khawājā* were at one time engaged in trade, although there is no explicit evidence in many of these cases. Some *khawājās* were involved in confiscations of merchants' properties, which suggests some connection to commerce, and the fact that other *khawājās* were connected with the administration of estates, waqfs, and taxation may also imply commercial experience.[25]

Opportunities for changing from merchant to bureaucratic careers probably varied over time. Although there is no statistical basis for the generalization, the first fifty to seventy-five years of the Mamluk period may for quite special reasons have been favorable to merchant mobility. Many traders held posts under the Ayyūbids when oportunities to come to the attention of the sovereigns of small principalities were greater, but the change of regime, the establishment of the large Mamluk forces, and territorial consolidation and expansion also stimulated a demand for administrative personnel. Merchants coming from abroad to make their fortune in Egypt or Syria or recent converts to Islam had good chances of entering official positions because their isolation from original homes and communities made them all the more reliable servants. In the remainder of the fourteenth century opportunities to enter the bureaucracy probably were fewer, though mid-century trading in military pay certificates offered some chance for rich merchants to buy themselves offices. In the fifteenth century, the absorption of private commerce by the state opened a new inlet for social mobility. Merchants who reached the post of *khawājā* were already within the administration and other offices were available to them. By this time direct entry into the trading services of the state was a normal career route for merchants bent on public offices.

Perhaps the most important factor in the entry of merchants into the government service was the patronage of emirs. People who served in the secretariat of emirs or in buying and selling operations were often placed in the state service, perhaps as a reward, perhaps as a way of packing the government with the emirs' clients. Purchase of office was another means of entry into the civil service and even into the military. The conservative chroniclers complained of how merchants and commoners bought posts in the auxiliary corps by purchasing negotiable pay tickets. In the fifteenth century merchants even bought their way into the Mamluk corps itself and became emirs.[26]

Skilled workers and even common laborers had similar opoprtunities. Positions in the bureaus and sometimes strikingly brilliant careers were accessible through patronage and purchase. A faithful and competent tailor, furrier, or butcher might persuade his patron to give him a secretarial job. Market people attached to military expeditions may have had good chances too. Once the skills were learned, the former worker was on his way to a career limited only by his own abilities, his talent for flattery and intrigue, and, above all, by the prestige and fortunes of his original patron. Many men had the good luck to transfer their allegiance to the Sultan, and thus to reach very high posts in the government.[27] These opportunities differed, however, from the chances of the merchants in one decisive way. Although they depended on patronage or purchase, the chances for merchants were part of a more natural and perhaps expected career pattern, an extension of their prior functions. In selling the emirs' grain, managing their storehouses, estates, and rents from urban investments, or even in supplying the large households, merchants were already performing quasi-administrative and bureaucratic tasks. Instances of upward mobility among craftsmen, however, do not reveal a normal career pattern so much as good fortune in patrons or business.

In the Mamluk Empire, cooperation between the state and the merchant class was essential. In many sectors of the economy, the merchants could not carry on their enterprises without state protection and cooperation. Nor could the Mamluk regime, with its vast economic interests, dispense with the services of the merchant elites. Most trade, however, apart from the international trade and large scale internal wholesaling, remained private and independent except from taxation. The result of merchant relations with the state in these special sectors was the absorption of the merchant elites into the regime where they took up the duties of office in the state bureaucracy and the Sultans' service. On the other hand, from their own point of view, this was a situation rich in opportunities for profit and social prestige which consolidated their status as notables in Muslim urban society. Standing astride the two realms of state and society, they became the intermediaries for the economic and social exchanges by which the Mamluks penetrated the urban world to draw forth its resources and by which the urban economy adjusted itself to the all-powerful presence of the Mamluk state.

THE ULAMA

Like the merchants, the ulama were at the same time leading notables of urban society and auxiliaries of the regime, but their importance in the dynamics of urban-Mamluk relations was still greater, for their relationship to the regime illustrates the interpenetration of state and society in politics and social organization as well as in economic life. The ulama, as we have seen, were the religious elites of the community, the undisputed interpreters of the divine law, and the administrators of the community's familial, commercial, educational, and legal affairs. They were not a separate class, but a body of people belonging to every social level, who permeated town society and helped give it cohesion and stability. Whatever their social position, the ulama were all those people recognized for their competence in learning.

The ulama, however, depended on the cooperation of the Mamluks and necessarily collaborated with them because the ultimate powers generated by the society were vested in Mamluk hands. The bulk of social wealth which in pre-modern society came from the control of the land was theirs, and contributions from their vast incomes were essential to the physical maintenance of the towns, the creation and endowment of great institutions of charity, learning, and worship, and support of the large community of scholars and divines who were the flower of the Muslim peoples. The ulama, whose own incomes were limited by institutions which tied them to the wills of previous generations or the rights of future ones, were in considerable measure dependent on the Mamluks for financial support. Since inheritance laws made difficult the accumulation of great free fortunes and waqfs ascribed resources to given purposes, the Mamluks could best meet new needs.

More important, the ulama looked to the Mamluk regime for the defense of the community. Lacking the skills of warfare, the organization, and above all as we shall see in the next chapter, a relation with the masses adequate to establish themselves as the sole rulers of the city, the ulama needed the assistance of outsiders to protect the community. They depended on a military regime for discipline in the towns, the suppression of heresy, and resistance to violence from criminals, rebels, and sometimes even the masses of the people. Above all, they depended on the regime for defense against the destruction of the community or the subversion of its true faith by foreign invaders who might be pagans, heretics, or Christian infidels.

The ulama, however, were not necessarily loyal to any particular regime, faction, or form of government. Any stable military order which would protect the community from harm was deemed appropriate. Their political doctrine held that a military state was necessary for the good order of society, and that in cases of civil war or interregnum loyalty to any particular regime had to be sacrificed if recognition of the apparent victor would minimize conflict. In case of invasions as well, the religious community was prepared to repudiate the Mamluks if they were defeated, and accept the apparent victor as their new sovereign. Loyalty to the good order of society transcended all else, and the ulama of the Syrian towns failed on several occasions to assist the Mamluks to defend their empire. Fearing the damage that war would bring and the internal chaos which would result from the sudden defeat and withdrawal of Mamluk forces, the ulama saw submission and cooperation with the conqueror as their duty.

In three crises, when the existence of the Mamluk state hung in the balance, the notables of Damascus deserted the prostrate Mamluk government. In 699/1299–1300 when the invading Mongols swept the

Mamluk armies and panic-stricken officialdom from Syria, the leading ulama promptly sent a delegation to Ghāzān to seek peace, amnesty, and assurances of security. Implicitly, they first tendered him recognition as the legitimate master and overlord of Damascus and Syria by omitting mention of the Sultan's name from the Friday prayers, and accepted at great and evident risk uncertain guarantees that the conqueror would protect the city against pillage and give it a true Muslim regime. Refusing to heed the protests of the governor of the citadel that the Mamluk government was still in power, they urged him to surrender. Without tangible protection except the closure of the city gates to the Mongol forces, Ghāzān was then formally recognized as ruler of Damascus. Capitulation was justified by the need to avert fighting for control of the town and consequent bloodshed and pillage. The choice proved shortsighted. The Mongols pillaged al-Ṣāliḥiyya and the villages of Dārayyā and al-Mizza, and plundered the city of its valuables.[28]

Nonetheless helplessness would again lead the ulama to appease the Tatars. In 803/1400, Tamerlane invaded Syria, and the Mamluk army withdrew from Damascus. The city was then of two minds. Rich notables and merchants and some of the ulama, more fearful of the costs of surrender than the risks of resistance, met in the governor's palace and decided to distribute arms and supplies to prepare the city for a siege. The common people and refugees from Aleppo, Hama, and Homs were also prepared to fight. Since it was fortified, stocked, and well-armed, Damascus held out for two days, but other elements of the ulama, led by Ibn Mufliḥ, urged that the city surrender and put itself at the mercy of the invader. The chronicler, Ibn Taghrī Birdī, accuses them of seeking jobs and special protection for their families, but the eagerness of the Ḥanbalī qadi to surrender may have been due to fear for the safety of the exposed quarters, such as al-Ṣāliḥiyya, where his associates were concentrated and where much of their property was located. The peace party, strengthened by preliminary conversations with Tamerlane, won out, and the ulama accepted his terms for a huge ransom. They not only turned over the city, but agreed to persuade the common people to accept him as Sultan. Subsequently, they acted as his agents for the collection of tribute, and the qadis, led by Ibn Mufliḥ, diligently confiscated property abandoned by people who fled the city. The government bureaus and scribes also served the victor. Nowhere was there a hint of resistance or obstruction or shame at the lack of it. The results were even more disastrous than the flirtation of the previous century. Damascus was systematically plundered and burned. Huge sums of money were taken, and many of the leading scholars and artisans were led into captivity.[29]

Again in 922/1517 the Ottoman victory was passively accepted by the notables of the Syrian towns. Sultan Selim sought the favor of the qadis of Aleppo by giving them gifts, and at Damascus, the sheikhs of the quarters decided not to fight. This time, however, the stability of the Ottoman Empire in the sixteenth century ushered in a period of repose.[30]

The ulama favored recognition of conquerors at any price and without delay, though they were well aware that marauders far from home were not likely to establish a permanent regime, but would exploit and pillage the helpless population. Yet the notables had little choice, and had to take their chances. For them, the dangers were no graver than those of an interregnum which would dissolve the fabric of the community into chaos and tyranny self-imposed by the absence of law and order. Indeed, in 699/1299, at the very moment of Mamluk defeat, the Mongols were needed to preserve order. Damascus was overcrowded with refugees from nearby suburbs and villages. Men closed their shops and even left their money behind, while women ran screaming in the streets without their veils. Ten to twenty people were killed in surges of the panic-stricken crowds when it was bruited that the Mongols had entered this or that part of the city and were putting it to fire and sword. Prisoners escaped the jails. Military equipment was sold in the streets at bargain prices while food rose precipitously. People stole when they could and settled old scores.[31]

Similarly in 803/1400, it was feared that Damascus, divided into bitterly opposed religious and ethnic communities, would burst into inter-communal warfare. One chronicler saw in the treacherous maneuvers to surrender the city a conspiracy of the Shi'ites for whom Tamerlane had issued a special patent. Hints of religious and communal tensions might well justify an immediate peace.[32] Again in 922/1517 the defeat of the Mamluks posed a similarly acute problem. The angry populace attacked the fleeing troops, while thieves and plunderers set to work on the houses and quarters of the rich.[33] Surrender and recognition of the victor were imperative because order was imperative. Local needs took precedence over imperial considerations. In such crises prior ties and old loyalties between regime and populace meant nothing at all, because the ulama were helpless to curb internal violence without the assistance of a military state.

In return for this essential protection the ulama legitimized the Mamluk regime. They joined in recognizing new Sultans, accepted as legitimate the transfer of the Caliphate from Bagdad to Cairo, and thus symbolized their loyalty. On a lower level, the arrival of a new governor in a city was occasion for the ulama and officials to pay their respects, accept his authority, and simultaneously confer their recognition and implicit promise of cooperation. To the people, the ulama preached obedience. Their unyielding doctrine held that any state was better than the natural state of war. Necessity compelled submission.[34]

In case of need, the ulama lent their authority to assist in the defense of the community. They volunteered for the counter-crusading wars against Armenia and the attacks against the pirate bases of Cyprus and Rhodes in the fifteenth century. When mass support was needed for defense against pirates, rebels, or invasion, leading ulama called on the populace to take up arms, and ordered scholars, teachers, and students to learn to shoot and be prepared to fight. In 699/1299 the qadis of Damascus opened the mosques and madrasas for military exercises, and the syndics of the group of descendants of the prophet also gathered their men in a paramilitary force. In time of danger the ulama exhorted Sultan, soldier, and commoner to come forward and defend the faith.[35]

The ulama not only offered invaluable political support to the regime, but favored the fortunes of emirs and Mamluks with whom they had especially good relations. They enlisted themselves as supporters of particular emirs because in the decentralized Mamluk polity services to the community were the work of individuals. Although it was rarely openly avowed, ulama probably assisted in court intrigues. In 814/1411 an example of their services came to light in a letter to the Sultan from the qadis, jurists, notables, and merchants of Tripoli attesting their satisfaction with the governor. In Mamluk civil wars, the support of the ulama, and with it massive popular backing, was often of decisive importance. Rebels and pretenders vied for recognition of the legitimacy of their claims, and sought *fatwās* or judicial opinions justifying rebellion. In addition, the ulama could offer even more direct help by accepting public offices under rebel emirs. The rebel emir Minṭāsh, in the civil wars of the 1390's, was aware of the importance of the ulama, and called on the chief qadis, the Sheikh of Islam, and other notable men of learning to support him. At a later date Nawrūz, the rebel governor of Damascus, tried to induce the qadis and jurists of the city to pronounce against Sultan al-Mu'ayyad Sheikh, which in this case they refused to do.[36]

The Mamluk regime required money as well as obedience and here too the services of the ulama proved essential. The stresses of frequent warfare often required extraordinary taxes, and the cooperation of the ulama in attesting the legality of tax demands was vital. Legally speaking, only they could permit a diversion of revenues intended for charities or the support of the religious community to meet pressing demands for military defense. Councils of qadis and high ranking ulama were thus called to authorize extraordinary loans or gifts to the Sultan from the endowed revenues in the orphan funds or other waqfs. Qadis and scholars were also consulted about levying extraordinary taxes on the merchant class. By authorizing the levies, they removed pretexts for resistance.[37]

They proved equally helpful in the actual collection of taxes. Many were officials in the bureaucracy and lent the prestige which inhered in them as representatives of Islam to the purposes of the state. Moreover, since the tax process often required statements of assets and certificates of payment, the qadis took oaths and certified the actual contributions. Professional witnesses who commonly recorded transactions and contracts and of course the market inspectors who collected taxes were simultaneously ulama and agents of the state in these functions. In the later decades of Mamluk rule, qadis and sheikhs of the quarters were invaluable intermediaries for the collection of taxes from a recalcitrant populace. Qadis represented the governor in his dealings with the sheikhs, and the sheikhs helped raise money from the people.[38]

Collaboration between the Mamluks and the religious notables ultimately entailed the quasi-integration of the ulama into the state apparatus. The most prominent ulama officers such as the chief qadis, army judges, the chief legal consultants, the head of the public treasury, and the market inspector were all state appointed. In addition, the chief sheikhs of the Sufis, the sheikh of Koran readers, leading professors, official preachers, administrators of hospitals, and prayer leaders all received official confirmation of their appointments. These appointments were most probably made on the recommendation of the leading local qadis and ulama and their confirmation in all except the most important offices was a formality. In an episode reported by Ibn Ṭūlūn, the qadis, jurists, and sheikhs of Damascus met to hear a decree of the Sultan removing the market inspector and syndic of the group of descendants of the prophet and consult on the nomination of a new syndic whom they recommended to the Sultan. The ulama in this instance made no recommendation for the appointment of a market inspector leaving this to the discretion of the ruler.[39]

The most important of these appointees were the chief qadis. They had vast personal authority among the ulama and in the urban community, and their selection by the state served to vest a certain measure of influence over the ulama community in the hands of the Sultan. At the same time it conferred an additional degree of prestige on the chief qadis. Unfortunately, judges' posts became venal offices in Mamluk times, possibly from the middle of the fifteenth century. As early as 679/1280 the governor of Damascus was paid a thousand dinars for the post of qadi, although the purchaser was removed twenty days later when the governor was deposed. But by the latter part of the Mamluk period payment for important judicial as well as other bureaucratic posts was common. Dismissals from office then followed not from outrage at an abuse, but from greed and desire to sell the offices once again.[40]

We have already seen from the point of view of the community how the chief qadis were primarily responsible for the organization of the schools of law. From the point of view of the state, as a sign of the incorporation of the whole orthodox establishment under the state umbrella, the Mamluks followed the precedent of Nūr al-Dīn* and the Ayyūbid princes by patronizing all four schools of law, and eventually by creating four chief qadis, one for each school. Cairo was given four qadis in 661/1262–63 and the honor was extended to Damascus in 663/1264–65, and in 748/1347–48 to Aleppo. In 811/1408 the privilege of having a chief qadi for each school also was granted to Jerusalem and Ramla. Each qadi was responsible for appointments to positions within the school, for the maintenance of discipline and religious standards, and for the management of its institutions and properties. Qadis were sometimes managers of schools and waqfs, and were always consulted about the disposition of educational and financial affairs.[41]

The second duty of the qadis was the organization of the judicial

* Nūr al-Dīn was ruler of Aleppo from 1147 and of Damascus from 1154 until his death in 1174.

services of their schools. The chief qadis not only held court themselves, but appointed deputies to carry on the normal judicial business of the towns. The power to make such appointments, however, was often subject to abuse, and from time to time the Sultans intervened to trim the bloated ranks of qadis' deputies. By 731/1331, the deputies of the chief qadis in Cairo had proliferated to fifty men, and the Sultan abolished the office. Ever after sporadic seesaw efforts were made to keep the judicial bureaucracy in hand. In 782/1380, the Sultan decreed a maximum of four deputies for each qadi, but some decades later in 819/1416 the number had risen to two hundred and the Sultan limited the Shāfi'ī and the Ḥanafī schools to ten, the Mālikī to five, and the Ḥanbalī to four. Yet in 842/1438–39, new limits had to be set on the swelling body of deputy judges. The numbers were restricted to fifteen for the Shāfi'ī school, ten for the Ḥanafī, and four each for the Mālikī and Ḥanbalī. Still in the last decades of the Mamluk period qadis had from fourteen to sixteen deputies.[42]

The qadis were also responsible for the organization of the professional witnesses, and similar disciplinary measures had to be taken from time to time to curb excessive expansion. Qadis were instructed by the regime to set limits to the numbers of witnesses that could occupy a shop in the markets and to select them only from their own schools. Other quasi-judicial posts such as the office of *wakīl* in charge of access to the qadis' chambers required close control too. The latter office was abolished when the *wakīls* were discovered to be taking bribes.[43]

The authority of the qadis extended as well to the administration of the cult and religious affairs. In the Mamluk period qadis were often appointed chief preachers in the mosques and some were designated chief sheikhs in charge of the Sufi sheikhs. It was very common for qadis to be teachers too. In community affairs, guardianships of minors or of unmarried women and management of the properties of people deemed legally incompetent also devolved on the qadis.[44]

The partial bureaucratization of the ulama body and their close association with the political and administrative concerns of the Mamluk state led to their employment in the state bureaucracy in other than ulama capacities. The qadis, who were most directly members of the state organization, were commonly employed by the Sultan in his private secretarial service in the office of *kātib al-sirr,* in his private treasury, and in the military bureaus. Some became viziers and others held scribal posts in various branches of the administration. In many cases the post of qadi was itself the culmination of an official rather than a religious career, for qualified secular administrators were often appointed to the post. Other qadis of course were prepared by a more strictly religious and legal experience. Many sheikhs and prayer leaders as well were at some point in their careers scribes and officials. So too religious functionaries such as the administrators of mosques and convents doubled as functionaries in the regular administration. The skills of the ulama were in many ways vital to the state, and the close collaboration of the joint elites made it likely that many would find state employment a means of support.[45]

Ties of patronage and mutual interest and of marriage and kinship between ulama and Mamluks were thus supplemented by a limited but nonetheless important state supervision. In addition to reinforcing the bonds between the elites, official organization of the ulama became a crucial element in the cohesiveness of Islamic urban society. State organization, which helped to manage the personnel, institutions, and properties of the religious community, confirmed the authority of the ulama chiefs and defined the obligations of their subordinates to them. It thus stiffened the structure of urban community life which was informally but vitally built around the normative and administrative authority of the ulama.

However, neither the state appointment of leading ulama chiefs, nor their tendency to take places in the bureaucratic services implied state control or rigid organization of the religious elite. Those who were not state appointees were under the supervision of the qadis and sheikhs who were, but nonetheless instead of close controls, a loose interplay of prestige, influence, and authority prevailed. The activity of the ulama remained basically unregulated and diffused throughout the society. Only a few were responsible to the Sultan, while others in charge of the daily religious and commercial functioning of the community retained a relative independence to the degree that their activities did not directly concern the state.

The residual independence of the ulama was confirmed by the way in which they earned their livings. Qadis, market inspectors, and administrators of course received salaries or stipends directly from the state. In 725/1325 a qadi was paid the equivalent of 198,000 dirhems, an official preacher 60,000, and professors from 30,000 to 60,000 dirhems annually. Most teachers and religious functionaries, however, were part-time stipendiaries of waqfs. Professors in madrasas commonly earned about five hundred dirhems a month while more modestly endowed chairs paid two or three hundred dirhems a month. Lesser ulama, sheikhs, prayer leaders, Koran readers, and others normally received from about twenty to one hundred dirhems a month from waqfs. At these salaries many of the ulama were extremely poor, and al-Maqrīzī estimated their incomes to be at the level of cultivators and workers. The Sufi beggars must have been poorer still.[46]

Other sources of support lay outside either salary system. Professional witnesses, legal experts, and some teachers were paid by fee for their services. Further income came from the gifts and small pensions which rich ulama, officials, and merchants provided for poor scholars and jurists. Many teachers and Sufis must also have subsisted on petty charity, by soliciting gifts or by being hired for the sake of the blessings of a holy man at some social or familial occasion.

Actually many earned their living from several of these sources as well as a number of part-time jobs. Judges for example earned a state salary, fees paid by litigants, and even stipends allotted for the supervision of mosques and schools. The amounts of the salaries paid to stipendiaries of waqfs indicate that teachers, muezzins, prayer leaders, Koran readers, and even administrators and servants were part-time employees. These stipendiaries were free to supplement their incomes by holding other posts in other waqfs and even to earn more money in crafts or trade.[47] Characteristically, the ulama, absorbed only part-time by many religious and administrative functions, and possessing transferable skills of literacy and knowledge of the Muslim holy law as well as a reputation for probity, moved through the life of the community, performing legal, administrative, religious, and teaching roles where necessary and where employment was available. The complexity and variability of their functions and incomes tied the ulama to the whole spectrum of classes, groups, and interests which made up the Muslim town. Very old ideals in Islam held that the ulama must be independent of state support and tainted money, and undifferentiated by their functions from the activities, concerns, and burdens of the rest of the people.

Thus, the ulama were closely tied to urban society by strong economic as well as familial and ideological bonds. They further shared its problems and interests because many of them and their families were merchants or craftsmen as we have shown. Others were rich notables who had to shoulder extraordinary taxes levied on waqfs as well as private property. Taxes on imports and transactions raised prices for them as for others, and they shared the concerns of the rich merchants and even of artisans who were their clients or colleagues. Finally, the masses of the ulama had much the same economic interests as did the mass of the common people, since many of the sheikhs, teachers, students, and mosque servants were among the poorer classes.

Thus there were limits to the absorption of the ulama into the state apparatus, and firm ties to the populace of the towns, which gave them a double part in public affairs. Their true destiny was to be intermediaries who not only negotiated, legitimized, and facilitated taxation, but also resisted, haggled, and defended against abuse. In principle they stood against confiscations without consent and proper compensation. In one spirited defense of the sanctity of private property, a qadi asserted that it was contrary to Islam to disturb property rights, for these were God given. Ulama also resisted the contention that all property belonged to the Sultan, and inveighed against the practice of eminent domain.

Moreover, insofar as their cooperation was essential for collecting taxes, they might refuse to do so. Insofar as their assent was necessary, they had occasion to resist. In 803/1400, when the Sultan wished to confiscate the money of both waqfs and merchants to pay for the army, the qadis refused to sanction the tax and the idea was dropped. Again in 827/1424, they opposed a supplementary tax on merchants, and otherwise resisted the innumerable abuses of lesser officials and called for the cancellation of illegal fees and the dismissal of offending emirs and tax collectors.[48]

Equally important, when negotiating taxes on behalf of towns or quarters, the ulama used their influence to reduce official demands. One sheikh obtained a promise from Sultan Baybars, never fulfilled, to remove certain taxes on Damascus. Another eventually wore down the governor and secured abolition of market fees in al-Ṣāliḥiyya. A more important success of this kind came in 711/1311. A tax to pay for fifteen hundred cavalry valued at five hundred dirhems each was laid on waqfs and private properties in Damascus, and everyone was threatened with the loss of four months' income. The notables protested and organized a public protest procession headed by a delegation of qadis, preachers, and other ulama. Roused to fury the governor seized and beat the leaders, but in the end the tax was reduced to four hundred horsemen, in accord with previous usage. In the late fifteenth century sheikhs of the quarters took a similar leading role in resisting taxation. They protected delinquent taxpayers and at times refused to raise the fees demanded of their quarters. Qadis in addition represented such special constituencies as the professional witnesses, and defended them too against abusive taxes.[49]

Furthermore, the ulama used their influence to protect the community in other ways. They protested the conduct of riotous Mamluks to the emirs and the Sultans. In time of civil war, they sought to pacify the fighting factions and to mediate the endless disputes of the emirs, as in the Damascus civil wars of 791/1389, and at Aleppo in 896/1491 when a Mamluk party appealed to the notables of the quarters to help settle the fighting, or a few years later when the ulama, qadis, and other notables appealed to a rebellious Mamluk faction to make peace with its rival. Finally, *in extremis,* they countenanced or even sponsored rebellion against the regime.[50]

The power of resistance must not, however, be exaggerated, and what we have described is a model of ways of acting and not an assessment of the effect of ulama protests. They were in fact helpless to stop any determined abuse, and their extraordinary commitment to a regime at any cost by and large led them to support the state rather than to stiffen the resistance of the community against it. The protection afforded by the ulama established long run limitations on abuse essential for the survival of the community, but in the short run these limits might be wide indeed.

CONCLUSION

The Mamluk emirs and the regime had an immensely important role to play in the Muslim city. Only they could be expected to defend it against assault. By their control of rural areas they were dominant in the urban economy, and by their patronage for both religious and commercial life they extended that dominance to the innermost recesses of the Muslim community. Faced with this established power, urban notables, ulama, and merchants, collaborated with the regime in order to realize the potential power inherent in their local status, to protect the religious and educational values of the community, and to help assure order and defend commercial interests. The Mamluk regime needed them to perform the myriad of complex services involving social discipline and control, administration of the intimacies of economic life, and preservation of the religious and cultural fabric of the community, which were tasks too subtle for their own efforts. The ulama in particular stood as intermediaries between the regime and urban society, indispensable to both because they formed the integrative and administrative class of the Muslim community, performing all the legal and political functions we normally associate in modern government with bureaucratic, judicial, and sometimes parliamentary structures. The whole economic and social infrastructure which supported the regime and from which it collected its revenues depended on their functioning. Only they had knowledge of the deepest recesses of communal life. Only they knew the populace, its resources, and the ways of getting things done. Only they could enable the Mamluk regime to penetrate the mysteries and labyrinths of the governed society. Analogously, the merchant notables lent their economic, banking, and administrative skills to the management of the household economies of the Sultans and emirs and to the exchanges between the regime and urban society.

The symbiosis of the Mamluks and notables created the governing order of the urban community. Subtle sanctions, courtesies, and the play of complementary interests replaced formal institutions by a system of accommodations in which the Mamluks managed regional and urban defense and economy while the ulama were the instrument through which the norms by which the society would be ruled were created, adjudicated, and enforced. This balance of forces, however, does not itself fully describe the polity of Mamluk cities, for the masses of the common people must now be weighed in.

CHAPTER V · THE POLITICAL SYSTEM: THE COMMON PEOPLE BETWEEN VIOLENCE AND IMPOTENCE

THE ESTABLISHED order of Mamluk cities was based on a condominium of two elites. The local notables were guardians of the values of Islamic society and were entrusted with the intricacies of local affairs, while the tasks of defense and control of the urban economy were vested with the Mamluks. Sometimes cooperative, sometimes antagonistic, this combination of Mamluk repressive and economic power and ulama and merchant social skills created the political order of the towns.

This order of society, however, did not fully meet the needs of the common people. The absence of centralized governmental institutions, the weakness of economic associations, and the imperfect inclusion of both internal urban communities and lumpenproletarian groups generated pressures for which the Mamluk-ulama order afforded no regular outlet. The result was that the frustrations of the common people characteristically expressed themselves in mob violence which articulated needs and demands not otherwise served by the city elites. Still, we should not think of violence as necessarily senseless and chaotic. Violent action fell into patterns which not only reflected the limitations of the social order, but served to integrate the common people into a more complex over-all form of social organization. Violence as controlled and channeled by the Mamluks and the ulama could often be made to serve, though with great stress and at high cost, to consolidate the existing form of society. Mass political violence ranged from protests against food shortages and high prices, to resistance to fiscal exploitation, to outright rebellion. In these respects, the paramilitary youth gangs of Damascus, called the *zuʿar,* are of special interest because they epitomized the methods by which popular resistance was organized and the methods by which it was controlled. More generally, mass participation in military affairs also posed special problems in the politics of the cities. Finally, distinct from the actions of the common people were the activities of lumpenproletarian groups which also had to be made compatible with the existing order of society. In each of these cases our task is to examine the cause and nature of mass public action; the character, organization, and purposes of the participants; and, finally, the means of manipulation and control by which mass violence was integrated into the political system of Mamluk Muslim cities.

ECONOMIC GRIEVANCES AND THE PROTESTS OF THE COMMON PEOPLE

The most important forms of mass violence were caused by economic hardship or oppression. A society based upon Mamluk military and economic power, the overarching but loosely organized schools of law, and all absorbing solidarities of family and quarter, left few channels for the articulation of economic concerns. In the markets, where men stood apart from their communities of origin, no intermediary bodies such as guilds existed for the expression of economic or social interests which cut across class lines but which were not the concern of the community as a whole. Nor were there fully responsible authorities competent to hear complaints from the common people. The Mamluks who controlled the economy had few or no direct ties to the masses while the ulama and merchants who were closer to the common people had little influence in policy matters save perhaps to appeal for redress of grievances.

In this situation demonstrations by the people of the markets became an important form of economic protest. Shopkeepers sought to defend their interests by strikes—by closing the markets in times of troubles. Such strikes were always protective in nature and never designed to advance new claims. Shopkeepers refused to do business in protest against arbitrary or excessive taxation. In food crises bread sellers and bakers closed down in their war of nerves with the market inspectors who sought to impose unwanted price ceilings. Refusal to trade in protest against coinage manipulation was also common, and represented a spontaneous strike based on recognition of self-interest against arbitrarily unfavorable monetary terms. Most commonly the markets were closed to defend against riots or the abuses of Mamluks who often stole the supplies they wanted. In all these cases, however, the Mamluks could exercise a controlling influence. They could break such strikes by threatening to plunder all shops which remained closed. They could, on the other hand, provoke such strikes too when it suited their interests. Emirs were accused of complicity in spreading panic in the markets in order to use economic troubles to embarrass the government. Governors sometimes closed them down in times of civil war to deny provisions to their enemies.

These strikes give no evidence of guild organization. The initiative of a few fearful shopkeepers or informal discussion among the notables sufficed to set them off. Despite the absence of strong internal solidarities, men who felt sympathies of common class and condition of life rose up together even without prior organization, articulated objectives, or expressed agreement over means and ends. Informal ties and feelings of solidarity led to common efforts at self-defense against abuse and for relief from hardship, but only natural spokesmen whose opinions were generally accepted in the markets sufficed to inspire these risings. However, though numbers alone gave the market people a vast potential power, weaknesses in inner organization limited their effectiveness. These strikes were useful, but limited by the informality of market organization and the inevitable economic pressures on individual shopkeepers in a free market.[1]

Closure of the markets, of course, was a special sort of protest available only to shopkeepers and not relevant in every situation. The most common kind of demonstrations which involved the populace as a whole were riots over food shortages and high prices. Riots crystallized around the bread shops, the ovens, and the docks, and guards had to be posted to prevent disturbances and the pillage of supplies. Sometimes mobs surged through Cairo and its outskirts in search of food. Emirs took care to guard warehouses and often transferred their food supplies under armed guard to their residences for greater security.[2]

Moreover, the masses turned to their political overlords for relief. Since they had neither formal means nor regular spokesmen to make representations to the Sultan, in Cairo they often gathered outside the gates of the citadel to clamor for his attention and call upon him to relieve their hunger, curb speculation, and replace the market inspectors responsible for the regulation of the grain trade. Conceivably a delegation might be admitted, though there is no explicit indication that this ever happened. In the great famine of 775/1373–74 a delegation of important commoners (*nās min al-ʿāmma*) petitioned the Sultan to remove the market inspector, but who they were and whom they represented is not clear. Sometimes the pleas of the mob would reach the Sultan's ear through an emir sent down to hear them, but as likely as not troops were sent instead to disperse the crowds. The pleas of commoners beneath the citadel were answered by punishment for creating a disturbance and insulting the Sultan.[3]

Deprived of consultation, further violence was the only means by which the populace could seek redress. The crowds held the market inspectors and other officials of the grain trade responsible for their hardship and attacked them bodily. They hoped by punishing the inspectors to force them to put pressure on grain hoarders, millers, and bakers, and make it unsafe for any official not ameliorating their lot to hold the post. Market inspectors were often stoned and beaten and grain crises sometimes saw a succession of *muḥtasibs* offered as scapegoats to the masses. Assault and demonstrations, however, rarely resulted in the assassination of market inspectors. Their culpability was never wholly apparent, and popular feeling could not easily crystallize great extremes of bitterness against them.[4]

On the other hand, other officials were murdered in violent outbursts. For example, at the end of the fourteenth century, the enraged populace of Damascus killed the administrator and broker, Ibn al-Nashū, for hoarding grain. Such direct attacks on hoarders were warning that the only recourse of the common people when starved was to defend their lives by taking life. Other assaults were common enough. For example, in 843/1439–40 in Damascus, the people raided the house of the governor and stoned his Mamluks. He had forced merchants bringing sheep to Damascus to sell them to him at below their true value, promising that in return he would excuse them from taxes. When he failed to keep his promise, the merchants cut off meat imports, and the angry masses assailed the governor until pacified by a qadi. In Cairo the reaction of some qadis was to recommend executions, but calmer heads prevailed and a message was sent both to reprove and to calm the populace. Almost never was the Sultan himself the object of such outbursts, though in the great famine of 694/1295 Sultan Kitbughā, in fear of attack by hunger stricken mobs, built a new hippodrome so that he would not be obliged to cross the most populous parts of the city on the way to military reviews.[5]

Assaults and riots of this sort had a spontaneous basis in the desperation of the masses, but they were not merely outbursts of anger and frustration. The riots played directly into the political situation in the towns. They were sometimes incited by people who distributed money to the commoners to provoke the demonstrations or to arrange the assassination or removal from office of their political opponents. For example, it was rumored that the murder of Ibn al-Nashū was instigated by his enemies. More important, the common people themselves expressed a political intention in these seemingly inarticulate demonstrations. Their riots made every bread shortage a crisis of confidence in the existing "ministry" by pressing the Sultan, in whose hands lay the power to curb abuses, to remove obnoxious officials, curb the speculations of the emirs, and reduce prices. If violence could not directly ameliorate the situation, it might at least enlist the efforts of the ulama or other officials to pacify the cities.[6]

In this struggle, the people had a number of advantages. Their demands could hardly be overlooked. The need for food was universal, and the potential for serious uprisings very great. Moreover, the interests threatened by the insistent popular outcry, though important collectively, were dispersed. The emirs and grain holders who favored high prices were not organized to make their collective weight effective, and represented nothing more than a sentiment opposed to restrictions. Other emirs caught short or fearful of plunder, and soldiers and minor officials themselves in straits, also hoped for relief. The market inspectors, moreover, were relatively minor officials both vulnerable to popular pressure and easily dismissed if a change of policy became necessary. Even in late Mamluk times when emirs bought the post, purchase itself made even powerful men vulnerable because a change of market inspectors benefited the Sultan's treasury a pretty sum. In any case, the more powerful the Sultan the further he could go in satisfying popular demands.

Other factors complicated the situation. Aside from the sentiment of the court and the clamor of the populace, the effect of prices on imports, the interests of grain holders and emirs outside of Cairo or other major cities, and the Sultan's own grain situation had to be considered. Every grain crisis thus became a political game raging around the Sultan without formal organs for articulation of the political struggle. As such it was typical of the life of Mamluk cities.

Another basic cause of violent protest was abusive taxation, but the actions which this elicited followed a different pattern. In Cairo, mass demonstrations were few and notably ineffective. Only occasional riots over taxes on sugar cane and general fiscal abuse are recorded, although in 871/1466–67, when a group of weavers who came to complain to the Sultan about forced purchases of natron were punished and paraded through Cairo as a warning, the rage of the common people spilled over, and they fought the Mamluks for custody of the unfortunate weavers.[7] The tax system, however, was so decentralized that particular abuses, no matter how widespread, could never rally general protest. Each particular case had to be appealed separately no matter how many times instances of a similar kind were repeated because the system varied so much in products taxed, manner of assessment, rates of taxation, regions of application, methods of collection, and agencies of administration. Delegations of notables or purchase of protection made better sense than public demonstrations.

In Cairo, mass pleas for the removal of abusive tax collecting officials were also uncommon. Occasionally, qadis, market inspectors, or lesser officials were removed because of popular protest, but petitioners often ran the risk of being themselves seized and beaten. Petitions to remove powerful emirs were even less likely to be heard because that was a delicate political matter which might set off currents of intrigue at court, and upset the balance of influence among the Mamluks. In the case of the grain trade, where weak officials or marginal interests were involved, popular protest might have its effect. In these cases, however, the structure of the state was in question, and the common people could not easily be represented in the balance of forces which controlled the distribution of high offices. Popular demonstrations were then likely to meet the hostility of the Mamluks. In 770/1368–69 a mob outside the citadel of Cairo demanding that the governor of Cairo and the head of the bureaus be turned over to them was dispersed by the Mamluks who ruthlessly butchered the helpless people whom they trapped inside the Sultan Ḥasan Madrasa. The Sultan's first response had been to send down an emir to hear the clamors of the crowd, but when the mob began to stone the soldiers guarding the entrance of the citadel, forbearance was put aside. Nonetheless, probably to avoid further difficulties, the governor was removed shortly afterwards. Again in 800/1397–98, when the common people clamored at the gates of the citadel for removal of a governor, the Sultan sent his Mamluks to drive them off.[8]

With riots and protests modeled after food disturbances excluded, the more usual response to fiscal abuse in Cairo was direct assault upon offending officials. Unable to influence the tax policies of the Sultans or the behavior of the emirs, assaults by the commoners at least guaranteed the circumspectness of the successor to an office if his memory was good and the price he paid not too high. Sporadic attacks directed against individual officials were common in Cairo. Mobs murdered abusive tax collectors or retaliated for Mamluk thefts by summary executions. Resentful crowds often stoned emirs who had fallen into disgrace and once even exhumed the body of a hated Mamluk to vent their anger.[9]

Yet, however widespread Cairo's grievances, they rarely attached to the Sultan himself. The populace acted as if he were innocent and only particular officials culpable. Although he might be deceived by advisers, the ruler was regarded as exempt from ill intentions, and the people expected that he would redress grievances once he was aware of the evil actions of his ministers. Moreover, the presence of the Sultan reduced Cairo outbursts to sporadic attacks, and removed justification for more general risings. A massive uprising against fiscal oppression in Cairo would have been an attack on the regime itself, a matter not to be taken lightly even by the mass of the people. The army was stronger in Cairo than elsewhere, and serious resistance or annoyance could and would be bloodily put down.

In the Syrian towns, however, the situation differed in important ways. As in Cairo, sporadic assaults were frequent. In the fifteenth century, city mobs often demanded that some abusive tax officials be turned over to them, but others met their fate more directly. For example, in 868/1463–64, the common people of Damascus simply seized and killed an official after his protector had died. In 880/1475–76 the Sultan's *wakīl* (agent) was attacked and his house burned, and in 893/1488 a mob stabbed and burned a man who had come with a royal decree increasing the tax on grain brokerage. Abuses of waqfs, and once the arrest of sheikhs who sought to prevent wine from being imported to Damascus, were also violently protested.[10] In Syrian towns, however, violent protests of this sort were likely to reach massive proportions. From assaults they mushroomed into attacks on the governors themselves. Covering their rebellion with protests of loyalty to the Sultan, the city mobs held the governors responsible for the whole of town administration and attacked them without impugning the regime. In the absence of the Sultan massive violence in the Syrian towns could be more effectively utilized than in Cairo. At Aleppo, for example, in 885/1480, when the governor wished to levy taxes to pay for an infantry expedition to Mardin, the people killed him as well as the Sultan's *wakīl* who advised the tax. Another Mamluk official escaped with his life only by directing the wrath of the mob against the *wakīl*. In general, nothing was more likely to provoke such extensive outbursts than refusal to hear petitioners. In Aleppo in 852/1448 villagers came to protest oppression to the governor, and he had them beaten and paraded in the city as an example. The common people rose up to rescue them and many were killed in the fighting which followed. According to one account, the mob even drove the governor out of the city. In 860/1456 two delegates were sent to the governor to complain of officials who were taking their money and abusing their women. The governor imprisoned one of them and riots ensued in which the populace killed three officials and burned their houses. The Sultan, however, confirmed the governor in his office and ordered the troublemakers arrested.[11]

Assaults on the governor in the Syrian towns were often transformed into organized popular resistance which amounted to rebellion against the state. In these cases limitations in the articulation of economic interests coincided with the weaknesses of the political order divided between Mamluk and ulama elites. Conflicts between the demands of the Mamluks and the common people sometimes strained the whole system of Mamluk-ulama collaboration to the breaking point. Popular resistance to abuse won the backing of the notables and became community or city-wide resistance to the Mamluk regime. While assassinations and sporadic outbursts were the work of the common people, outright rebellions of the town populace were usually led by the ulama. The chronicles attribute the former to the commoners but the latter to the people as a whole—the *ahl* of the cities.

The Syrian towns were better able to organize for such general resistance than Cairo. Evidently the more cohesive internal communities of the smaller towns gave them an organizational potential which Cairo, a larger metropolis, with transient populations of soldiers, officials, and rootless migrants, lacked. In Syrian towns, the quarters emerged as important units of action. For example, in 821/1418 the people of a quarter in Tripoli stoned the governor when he tried to collect money at an unfair exchange ratio between gold and copper. Nonetheless, they were eventually forced to pay, and many of the notables went to Cairo to buy copper, thus reducing the price of gold. The organized al-Ḥawrānī faction of Aleppo had a long history of attacks on abusive officials, and in 889/1484, there was fighting in Aleppo between the common people and Mamluks in which an officer was killed and a quarter burned.[12]

In Damascus as well, the quarters were centers of resistance. From the 880's/1475–85 the suburban quarters resisted the government, murdered officials, and refused to pay fines and indemnities. Al-Shāghūr and al-Ṣāliḥiyya were particularly vociferous, but they were not alone. In 886/1481, the people of Sūq al-Ṭawāqiyyīn and Sūq Jaqmaq remonstrated in the Umayyad Mosque, which resulted in shootings by Mamluk archers.

"Suburban" villages were similarly embroiled with the government. Al-Mizza fought the Mamluks for years on end. Its notables were arrested, money demanded, and protests in the mosques of Damascus were followed by further arrests, beatings, and demands for ransom. In revenge the villagers assassinated oppressive emirs. Al-Qābūn was in similar straits. When in 899/1493–94 emirs seized a sheikh of al-Qābūn, great crowds of common people and Sufis gathered outside his prison. The governor drove them into the mosque, and his Mamluks killed some seventy people and then plundered the village.[13]

The strength of communal life in the Syrian towns had one further consequence. Resistance and rebellions came to be organized not only within the quarters, but on a city-wide basis. Civil wars between the Mamluks often brought such rebellions to a head, but these cases were complicated, as we shall see, by divisions within the cities. In the great civil wars which began in 790/1388 Damascus and Aleppo were divided by disputes between popular factions. However, at Tripoli in 802/1399–1400, a firm and unified popular resistance to the rebel governor Tanam developed because of his extortionate demands for money. One source mentions taxes of 650,000 (units unspecified, probably) dirhems. At the same time agents from Egypt tried to win the population to Sultan Barqūq, but they were seized and executed by the rebels who claimed that they were European spies. When the truth was discovered, rebellion broke out led by the qadis, jurists, and other ulama. A number of the leading notables and between seven hundred and a thousand of the common people lost their lives. Many notables fled to Egypt, but in the end the rebellion was nonetheless victorious.[14]

True rebellions apart from the immediate circumstances of the civil wars, but probably inspired by the general hardships of the period, were also common. In 799/1397, Kerak rebelled against its governor, and Damascus in 804/1401 actually drove the governor out of the city. A most striking episode was the rising of Hama in 811/1408, when market people protested the detention of sixty men as hostages for an unsolved murder. People closed the markets, gathered outside the city, and re-entered in groups of a hundred. The crowd's mood soon led to plundering and stoning of officials as the latter scurried to the protection of the citadel, or closed their lanes and streets, stocking in supplies. Some four thousand people milled about in an ugly temper while the emirs tried to assure the mob that nothing would be taken from them as ransom for the hostages. On another occasion, in 816/1413, the extortions of Governor Nawrūz led to a rebellion at Aleppo which locked him out of the city, where the Bānaqūsā populace fought him and forced him to flee. Later in the century, a severe battle at Hama in 848/1444–45 cost the lives of a hundred and twenty townspeople and twenty Mamluks, and compelled the transfer of the governor to Alexandria.[15]

Not until 882/1477–78 did the new and rising tide of military and economic difficulties again provoke town rebellions in Syria. First, the governor of Hama was driven out by the common people, and at Aleppo in 896/1491, several functionaries and a hundred commoners were killed before the governor could put down the rising. In 898/1492–93 there were severe disorders in Damascus and the governor was stoned. Two years later at Hama, the subjects, oppressed by a governor who had burned some of their houses, struck back. The Sultan sent reinforcements from all over Syria to rescue him, and permitted the troops to plunder the town. In 912/1506–07 Kerak revolted and drove out the governor, but the crowning episode was Aleppo's refusal to permit the Mamluk army defeated by the Ottomans to take refuge in the city. Taking advantage of the Mamluk defeat, the populace denied its 257-year-old regime possession of Aleppo.[16]

The actual part of the notables in these rebellions was seldom described in detail but their support was vital to success. The qadis of Bānaqūsā and the ulama of Tripoli not only sanctioned the rebellions, but actually led the movements. In Damascus, sheikhs of the quarters and villages similarly protested on behalf of their communities. The Mamluk regime well recognized the importance of local notables in inspiring these rebellions and held them responsible for such outbursts. For example, at Alexandria in 727/1327 trouble started with a fight between some European merchants and Muslims, adding strong religious and communal feeling to the conflict. The governor of the city, on receiving word of the fight, extricated the Franks and then locked the gates. The people trapped outside and forced to leave their goods and slaves unprotected prevailed upon him to open the gates, but hot tempers led to a clash. The governor was assaulted and a qadi issued a judicial opinion authorizing a rebellion in which many people were killed. Other accounts see this revolt as an outburst of the weaving and commercial interests of the city against taxation and the competition of European imports. This was in any case an uprising of the populace as a whole, and when forces finally arrived from Cairo to restore order, they held the notables of the city responsible for a failure of social discipline. Officials were dismissed for having condoned the riots, and qadis, merchants, and property owners were fined. No one was allowed to leave the city as the weighing and measuring for the confiscations went on.[17]

Ulama leadership was vital because it helped create coherent pressures. Only with their help could the common people forcibly overthrow oppressors without recourse to uncertain appeals, clamors, and demonstrations. In effect, this meant that rebellion was not a weapon of the market people in defense of economic interests, but really an instrument of the notables supporting community-wide risings against general grievances. In Cairo, to the degree that the masses of the markets remained atomized or bound to each other merely by force of sentiment and common interest, they were unable to force their will on the government or have their wishes anticipated in any regular way. Taken alone, the main force of the common people was limited to the protest of individual grievances. In Syrian towns, ulama leadership made communal risings against generally felt grievances possible, but in the existing political context resistance to fiscal abuse was restricted to rebellions whose limited objective was to replace one body of officials with another, presumably, more congenial group. Weaknesses in the organization of the commoners, and perhaps still more important, the implicit collaboration of the urban elites with the Mamluk regime inhibited more revolutionary developments. Though the ulama and merchant classes would resist the state, their long-term interests depended on the preservation of a stable military order. They would resist to force the Mamluk state back into the mold of their implicit condominium, but never to completely destroy the relationship.

THE ROLES OF THE DAMASCUS ZUʿAR

A special problem in the management of popular resistance was posed by the *zuʿar* of Damascus. The term appears for the first time at the end of the fifteenth century to designate organized gangs of young men in the quarters of the city. The phenomena is no doubt older than the use of the term, for the *zuʿar* seem to have been the fifteenth century counterparts of the Syrian militias called *aḥdāth* which were active in the pre-Mamluk period.[18] The *zuʿar* are of particular interest because they were the most highly organized groups in the Mamluk cities and, because of their paramilitary organization, they were potentially a powerful counterpoise to Mamluk control. Therefore, the dynamics of the relationships among the *zuʿar,* the Mamluks, and the rest of the urban population exposes important aspects of the character of popular resistance, and the ways in which the Mamluks could channel this resistance in accord with Mamluk interests and the established order of society.

The *zuʿar* were self-consciously organized gangs of young men, probably bachelors, who wore a distinctive hair style called the *qarʿānī* and robes worn over their shoulders as a kind of uniform. In common usage they were called the *zuʿar* (scoundrels), *ahl al-zaʿāra* (evil people), *ghawghāʾ al-zuʿar* (rabble of the *zuʿar*), *ghawghāʾ al-ḥārāt* (rabble of the quarters), and *awbāsh min al-zuʿar* (riff-raff of *zuʿar*), all pejorative terms, for, as we shall see, they were a turbulent part of the population. Otherwise we know very little about them. At least some of the *zuʿar* were shopkeepers. One is identified as a carpenter, another as a broker, and a third was named the spinner or thread seller. One of the *zuʿar* chiefs was called Ibn al-Ṭabbākh, the son of the cook.[19]

These gangs were organized in the quarters outside the city walls and in surrounding villages. Al-Shāghūr, al-Qubaybāt, Maydān al-Ḥaṣā, al-Ṣāliḥiyya, Bāb al-Jābiya, al-Mazābil, Bāb al-Muṣallā, and the districts of Maḥalla JāmiʿḤasan and al-Suwayqa were the *quartier louche* of Damascus, districts which still contained populations with rural backgrounds, not fully incorporated into the city. One reference associates the *zuʿar* with the Qays, one of the fighting tribal groups of Syria.[20] These districts formed, in proportion to the intensity of their own solidarity, a natural mold for shaping the turbulent youthful elements within them. They were grounded in the quarters, but were not part of their regular structure. The quarter was the special field of action in Muslim society in which men were sure of each other. It was not the essence of the solidarity nor the bond of unity, but the boundary for recruitment and organization.

The *zuʿar* of each quarter were led by *kabīrs* or chiefs. In the period between 902/1496–97 and 911/1505–06 we know of four *kabīrs* of the *zu'ar* of al-Shāghūr. In 903/1497–98, one Quraysh, a *sharīf,* a descendant of the prophet was mutilated by the Mamluks. His successor from 904/1498–99 to 907/1501–02 was also called al-Sayyid Quraysh, and from 907/1501–02 Ibn al-Ṭabbākh was *kabīr.* His successor in 910/1504–05 was known as Abū Ṭāqiyya. Other *kabīrs* of the quarters were al-Jāmūs who headed the al-Ṣāliḥiyya *zu'ar* until 907/1501–02, Ibn al-Ustādh, *kabīr* of the *zu'ar* of Maydān al-Ḥaṣā from 907/1501–02 to 913/1507–08, Abū Bakr ibn al-Mubārak, chief of al-Muṣallā, and Samkarī, head of the Bāb al-Jābiya, executed in 911/1505-06. Other *kabīrs* whose names we know are al-Shahāb Ibn al-Maḥawjib (?), al-Sayyid Ibrāhīm, al Qāḍī Taqy al-dīn Qāḍī Zar', Ismā'īl ibn al-Qarawānī, and the chiefs of a *zu'ar* gang of thieves not identified by quarter, Humayl and Fuṭaym al-Akbā'ī.[21]

From these names at least a few conclusions may be drawn. First of all, a number of the *zu'ar* chiefs were styled *sharīf, sayyid,* or *quraysh,* descendants of the prophet. Most of them seem to have been commoners, for none bore the honorific titles given middle-class notables. We cannot see a clear religious inspiration in their authority, though some element of family prestige or cultic importance may have been a factor in their ascendancy. It seems unusual to find that a qadi was chief of the *zu'ar,* but other ulama were associated with the young men's gangs. One of the *zu'ar,* Ibn Kasār, was titled *al-Khaṭīb,* the preacher. Ulama leadership seems paradoxical, but as we shall see, not altogether inconsistent with the *zu'ar* activities. The only other one of the *zu'ar* who was prominent in the established order of society was al-Muhtadī, who was also the sheikh of Maydān al-Ḥaṣā. Otherwise the sheikhs of the quarters were not also chiefs of the *zu'ar.* Though the relations between the *zu'ar* and the quarters were close the two offices and the interests represented were quite separate.[22]

The sudden activity of the *zu'ar* after 890/1485 was the result of economic decline and political disintegration. In time of distress the unemployed and the destitute grew in numbers, swelling the ranks of the marginal members of the society. With Mamluk controls seriously weakened, and the population of Damascus seething with resentment and revolt, this popular element of half-communal, half-criminal character came forth to play a part which was characteristic both of the potentials for resistance to the established order of society and its limitations. The relations of the *zu'ar* to their fellow townsmen, notables, and the Mamluk regime bring into clear relief how violence was generated, how it was controlled, and how it was even made to serve continued Mamluk domination.

On the one hand, the *zu'ar* represented the interests of quarters and defended them against abuse. They frequently assaulted rapacious tax collectors. In 902/1498–99 they attacked the agents of the Mamluk chamberlain, and in an extraordinary incident later in the same year, incited and bribed by the ulama to attack their oppressors, killed over thirty people in al-Ṣāliḥiyya including the police chief and more than a hundred men in the city itself. From time to time the *zu'ar* murdered other tax collectors, and it is probable that many assaults in this turbulent epoch not specifically attributed to them were also their doing.[23]

More dramatically, the *zu'ar* were the backbone of massive resistance to taxation, and led in barricading the streets and fighting the Mamluk troops. Resistance to taxation was simultaneously resistance to their own dissolution for one was the *sine qua non* of the other. In 907/1501–02 the *zu'ar* of the quarters waged an all-out battle with the governor of the city, resisting threats to disband them and tax demands on the quarters. The trouble broke out when the *zu'ar* of al-Ṣāliḥiyya came armed with their chief al-Jāmūs to meet the new governor. Passing through the quarter of Maydān al-Ḥaṣā, they abused several of its residents. The governor seized the moment to order the dissolution of the *zu'ar,* the execution of their chief, and following up his advantage, imposed heavy taxes on the quarters. The inhabitants of Maydān al-Ḥaṣā, and al-Shāghūr, however, met to protest and swore to resist. A crowd from al-Shāghūr attacked the troops, and fighting spread to al-Qubaybāt. Other *zu'ar* arrived, marching, as it were, to the sound of the guns. Armed, they refused to attend prayers, and barricaded the quarters. The Mamluks had the worst of another skirmish, and the governor, unable to maintain order, sent qadis and the Sheikh of Islam to parley.

In the negotiations which followed, the sheikhs of the quarters and the chiefs of the *zu'ar* treated separately with the governor. The former demanded cancellation of various burdensome taxes including the monthly market inspector's tax and taxes on houses, and also the execution of certain tax collectors. The governor proclaimed the abuses abolished, but evidently the sheikhs could not speak for the *zu'ar.* Murders of rapacious officials continued, and the governor was forced to recognize the special organization of the *zuʿar* and to make his peace with them as well. In an interview with Ibn al-Ṭabbākh, the chief of the *zuʿar* of al-Shāghūr, the governor conceded that only people directly responsible would have to pay blood money for crimes or assassinations committed in the quarters and that the districts as a whole would be spared. An implicit alliance between the sheikhs of the quarters and the chiefs of the *zuʿar* won this victory for both. The sheikhs, standing between the populace and the regime, must have found it to their advantage to connive at the existence of the *zuʿar* who better than they could organize opposition, and use them as a balancing element, without being wholly responsible, to sustain their own freedom of maneuver.

However, trouble soon broke out again over new taxes. The *zuʿar* leaders of al-Shāghūr and Maydān al-Ḥaṣā were arrested, and Ibn al-Ustādh was killed. The others barricaded their quarters while the Mamluks attacked al-Shāghūr, killing several of the *zuʿar*. The *zuʿar* of other quarters rallied to assist al-Shāghūr, but they were routed and the quarter burned. The governor then extended a general amnesty, but refused it to this most rebellious district. Abū Bakr ibn al-Mubārak of al-Muṣallā quarter was pardoned, but a chief of al-Shāghūr was arrested and executed.[24]

In these cases resistance came not only from each quarter, but from the *zuʿar* of the city as a whole. In 907/1501–02 the chief of al-Shāghūr gathered men from the villages and other quarters to do battle with the Mamluks and again in 910/1504–05 Abū Ṭāqiyya, chief of al-Shāghūr, united the *zuʿar* of various quarters and villages to intimidate the Mamluks. Yet despite this temporary solidarity in resistance to the regime, the *zuʿar* of the quarters were fundamentally hostile to each other. Reflecting the disputes of their districts *zuʿar* were often embroiled in factional battles. In 893/1488 a parade of *zuʿar* of al-Shāghūr through the Ḥārāt al-Mazābil ended in a fight in which ten men were killed. In 902/1496–97 the *ghawghāʾ* of al-Shāghūr and Maydān al-Ḥaṣā made the quarter of Bāb al-Shāghūr a battleground. The markets closed in fear of plunder until the emirs divided the parties. These battles resumed in the following year, and the quarters endured three days of fighting until the troops finally pacified the city. In later years the feuds of al-Shāghūr and Maydān al-Ḥaṣā broke out again into open fighting. Occasional efforts to reconcile the *zuʿar* of the various quarters were of little avail. In 902/1488 the *zuʿar* of Maḥalla al-Qaṭāʾiʿ made a feast for the *zuʿar* of al-Shāghūr, al-Mazābil, and other quarters, which the chiefs attended, but the reconciliation was short-lived. Soon after the *zuʿar* of al-Qubaybāt attacked the Maydān al-Ḥaṣā. Although the *zuʿar* might unite under stress of extreme provocation, they were hostile to each other. The most powerful of popular forces dissipated their energies in futile bickering.[25]

Nor was the alliance of the *zuʿar* with the rest of their own quarters reliable. The *zuʿar* rose out of the districts, but remained an antithetical force within them. In disputes between the quarters and the government they formed a coalition, but otherwise the *zuʿar* abused the quarters as well as defended them. They were criminals, assassins, thieves, and pillagers who preyed on the people for their livelihoods. They were responsible for innumerable assassinations which unfortunately remain inexplicable. Feuds between quarters may have been the cause of some. For example, in 910/1504–05 a young *sharīf,* Ibn al-Sayyid Aḥmad al-Ṣawwāf, was killed and in revenge the *ghawghāʾ* attacked the Ḥārāt al-ʿAbīd. In other cases *zuʿar* gangs were hired as killers in the feuds of others. Other crimes were motivated by purely criminal considerations. Gangs of *zuʿar* thieves operated in the city, and they were widely feared as plunderers. In 903/1497–98 emirs transferred their goods to the citadel to protect them from the troublemakers of the quarters, and barricades were erected at the gates of the districts for fear of the *zuʿar.* In 922/1516, freed from restraint by the collapse of the Mamluk Empire, the *zuʿar* began again to pillage in Damascus and to attack fleeing soldiers. They plundered and burned quarters which failed to buy them off, and many officials left for Egypt with the retreating Sultan in fear of their lives. Even after the arrival of the Ottomans, *zuʿar* continued to attack Mamluk emirs.[26] Throughout these decades the notables were terrorized and bedouin chiefs no longer dared make their residence in Damascus.

Aside from crude assaults, *zuʿar* criminality reached a degree of sophistication in protection rackets and other financial crimes. The *zuʿar* evaded taxes, for example, and made others pay in their stead. They forced some merchants to pay them protection money to stay in business while at other shops they installed accomplices to do business on their behalf, protecting them against taxes and forcing purchasers to pay excessive prices. The *zuʿar* were the organized racketeers of early sixteenth century Damascus.[27]

The *zu'ar* thus appear in two dimensions. Their partial isolation from the rest of urban society, self-conscious defiant organizations, special signs and identifications, and their riotous violence in the city gave these gangs a lumpenproletarian aspect. On the other hand, they were also representative of the communal life of Damascus. Attached to the quarters in which they were organized, many of the *zu'ar* were artisans or shopkeepers, and thus, unlike the true lumpenproletarians, affiliated to the working population. Moreover, although most of their leadership was drawn from the common people, religious and communal notables were involved in their movement.

To blunt the dangerous thrust of *zu'ar* power the Mamluks took this double aspect into account. The Mamluks enrolled these gangs into their armies as auxiliary infantry. Impelled by the stress of continuous warfare against foreign enemies and bedouins, the Mamluks required military support from the populations of Syria. A period of intensive recruitment in the towns and taxation of the quarters to pay for supplementary military help began in 890/1485 because of the struggle with the Ottoman Empire over Adana and Tarsus. In 893/1488 the *zu'ar* of al-Shāghūr were reviewed in formal procession, and in 895/1490 some three thousand men of the quarters gathered for infantry duty were reviewed, fully equipped and armed, in public ceremonies. In each subsequent military crisis, the *zu'ar* auxiliaries were reviewed and probably paid by the governors or leading emirs for wars or campaigns against bedouin tribes and to pacify village rebellions and quarrels. The *zu'ar* were reviewed for military expeditions in 906/1500–01, 910/1504–05, 913/1507–08, and 914/1508–09, when they joined in an expedition to the Hauran. Even after the Ottoman conquest of Damascus the *zu'ar* continued to serve the new regime in this way. For example, in 927/1521 the Ottoman governor of Damascus, to raise support for his rebellion, urged the people to fight to defend themselves and their families against the Turks. He called out the young men of the quarters and ordered them to form an *'arāḍa*—a line up in review in arms. He then appointed a commander for each group. The *zu'ar* were also used for ceremonial parades, and formed part of the cortèges organized to greet newly arrived governors, ambassadors, or other high ranking dignitaries.[28]

The Mamluks armed and equipped the *zu'ar* gangs, honored their chiefs, and probably paid them for their loyalties in order to utilize the gangs as paramilitary reserves. If the Mamluks did not actually create the organization of the *zu'ar,* their policies contributed decisively to consolidating the factions. The result was the strengthening of the *zu'ar* and the evolution of ever more intimate relations between them and the Mamluks.

This intimacy was reinforced by the fact that the *zu'ar* were useful in civil as well as foreign wars, and as a result they were cultivated by individual emirs and factions as well as by the regime as such. In 903/1497–98, in anticipation of fighting, the *zu'ar* were organized as auxiliaries and reviewed in the hippodrome along with the regular troops. Al-Qubaybāt and Maydān al-Ḥaṣā backed the rebels while al-Shāghūr and al-Ṣāliḥiyya supported the regime. The rebel emir Aqbirdī lived in al-Qubaybāt, and the *zu'ar* who backed him were his men and clients; but other quarters probably chose sides in response to their own long-standing antagonisms. The Mamluks were quick to exploit the city's tensions. The result was bloodshed and a good deal of pillaging which reflected these inter-communal hostilities as much as the passions of battle and the evils of sheer brigandage. Only with the arrival of troops from Egypt and a new governor, Kurtbāy, who dispersed the *zu'ar* his enemies had organized and forbade them to bear arms, was order restored. Kurtbāy simultaneously tried to raise auxiliaries from the populace, but because the *zu'ar* were opposed to him, he called on skilled craftsmen and tradesmen—masons, millers, turners, and shoemakers—to assist him in pursuit of the rebels. Their help, however, was grudgingly rendered. Carpenters and masons fled Damascus rather than be conscripted. The quarrels of the emirs were not their business.

In the threatened civil war of 910/1504–05, the *zu'ar* again had an important part to play. They were asked to swear allegiance to the Sultan and in return they required that an *amīn* be appointed in each quarter. The significance of the demand is hard to appraise. It would seem that the appointment of an *amīn* as a commander implied official recognition of the auxiliary status of the *zu'ar*. It could also have been a guarantee of Mamluk protection for the quarters in case of fighting. In any case, the *zu'ar* of the Maydān al-Ḥaṣā and al-Qubaybāt were reviewed in the hippodrome. The *zu'ar* of al-Shāghūr, of other quarters, and the surrounding villages, however, emboldened by the weakness of the state and their own growing power, set out to pillage. The rebel emir Arikmās supplied them with arms. To pacify them, they were also reviewed, and marching in better discipline than the regular soldiers, their strength, good order, and superiority to the Turks was universally recognized. The *zuʿar* were given robes of honor, and they boldly demanded regular pay. The governor, however, strengthened by reinforcements from Egypt, later gave warning that he would not tolerate violence. Intimidated by the new forces, the *zuʿar* remained quiet.[29]

To sustain these factional ties between Mamluks and the *zuʿar,* the emirs cultivated personal followings. The *zuʿar* were hired as gangsters. In 904/1498–99, *zuʿar* murderers were arrested, and discovered to be in the service of ʿAlī ibn Sharbāsh, who was the brother-in-law of an emir. Similarly, in 910/1504–05 when *zuʿar* killed a sheikh in his *zāwiya,* it was bruited that the assassins were doing the bidding of a leading emir. Emirs also employed the *zuʿar* as hoodlums to intimidate their opponents and extort money. Arikmās, a Mamluk official in Damascus in 911/1505–06 who had a large following of *zuʿar* in the civil wars of 910/1504–05, is particularly interesting as their patron. One of the *zuʿar* who marched in his reviews and was also head of a criminal gang, Fuṭaym al-Akbāʿī, was the husband of a servant of Arikmās. In this case, the ties of patronage between *zuʿar* and emirs took a classic form. Arikmās is said to have hired a great number of people besides his Mamluks, and he gave them a free hand in Damascus, being unwilling to check their powers and alienate their support. Thus when the *zuʿar* of al-Shāghūr led by Abū Ṭāqiyya began to fortify their quarter by building new doors he was reluctant to intervene. Only the pressure of other emirs who threatened to denounce him to Cairo forced him to make the *zuʿar* desist. Emirs like Arikmās had turned the *zuʿar* from the infantry auxiliaries of the state to personal followers. This was one more dimension in the complexity of the *zuʿar*'s political roles in Damascus and the relations between the populace and the Mamluks.[30]

The tangle of these conflicting *zuʿar* roles governed the rhythms of Damascus' social history in the latter decades of Mamluk rule. When the *zuʿar* emerged after 890/1485 the regime itself fostered their cohesion, and made them a prominent factor in the balance of city politics. Military employment and reviews increased their self-conscious strength. The result was the intensification of inter-communal fighting between the quarters and rising levels of criminal violence. So long as the Mamluks needed the *zuʿar,* they had to give them a free hand within the city. Inter-communal violence and *zuʿar* crimes reached a peak in the civil war of 903/1497–98, and the new governor, Kurtbāy, sought to check their powers by disarming and disbanding the gangs. His efforts yielded few results. The *zu'ar* continued to be organized by the regime for ceremonial and military needs. The dangers of this policy became evident in 907/1501–02 when the *zu'ar* sponsored a massive popular uprising against the government. Subsequent efforts to disband them again proved short-lived. Individual emirs had important interests in the cultivation and protection of these gangs, and military reviews and official receptions resumed again. The divisions of the emirs prevented any consistent policy towards the *zu'ar,* and the civil war of 910/1504–05 again strengthened them. Each review in the hippodrome served to heighten a self-important estimate of their own discipline and power as a match for that of the regular troops. Indeed, the *zu'ar* came to despise the Mamluks and the government. Thus, when the regime felt strong it ceased to appease and purchase silence or support, but seized and executed the *zu'ar* leaders. The governors tried to disarm the *zu'ar* they had armed, disperse the men they had gathered, dissipate the forces they had sponsored. It was a matter of grave importance to keep them in check. Their organization, participation in the clienteles of emirs, and resistance to taxation often implied a direct threat to Mamluk control of Damascus. The emirs who were tolerant of their depredations against the rest of the population as a way of buying their support were also fearful that the strength of the *zu'ar* would be turned against them.[31]

These tangled relations of the *zu'ar,* the Mamluks, and the rest of the population formed a pattern of actions by which *zu'ar* violence became part of the political equilibrium of Damascus. They sometimes emerged as the fiercest and best organized enemy of the state. They defended the quarters, defied taxation, and murdered officials, but this protection was basically directed at weakening the government and strengthening themselves. The unscrupulousness of the *zu'ar* in seeking their livelihood gave the Mamluks means to divert, control, and even exploit *zu'ar* powers for their own purposes. The *zu'ar* were enrolled and paid as Mamluk auxiliaries and clienteles. If the government could neither crush them nor buy their acquiescence, it chose as a middle ground to permit the *zu'ar* to prey on the rest of the city, which they were equally ready to exploit. The regime had found a way to control and channel the violence of the lower classes, making use of them whenever suppression failed, and dividing their interests between opposition and cooperation. Because the *zu'ar* did not seek any regular position in Muslim society, but sought to stand in the interstices between the populace and the regime and to be parasites upon both, there could under the circumstances be no political challenge rising out of the quarters. By this double relation of resistance and cooperation the potential for organized political action by the quarters was inhibited, and systematic resistance prevented from emerging. The revolutionary potential of the alienated *zuʿar* was broken. Instead they accepted the terms of this rough system. Political violence was converted into merely criminal violence. Through patronage of lower class elements the Mamluks could check their power and govern the towns.

MAMLUK CONTROLS OVER POPULAR MILITARY ACTIONS

Even apart from specific instances of popular resistance, or of *zuʿar* opposition to Mamluk authority and Mamluk taxation, popular military experience, and the possibility of independent popular forces, posed a more general potential threat to Mamluk hegemony. The Mamluks had to rely on popular participation in the defense of the cities, in foreign campaigns, and especially in Mamluk civil wars. Even though war was waged from horseback, infantry were used for seige labor and as diversionary fodder to absorb the blows of the enemy and entangle him while the elite of the defenders sought the victory from horseback. All mass military activities, then, had to be closely supervised by the Mamluks to prevent the experience of the townspeople from being used against them. If violent resistance from a bellicose population could not be avoided, at least the organization of regular military action was never to fall to the independent aegis of the common people.

Popular military experience was nonetheless extensive. In defense of their cities against the Mongols, commoners were enrolled by the Mamluks at Damascus and Aleppo in 658/1260, and in 680/1281 at the battle of Homs. In the wake of the latter battle, auxiliary military manpower was raised in the markets of Damascus and efforts were made to teach the shopkeepers, students, and sheikhs how to use the bow and arrow. The *ʿarīfs* of the markets were ordered to write down the numbers of men available and to assist in organizing the training. Again in 699/1299 the Damascus common people took a large part in the defense of the city. After the Mamluk defeat, they took courage to attack the occupying forces when it was rumored that a relief army was coming from Egypt. When the Mongols retreated, the populace was organized to defend the city in anticipation of another attack. The

ʿarīfs arranged military exercises, but a commander was assigned by the Mamluks to lead each suq. Not only the shopkeepers and artisans, but, with the help of the ulama, the sheikhs and students were trained to fight. Fifty thousand men are reported to have armed themselves as best they could for the impending struggle with the returning Mongols. In later decades Alexandria was defended by shopkeepers and youths against the Franks, and in the fateful year 803/1400, the common people of Damascus and Aleppo who joined the Mamluk armies to resist the invasion of Tamerlane were swept aside by the onslaught.[32]

Not only local defense but foreign campaigns required infantry which the Mamluks recruited from the common people. Cairo beggars campaigned in the counter-crusading wars in Syria. In 785/1383 popular levies were raised in Aleppo and paid a thousand dirhems a man to fight the Turkomans. The late fifteenth and early sixteenth century wars against the Ottomans, and efforts to suppress the bedouins in Syria, also required auxiliary levies. Aside from the bedouins or Turkomans who commonly joined the armies, the Mamluks raised infantry in the villages of the Nablus region and from the populations of Damascus and Aleppo. The *zuʿar* and other infantry units were sometimes conscripted by requiring each quarter to present men or hire substitutes, and their wages were often paid by a tax on populations of the quarters.[33]

The freely given help of individuals also bolstered Mamluk forces. The tradition of the holy war in Islam inspired ulama, Sufis, and poor sheikhs and students to enroll in Mamluk expeditions, and fostered cooperation between the regime and the populace. They supported the counter-crusading wars, and volunteers fought against Armenia. When the fifteenth century counter-crusade brought Muslim vessels to Cyprus and Rhodes, volunteers again went out to fight the Franks. No campaign, however, aroused more religious feeling than the war against the heretics of the Kasrawān Mountain in the Lebanon. The ulama preached to rouse the fury of the masses, and even the peasants went to fight the mountain peoples.[34] In all these cases the populace played an auxiliary role in campaigns organized by the Mamluks.

Even more indicative of Mamluk power to manipulate the military potential of the urban commoners was their success in enrolling the masses in Mamluk civil wars. Auxiliaries to fight with stones and arrows, pillage and harass opposing troops, and retrieve expended weapons were often important to the outcome of factional struggles.

Although the common people were usually devoid of any political ambitions, the Mamluks drew them into participation. In most of these events in fourteenth century Cairo there was no pattern of popular support or opposition to the regime. The mobs had no will of their own. Amorphous popular involvement in civil wars was first recorded after the death of Sultan Nāṣir Muḥammad in 1341 and was a factor in Cairo in every major crisis for the rest of the century. In the strife of 742/1341–42 and 743/1342–43 the common people backed both of the Mamluk factions, and again in 768–70/1366–68 and 781–83/1379–81 the emirs rallied help from the masses.[35]

In the great civil wars which began in 790/1388, the common people of every major town became involved. Social conditions in the different cities evidently had a part in the formation of Mamluk clienteles and the behavior of the common people. In Cairo the mobs fought for both Sultan Barqūq and his rivals, Yalbughā al-Nāṣirī and Minṭāsh, switching sides with the tides of victory or shows of bribes or chances of plunder. The populace behaved as an amorphous mass seeking only the most immediate monetary gains, having no deep attachments to any party. The mobs first backed Sultan Barqūq, but then divided, some deserting to the rebels. With the victory of the rebels and the succession of Yalbughā al-Nāṣirī to the Sultanate, he and Minṭāsh came to blows. Using the authority of his office, Yalbughā instructed the populace to pillage Minṭāsh. Again, however, bribes bought popular help for Minṭāsh as well. In this chaos the return of Barqūq recreated his popular following. Minṭāsh neglected the masses while Barqūq was again diligent in buying popular favor.[36]

On the other hand, the Syrian towns appear to have been much better organized, less volatile, and more consistently motivated by important political and social considerations. Damascus was polarized between two factional groupings called the Qays and Kalb, and this underlying tension divided the populace, the Qays faction backing Sultan Barqūq and the Kalb, including the quarters of Maydān al-Ḥaṣā, al-Ṣāliḥiyya, and al-Shuwayka, supporting Minṭāsh. Other elements of the common people also opposed the Sultan and supported the rebels.

The civil wars brought the latent tensions to the fore by first enlisting a substantial part of the population on the side of Minṭāsh. From 791/1389 a majority of the common people seem to have backed him consistently through three years of hardship, sieges, and battles against the forces of Sultan Barqūq and their fellow citizens. The city and the surrounding villages resisted Barqūq's efforts to regain control of Syria in 791/1389, and later on the common people rebelled when Barqūq's governor happened to be absent from the city. This was a sustained and determined popular rebellion against the legitimate Sultan, motivated by a staunchly political opposition. Its immediate cause was mistreatment of the populace and the wanton damage done to many of the quarters by Barqūq's soldiers, but a more general and profound disappointment with his regime is evident. Barqūq's reign introduced a period of increasing hardship. The rapacious Circassian Mamluks came to power, and the first signs of agricultural decline, monetary inflation, and severely abusive taxation dated from this time. Mamluk abuses in Damascus crystallized an abiding dissatisfaction and conviction that a change of Sultan might benefit everyone. Many Damascenes took advantage of the civil wars to throw their support to the side from which they had the most hopes for the future. Unfortunately the result was not only to win the enmity of the Sultan but to awaken the hostilities latent within the populace itself.

Despite these strong feelings the people of the city were not always eager to become involved in Mamluk battles. Mamluk efforts to organize and arm the populace were prerequisites to their active participation in the civil wars. Minṭāsh deliberately organized the Maydān al-Ḥaṣā quarter and armed it to fight on his behalf while in another case the Governor al-Nāṣirī, defending the city for Barqūq in 793/1391, induced the qadis to organize the populace group by group (*ṭā'ifa*), market by market, and quarter by quarter according to the city's natural communal bodies to fight against Minṭāsh. The people of al-Ṣāliḥiyya, sympathetic to Minṭāsh, were perplexed by the pressures which came from both sides to make them join wearying and costly battles. In Damascus, not volatile and easily bought mobs, but a complicated interplay of local hostilities, the interests of the notables, and the feelings of the population about their prospects under one or another Mamluk regime motivated participation in the civil wars.

Aleppo exhibited a similar basis for her participation in the wars. Deep standing divisions within the population of the city had created two factions. The Bānaqūsā district outside the walls, led by its own qadis and sheikhs, backed Minṭāsh in 791/1389 in a struggle embittered by prior antagonisms. Its Shāfi'ī qadi is said to have preached against the vices of the ulama, presumably of the Bānaqūsā quarter's opponents, but the Banāqisa were defeated and the qadis who participated in the resistance executed. In the following year Minṭāsh appeared at Aleppo and again the Banāqisa backed him. Together they besieged the citadel, but when Minṭāsh was forced to withdraw, the defenders took their revenge, pillaging the quarter and executing some eight hundred people. Betrayed by their passions into disaster, the Banāqisa were ruthlessly suppressed by the victors.[37]

In the civil wars which followed the invasions of Tamerlane, the common people were equally active on one or another or on both sides. The populace of Aleppo backed Governor Nawrūz against Sultan Faraj in 809/1406, but at Damascus three years later the people sided with Faraj until his death in 815/1412. In Cairo many of the common people also shared in the fighting. Other instances occurred sporadically in the fifteenth century. In 842/1438–39, the populace of Aleppo was enlisted to fight the rebel Governor Taghrīwirmish. The people plundered his headquarters, stoned the rebels when they besieged the city, and drove them off with bows and arrows. At Antioch too, peasants resisted Taghrīwirmish with arrows and stones, and fighting in Cairo at the same time also involved the commoners. Again at the beginning of the sixteenth century Damascus rebellions attracted the masses.[38]

In all these cases popular support for emirs and the Sultan was actively solicited, and the inducements were of various kinds. Though the masses were unorganized, their sheer numbers gave them an implicit leverage to extract some concessions from the Mamluks. Money had to be paid for agitators to monger rumors, incite riots, and organize street demonstrations and rallies. When emirs in Damascus prepared a rebellion in 695/1296, they not only took the precaution of stocking the citadel with food and arms, but increased their "benefactions" to the common people. Beggars and the *zuʿar* were similarly favored to create useful clienteles, and a Sultan once even gave robes of honor to bath servants. At other times emirs were accused of plotting rebellion and sending messages to the markets to stir up popular support.[39]

Tax remissions were another way of winning the sympathy of the masses. In the desperate moments of 791/1389, Sultan Barqūq, in response to an initiative of the rebels, abolished taxes to rally support for his tottering throne. Similarly, in 815/1413 to win the common people of Damascus to his side, a rebel emir canceled market fees and illegal duties. Emirs might also try to win support by acquiring a reputation for good deeds. At one time the populace of Aleppo interceded for the Emir Taghrīwirmish who had taken care of the grand mosque and earned the favor of the ulama and Sufis. In 865/1460–61 Governor Jānam, whose rebellion the hostility of the Damascus mobs had once defeated, set out on his return to win popular favor by good deeds. He saw to it that if a man's goods were stolen he got them back; or if the goods were found in the possession of a broker, he paid for them. Sympathies turned to him and the populace was won over. In this competition for favor the Sultan generally had the advantage of popular veneration for his office.[40]

The most important inducement offered by the Mamluks to the common people was the opportunity to plunder the property of defeated emirs. In tense civil war times, restless crowds stood hungrily on the edge of violent action, until official proclamations, affording immunity from prosecution, authorized them to plunder. The emirs made thieves of the common people in order to harass the enemy, destroy its fortunes, and of course reward the mobs for their assistance in the struggles. The right to plunder was simultaneously a means of guiding the impulse to violence in ways beneficial to the Mamluks and of rewarding the commoners for their assistance.

Thus in 673/1274–75, Sultan Baybars gave the properties of a disgraced emir over to plunder, and in 742/1341–42 the common people plundered Emir Qawsūn, taking their revenge for the execution of a number of commoners he had caught trying to rob his property. Ever after pillage accompanied the disgrace of emirs or civil war among the Mamluks. There were episodes in 748/1347–48 in Damascus and in 752/1351, 759/1358, and 761/1360 in Cairo when neither houses, religious endowments, nor shops of emirs were spared. Skirmishing in Cairo in 768/1366–67, 769/1367–68, 770/1368–69, 781/1379–80, and 782/1380–81 also called the common people to plunder, and in the great civil wars around the turn of the century, in 792/1390, 800/1397–98, 802/1399–1400, and 803/1400–01 the common people again looted houses of defeated emirs. Other sporadic episodes occurred in the fifteenth century. So much was pillage expected in civil wars that in 872/1467–68 the crowds got out of hand and plundered a fallen emir without the permission of the Sultan or any high official.[41]

Generally, pillaging was a special circumstance and both the inspiration and the opportunity were created by the Mamluks themselves. Permission to pillage served them well, for it created bonds of complicity and a syndrome of expectations which tied the mobs to the will of the emirs. Hope of spoils, and the irregularity and uncertainty of the benefit, sensitized the masses to cooperation with the regime. It did not, however, foster lawlessness or render the notables insecure in their own holdings, but on the contrary, it worked to protect the victors by satisfying greed at the expense of the losers.

The behavior of the common people in these situations is important evidence about the character of the population involved. The working population, the common people proper, indulged in looting only when authorized by the Mamluks in circumstances of civil wars. Their pillaging was almost entirely directed against defeated emirs, and the markets and property in general were safe. Occasionally hunger would lead to the looting of bread shops in time of famine; other social stresses might provoke attacks on Christians and foreigners. But even religious and social resentments which resulted in the plunder and destruction of churches and synagogues never went so far as pillage of non-Muslims generally for the sake of robbery alone. The Mamluks were able to protect the minorities by subjecting them to state organized extortions or limited punishments as a substitute for mob violence. Social tensions might also result in assaults on foreign merchants or ambassadors, European or Persian, but these situations mark the limits of pillage by the common people. They were not a wholly unruly mob of thieves, and unlike the beggars, slaves, and thieves of the city who formed the lumpenproletarian class may be distinguished by their restraint. Unlike the criminal and lumpenproletarian elements, the common people proper were never a threat to property as such.[42]

Aside from such simple temptations, other important social conditions influenced the ability of the emirs to form parties among the common people. We have mentioned the divisions in Damascus and Aleppo. Citizen-bedouin antagonisms also influenced the formation of party ties. Emirs who relied on bedouin auxiliaries for support were likely to find themselves embroiled with the townsmen. For example, Turkoman intervention on the side of rebellion in 753/1352 may have influenced the Bānaqūsā quarter of Aleppo to join the rest of the city in resisting the rebels, while in the Damascus area, the common people also fought and captured Turkomans. Aleppo in 810/1407 resisted a Dulghādir attack for similar reasons just as in 842/1438–39 it opposed Taghrīwirmish because his rebellion represented a bedouin assault on an urban community. At another time, in Damascus, fighting broke out between townsmen and bedouin tribesmen brought in to support the claims of one of the contending factions. The populace taunted the tribesmen, stoned them, and killed their sheikh in a welling over of resentment at the arrival of bedouins to police and lord it over townsmen.[43]

Thus in summary, all truly military actions in which the populace took part were organized by the Mamluks. Lack of inner organization and the diversionary claims of the Mamluks stood in the way of popular militias. The populations of the cities were capable of resentful rebellions, but without independent military organization, the effectiveness of popular protests was limited and subject to manipulation. Moreover, the most potent weapon of the common people short of military revolution—the threat of attack on property—was diverted and scarcely used at all save at the behest of the Mamluks. Mass grievances against the established order were satisfied by the occasional sacrifice of the houses and possessions of emirs marked out in any case for elimination. The use of violence by the masses was diverted from any permanent or revolutionary achievements. The common people were a force to be reckoned with, but not an interest to be consulted.

THE CONTROL OF LUMPENPROLETARIAN VIOLENCE

Another threat to the established pattern of social organization came not from the common people, the masses of the working population, but from the lumpenproletarian elements. Limited in its capacities to express and satisfy the economic claims of the common people, Muslim-Mamluk urban society also fell short of incorporating marginal social bodies into the ulama-centered social order. Lumpenproletarian groups resisted assimilation to the nexus of economic, social, and religious ties which unified the rest of the society. Criminal and racketeer elements, runaway slaves and soldiers, and begging Sufi "friars" organized counter-societies in defiance of official ties. The result was criminal violence, but the facts of murders, thefts, extortions or the wine, hashish, and prostitution rackets are not themselves of interest to us. We are concerned, rather, with the ways in which criminal activity was organized in relation to the rest of society, and the means by which it was prevented from totally disrupting urban life. In some respects, criminal violence was even made to serve Mamluk interests in the control of urban society.

In times of political and social hardship organized gangs of criminals called *al-mansīr* or *al-ḥarāmiyya* came to the fore in Mamluk cities. In Damascus in 695/1296, a gang of forty men broke into the markets to the astonishment of bystanders who first mistook the band for a wedding procession. Especially in the last decades of Mamluk rule when the weakness and absorption of the regime in foreign wars gave thieves greater scope for their depredations, these gangs were active in Cairo and Damascus. Groups of up to one hundred men led by a *kabīr* or *ra's* attacked isolated sanctuaries and cemeteries making life on the periphery of the city all but impossible, and invaded the quarters of the cities, demanding protection money and often selecting particular houses for plunder. Conceivably, they were hired for assassinations or were motivated by feuds of their own, though generally pure brigandage was the reason. Other relations with the populace of the towns are obscure, but an episode in Damascus suggests some connection of criminal gangs to quarters of the city. In 916/1510–11, the head of such a gang (called *mansīr al-ḥarāmiyya* in this case), a doorkeeper, was seized with some of his followers and fined for having sullied a review of the *'arīf* of his quarter. The source is too cryptic for us to fully see the relation of the gang to the quarter, but suggests that the chief and his followers were reviewed, and were expected to muster for review by the *'arīf* of their quarter. Are the thieves in this case to be identified with the *zu'ar,* or are they a separate and officially recognized organization? We cannot say.[44]

Gangs of black slaves as well as thieves created their own social organizations, and troubled the cities by pillaging. At the very beginning of the Mamluk period Negro stable hands and pages ran amuck in Cairo stealing weapons and horses. Under the heretical banner of a man named Kūrānī, possibly a Sufi sheikh, they rebelled as Shi'ites against the officially Sunni society. In the fifteenth century, the decline of the Mamluk state and its powers of discipline over its own troops and retainers again permitted the slaves to get out of hand. As slaves drifted away from the households of their masters in Cairo, slave riots became frequent occurrences. With the old cadres ruptured, efforts to establish new organizational forms appeared, and a curious report tells of how renegade slaves set up a government of their own, replete with officials and an enthroned Sultan to rule absolutely and judge among them. They offered refuge to other slaves, ransomed their fellows, and may have numbered as many as two thousand men. Surprisingly, this shadow state maintained discipline among its own members, and for a time according to some accounts was not a threat to public order. Eventually, however, following the inevitable history of politics, the slaves divided into opposing bodies led by rival claimants to a beggar's throne. The fugatives, now disunified and troublesome, were seized by their masters, and sold and exported to Turkey. Perhaps in the slaves' minds there was magic in imitating the state, not for any political purpose, but to ease the inchoate yearning of men isolated and abandoned to find some solidarity, belonging, and dignity.[45]

Slave gangs also troubled the cities by pillaging. Slaves joined in the fighting of emirs, and slave riots in Cairo, often provoked by shortages in food supplies or delays in salary payments, ended in stealing turbans, raiding shops, and even attacking the women's baths. Tensions between the blacks and the Mamluk recruits seemed particularly high, and led to serious street battles. Slaves were thus forbidden to bear weapons, and the Mamluks urged not to look for trouble either.[46]

The regime was, of course, responsible for the suppression of crime and violence, but there is reason to believe that the attitudes of emirs were sometimes ambiguous. Governors in charge of police often gave a free hand to evildoers and thieves. In 728/1327–28, the governor of Cairo sold "deputyships" for a hundred dirhems a day and allowed the purchasers to recoup as they might. At another time, in 864/1460, the governor of Cairo gave Mamluk thieves a free hand, claiming that he had no jurisdiction over them. He was accused of being an *ḥarāmī* himself. Other emirs may also have found the criminal gangs of use as hired assassins.[47]

More openly, the Mamluks tolerated and even profited from certain other criminal activities. Taverns, prostitution, and hashish were taxed even though the tax farms were strictly speaking illegal. However often ordinances were issued to abolish the farms, and however bitter the protests of the respectable ulama, the weaknesses of men and the immense value of the farms kept them in existence. In the latter part of the thirteenth century and in the early decades of the fourteenth, Cairo tax farms on wine and prostitution were worth a thousand dinars a day. The Damascus farm was worth 700,000 dirhems a year to the state, and a million to the tax farmers, and the tax there was even part of the salary of the governor. At Tripoli in 717/1316, the tax on prostitution brought in 70,000 dirhems a year. The Sultan himself was not above profiting from the illicit trades. His privy purse controller made 30,000 dinars a year on the wine imported into Alexandria and until the destruction of a Cairo prison, *al-khizānat al-bunūd* in 744/1343–44, the Sultan profited from the production of 32,000 jars of wine annually, pork sales, and prostitution organized by the prisoners.

None of the frequent cancellations of the tax farms put an end to the role of the regime in vice. At the beginning of the fifteenth century there was still a tax on prostituted slaves. In 826/1423 the governor of Damascus resisted efforts of a qadi to abolish the tax on wine making, and in 831/1427–28 and 868/1464 the bureaus for the wine and hashish taxes were again ordered closed. In 876/1471–72 the governor of Cairo was still behind prostitution and other emirs profited from the wine trade.

This taxation was important not only for revenues, but for the complicity which it created between the emirs and the underworld. Access to lumpenproletarian realms was the basis of control, and as we shall see, for the potential utilization of criminal activity to embarrass the rest of the urban population and enforce its dependence upon the Mamluks.[48]

There were other sources of organized and criminal violence in Mamluk cities, of which the *zuʿar* of Cairo are a noteworthy example. Though they bear the same name as the *zuʿar* of Damascus, the very incomplete evidence we have suggests that they were different in character, more properly a lumpenproletarian group and less closely attached to local society than the *zuʿar* of Damascus.

In Cairo, the *zuʿar* appear almost wholly as criminals and thieves recruited among slaves and servants, some of whom were free men and others not. The first episode in which the term is used describes how eunuchs, slaves, and *zuʿar* came to blows in the Cairo baths, and how the outbreak led to the pillaging of shops. Evidently this was carried out with impunity for the pillagers were saved by their friends from arrest. The *zuʿar* were organized into gangs of thugs who sometimes fought each other in broad daylight to the consternation of the Mamluks. Gangs of *zuʿar* were also known in Alexandria. In 803/1400 a gang, led by a *kabīr* named Abū Bakr who was a slave, was hired to intimidate a sheikh who had refused to yield to extortionate demands. Another source reports that the gang was hired to assassinate the governor who seized and beat Abū Bakr and reported the machinations of his enemies to Cairo.[49]

The main activity of these gangs was to hire themselves out as auxiliaries of the Mamluk factions in time of civil war for the sake of gifts and above all for a free hand to plunder the quarters and markets of Cairo. The *zu'ar* fought for Sultan Barqūq on his accession, stoned his enemies, pillaged their houses, and were in turn protected by the Sultan from arrest or harassment by the governor of the city. The fighting of 791/1389 gives the most complete picture we have of their activities. The outbreak of civil war set the *zu'ar* and other thieves free to terrorize the city. By order of the Sultan weapons were distributed to the *zu'ar* and *al-'āmma* (the common people) to strengthen his hand against the rebellious army from Syria. The *zu'ar* joined the fighting emirs but in the tumult, with the governor of Cairo too occupied to restrain them, they were free to roam the city. The markets and *qayṣariyyas* were guarded, but the *zu'ar* filled the center of Cairo and plundered soldiers of their clothes and weapons. So long as Barqūq held the upper hand there seems to have been some restraint, but with the tide of battle turning in favor of Yalbughā al-Nāṣirī, the *zu'ar,* and other thieves and riffraff, the dregs of the common people, joined Turkomans brought from Syria to attack the houses and stables of emirs, and plunder the quarters of Cairo. The *zu'ar* even set the prisoners, peasants and assassins both, loose on the city. Emirs, notables, merchants, and Jews were attacked. Eventually, however, the city organized to defend itself. The quarters arranged patrols, and merchants appealed to the regime for protection. With the termination of the fighting between Barqūq and Yalbughā al-Nāṣirī, Cairo had a brief respite.

A second round of troubles began with the outbreak of fighting between the factions of the victorious rebels. Minṭāsh to support his rebellion against Yalbughā gathered commoners, *zu'ar,* and thieves, personally appealing to them for support. While *al-'āmma* fought for him, the *zu'ar, al-ḥarāmiyya,* and other thieves set out to plunder. To keep their cooperation Minṭāsh called on the *zu'ar,* wrote down their names and quarters, appointed *'arīfs* (syndics), and distributed 60,000 dirhems. They were only further emboldened to steal and kill. With order again breaking down, the common people appealed for protection and the notables demanded the dismissal of the governor and the suppression of the *zu'ar.* Guards were again posted in the quarters, and finally eight *zu'ar* chiefs from al-Ḥusayniyya and six from al-Ṣalībiyya quarters were arrested. They were imprisoned, and the *zu'ar* were henceforth forbidden to bear arms. In the following year, however, at the defeat of Minṭāsh, rioting again broke out in Cairo and the Turks, *zuʿar,* and commoners pillaged the houses of the defeated party.[50]

This was not the last civil war which brought the *zuʿar* into action, fighting for the emirs and plundering the city. Such events took place in 801/1398, 802/1399, 813/1410, and 832/1428–29, and each time the *zuʿar* were joined by thieves to pillage vulnerable and especially outlying areas. A decade later Sultan Jaqmaq also purchased the support of the *zuʿar* and the common people in his struggle for the Sultanate and used them to pillage his enemies. In the latter half of the fifteenth century Cairo continued to be plagued by the *zuʿar* and subject to their riots and fighting. The *zuʿar* even fought the Mamluks. With the weakening of the regime, it became impossible to pacify Cairo, in part because the *zuʿar* were necessary auxiliaries in the Mamluk civil wars and infantry support for military expeditions. They were needed to fight the Ottomans, and once they were even paid thirty dinars a man to enroll in an expedition.[51]

Surveying these activities, are the *zuʿar* to be distinguished from other segments of the common people? Does the word have any more precise significance than other pejoratives such as *awbāsh* (lowly) or *ghawghā'* (rabble)? Does it in fact signify anything other than *al-ʿāmma*—the common people? Such words as *zuʿar, awbāsh, ghawghā'* and *al-ʿāmma* are very elastic, and are used both as descriptive and as pejorative expressions. Moreover, even though close examination of contexts suggests that the term *al-ʿāmma* is preferred for situations involving violent protests and demonstrations caused by widespread economic or communal grievances, and that the other terms are preferred in contexts involving more purely criminal acts, it often seems impossible to say whether the word chosen is governed by the character of the participants or by the nature of the events. We can not always be sure *al-ʿāmma* always means working people, for surely many food and tax riots brought lumpenproletarians into the streets. Nor can we be sure that the use of *awbāsh, ghawghā',* or *zuʿar* excludes the workers and market people from participation in criminal acts. Still, some contexts do make clear distinctions about the character and roles of the participants, and there is evidence to suggest that the term *zuʿar* is at least sometimes used to refer to a specific sub-group, and not to troublemakers in general.

Moreover, some evidence points to special *zuʿar* solidarities. Apart from gangs, the *zuʿar* of Cairo were associated with certain quarters of the city. In particular, they came from al-Ḥusayniyya, a large district outside the walls of the city, beyond the Bāb al-Naṣr and near the cemeteries. Al-Maqrīzī, in his description of Egypt, reports that al-Ḥusayniyya was settled by refugees from Mesopotamia and Syria fleeing the Mongol invasions in the thirteenth century. Of course by the fifteenth century it was thoroughly built up, and emirs made it their residence, but al-Ḥusayniyya continued to be socially as well as geographically a marginal district. In 864/1460, for example, statistics on deaths in Cairo did not include this quarter or a count of burials in its cemeteries. Another district with which the *zu'ar* were identified was called al-Ṣalībiyya, but we know nothing about it save that it was the name of a street of shops. Precisely what part the quarters played in the lives of the *zu'ar* is unclear. The chiefs of the *zu'ar* were well enough established in their districts for the Mamluks to make the quarters responsible for their arrest after the rioting of 791/1391, but there is no further evidence about organization within the quarters.[52]

Another episode, however, also suggests distinct *zu'ar* organizations related to the quarters of the city. In 790/1388, to celebrate the restoration of Barqūq to the Sultanate, decorated wooden castles were built in each quarter of Cairo. The people named a governor for each of these stands and created officials and a postal service for communication between the quarters. Ceremonials imitated the trappings of the state. This horseplay, however, soon led to mischief by the *zu'ar* and people of al-Ḥusayniyya, and the Sultan ordered the decorations and mock castles torn down. May we see the quarters as the locus of *zu'ar* organizations which in this case mimicked the forms of the state to achieve a fuller and more independent social life than that afforded by their gangs?[53]

There is one final indication of special, organized solidarities among the Cairo *zu'ar*. In 770/1368–69 the *ghawghā' min zu'ar al-'āmma,* literally "the rabble of the *zu'ar* of the common people," gathered outside of Cairo in the area of the Bāb al-Lūq for games called the *shalāq*. A man was killed, and the troops flogged several people. Outraged, the common people gathered beneath the citadel to protest the governor's actions to the Sultan. They stoned the governor and the crowds were ridden down by the Mamluk horsemen.

The interest of the episode lies in the association of the *zu'ar* with the *shalāq*. The *shalāq* were games we know were played at Aleppo in the thirteenth century. Aleppo was divided into two factions for the games, and as we have seen, the factions may have been associated with the later moieties into which the political and social struggles of the Mamluk period divided the city. The participation of the *zuʿar* in the games of the *shalāq* suggests, though no confirmation is yet available, associations of some political and social consequence. Young men's gymnastic clubs of the sort common in the Persian world come to mind. The evidence on the *zuʿar* of Cairo, however, is not adequate for us to reach any more definite conclusions.[54]

The Cairo *zuʿar,* then, were riotous lumpenproletarian gangs, quite probably a fairly distinct body within the general population. Compared with the *zuʿar* of Damascus their association with the quarters seems superficial, and their organizations very much less developed. When Minṭāsh sought to raise *zuʿar* help in Cairo he had to make lists of individuals and appoint commanders for the *zuʿar* whereas in Damascus the *zuʿar* of the quarters were previously organized and enrolled and reviewed by the Mamluks as units. Moreover, the Cairo *zuʿar* were a still less reputable part of the population than their Damascus counterparts. They were associated with slaves and thieves while the *zuʿar* of Damascus included shopkeepers and minor religious figures as well. The two groups may represent variations in the form of young men's associations, with the Cairo *zuʿar* belonging to a less highly structured social world while the Damascus *zuʿar,* though an aberrant body, showed more highly institutionalized organization and relations to the rest of society. However, to a degree, they played analogous roles in the politics of the city. As in Damascus, the Sultan and the emirs abetted *zuʿar* violence in Cairo, for they needed help in both civil and foreign strife and were willing to buy that help by permitting the *zuʿar* to prey on the rest of society. *Zuʿar* violence was taken under the aegis of the Mamluks and turned back against the larger society, and their proclivities ran to collusion with the Mamluks rather than the defense of the respectable elements of society against the regime. What organized forces existed among the masses were thus contained within the existing political order.

The public activities of another lumpenproletarian element show the same tendencies to violence and similar Mamluk efforts to channel this violence for their own ends. These were the *ḥarāfīsh* who were beggars found in all the major cities of the region—Cairo, Damascus, Aleppo, Jerusalem, Mecca, Homs, and Hama. They lived in houses, booths, mosques, and on the streets. In Jerusalem there was even a place called the steps or way of the *ḥarāfīsh*. Some of them, however, seem to have lived or roamed in rural districts outside the cities.[55]

The *ḥarāfīsh* lived on the largess of the Sultan, emirs, and the rich. In times of famine they were among the poor souls gathered to be fed by the charity of the Sultan, or along with the poor Sufis and other beggars to be distributed among the emirs. In 662/1264 and in the great famine of 775–76/1373–75 such provision was made to feed the *ḥarāfīsh* who were ordered, on pain of death, not to appeal for further alms. Even apart from such crises, the Sultan and emirs frequently gave them alms. To celebrate the circumcision of his son, Sultan Baybars invited emirs, soldiers, and his subjects to bring their children to be circumcised on this joyous occasion. To each child of a *ḥarfūsh* he gave one hundred dirhems and a sheep. Distributions of alms were also common without special cause. At the end of the Mamluk period, *ḥarāfīsh* in Cairo, both men and women, received two silver coins each. Leading emirs also made it a practice to give alms, and the emir Ṭushṭu of Damascus had a large following among the *ḥarāfīsh* to whom he gave generously. Visiting dignitaries, such as the Tatar ambassadors of 732/1332, eager to ingratiate themselves in Cairo, gave gifts to the Sultan and alms to the Sufis and *ḥarāfīsh*. Finally, provision was once made for them in waqfs. In 748/1347 a waqf was left in Damascus for their relief.

Despite organized alms giving, Cairo and other towns teemed with *ḥarāfīsh* who begged in mosques and from passers-by on the streets. They used to cry out, cursing vilely, to the embarrassment of respectable Muslims. In the mosques their loud shouts sometimes interrupted the prayers until they were silenced by gifts. They were, as may be imagined, miserably poor, and many are known to have died of exposure during unusually cold Cairo winters.[56]

Surprisingly, however, *ḥarāfīsh* are described as able-bodied men, unemployed by force of circumstances and more probably by intention. Begging was their regular work, but often they were called to hard labor. *Ḥarāfīsh* were impressed in 723/1322–23 to labor on the canals, and so many were rounded up that they were no longer to be found in Cairo. A decade and a half later they were again taken from their usual haunts and set to work without pay hauling dirt alongside prisoners, but in 748/1347–48 the policy of the government changed and all workers were offered a dirhem and a half and three loaves of bread a day. Not only was the hardest labor assigned the *ḥarāfīsh,* but the most distasteful. In the Cairo plague of 694–95/1295–96 the *ḥarāfīsh* brought in abandoned bodies for a quarter of a dirhem or buried them at night for half a dirhem. They were menials who could be bought by retailers and peddlers to capture and remove dogs from the city, a task the shopkeepers disdained for themselves. These were tasks for the *ḥarāfīsh* because in the eyes of the respectable to be one of the *ḥarāfīsh* meant not only to be poor, but to be depraved, barbarous in speech and dress, an hashish addict—the lowest of the low in the mélange of the urban lumpenproletariat. They were called the *sūqa*—the rabble of the towns.[57]

In the thirteenth and fourteenth centuries, these beggars and menials formed a turbulent and dangerous mob. At the capture of Antioch in 666/1268, *ḥarāfīsh* plundered the city. In 680/1281, *ḥarāfīsh* who came with the army from Cairo plundered the army's supplies of food, weapons, and clothing when the regular forces left them behind and went out to fight the Mongols. A generation later in 699/1299–1300 they began to plunder Damascus at word of the defeat of the Mamluk armies by Ghāzān. They stole woodwork, doors, marble, and utensils, disposing of them at low prices, and plundered the gardens in outlying villages. Three years later another Mongol invasion renewed fear of plundering by the *ḥarāfīsh*. Decades later their strength appears undiminished. In 738/1338 in the absence of the governor, some seven hundred *ḥarāfīsh* complained to a high ranking emir that they had been abused by his horsemen. To avoid further trouble the emir sent troops out of the city rather than test the will of the riotous *ḥarāfīsh*. Ibn Baṭṭūṭa estimated that there were thousands of them at about this time. A decade later, however, when alms distributions resulted in riots, the governor dealt harshly with the plunderers, mutilating some, executing others, and dispersing the rest to Homs, Hama, and Aleppo.[58]

In Cairo as well as Damascus, *ḥarāfīsh* riots were feared. They joined in the popular riots which destroyed Christian churches in 721/1320–21, and in the grain crisis of 736/1336 *ḥarāfīsh* as well as other commoners attacked hoarders. Some years later, *ḥarāfīsh* were rounded up and jailed to prevent them from taking advantage of a great conflagration by looting the city while it was engaged in fighting the fire.[59]

While the *ḥarāfīsh* generally constituted an unruly element in the life of the towns, the force of these beggars, like that of other popular elements, was in some circumstances actually of use to the Mamluks.

Generosity in alms giving created a claque in the city mobs for favored Sultans and emirs. In 697/1298 *ḥarāfīsh* clamored in the streets at the passing of the Sultan to wish him well for recovery from an accident. At another time they joined mobs which supported the return of Sultan Nāṣir Muḥammad in 709/1309–10 and hooted and stoned the anti-Sultan, Baybars II, when he was forced to flee the city. *Ḥarāfīsh* in 740/1339–40 again demonstrated in the markets singing their songs at the fall of al-Nashū, the Sultan's oppressive minister. Unfortunately, the inspiration and circumstances of this seemingly political demonstration are unknown.

Ḥarāfīsh were also loyal to favored emirs. In Damascus in 727/1326, the emir Ṭushṭu, imprisoned twice, was both times rescued by the clamor of mobs of *ḥarāfīsh* to whom he had generously given alms. In similar circumstances some decades later, the *ḥarāfīsh* and common people of Damascus gathered to congratulate the chamberlain on his release from prison. Presumably, he too had bought their support.[60]

Beggars, moreover, joined with *zu'ar* and other commoners to fight as auxiliaries in Mamluk civil wars. Recruited by the emirs, they fought and plundered on behalf of their sponsors. More regularly, the *ḥarāfīsh* were enrolled in the army for the counter-crusading wars in Syria and later for the invasions of Armenia.[61] The thrust of their potentially antisocial turbulence was put to the use of the Mamluks. By their indirect and incomplete patronage, the Mamluks were able to channel some of *ḥarāfīsh* strength into support of their own interests. Thus was this mob of beggars controlled in the fourteenth century.

By the fifteenth century, however, the portrait of the *ḥarāfīsh* began to take on new dimensions. The rough mob of the earlier epoch appears more and more organized into groups. Ibn Baṭṭūṭa referred to them as a *ṭā'ifa,* a group, in the early fourteenth century, but only later does evidence of their organization under the leadership of sheikhs or "sultans" become unmistakable. The first sheikh appearing in the chronicles was one Amīr 'Alī who was called sheikh of a *ṭā'ifa* of *jud'aydiyya* (beggars) and sultan of the *ḥarāfīsh.* He died in 791/1389. In 801/1398–99, the death of sheikh 'Abd-allāh, sheikh of the *ḥarāfīsh,* is mentioned in the sources. Sheikhs of *ṭawā'if* (societies) of the *ḥarāfīsh* appear again to organize the distribution of alms and the discipline of the beggar groups.[62]

It seems equally certain that the *ṭawā'if* of *ḥarāfīsh* were dervish orders. For example, in 875/1470–71 a delegation of commoners went from Jerusalem to Cairo to petition the Sultan, and one of the delegates was a man who took part in dervish rites. According to the chronicle, he beat the drum with the *ḥarāfīsh* and cried out like a horse. Furthermore, in 895/1490 the sultan of the *ḥarāfīsh* of Damascus went to Cairo where the Mamluk Sultan mediated a dispute between him and his wife and reconciled the couple. On his return to Damascus Ibn Sha'bān was greeted by *awbāsh* (low people) who beat drums, applauded his arrival, and raised up yellow banners, parading before him. His wife was similarly greeted by about two hundred women dressed in yellow headbands with the same ceremonial. The resemblance to dervish orders seems unmistakable.[63] In the fifteenth century, if not earlier, the *ḥarāfīsh* were organized fraternities of Sufi beggars.

Many individual *ḥarfūsh* or sheikhs of the *ḥarāfīsh* are described in ways which imply membership in a special fraternity. For example, a sheikh from a leading Damascus family who died in 688/1289 gave up teaching in a madrasa to become a *ḥarfūsh*—not merely a beggar—for the biography reports that he threw himself into a style of life imitating their dress and *ṭarīq* (habits or perhaps the Sufi way). He took hashish and became depraved in the view of the ulama, opting not only poverty but a new identity. Other evidence more firmly identifies the *ḥarāfīsh* as Sufi divines. In 801/1398–99, sheikh 'Abd-allāh, who spoke and dressed in the special fashion of the *ḥarāfīsh* and whose biographer considered him a heretic, died. This man lived in deserted mosques and celebrated in poetry a freely accepted, poverty stricken, lonely existence.[64]

However bizarre it may seem, these mendicant friars of the Muslim world were associated with the lumpenproletarian dregs of society. Being Sufis did not change their status or make them any less violent. In the fourteenth century the *ḥarāfīsh* were connected with despised menial laborers and so too in the fifteenth their cohorts were menials and criminals. One sheikh of the *ḥarāfīsh,* Ibn Fa'alātī, who succeeded to the chieftainship in 855/1451, came from a family of street entertainers and was himself brought up as a wrestler. Having acquired a bit of learning to distinguish himself from the common people, he rose to be the sheikh. In the delegation from Jerusalem, the *ḥarāfīsh* were joined by a burial worker and bath servant who collected dung for fuel, and worse, in Damascus in 888/1483 the sultan of the *ḥarāfīsh,* Sheikh Muḥammad Sha'bān, defended the wine and hashish places around the citadel against a party of pious sheikhs inspired by the injunctions of Islam. In response the religious sheikhs attacked the house of the sultan, the market inspector, and a leading emir and got hold of their enemy, whose fate is not described. Conceivably the Damascus *ḥarāfīsh* in defending the taverns and hashish parlors were protecting their own livelihood in the low life of the city. They were Sufis, but also vagabonds and street entertainers, divines who stood outside respectability and belonged socially and religiously to the marginal strata of urban society.[65]

On the other hand, the smattering of their ulama learning and Sufi affiliations brought to the lowest reaches of society at least some version of the Islamic religious world, and the *ḥarāfīsh* and their families remained in touch with the larger society. The son of a sultan of the *ḥarāfīsh* was an entertainer and minor scholar. Sometimes officials and emirs were called Ibn Harfūsh, which suggests a beggar's origin and subsequent rise to a regular place in society. The Sufi beggars served to hold the lumpenproletarians in touch with the larger social world of the cities.[66]

The improved organization of the beggars' orders in the fifteenth century facilitated their control by the Mamluk regime. Like the *zuʿar* and like the common people in general, they were limited by liaisons and patronage of the regime to actions which could be well accommodated and assimilated by the society. In the fourteenth century a loose patronage kept watch on the turbulent *ḥarāfīsh,* but in the fifteenth their chiefs, the sultans and sheikhs of the *ḥarāfīsh,* were in charge of their discipline. The title sultan of the *ḥarāfīsh* first appeared in 791/1389 when the sultan of the *ḥarāfīsh* was sent by the Mamluk Sultan with the armies of Syria to reconcile the vow of the army that it would not march without the Sultan with the unwillingness of the Sultan to go. The basic duty of the sultans of the *ḥarāfīsh,* however, was to supervise the distribution of alms and discipline the beggars. In 841/1438 when the anger of the Sultan was roused by their bad behavior he ordered the sultan and sheikhs of the *ḥarāfīsh* to forbid able-bodied men from begging, insulting passers-by, and embarrassing Muslims before their Christian and Jewish neighbors. Those who had no trade were to be put to work on the canals.

The sultans also organized the *ḥarāfīsh* for ceremonials. In 885/1480–81 *ḥarāfīsh* marched in the procession of a Damascus qadi who was being awarded a robe of honor, and at other times they joined the troops and qadis in welcoming visiting emirs to Damascus and presenting robes of honor. These ceremonial duties were regarded by the chronicler, Ibn Ṭūlūn, as an unprecedented breach of custom, but they seem to have quickly taken root. In 922/1516 the sultan of the *ḥarāfīsh* marched in a great Cairo military parade on the departure of an expedition to Syria, following after the ulama, the physicians, and the artisans. From his first joking introduction to the Sultan's armies in 791/1389, participation in ceremonies of state had become a regular duty of the *ḥarāfīsh* sultan.[67]

A final purpose for the organization of the beggars is intimated but nowhere spelled out in the chronicles. However much they belonged to the despised and marginal elements of the society, beggars had a profession. They were without work, but they earned a living, and to earn a living was to be subject to taxation. In the Ottoman Empire beggars were organized into guilds and subject to state discipline, and in medieval Europe beggars also formed guilds. So too, for Mamluk times, there are faint indications that beggars were organized in order to be exploited. Visitors to Cairo in the late fifteenth century remarked on thieves and prisoners going about chained together begging for alms because they were obliged to give the Mamluk Sultan two or three *madines* (silver dirhems) a day. The prisoners were farmed out to earn money for their jailers, and the *ḥarāfīsh* may have been used in a similar way. There is one instance mentioned in which pages of the Sultan's court took money from the *ḥarāfīsh*.[68]

Thus in the fifteenth century the loose patronage of the Sultan and emirs evolved into regular state supervision for the distribution of alms and ceremonial functions. From the appearance of the sultan at the end of the fourteenth century throughout the remainder of the Mamluk period, the *ḥarāfīsh* scarcely appear in their earlier violent roles. Better organized, they were better supervised as well.

CONCLUSION

The Mamluks who administered the towns by means of their tacit alliance with the notables consolidated their control by channeling all potential popular resistance into actions which bore no threat to Mamluk hegemony. Violent outbursts of the markets' populations were dissipated into all but fruitless protests. Resistance of the quarters was brought to heel by the satisfaction of immediate grievances and by winning the notables back to cooperation with the Mamluks. Even Mamluk civil wars failed to afford an occasion for popular uprisings against the regime because the Mamluks exploited the shortsighted greed of turbulent and miserable mobs to turn them against each other and against other Mamluk factions. As long as the opportunity to plunder was controlled by the Mamluks the masses could be manipulated in a way which forestalled their being organized against the regime. At the same time organized gangs of *zuʿar* and other marginal or criminal groups were manipulated to channel their potential for violent resistance to the state towards purely predatory and self-interested objectives. Atop the religious and class divisions of the cities, the Mamluks rendered the masses politically helpless by fostering their division into clienteles.

Thus, rebellions and crimes never sought to change the government but only to ameliorate specific wrongs. As such they belonged to an equilibrium of political actions among the Mamluks, their officials, the notables, and the various classes of the common people. The people were not utterly alienated, but only imperfectly assimilated into the society. They had severe grievances, but accepted limited objectives which could be accommodated by the Mamluks and the notables. A true proletariat, productive of new ideologies and communal forms, and so resentful of disinheritance as to wage war on the established order, never developed in Muslim cities. The *zuʿar,* the *ḥarāfīsh,* and the commoners generally all had interests in common with the Mamluk regime as well as in opposition to it. The politics of the excluded became part of the politics of inclusion. The lower classes were caught between violence and impotence.

CHAPTER VI · CONCLUSION: SOCIETY AND POLITY IN MEDIEVAL MUSLIM CITIES

In this study I have tried to examine the configuration of elements out of which the social and political life of Muslim Arab cities was built. The complexity of this pattern rises not only from diversity of classes and interests, but also from the various mechanisms by which city life was organized. Traditional social forms of action existed side by side with voluntary purposive associations. Legal and adjudicated norms were found together with rights and responsibilities ascribed by tradition and status. Bureaucratic organization and patronage-clientage bonds were simultaneously means of government. These forms are found in both Muslim and European cities, but the differences between European and Muslim towns cannot be summed up in the dichotomy of communes versus bureaucracy. Communes did not embrace all of the public life of European cities any more than the Mamluk state excluded all associational life. The commune should not conjure up images of democratic harmony, nor should the term "oriental despotism" evoke images of spiritless and prostrate towns.

European and Muslim urban societies had by the late middle ages evolved two differing over-all urban social configurations. Muslim society tended to be relatively undifferentiated. The innumerable roles which must be played in any functioning society were not the responsibility of specialized persons or agencies. All of the crucial political, economic, cultural, and religious roles of the society were entrusted to a broad and undivided class of professional, religious, and commercial notables. The extension of the Shari'a to virtually all communal concerns created one unspecialized stratum for the performance of adjudicative and administrative roles essential to the maintenance of society. Barriers of class stratification were reduced by relative ease of mobility and by the overlapping of the ulama with all the milieus and classes and communities of the cities. Even the isolated Mamluks married into families of ulama, shared the concerns of the ulama, and respected their values. Even the despised lumpenproletarian classes might be represented in the ulama by the disreputable sheikhs and Sufis who had at least some smattering of Islamic learning, and who represented in faint echo the basic ethos of the society. The ulama were diffused throughout the society. Through them all classes and groups found common social affiliations.

Other solidarity ties cut across class lines, and knit together men of diverse status and functions. Ties of patronage bound servants to masters, workers and craftsmen to customers, professionals to clients, and ultimately all men to the Mamluk state. Family, residence in a common quarter, and ethnic or religious community united men of high and low rank. Affiliation to the law schools, circles of sheikhs, scholars, and Sufis bound men of different station.

By contrast, European urban society was much more highly segmented. Strong cultural and emotional underpinnings supported interests and functions in dividing the classes of the society. The nobility was virtually a caste apart, with its own ethic, occupation, and internal system of feudal law and obligations. Even more than the Mamluks the nobles were divorced from contact with urban society. Their ties with the church were close, but ties with the bourgeoisie were scarcely formed. The church too was set apart from the society as a whole by its sacramental character and the special dedication and commitment of its members to the life of the world beyond.

Furthermore, the commercial classes, in a feudal and religious atmosphere hostile and unreceptive to commerce and the demeaning functions of earning a living from work or trade, developed their own interests and the cultural, legal, and familial systems essential to sustain their activities. Legal and professional classes in Europe also began to emerge as specialized and distinct groups. At another level, extremely close and exclusive guild ties isolated the artisanate from other classes.

The differences in social organization were at the root of important political differences. In the fluid situation of Muslim towns, public or political life was no more differentiated from the mass of religious, economic, familial, and communal concerns than were any of the other functions from each other. Public affairs fit into the comprehensive structure of these overlapping solidarity and functional ties. They were carried on by the part-time initiative of the society as a whole, and by its notables in particular. Public duties were left to the consultation of relevant parties. Traditional norms and pious principles, and the ties of obligation inherent in the system of relations as a whole, governed the carrying out of these initiatives. More specialized agencies could not exist.

In Europe, however, a highly divided society required formal agencies for the defense of special interests or the coordination of diverse interests within the towns. In Muslim society, which did not cultivate purposive voluntary associations, and whose social life was not so highly segmented as to foster a keen sense of isolation and independent objectives, communes could not develop. Administrative and bureaucratic forms of organization were equally irrelevant except for the central government. The personal loyalties essential to the Mamluk military system militated against it. Hierarchical management of the society was also impossible when administrators could not be found whose loyalties were basically with the regime. There was no base for administration, for there were no agents free of other roles, functions, and social commitments. Insofar as the cooperation of local notables was needed, it would have to be won on a different and unbureaucratic basis. In the Muslim world politics was not defined in terms of institutions or structures. Politics as the task of coordinating different purposes, people, and interests for the sake of some common goal was defined in terms of networks of overlapping and crisscrossing relationships which were typical of urban life in general.

Thus, political ties took the form of patronage-clientage relations, relations between two people such that one protected and sustained the other, who in turn provided his patron with certain resources or services. Patronage relations were in principle mutual, but they entailed an element of dependency for the client. While the patron had others who could supply the resources and services he needed, the client risked safety and his life if he abandoned the patron. In the towns we have studied, social interests were coordinated by the exchange of values between different levels of the society.

In this fluid system of political relationships the Mamluks and the Mamluk regime had a vital part to play. They became the focus of patronage ties which extended to every class of the society. The Mamluks governed not by administration, but by holding all of the vital social threads in their hands. They established direct ties to the ulama, high and low, to merchants, to the common people of the quarters and markets, and finally to the lumpenproletarians of the city. An alien caste of Turkish and Circassian soldiers, the Mamluks by their functioning in the society nonetheless became important participants. Moreover, the loose organization of the Mamluk state and its emphasis on a decentralized network of households accorded with the loose fabric of Muslim urban society, and even reinforced its basic disaggregative tendencies and its social and cultural bias toward unstructured social action. The Mamluks who preferred these decentralized means gave no encouragement to the formation of an organized opposition. Again contrast with Europe is illuminating. Struggles with the highly institutionalized empires of Germany, feudal principalities, or the Roman church encouraged the urban opposition to develop some institutional form to assure its own cohesion in the conflict. Faced with highly developed structures of political coordination, similar structures were essential to resist them.

The powers and the resources which sustained the leading role of the Mamluks stemmed from their economic preponderance in the cities. The Muslim towns depended for their food supply and raw materials on the productivity of their own hinterlands. The basic resources in the urban livelihood depended on control of the land, and in the total economy trade and commerce, though of great importance, were not decisive. Control over essential resources was vested in the Mamluk regime, and because the Mamluk households were located in the towns, mastery of the countryside was converted into direct political control of the cities. The Mamluks lived off the land, but they lived in the towns. Moreover, the state's powers of taxation were diverted to the leading Mamluk governors and officials. Rural wealth was delivered in kind to the emirs who became important intermediaries in the grain trade, and were permitted to exploit their marketing opportunities for personal gain. Similarly urban taxes were turned over to private farming by the Mamluks.

By contrast, the European cities avoided dependence on local feudal or imperial regimes. For them, trade and its secondary repercussions created an economic basis for independence. They did not depend on their immediate hinterlands, but sustained themselves by extensive trading activities which dealt not only in luxury goods but in food and raw materials. The great mercantile European cities found the goods to feed their populations and to keep them employed by hauling grain, meat, wine, salt, oil, cotton, and alum from abroad. Trade, moreover, indirectly strengthened the naval construction industries, and encouraged advances in manufacturing and banking techniques. These towns were more than a match for decayed imperial and feudal regimes which were forced to evacuate the towns, withdraw to the countryside, and relinquish direct control. In Europe, economic revolution and favorable political circumstances resulted in civic independence.

In Muslim towns the system of patronage ties emanating from the Mamluks prevented comparable developments. It had two main orientations. On the one hand, it was essential to enlist the cooperation of the notables of the cities in government. The professional middle classes, who had the necessary technical skills, social importance, and moral and religious prestige were indispensable intermediaries for the administration of the communities. Vis-à-vis the lower classes, the problem was different. Here the ties of the Mamluks to the common people and the lumpenproletarians were designed to curb and manage the potential for violence inherent in the masses. These two sets of intimate relations formed a pattern of government which prevented the development of alternative regimes.

In the first place, the Mamluks patronized the notables by the general maintenance of the urban community. They defended it in war, and they turned rural wealth to urban uses. The Mamluks built and maintained the water works, repaired streets and public spaces, invested in commercial properties, and above all endowed the religious, educational, and philanthropic life of the community. The ulama were dependent on the Mamluks for indispensable structural capital and great reserves of permanently endowed funds. More directly, they depended on the Mamluks for a large component of their status in the community. To be a notable meant to share in the authority of the regime and the right to make appeals and representations to the government. It meant access to offices and resources without which notables could not validate their potential leadership in the community as a whole. Without this access they would themselves be deprived of resources essential for maintaining their position as leaders of the populace.

Similarly, the Mamluks protected the interests of the merchant class. The security of trade in general depended on the state. Merchants also found employment in the households of emirs and the Sultan. By access to office, employment, and commercial opportunities the state conferred on the patrician merchant class some of the prestige and position it had in the larger community.

In return the notables gave the Mamluks their support. As the religious leaders of the society and the authoritative interpreters of Islamic law and values, the ulama recognized and legitimized the regime and persuaded the people to obey its commands. As the managerial, professional middle classes of the community, its judges, lawyers, property managers, and witnesses, they assisted the Mamluk regime in taxation and in the performance of the intricate administrative and adjudicative tasks which the regime itself was unable to comprehend. The merchant notables also aided in taxation and performed administrative and brokerage roles essential to the economy of the towns and the state.

Mamluk patronage, it should be emphasized, was not extended from the regime to the community as a whole. Except for the activities of the Sultan, Mamluks made their donations to the ulama not as a matter of state policy, but in accord with personal interests and objectives. Their contributions were given in particular places to particular circles of ulama, judges, and sheikhs who would administer and staff the institutions. Sometimes these were gifts to embellish quarters or districts of the towns. The notables, on the other hand, were not generally enrolled in a bureaucracy, but directly served the needs of the governors and the leading emirs. These personal ties between the contributing Mamluks and their clients were the key to the system.

The second set of supervisory and patronage ties ran directly to the masses of the common people. The Mamluks organized the military activities, public labor, and ceremonial responsibilities of the people of the markets. They enlisted them in civil wars by offering bribes and opportunities to plunder defeated emirs. The lumpenproletarians were equally well bound to the regime. By satisfying minimal objectives, conniving at criminality and violence, and employing the dangerous elements as supporters of the emirs, the Mamluks were able to channel and exploit the demands of the lowest classes. The strong organizations of bachelors, peripheral quarters of the cities, and criminals, slaves, and beggars were checked by appeasement and supervision.

These direct ties of the Mamluks to all classes created a configuration of relationships by which they ruled the society. Having enlisted the cooperation of the notables, atomized the common people, and contained lumpenproletarian violence, the Mamluks by the logic of these relationships prevented the formation of alternative configurations of rule.

On the one hand, the development of a unified and independent middle class was impossible. The emergence of the type of class associations on which the European communes had been based was impossible so long as many important notables found it in their interests to collaborate with the regime. On the other hand, Mamluk ties to all classes prevented a dangerous union of the notables and the lower classes which might exclude the Mamluks from effective control of the towns. Ulama cooperation with the regime deprived the populace of its natural leadership. Without the ulama effective resistance was impossible to organize. With the ulama only limited objectives would be countenanced. They led rebellion only to coerce the regime back within the limits required by the long-term safety of the community.

At the same time the Mamluks themselves cut off the ulama from the common people. By direct supervision and patronage of lower class elements they deprived the notables of universal support. The Mamluks even used their control of the masses to constrain the notables. Mamluk access to the nether world of the towns made them the ultimate arbiters of the use of violence. The notables were isolated from important elements of the lower classes and dependent on the Mamluks for security of person and property. Neither a cohesive middle class nor mass movements of notables and commoners were likely to develop in this situation. The Mamluks alone were the focus of a diffuse system of social and political relations which excluded the formation of other loci of aggregation.

This system of relations constituted the government of Muslim towns. It was a way of adapting Muslim urban society to Mamluk domination. By these relations an alien regime and the society it ruled came to interpenetrate and form one political and social whole.

APPENDICES · BIBLIOGRAPHY · NOTES · INDEX

APPENDIX A · WAQFS (ENDOWMENTS FOR RELIGIOUS, EDUCATIONAL, OR PHILANTHROPIC PURPOSES)

Date	Institution	Location	Donor	Property	Source
676	madrasa	Damascus	Sultan	grain, storehouse, pottery factory, houses, upper floors, khan, villages, qayṣariyya	**210**, XII, 230, XIII, 57-58.
682-83	madrasa	Cairo	Sultan	qayṣariyya, shops, bath, land rents	**61**, III, 46a; **166**, VIII, 8-9.
686	madrasa	Jerusalem	Sultan	building, upper floors	**208**, XLIII, 200.
686	madrasa	Damascus	wife of emir	village, bathhouses	**210**, XIII, 55-56.
689	khan		emir	khan	**186**, p. 3.
690	khan		governor	khan, shops, slaughterhouse	**221**, pp. 1-3; **210**, XIII, 98-100.
690	sanctuary	Hebron	Sultan	villages	**210**, XIII, 95-97.
695	tomb	Damascus	emir	shops, khan	**210**, XIII, 149.
695	madrasa khānaqā	Jerusalem	emir	ovens, mills, houses, soap factory, shops, paper factory, bath	**208**, XLIII, 214; **210**, XIII, 146-48.
696	school	Damascus	official	land, house, grain storeroom, upper floors, stable	**210**, XIII, 162-63.
696	khānaqā		emir	upper floors, khans, land	**121**, V, 286-87; **210**, XIII, 164-65.
699	khānaqā	Damascus	ulama	shops, mills, soap factory, land, hall, stores	**99**, p. 17.

APPENDIX A · (*Continued*)

Date	Institution	Location	Donor	Property	Source
703	mosque	Aleppo	emir	land, bath, houses	**110**, p. 71.
719	mosque	Ḥiṣn al-Akrād	emir	land, khan, bath, stores, oven, mill	**230**, p. 28.
719	school	Ḥiṣn al-Akrād	emir	buildings	**230**, p. 30.
722	madrasa	Damascus	emir	qayṣariyya, houses, upper floors, khan	**210**, XIV, 181-82.
723	mosque	Damascus	merchant	press, shops	**210**, XIV, 193-94; **121**, VI, 228.
727	tomb		wife of emir	land, shops, house, upper floors, stores	**210**, XIV, 234-35.
731	mosque	Damascus	governor	granary	**46**, p. 245; **34**, yr. 731; **39**, p. 26.
732	madrasa	Damascus	qadi		**119**, I, 431.
733	madrasa	Damascus	emir	house	**119**, I, 436.
734	tomb	Damascus	emir	villages	**119**, II, 231.
736	mosque	Tripoli	emir	gardens, stores, khan	**230**, pp. 87-88.
736	tomb	Tripoli	emir	upper floors, qayṣariyya, stores, land	**230**, p. 92.
736	mosque	Damascus	governor	shops	**46**, p. 492.
737	madrasa	Aleppo	emir		**23**, p. 212b.
738	school	Damascus	merchant	market, bath, lands	**176**, XIV, 181.
739	school	Damascus	governor	shops, rooms, stable, land	**121**, III, 315.
741	mosque	Safad	emir	upper floors, stables, bath, land	**210**, XV, 201-02.
749	mosque	Damascus	merchant	hall, khan, qayṣariyya, house, land rents, stable	**119**, II, 223-24.
749	mosque	Damascus	governor	qayṣariyya, baths	**176**, XIV, 223.
755	hospital	Aleppo	governor	villages	**101**, II, 103.

APPENDIX A · (*Continued*)

Date	Institution	Location	Donor	Property	Source
760	mosque	Tripoli	emir	shops, houses, oven	**230**, pp. 110-11.
773	mosque	Aleppo	emir	bath, oven, khan, press, shops	**110**, p. 170; **125**, II, 451.
775	madrasa	Tripoli	wife of governor	qayṣariyya, stores, upper floors	**230**, pp. 116-17.
782	zāwiya	Aleppo	emir	house	**123**, p. 114.
784	khānaqā	Damascus	emir	shops	**119**, II, 190.
786	madrasa	Damascus	merchant	hall	**36**.
786	mosque	Gaza	emir	hall, house	**217**, XI, 148-49.
787	madrasa	Aleppo	emir	house, stables, shops	**123**, pp. 100, 171.
788	sanctuary	Jerusalem	Sultan	caravansary	**208**, XLIII, 300.
797	mosque	Gaza	emir	qayṣariyya, shops, house	**217**, IX, 220-21.
799	mosque		Sultan	cash	**73**, p. 314b.
eighth	school	Gaza	emir	shops, mill	**217**, XI, 150.
cen-	madrasa	Akrād?	emir	wells, cistern	**217**, XI, 150-51.
tury A.H.	madrasa	Tripoli	wife of emir	soap factory, oil press, mill, market area, house, room	**230**, pp. 136-37.
	madrasa	Aleppo	merchant	khan, bath	**123**, p. 53.
	hospital	Tripoli	emir	house, markets	**230**, p. 34.
802	zāwiya	Damascus	official	shops, upper floors	**119**, II, 204; **121**, V, 394.
806	mosque	Aleppo	governor	stores, shops, qayṣariyya	**110**, p. 69.
808	madrasa	Damascus	emir	shops, land	**119**, I, 427.
813	madrasa	Damascus	emir	hall for oil	**119**, I, 233.
813	mosque	Damascus	emir	shops	**119**, II, 422.
817	madrasa	Damascus	khawājā merchant	house, qayṣariyya, shops, upper floors, stables, land	**75**, yr. 816.
818	zāwiya	Aleppo	merchant	bath, hall	**101**, II, 74.
820	mosque	Damascus	emir	shops, rents, gardens	**119**, II, 592; **111**, I, 61.

APPENDIX A · (*Continued*)

Date	Institution	Location	Donor	Property	Source
824	khānaqā	Damascus	emir	market, mill, khan	**121**, IV, 249.
824	khānaqā	Damascus	Sultan	baths	**121**, IV, 296.
824	madrasa	Aleppo	emir	market	**101**, II, 78.
826	school	Damascus	emir	house, stables, rooms, khan, shops	**121**, VI, 299-300.
829	madrasa	Aleppo	emir		**123**, p. 55.
833	mosque	Damascus	Sultan	cash	**119**, II, 407.
836	tomb	Damascus	emir	house, village	**119**, II, 231.
840	school	Aleppo	emir	land, market	**125**, V, 160; **211**, II, 359.
862	mosque	Aleppo	ulama	shops, land, khan, house	**101**, II, 100.
863	madrasa	Damascus	merchant	khan, hall, shops, upper floors	**121**, III, 264-66.
865	madrasa	Damascus	ulama	shops, house, land, rents	**119**, I, 412.
871	zāwiya	Aleppo	Sultan	house	**520**, pp. 259-63.
883	madrasa	Damascus	Sultan	shops	**29**, p. 72a.
890	madrasa	Damascus	emir	qayṣariyya	**185**, p. 35; **29**, p. 111a.
893	madrasa	Damascus	qadi		**54**, p. 183b.
ninth	tomb	Aleppo	emir	market	**123**, p. 127.
cen-	school	Aleppo	ulama		**123**, p. 131.
tury A.H.	madrasa	Aleppo	qadi	mills, qayṣariyya, bath	**101**, II, 111.
	khānaqā	Damascus	ulama	shops	**119**, II, 164.
	mosque	Aleppo	khawājā merchant	soap factory	**123**, p. 52.
	khānaqā	Aleppo	governor	khan, village, bath	**123**, p. 114.
	zāwiya	Aleppo	emir	market, villages	**123**, p. 120.
910	zāwiya	Damascus	ulama	bath	**181**, p. 279.
921	zāwiya	Damascus	ulama	house	**181**, p. 387.

APPENDIX B · INSTITUTIONAL CONSTRUCTIONS AND REPAIRS—DAMASCUS

Date	Type	Builder	Comment	Source
658	zāwiya	Sultan	in citadel	**106**, p. 40.
661	zāwiya	ulama		**111**, I, 194.
662	mosque	emir	restored 803-04, 846-47	**525**, p. 66; **210**, XII, 87-88.
663	ribāṭ	emir		**119**, II, 193.
665	madrasa	emir		**106**, p. 245; **119**, I, 441.
668	mosque	governor		**105**, p. 78.
668	Umayyad mosque	Sultan	1,000 dinars for marble	**106**, p. 79.
670	ribāṭ	merchant		**115**, pp. 156-58; **106**, p. 196.
674	madrasa	ulama		**119**, I, 275.
677	madrasa	governor	cost 60,000 dirhems	**188**, I_2, 162; **166**, VII, 97.
677	madrasa	emir		**119**, I, 468; **79**, p. 122b; **10**, I, 76b; **13**, II, 62b.
677	khānaqā	emir		**119**, II, 161-62; **64**, p. 177a; **166**, VII, 119.
677	khānaqā	emir		**119**, II, 171; **166**, VII, 116.
678	Umayyad mosque		repairs	**10**, I, 84b.
679	zāwiya	ulama		**111**, I, 196.
680	madrasa	ulama-official		**176**, XIII, 296; **210**, XII, 228; **13**, I, 66a; **119**, I, 496; **10**, I, 102b; **79**, p. 171b.
682	school			**119**, I, 74.
682	hospital	Sultan	with waqfs	**525**, p. 52; **210**, XIII, 13.
684	zāwiya	ulama		**111**, I, 193.
686	medical school			**119**, II, 133.

APPENDIX B · (*Continued*)

Date	Type	Builder	Comment	Source
686	school	wife of emir	waqfs	**210**, XIII, 55-56.
687	madrasa	qadi		**115**, pp. 156-58; **119**, II, 8-9.
688	zāwiya	ulama		**111**, I, 196.
689	madrasa	merchant		**121**, III, 389.
690	madrasa	emir		**64**, pp. 183b-184a.
691	mosque	governor	in citadel	**10**, I, 183a-b.
693	mosque			**176**, XIII, 333; **103**, p. 153.
694	madrasa	merchant		**105**, p. 46; **103**, p. 197.
694	mosque	governor	built with bath and market	**34**; **14**, p. 117a.
696	school	ulama		**120**, p. 44.
697	school khānaqā	official		**176**, XIII, 351; **119**, I, 72.
697	khānaqā	emir		**210**, XIII, 164-65; **125**, IV, 532.
698	mosque			**14**, p. 123b.
698	ribāṭ, school	emir	house given as waqf	**176**, XIV, 4; **10**, I, 281a; **119**, I, 64; **34**.
699	khānaqā	ulama		**119**, II, 191; **99**, p. 17.
701	mosque	emir		**103**, p. 237.
701	school	ulama		**120**, p. 50.
702	madrasa	ulama	restored	**210**, XIII, 237; **176**, XIV, 30.
704	madrasa		repaired	**34**; **176**, XIV, 34.
704	mosque	ulama	converted church	**119**, II, 325.
706	mosque	governor		**176**, XIV, 42; **187**, II, 29-30; **203**, p. 153; **37**, I, 233; **119**, II, 435; **23**, p. 124a; **19**, p. 117a; **80**, IV, 123a-124a.
709	mosque	merchant	conversion of old building	**121**, VI, 237; **532**, II, 43.
710	zāwiya	ulama		**111**, I, 194-95; **119**, II, 202.

APPENDIX B · (*Continued*)

Date	Type	Builder	Comment	Source
717	madrasa	emir	restored; waqf	**34**.
718	mosque	official		**187**, II, 184; **119**, II, 416; **23**, p. 155a-b; **34**; **97**, p. 238; **38**, p. 118b; **3**, I, 4a.
718	mosque	governor		**176**, XIV, 84; **119**, II, 425; **23**, pp. 155a-b; **34**; **38**, p. 118b; **153**, II, 173; **3**, I, 4a-5a.
718	mosque	qadi		**203**, p. 182; **3**, I, 4a; **38**, p. 118b; **97**, p. 238.
719	Umayyad mosque		10,000 dirhem repairs	**34**; **10**, II, 295b.
720	mosque	ulama		**119**, II, 442; **176**, XIV, 96.
721	mosque			**34**; **97**, p. 238; **90**, II, 402.
723	school	ulama		**119**, II, 55.
723	mosque	merchant		**210**, XIV, 193-94; **121**, V, 276.
726	madrasa		with waqf	**48**, p. 19; **34**; **38**, p. 181a; **119**, I, 232.
728	school	emir		**119**, I, 59.
728	school	governor		**119**, I, 123; **176**, XIV, 133.
728	Umayyad mosque	governor	repairs	**38**, pp. 190a-b, 196a, 202b; **121**, VII, 214; **153**, II, 183-84; **46**, pp. 11, 152-53.
729	ribāṭ, school	official		**111**, I, 85-86; **176**, XIV, 147-48; **115**, p. 149; **119**, I, 96.
730	zāwiya	emir		**203**, p. 220.
730	Umayyad mosque	governor		**48**, p. 199.
730	ribāṭ	governor		**149**, IV, 101.
732	mosque	emir		**38**, p. 7a.
733	mosque	qadi	restored	**119**, II, 440.

APPENDIX B · (*Continued*)

Date	Type	Builder	Comment	Source
733	madrasa	emir		**119**, I, 436.
734	mosque	emir		**119**, II, 325; **176**, XIV, 168.
734	mosque	merchant-official		**176**, XIV, 167; **119**, II, 438-39.
734	mosque		restored	**34**; **210**, XV, 34-35; **46**, p. 369; **111**, I, 16.
734	madrasa			**48**, p. 372.
734	madrasa	merchant		**121**, IV, 460.
734	madrasa	merchant		**119**, II, 7-8.
735	school	merchant khawājā		**34**; **149**, IV, 115; **176**, XIV, 171; **120**, p. 39.
735	mosque	merchant, ulama	waqf	**176**, XIV, 171; **119**, II, 246; **182**, III, 18.
735	school	merchant		**121**, III, 286.
735	mosque		in citadel	**176**, XIV, 170; **119**, II, 442-43; **182**, II, 7.
736	mosque	emir		**48**, p. 498; **119**, II, 421.
736	khānaqā	emir		**48**, p. 504.
737	zāwiya	ulama		**111**, I, 196.
738	school	merchant	restored	**176**, XIV, 181; **119**, I, 128; **34**.
738	madrasa	emir		**532**, II, 43.
739	school	governor		**176**, XIV, 184; **210**, XV, 115.
740	mosque	governor	restored	**59**, p. 27b; **187**, II, 510; **23**, p. 223b.
741	minaret	governor	restored	**176**, XIV, 189; **210**, XV, 202.
741	khānaqā	emir		**119**, II, 168.
745	mosque			**203**, p. 247.
745	mosque	emir		**210**, XV, 241; **176**, XIV, 216.
746	school	emir		**119**, I, 128.
746	madrasa	emir		**119**, I, 236.
748	mosque	emir (governor)		**187**, II, 756; **119**, II, 423.
748	school	ulama		**111**, I, 155.
748	madrasa	emir		**105**, p. 46.
748	madrasa	emir		**115**, pp. 156-58.

APPENDIX B · (*Continued*)

Date	Type	Builder	Comment	Source
749	madrasa	merchant		**176**, XIV, 181; **39**, p. 49b.
749	madrasa	merchant		**176**, XIV, 227; **525**, pp. 68-72; **119**, II, 223-24.
749	mosque	emir		**176**, XIV, 228.
750	mosque	emir		**176**, XIV, 232-33.
751	madrasa	emir		**176**, XIV, 233.
751	school			**176**, XIV, 233.
757	mosque	governor		**176**, XIV, 256.
761	madrasa	emir	restored	**121**, IV, 248.
761	madrasa	emir		**176**, XIV, 269; **119**, I, 489.
762	madrasa	merchant khawājā		**1**, I, 68a; **180**, V, 182.
763	mosque-madrasa	emir		**119**, I, 600-03.
765	Umayyad mosque	Sultan-governor	repairs	**21**, I, 74a; **176**, XIV, 309; **56**, II, 7b; **25**, p. 427.
767	school	ulama		**176**, XIV, 315.
773	madrasa	emir		**26**, I, 4b.
774	madrasa	official		**90**, II, 104; **119**, I, 340.
776	mosque	emir		**119**, II, 444.
784	khānaqā	emir		**119**, II, 189.
790	mosque	merchant		**111**, I, 55-60.
794-95	mosque	emir	repairs	**177**, pp. 116a, 136a-137a.
796	mosque	merchant	repairs	**203**, pp. 204-205.
802	zāwiya	official	with waqf	**119**, II, 204.
802	mosque	emir		**119**, II, 204.
806	mosque	governor	restored	**22**, p. 196.
806 or 856	zāwiya	ulama		**111**, I, 203-05; **119**, II, 202-03.
808	madrasa	emir	with waqf	**203**, p. 200; **119**, I, 426.
809	mosque		restored	**525**, pp. 17-18.
811	mosque	emir		**203**, p. 245.
811	mosque	emir		plaque on site.
813	mosque			**203**, pp. 200-01.
813	mosque	emir	restored	**203**, p. 253; **119**, II, 422.
814	madrasa	emir		**119**, II, 232.
813-14	madrasa	qadi		**119**, I, 234.

APPENDIX B · (*Continued*)

Date	Type	Builder	Comment	Source
815	mosque		repairs	**119**, II, 401.
816	madrasa	emir	restored	**119**, I, 313.
816	khānaqā	qadi		**119**, II, 37-38.
817	madrasa	khawājā merchant	with waqf	**111**, I, 71-75; **119**, I, 150; **121**, III, 387; **115**, p. 150; **26**, II, 131b.
817	mosque	merchant		**119**, II, 428.
817	mosque	official	restored	**119**, II, 431; **203**, p. 224.
818	mosque	Sultan		**119**, II, 426.
819	mosque	emir		**203**, p. 198.
820	madrasa	emir	gift of waqf	**119**, I, 326; **111**, I, 61-63.
821	madrasa			**119**, I, 430.
822	khānaqā	emir		**121**, IV, 248; **180**, VI, 552.
824	mosque	emir	in citadel, repairs	**119**, II, 443.
824	zāwiya	emir	gift of waqf	**119**, II, 200-01.
824	mosque	Sultan	repairs	**46**, p. 108; **525**, pp. 7-8.
825	mosque	emir		**203**, p. 204; **523**, pp. 21-25.
826	school	emir	with waqf	**121**, VI, 299-300.
829	zāwiya	ulama		**203**, p. 208.
830	mosque		repairs	**119**, II, 406.
830	mosque	Sultan		**525**, pp. 76-78.
830	mosque	qadi		**119**, II, 428-29; **374**, p. 419.
831	minaret	qadi		**119**, II, 305; **525**, pp. 76-78.
832	mosque	emir	enlargement	**119**, II, 430.
833	school	qadi		**120**, pp. 25-26.
833	mosque		repairs	**119**, II, 407.
836	khānaqā	qadi	house given as waqf	**119**, II, 141-42; **111**, I, 184-87.
842	mosque	merchant		**121**, VII, 245, 278.
842	mosque	emir		**119**, II, 440.
844	mosque	khawājā merchant		**119**, II, 291-92; **203**, p. 253; **111**, I, 74-75; **121**, VI, 261-63.
847	school	khawājā, official		**111**, I, 71-75; **120**, p. 31.

APPENDIX B · (*Continued*)

Date	Type	Builder	Comment	Source
850	zāwiya	ulama (Sufi)		**111**, I, 206-07.
850	zāwiya	emir		**111**, I, 208.
850's	zāwiya	ulama		**111**, I, 201-02.
851	mosque	emir		**125**, III, 46.
853	school	khawājā		**119**, I, 9; **197**, p. 275; **30**; **111**, I, 71; **121**, V, 260-61.
857	mosque	emir		**203**, pp. 230-31.
860	mosque	ulama		**203**, p. 189.
862	khānaqā	khawājā merchant		**119**, II, 173-74; **203**, p. 257; **95**, IV, 117; **121**, V, 291.
867	madrasa-khānaqā	emir		**119**, I, 501; **111**, I, 53-54.
868	madrasa	merchant-qadi		**203**, p. 215; **525**, pp. 76-78; **120**, pp. 42-43.
870's	zāwiya	ulama	house	**111**, I, 202-03.
872	madrasa	qadi		**111**, I, 87-88.
876	mosque	emir	repairs	**54**, p. 88b.
878	mosque			**54**, p. 168a.
878	school	qadi		**120**, pp. 27-30.
879	mosque		reopened	**54**, p. 159a.
880's	zāwiya	ulama		**111**, I, 210.
884–86	Umayyad mosque	Sultan, emir	restored	**29**, pp. 75-96; **67**, pp. 58a-b; **7**, pp. 46-47b; **181**, pp. 5, 14, 34, 42.
885	mosque	emir		**203**, p. 210.
887	zāwiya	emir		**203**, p. 221.
887	madrasa	khawājā		**113**, p. 33.
888	madrasa	emir		**29**, p. 104b.
890?	zāwiya	khawājā		**111**, I, 209.
890	school	governor	restored	**185**, p. 35.
890's	zāwiya	ulama		**111**, I, 208.
891	zāwiya			**54**, p. 181b.
892	mosque	quarter	enlarged	**181**, pp. 77, 107.
892	madrasa	governor	waqf of house	**119**, I, 564-65; **203**, p. 244; **181**, p. 79.
893	minaret	Sultan	Umayyad mosque	**29**, pp. 147b-148a; **525**, pp. 17-18; **181**, pp. 54, 107.

APPENDIX B · (*Continued*)

Date	Type	Builder	Comment	Source
895	mosque	merchant and emir	repairs	**181**, p. 117.
896	mosque	emir	repairs	**181**, p. 137.
900	zāwiya	ulama		**111**, I, 209-10.
903	mosque	merchant	enlarged	**181**, p. 198.
905	zāwiya	qadi		**111**, I, 205-06.
906	mosque			**182**, IV, 22-23.
907	mosque			**203**, p. 231.
915	zāwiya	ulama		**111**, I, 210.
921	madrasa	governor		**185**, p. 135; **30**; **525**, pp. 76-78.
922	zāwiya	ulama		**119**, II, 217-18.
923	mosque	Sultan		**111**, I, 63-64.
923	madrasa			**525**, p. 66.
	zāwiya	ulama		**111**, I, 210.
	zāwiya	ulama		**111**, I, 209.
	mosque	merchant		**121**, VII, 277-78.

APPENDIX C · INSTITUTIONAL CONSTRUCTIONS AND REPAIRS—ALEPPO

Date	Type	Builder	Comment	Source
before 676	grand mosque	Sultan	repairs	**211**, I, 172; **125**, II, 336-37.
684	grand mosque	Sultan-governor	repairs	**166**, VII, 250; **210**, XIII, 41-42; **125**, II, 336-37; **211**, I, 172.
695	mosque	ulama		**210**, XIII, 120.
699–709	grand mosque	governor	repairs	**211**, I, 172; **142**, p. 97.
700–08	madrasa, ribāṭ, school, mosque	governor		**226**, p. 179; **210**, XIV, 33; **125**, IV, 581.
708	mosque	son of merchant		**101**, II, 101.
710	mosque	ulama		**210**, XIV, 45-46.
711	grand mosque	governor	repairs	**210**, XIV, 59; **101**, II, 243; **125**, II, 170, 337.
718–23	mosque	governor		**210**, XIV, 129; **211**, II, 325-26; **523**, p. 86; **110**, p. 67.
714–27	grand mosque	governor	repairs	**211**, I, 172; **142**, p. 97.
727	madrasa	qadi and Sultan		**110**, p. 67; **101**, II, 139; **125**, IV, 283.
731–39	grand mosque	governor	repairs	**211**, I, 172; **210**, XV, 75; **101**, II, 243, 248, 250.
733	mosque	emir		**210**, XV, 24; **125**, V, 558.
739	mosque	emir		**210**, XV, 115-16.
739	madrasa, khānaqā	soldier	repaired	**125**, IV, 511.
741	grand mosque	governor	repairs	**211**, I, 169; **210**, XV, 205; **101**, II, 242.

APPENDIX C · (*Continued*)

Date	Type	Builder	Comment	Source
742	mosque-tomb	emir		**125**, II, 403-04; **101**, II, 76.
743	mosque	emir	restored	**210**, XV, 236-37; **110**, p. 72; **125**, IV, 586.
743	madrasa	emir		**110**, p. 171; **101**, II, 373.
743	mosque	ulama		**125**, IV, 580.
before 745	madrasa	official		**149**, IV, 142.
748	mosque	merchant	restored	**123**, p. 141.
750	madrasa			**125**, V, 13.
751	minaret			**211**, II, 330; **110**, p. 72; **101**, II, 207-08.
755	hospital	governor		**101**, II, 103; **234**, pp. 49-51; **492**, p. 194; **520**, p. 178; **125**, II, 436; **110**, p. 67; **23**, p. 280a.
756	mosque			**125**, V, 18; **523**, p. 90.
765	madrasa			**211**, II, 340; **523**, p. 90.
769	mosque	governor		**211**, II, 344; **523**, p. 90; **24**, p. 49b; **69**, p. 35; **110**, p. 68; **25**, p. 439; **125**, II, 443; **101**, II, 109.
771	mosque, minaret		restored	**125**, V, 303.
773	mosque	emir		**211**, II, 347; **110**, p. 170; **125**, II, 451.
774	madrasa	emir	repaired	**211**, II, 347-48.
775	mosque		restored	**125**, V, 55.
777	mosque			**69**, p. 1.
778	school	ulama		**125**, V, 62.
780	mosque	ulama		**125**, V, 89; **211**, II, 350; **110**, p. 71; **101**, II, 381.

APPENDIX C · (*Continued*)

Date	Type	Builder	Comment	Source
782	khānaqā	official	north of city	**125**, V, 81.
782	zāwiya	official		**125**, V, 84.
786	school	merchant		**50**, I, 632; **125**, V, 92; **51**, II, 232b-233a; **90**, II, 353.
787	madrasa	emir		**125**, V, 94-95; **110**, p. 171.
788	mosque	governor		**211**, II, 353.
790	zāwiya	merchant		**101**, II, 74.
790's	mosque	emir		**110**, p. 68.
792	madrasa		restored	**523**, p. 91; **125**, V, 107.
796	madrasa	qadi		**211**, II, 354.
797	grand mosque	governor	repairs	**211**, II, 172.
797	mosque	emir		**211**, II, 356; **110**, p. 69; **125**, II, 481-82; **101**, II, 131-32.
799	zāwiya	ulama		**211**, II, 359-61.
801	mosque	emir		**211**, II, 362-66; **110**, p. 69; **523**, p. 92.
801	mosque			**523**, p. 92.
804	zāwiya	emir		**125**, V, 149-51.
807	zāwiya	khawājā merchant		**125**, V, 145-46.
809	mosque			**523**, p. 92.
811	mosque	governor	completion of work begun in 801	**125**, II, 512; **211**, II, 364-66.
819	hospital	governor	reopening	**211**, II, 367.
820	mosque, school	governor		**125**, II, 518; **110**, p. 172; **101**, II, 78.
820's	zāwiya	mamluk	repairs	**123**, p. 116.
824	grand mosque	governor	repairs	**211**, II, 172.
828	madrasa	qadi		**211**, II, 368; **523**, p. 93; **110**, p. 173; **101**, II, 111; **374**, p. 419.
828	mosque	ulama	repairs	**374**, p. 419; **101**, II, 333-34; **125**, VI, 103.

APPENDIX C · (*Continued*)

Date	Type	Builder	Comment	Source
830	mosque	governor	enlargement	**101**, II, 285-86.
831	zāwiya	official		**125**, V, 184.
833	madrasa	ulama	repairs	**374**, p. 420; **101**, II, 139-40.
840	hospital		repairs	**374**, p. 420; **503**, p. 110.
841	madrasa or zāwiya	governor		**110**, p. 172; **101**, II, 363; **125**, III, 41-42.
841	zāwiya	ulama		**125**, V, 221.
842 or 846	mosque	ulama		**125**, III, 38, V, 249; **211**, II, 379-380.
846	grand mosque		repairs	**211**, I, 172.
849	school	ulama	built in khānaqā	**125**, V, 239-41.
852	mosque	qadi	repairs	**125**, III, 48-49, V, 215-19.
854	mosque	ulama		**211**, II, 379.
854	madrasa	qadi		**101**, II, 105.
855	mosque	ulama		**101**, II, 67.
870	mosque	ulama		**211**, II, 382.
880's	madrasa			**125**, V, 308.
882	madrasa			**101**, II, 209.
883	mosque	governor	restored	**211**, II, 385; **101**, II, 131.
897	mosque	ulama	restored	**211**, II, 397; **125**, V, 341.
910	madrasa	emir		**125**, III, 115.
	zāwiya	merchant		**125**, V, 378-79.
	mosque	khawājā		**123**, p. 57.
920	mosque	emir		**234**, pp. 53-54.
ninth century A.H.	khānaqā	khawājā merchant		**123**, p. 117.
	mosque	merchant		**123**, pp. 52-53.
	mosque	merchant		**123**, p. 55.
	mosque	merchant		**123**, pp. 52-53.
	madrasa	ulama	restored	**125**, IV, 507-08.

APPENDIX D · KĀRIMĪ (MERCHANTS IN THE SPICE TRADE)

Each entry appears in the following form: the date of death and name of the merchant followed by his titles, offices, and ranks; the locality of his activities; his religious education or affiliations; and other information. References to the sources follow in parentheses.

700, al-Takrītī
witness; Yemen; nephew was witness and kārimī; gave loan to officials in 687. (**37**, II, 372; **152**, p. 57.)

700, Jamāl al-dīn
ṣadr; Yemen; son was kārimī. (**152**, p. 60; **189**, XX, 662; **362**, p. 106.)

703, Ibn 'Awaḍ
(**362**, p. 106; **210**, XIII, 248.)

705, Ibn 'Affān
(**362**, p. 107; **189**, XX, 620-22; **152**, pp. 132-33.)

707, al-Damāmīnī
ra'īs; Alexandria; muḥaddith; descendant was poet and professor, gave loan in 687. (**362**, pp. 107, 111; **41**, IV, 110a; **43**, p. 258; **37**, II, 372; **90**, III, 186.)

712 or 714, al-Takrītī
ra'īs al-kārimī, ṣadr, official; Alexandria, Yemen, India; muḥaddith, calligrapher; endowed madrasa, father of kārimī, honored by Sultan. (**90**, II, 406, 410; **50**, II, 9a; **51**, I, 9a; **34**, yr. 712; **362**, p. 109.)

713, Ibn Qayṣur
khawājā; Aleppo, China, Alexandria, Bagdad, India; father a Jew, started as tailor then traveling merchant, came to Egypt in 704 with 400,000 dinars in goods and 500,000 dirhems after paying a fine of 300,000 dirhems in Yemen, acquired six capital funds of 200,000 dinars and paid zakāt of 40,000 dinars, endowed madrasa or school in Alexandria. (**93**, p. 207; **362**, p. 108; **41**, IV, 70a; **90**, II, 383-84; **187**, II, 132; **34**, yr. 713; **321**, pp. 56, 70.)

714, Ibn Kuwayk
Alexandria, Damascus; father of ḥadīth teacher, relative of poet. (**65**, p. 64b; **362**, pp. 107, 108; **90**, IV, 252; **41**, IV, 64b; **34**, yr. 714.)

723, al-Takrītī
Damascus, Alexandria. (**90**, III, 327-28; **362**, p. 109.)

723, Muhya al-dīn
wazīr of Yemen; Mecca, Yemen; poet and author; Rasūlids invested 150,000 dinars with him, associate of Sultan. (**362**, p. 109; **335**, p. 72; **90**, IV, 419; **374**, pp. 233-34; **34**, yr. 723.)

725, al-Fāriqī
inherited money, father of scholar. (**90**, III, 315-16; **362**, p. 110.)

731, al-Damāmīnī
ṣadr; Damascus, Egypt; muḥaddith; endowed madrasa, 100,000 dinar fortune, brother of kārimī. (**187**, II, 340; **176**, XIV, 156; **362**, p. 111.)
734, Ibn Kuwayk
ra'īs al-kārimī; Damascus; imām, muḥaddith; endowed madrasa, kārimī family, ancestor of scholars, made loan to king of Mali. (**153**, II, 187; **362**, pp. 110-11; **90**, II, 405; **142**, II, 356.)
747, al-Fāriqī
administrator; Yemen, Egypt; son of kārimī. (**362**, p. 112; **152**, pp. 233-34.)
752, Ḥasan
khawājā; Damascus, Bagdad; ḥadīth; endowed madrasa. (**90**, II, 55; **51**, II, 145a; **50**, I, 391-92.)
754, Ibn Kuwayk
a'yān al-tujjār, kārimī; Cairo, Mecca; endowed madrasa and school, son wasted 70,000 dinars. (**362**, p. 112; **90**, III, 429.)
776, Ibn Musallam
ra'īs, kabīr al-kārimī, khawājā; Egypt, India, Yemen, Abyssinia; father was a porter, then a merchant, he married daughter of muḥtasib, became richest man of his time, owned slaves, gave 16,000 dinars, land, and a house for a madrasa, left each son 20,000 dinars, son, a kārimī, offered 50,000 dinars to Sultan to have his father's inheritance, daughter married a kārimī. (**335**, p. 70; **362**, pp. 112-13; **93**, p. 362; **42**, III, 306a-b; **1**, I, 88b, 104b; **90**, IV, 257; **180**, V, 281, VI, 812-13; **116**, II, 401.)
777, al-Bālisī
father a great merchant and ra'īs. (**26**, III, 26b.)
787, al-Kharrūbī
ra'īs al-tujjār; Yemen, Egypt; ḥadīth; gave 1,000 dinars to sheikh, endowed madrasa, uncle owned sugar factory, owned a house, other merchants and ulama in his family, father lived in a zāwiya. (**90**, I, 450-51; **180**, V, 434; **116**, II, 427; **42**, III, 484b.)
789, al-Maḥallī
brother of kārimī, brought gifts to Yemen. (**362**, p. 116.)
796, Ibn Musallam
son of kārimī, lent money to Barqūq. (**169**, I, 302; **362**, p. 117; **26**, III, 123b.)
797, al-Hibī
(**362**, p. 117.)
799, al-Qāhirī
dallāl for cloth; muḥaddith; changed from trade to teaching, doubtful case. (**362**, p. 113.)
803, Ibn Ajjam
simsār fī al-kārim; owned sugar factory and made it a funduq. (**104**, IV, 44-45; **362**, p. 117.)
803, al-Ma'alī
bought sugar factory. (**104**, IV, 44.)
803, al-Kharrūbī
khawājā, a'yān al-tujjār, kārimī; endowed madrasa, repaired ḥaram for 100,000 dirhems, father and grandfather were merchants, Sakhāwī family,

lent money to Barqūq. (**362**, p. 116; **26**, III, 169b-170a; **169**, I, 340; **41**, IV, 132a; **95**, V, 240; **93**, p. 233; **56**, II, 191b.)

806, al-Maḥallī
ra'īs al-tujjār, khawājā, tājir al-khāṣṣ al-sharīf, ambassador to Yemen, tājir Sulṭāniyya; Yemen, Egypt; qadi, shāfi'ī; traded for his father-in-law, restored mosque, endowed madrasa and ḥaram, owned slaves, houses worth 50,000 dinars, related to qadi, son dissipated fortune. (**92**, p. 111; **56**, II, 207b; **41**, V, 23b-24a; **93**, p. 9; **169**, I, 302, 326; **166**, IX, 458; **26**, III, 204b; **46**, p. 51a; **116**, II, 368; **180**, V, 571, VI, 122; **321**, pp. 47-48; **95**, I, 112-13, V, 29.)

806, Ibn al-Maḥallī
Yemen. (**362**, p. 118; **26**, III, 204b.)

820, al-Rūkī
kabīr al-tujjār, kārimī; Mecca, Cairo; father of merchant. (**362**, p. 118; **95**, III, 178.)

820, al-Akfahsī
Damascus, Mecca, Hormuz, Herat, Samarkand; ḥadīth, poet. (**362**, p. 119.)

822, al-Kharrūbī
khawājā, kabīr; dissipated fortune of his family, married daughter of kārimī who taught ḥadīth. (**362**, p. 116; **197**, p. 107.)

829, Ibn Suwayd
witness; Yemen; shāfi'ī or mālikī; endowed madrasa, father a Coptic chicken peddler, circle of students and merchants. (**362**, p. 119; **95**, III, 101.)

829, al-Tabrīzī
tax collector in Jidda; ulama and merchants in his family. (**374**, p. 207.)

830, al-Kurdī
(**362**, p. 123.)

838, Ibn al-Hilis
Aden, Cairo; ḥadīth. (**362**, p. 123; **95**, XI, 19-20.)

844, al-Kīlānī
khawājā, merchant of court, repaired ḥaram; Syria, Egypt; sheikh; brought spice for Sultan. (**26**, II, 24a; **362**, p. 124; **374**, p. 222.)

851, al-Māḥūrī
khawājā, nāẓir al-Azhar; Cairo, Mecca; owned house. (**197**, p. 198; **362**, p. 124.)

851, al-Qabbānī
Koran reader. (**362**, p. 124.)

851, al-Halwānī
(**362**, p. 124.)

APPENDIX E · TĀJIR-KHAWĀJĀ (MERCHANTS WITH OFFICIAL RANKING)

Each entry appears in the following form: the date of death and name of the merchant followed by his titles, offices, and ranks; the locality of his activities; his religious education or affiliations; and other information. References to the sources follow in parentheses.

735, al-Sinjārī
Damascus, Cairo; gave waqf for school. (**121**, III, 263-64; **176**, XIV, 171; **34**, yr. 735; **119**, I, 13; **149**, IV, 115.)

762, al-Salāmī
Damascus; muḥaddith; gave waqf for madrasa. (**1**, I, 68a; **180**, V, 182; **56**, II, 4a.)

778, al-Is'ardī
a'yān al-tujjār; owned khan. (**56**, II, 47b.)

790, 'Alī and 'Uthmān
captured by Genoese pirates with family of Sultan. (**26**, III, 92b, 95b; **46**, pp. 18a-b; **3**, I, 147b; **166**, IX, 38, 49.)

792, al-Ḥarrānī
muḥaddith. (**26**, III, 106b.)

795, Yūsuf b. 'Alī
ra'īs; Aleppo; waqf of books. (**50**, II, 442.)

826, al-Is'ardī
Damascus; endowed madrasa, married daughter of Ibn al-Muzallaq. (**121**, III, 387; **111**, I, 73-74; **26**, II, 131b; **119**, I, 150-51.)

848, Ibn-al-Muzallaq
tājir al-khāṣṣ, ra'īs al-khawājā, ra's al-tujjār, kabīr; Damascus; gave waqf of khans, endowed khānaqā, owned 1.8 million dirhems and property and goods in fortune, father a brick worker, sons were qadis, khawājās, and officials, negotiated with bedouins to protect trade. (**111**, I, 74-75; **119**, II, 290-91; **56**, III, 13b; **121**, III, 279, VI, 261-63; **197**, pp. 112-13; **374**, pp. 150, 192-93, 208, 235-36; **95**, III, 85; **125**, V, 146; **179**, p. 24; **46**, p. 187a.)

841 (active in), Badr al-dīn
Mecca; Muzallaq family, honored by Sultan. (**46**, p. 167b; **374**, p. 175; **1**, II, 4b.)

841, al-Sirāj
Damascus, Aleppo; shāfi'ī, muḥaddith; gift of 500 dinars for ḥaram of Mecca, Muzallaq family. (**95**, VI, 120.)

848, al-Shaybānī
Mecca. (**95**, I, 59.)

848, Nūr al-dīn
a'yān al-tujjār, khawājā; Mecca, Jidda. (**197**, p. 101.)

850, Shihāb al-dīn Aḥmad
trader, shāh-bandar, government agent in India; repaired ḥaram of Mecca, friend of merchants and poets. (**362**, p. 124.)
852, Shihāb al-dīn
a'yān al-tujjār; Aleppo; repaired mosque. (**123**, p. 42; **125**, V, 217.)
855, 'Abd al-Karīm
traded; Hormuz, Yemen, Mecca; owned house. (**95**, IV, 319.)
856, al-Wajīh
traded; Damascus, Mecca, Calcutta; owned house. (**95**, IV, 55.)
?, al-Dawrī
Aleppo; endowed khānaqā. (**123**, p. 117.)
862, al-Naḥḥās
Damascus, Mecca; endowed khānaqā. (**119**, II, 173-74; **195**, VI, 117; **121**, V, 291.)
862, Nūr al-dīn 'Alī
a'yān al-tujjār; Damascus; son of khawājā. (**95**, V, 307; **30**, yr. 862.)
863, al-Anṣārī
Mecca; brother of qadi. (**180**, VII, 618-19; **95**, II, 32.)
864, Ibn Sālim
a'yān al-tujjār; Damascus. (**30**, yr. 864.)
864, al-Abūkīrī
traded; Mecca, Calcutta; owned house. (**95**, VII, 101.)
873, Shihāb al-dīn ibn Muzallaq
a'yān al-tujjār; Damascus; generous to ulama. (**95**, II, 147; **30**, yr. 873; **169**, II, 100.)
873, al-Nāṣirī
wakīl, dawādār of Aleppo; from merchant to official, brother a merchant. (**95**, II, 257.)
875, al-'Ajamī
kabīr; Egypt, Rum; fortune in jewels and copper confiscated. (**54**, p. 58a.)
876, al-Marāhalī
investigated in Cairo. (**54**, p. 96a.)
878, Ibn Muzallaq
trade, nāẓir al-jaysh, muḥtasib, ra'īs, qadi; Damascus, Aleppo, Mecca, Cairo; son succeeded him as nāẓir al-jaysh. (**95**, III, 126; **374**, pp. 208, 236; **197**, p. 113; **179**, p. 24; **30**, yrs. 857, 878.)
878, al-Baṣrī
traded, official in Hormuz; Mecca, India. (**95**, V, 165.)
879, 'Abd al-Raḥman al-Baṣrī
traded; India. (**95**, IV, 87.)
881, al-Ṭahṭāwī
trader; Mecca; owned house. (**95**, VI, 27.)
886, Khalīl
(**29**, p. 87b.)
891, al-'Ajamī
Mecca; associate of sheikhs, left money to qadis. (**95**, VI, 61.)
895, 'Īsā al-Qārī
kabīr al-tujjār; Damascus; dealt in spices for the Sultan, generous to Sufis, son inherited his fortune. (**181**, pp. 125, 128, 132.)
897, al-Turkamānī

ra'īs; India, Aleppo; gave qayṣariyya as waqf for poor, married daughter of qadi, owned house, rebuilt roof of mosque, son was qadi. (**125**, V, 341; **28**, pp. 45a-b.)

901, Ibn Mahfūz
a'yān al-tujjār, ambassador to Florence. (**282**, p. 212.)

920, al-Ḥalabī
a'yān al-tujjār; wealth confiscated. (**169**, IV, 373.)

KHAWĀJĀ-TĀJIR AL-SULTĀN

854, Ḥasan
Alexandria; wealth confiscated. (**197**, pp. 209, 328; **179**, pp. 97, 156.)

854, al-Tawrīzī
tājir of Alexandria; 100,000 dinars confiscated. (**197**, p. 345; **95**, III, 133.)

874 (active in), Khawājā
ṣāḥib al-Sulṭān. (**45**, p. 62b.)

876 (active in), Shams al-dīn
ṣadīq al-Sulṭān, ṣāḥib al-Sulṭān. (**54**, pp. 96b, 107b.)

877, Ibn Mūsā
traded in spices; owed Sultan 30,000 dinars. (**45**, p. 191a.)

889, Ibn 'Ulayba
nāẓir. (**45**, p. 195b; **362**, p. 127.)

BIBLIOGRAPHY

CLASSIFICATION OF CONTENTS

I. *Primary Sources*

A. Manuscripts

B. Printed Sources

1. Administrative Manuals
2. Biographical Dictionaries
3. Descriptions of Towns
4. Economic and Social Texts
5. Geographies
6. Histories and Chronicles
7. Inscriptions
8. Travelers' Accounts and Western Sources
9. Treaties

II. *Secondary Works*

A. Art History
B. Economic History
C. History of Syria and Egypt
D. The Mamluk State
E. Mediterranean Cities and Trade
F. Muslim and Mamluk Cities
G. Social History

III. *Bibliographies*

ABBREVIATIONS

AIEO	Annales de l'Institut d'Études Orientales, Algiers.
BEO	Bulletin d'Études Orientales, Beirut.
BIE	Bulletin de l'Institut Égyptien, Cairo.
BIFAO	Bulletin de l'Institut Français d'Archéologie Orientale, Cairo.
BSOAS	Bulletin of the School of Oriental and African Studies, London.
JA	Journal Asiatique, Paris.
JAOS	Journal of the American Oriental Society, New Haven.
JESHO	Journal of the Economic and Social History of the Orient, Leiden.
JRAS	Journal of the Royal Asiatic Society, London.
RAAD	Revue de l'Académie Arabe de Damas, Damascus.
REI	Revue des Études Islamiques, Paris.
ZDMG	Zeitschrift der Deutschen Morgenländischen Gesellschaft, Leipzig-Wiesbaden.

Indented entries in Section I are other copies of the manuscript indicated in the preceding entry. In other sections of the bibliography, secondary versions, extracts, translations, or commentaries are indented under the title of the most important edition.

I. *Primary Sources*

A. MANUSCRIPTS

1. 'Abd al-Bāsiṭ. Dhayl Nayl al-Amal fī Dhayl al-Duwal. 2 vols. MS Bodleian, Oxford, nos. 803, 812.
2. Awrān min Kitāb fī ta'rīkh qhayra Marabata. MS Ma'had al-Makhṭūṭāt al-'Arabiyya, Cairo, Ta'rīkh, no. 922.

3. al-'Aynī, al-'Iqd al-Jumān min Ta'rīkh al-Zamān. 2 vols. MS Suleymaniye, Istanbul, nos. 830, 835.
4. MS Serai, Istanbul, no. 2911.
5. MS Oriental Institute, Leningrad.
6. ——— Sayf al-Muhannad fī Sīrat al-Mālik al-Mu'ayyad. MS Bibliothèque Nationale, Paris, no. 1723.
7. al-Bā'ūnī, al-Lamḥa al-Ashrafiyya wal-Bahja al-Saniyya. MS Bibliothèque Nationale, Paris, no. 1615, foll. 30-50.
8. Baybars al-Manṣūrī. Zubdat al-Fikra fī Ta'rīkh al-Hijra al-Nabawī. MS Bodleian, Oxford, no. 704.
9. al-Bayrūtī. Ta'rīkh. MS Bodleian, Oxford, no. 712.
10. al-Birzālī. Ta'rīkh al-Musammā bil-Muqtafī. 2 vols. MS Serai, Istanbul, no. 2951.
11. al-Dhahabī. Ma'rifat al-Qurrā' al-Kibār 'ala al-Ṭabaqāt wal-A'ṣār. MS Bibliothèque Nationale, Paris, no. 2086.
12. ——— Ta'rīkh al-Islām. MS Köprülü, Istanbul, no. 1020.
13. 2 vols. MS Bodleian, Oxford, nos. 654, 656.
14. MS Dār al-Kutub al-Miṣriyya, Cairo, Ta'rīkh no. 42.
15. al-Ḥalabī. Tadhkirat al-Nabīh fī Ayyām al-Manṣūr wa Banīh. MS British Museum, London, no. Add. 7335.
16. Hujjat Waqf. MS Dār al-Kutub al-Miṣriyya, Cairo, Ta'rīkh, no. 9227.
17. al-Ḥusaynī. al-Ta'rīkh al-Musammā bil-'Ibar lil-Ḥafiẓ al-Dhahabī ma'a Dhayl. MS Köprülü, Istanbul, no. 1048.
18. al-Dhahabī. al-'Ibar fī Khabar Man 'Abar. MS Bibliothèque Nationale, Paris, no. 5819. Continuation by al-Ḥusaynī.
19. Ibn Asbāṭ al-Gharbī. Ta'rīkh Miṣr. MS Bibliothèque Nationale, Paris, no. 1821.
20. Ibn Duqmāq. Jawhar al-Thamīn fī Sīrat al-Khulafā' wal-Salāṭīn. MS Bibliothèque Nationale, Paris, no. 5762. Abbreviated with continuation.
21. 2 vols. MS Bodleian, Oxford, nos. 648, 680.
22. MS Dār al-Kutub al-Miṣriyya, Cairo, Ta'rīkh Taymūr no. 1492.
23. Ibn Ḥabīb. Durrat al-Aslāk fī Dawlat al-Atrāk. MS Bibliothèque Nationale, Paris, no. 1719.
24. MS Bodleian, Oxford, no. 739.
25. Vol. III. MS Dār al-Kutub al-Miṣriyya, Cairo, Ta'rīkh no. ḥ 617.
26. Ibn Hajar al-'Asqalānī. Inbā' al-Ghumr bi Abnā' al-'Umr. 3 vols. MS Bibliothèque Nationale, Paris, nos. 1601-1603.
27. Ibn al-Ḥanafī. Tawḍīḥ Manāhij al-Athwār wa Taftīm Mabāhij al-Azhār. MS British Museum, London, no. OR 4306.
28. Ibn al-Ḥanbalī. Durr al-Ḥabab fī Ta'rīkh A'yān Ḥalab. MS Bibliothèque Nationale, Paris, no. 2142.
29. Ibn al-Ḥimṣī. Ḥawādith al-Zamān wa Wafayāt al-Shuyūkh al-Aqrān. MS Feyzullah, Istanbul, no. 1438.
30. MS Ma'had al-Makhṭūṭāt al-'Arabiyya, Cairo, Ta'rīkh no. 222. No pagination.
31. Ibn Iyās. 'Uqūd al-Jumān fī Waqā'i'. MS Aya Sofya, Istanbul, no. 311.
32. Ibn Malā. Nihāyat al-Adab min Dhikr Walāt Ḥalab. MS Ma'had al-Makhṭūṭāt al-'Arabiyya, Cairo, Ta'rīkh no. 1294.
33. Ibn Qāḍī Ajlūn. Kitāb al-Kunz al-Akbar fī al-Amr bil-Ma'rūf wal-

Nahī ‘an al-Munkar. MS Zāhiriyya, Damascus, majmū‘, no. 8, pp. 98-104.

34. Ibn Qāḍī Shuhba. al-‘Alam bi Ta’rīkh al-Islām. MS Bodleian, Oxford, no. 721. No pagination.

35. ——— Dhayl ‘ala Ta’rīkh al-Islām. 2 vols. MS Bibliothèque Nationale, Paris, nos. 1598-1599.

36. Ibn Shajar al-Tadmūrī. al-Sukkariyya fī al-Sukkariyya. MS Zāhiriyya, Damascus, majmū‘ no. 128.

37. Ibn Shākir al-Kutubī. ‘Uyūn al-Tawārīkh. 2 vols. MS Dār al-Kutub al-Miṣriyya, Cairo, Ta’rīkh nos. 949, 1497.

38. MS Karaçelebi, Istanbul, no. 276.

39. MS Serai, Istanbul, no. 2922.

40. Ibn Shiḥna. Rawḍ al-Manāẓir fī ‘Ilm al-Awā’il wal-Awākhir. 2 vols. MS Bibliothèque Nationale, Paris, nos. 1537-1538.

41. Ibn Taghrī Birdī. al-Manhal al-Ṣāfī wal Mustawfā ba‘d al-Wāfī. 5 vols. MS Bibliothèque Nationale, Paris, nos. 2068-2072.

42. 3 vols. MS Dār al-Kutub al-Miṣriyya, Cairo, Ta’rīkh no. 1113.

43. al-‘Irāqī. al-Dhayl ‘ala Kitāb al-‘Ibar. MS Dār al-Kutub al-Miṣriyya, Cairo, Ta’rīkh no. 5615.

44. al-Ja’farī. Bahjat al-Sālik wal-Maslūk fī Ta’rīkh al-Khulafā’ wal-Salāṭīn wal-Mulūk. MS Bibliothèque Nationale, Paris, no. 1607. Same text as Anhaj al-Ṭarā’ik, MS Bibliothèque Nationale, Paris, no. 1815.

45. al-Jawharī. Inbā’ al-Haṣr fī al-Abnā’ al-‘Aṣr. MS Bibliothèque Nationale, Paris, no. 1791.

46. ——— Nuzhat al-Nufūs wal-Abdān fī Tawārīkh al-Zamān. MS Dār al-Kutub al-Miṣriyya, Cairo, Ta’rīkh no. m 116.

47. al-Jazarī. Ḥawādith al-Zamān. MS Bibliothèque Nationale, Paris, no. 6739.

48. ——— Kitāb Ta’rīkh Jalīl Dimashq wal-Shām wal-‘Irāq wa Miṣr wal-Ḥabasha. MS Dār al-Kutub al-Miṣriyya, Cairo, Ta’rīkh, no. 995.

49. ——— al-Mukhtār min al-Ta’rīkh. MS Köprülü, Istanbul, no. 1147.

50. al-Jibrīnī. al-Durr al-Muntakhab bi-Takmilat Ta’rīkh Ḥalab. 2 vols. MS Aḥmadiyya, Aleppo, no. 1214.

51. 2 vols. MS Bibliothèque Nationale, Paris, nos. 2139, 5853.

52. Kitāb Majmū‘a min al-Tawārīkh. MS Serai, Istanbul, no. 3057. History of Dulghādir.

53. Kitāb Sīrat al-Sulṭān al-Shahīd al-Mālik al-Zāhir Jaqmaq. MS Serai, Istanbul, no. 2992.

54. al-Kitāb fī Ta’rīkh. MS Dār al-Kutub al-Miṣriyya, Cairo, Ta’rīkh no. 5631.

55. Kitāb Ta’rīkh al-Salāṭīn wal-‘Askar. MS Bibliothèque Nationale, Paris, no. 1705.

56. al-Maqrīzi. al-Sulūk li-Ma‘rifat Duwal al-Mulūk. 3 vols. MS Aya Sofya, Istanbul, nos. 3372, 3374, 3375.

57. Mujīr al-Dīn al-‘Ulaymī. Dhayl al-Ins al-Jalīl bi Ta’rīkh al-Quds wal-Khalīl. MS Bodleian, Oxford, no. 853.

58. ——— al-Ta’rīkh al-Mu‘tabar fī Anbā’ man ‘Abar. MS British Museum, London, no. OR 1544.

59. al-Mu'minī. Futūḥ al-Naṣr fī Ta'rīkh Mulūk Miṣr. MS Dār al-Kutub al-Miṣriyya, Cairo, Ta'rīkh no. 2399.
60. al-Nu'aymī. Mudhakkarāt Yammiyya Dawwana bi-Dimashq. MS Ẓāhiriyya, Damascus, no. 4533.
61. al-Nuwayrī. Nihāyat al-'Arab fī Funūn al-Adab. 3 vols. MS Bibliothèque Nationale, Paris, nos. 1577-1579.
62. Nuzhat al-Insān fī Dhikr al-Mulūk wal-A'yān. MS Bibliothèque Nationale, Paris, no. 1769.
63. al-Ṣafadī. Nuzhat al-Mālik wal-Mamlūk. MS British Museum, London, no. OR 6267.
64. al-Ṣafadī, Khalīl ibn 'Abd-allāh. Tuhfat Dhawī al-Albāb fī man Ḥakama bi Dimashq min al-Khulafā' wal-Mulūk wal-Nuwwāb. MS Bibliothèque Nationale, Paris, no. 5827.
65. al-Ṣaqā'ī. Tālī Kitāb Wafayāt al-A'yān. MS Bibliothèque Nationale, Paris, no. 2061.
66. al-Sakhāwī. Dhayl Duwal al-Islām. 2 vols. MS Bodleian, Oxford, nos. 843, 853. Vol. I, no pagination.
67. ——— al-Durra al-Muḍi'a fī al-Ma'āthir al-Ashrafiyya. MS Bibliothèque Nationale, Paris, no. 1615, foll. 51-62.
68. al-Salāmī. al-Mukhtaṣar al-Tawārīkh. MS Dār al-Kutub al-Miṣriyya, Cairo, Ta'rīkh no. 1435.
69. Sibṭ ibn l-'Ajamī. Kunūz al-Dhahab fī Ta'rīkh Ḥalab. Vol. III. MS Dār al-Kutub al-Miṣriyya, Cairo, Ta'rīkh Taymūr, no. 60.
70. al-Suyūṭī. Badā'i' al-Zuhūr fī Waqā'i' al-Duhūr. MS Bibliothèque Nationale, Paris, no. 1552.
71. Ta'rīkh al-Amīr Yashbak al-Ẓāhirī. MS Dār al-Kutub al-Miṣriyya, Cairo, Ta'rīkh no. ḥ 11658.
72. Ta'rīkh al-Mālik al-Ashraf Qāyitbāy. MS Bibliothèque Nationale, Paris, no. 5916.
73. Ta'rīkh al-Sulūk fī Khilāfa wal-Mulūk. MS British Museum, London, no. OR 6854.
74. Tashrīf al-Ayyām wal-'Uṣūr bil-Sīrat al-Sulṭān al-Mālik al-Manṣūr. MS Bibliothèque Nationale, Paris, no. 1704.
75. Waqf. MS National Museum, Damascus. 3 rolls on display.
76. Waqf. MS Ẓāhiriyya, Damascus, no. 4838.
77. al-Yāfi'ī. Mir'āt al-Janān wa 'Ibrat al-Yaqẓān fī Ma'rifat Ḥawādith al-Zamān. MS Bibliothèque Nationale, Paris, no. 1591.
78. al-Yūnīnī. Dhayl Mirāt al-Zamān. MS Bodleian, Oxford, no. 700.
79. MS Dār al-Kutub al-Miṣriyya, Cairo, Ta'rīkh no. 1516.
80. Vols. II-IV. MS Serai, Istanbul, no. 2907 E.

B. Printed Sources

1. *Administrative Manuals*

81. Mantran, Robert and Jean Sauvaget. *Règlements Fiscaux Ottomans: Les Provinces Syriennes.* Paris, 1951.
82. Moberg, Axel. "Regierungspromemoria eines Ägyptischen Sultans," *Festschrift E. Sachau.* G. Weil, ed. Berlin, 1915. pp. 406-21.
83. al-Nuwayrī. *Nihāyat al-'Arab fī Funūn al-Adab,* vol. VIII. Cairo, 1931.
84. al-Qalqashandī. *al-Ṣubḥ al-A'shā.* 14 vols. Cairo, 1914–1928.

85. Sauvaire, Henry. "Extraits de l'Ouvrage d'el Qalqachandy," *Mémoires de l'Académie des Sciences, Belles-Lettres, et Arts de Marseille* (1885–1887), 79-111.
86. al-'Umarī. *al-Ta'rīf bil-Muṣṭalaḥ al-Sharīf*. Cairo, 1312 A.H.
87. al-Zāhirī. *Kitāb Zubda Kashf al-Mamālik*. P. Ravaisse, ed. Paris, 1894.
88. Gaulmier, Jean, ed. *La Zubda Kachf al-Mamālik de Khalīl aẓ-Zāhirī*. Beirut, 1950. French translation.

2. *Biographical Dictionaries*

89. Gabrieli, G. "Indice Alfabetico di Tutte le Biografiche Continute nel Wāfī bi-l-Wafavāt di al-Ṣafadī," *Rendiconti Della Reale Accademia Dei Lincei*, Rome, Ser. V, vol. XXII (1913), 547-77, 581-620; vol. XXIII (1913), 217-65; vol. XXIII (1914), 191-208; vol. XXIV (1916), 551-615; vol. XXV (1916), 341-98, 1165-84.
90. Ibn Ḥajar al-'Asqalānī. *al-Durar al-Kāmina*. 4 vols. Hyderabad, 1348–1350 A.H.
91. Ibn Shākir al-Kutubī. Fawāt al-Wafayāt. 2 vols. Cairo, 1951.
92. Ibn Taghrī Birdī. *al-Manhal al-Ṣāfī*, vol. I. Cairo, 1957.
93. Wiet, Gaston. *Les Biographies du Manhal Safi*. Cairo, 1932.
94. al-Ṣafadī. al-Wāfī bil-Wafayāt. ed. Ritter, Hellmut, and Sven Dedering. *Das Biographische Lexicon des Ṣalāḥaddīn Ḫalīl ibn Aibak as-Ṣafadī*. Bibliotheca Islamica, VI a-c. 3 vols. Istanbul, Damascus, 1931–1953.
95. al-Sakhāwī. *al-Ḍaw' al-Lāmi'*. 12 vols. Cairo, 1353–1355 A.H.
96. al-Suyūṭī, Jalāl al-Dīn. Naẓm al-'Iqiyān fī A'yān al-A'yān. tr. Hitti, Philip. *Who's Who in the Fifteenth Century*. New York, 1927.

3. *Descriptions of Towns*

97. al-Arbalī. ed. Dahmān, Muḥammad Aḥmad. "Madāris Dimashq wa Ḥammāmātiha," *RAAD*, XXII (1947), 232-46, 320-33.
98. al-Badarī. *Nuzhat al-Anām fī Maḥāsin al-Shām*. Cairo, 1341 A.H.
99. Dahmān, Muḥammad Aḥmad. *Jabal Qāsiyūn*. Damascus, 1946.
100. Fleischer, Michael. "Meschàka's Kultur-Statistik von Damaskus," *ZDMG*, VIII (1854), 346-74.
101. al-Ghazī. *Nahr al-Dhahab fī Ta'rīkh Ḥalab*. 3 vols. Aleppo, 1923–1926.
102. Ibn 'Abd al-Hādī. *Ḥammāmāt Dimashq*. S. Munajjid, ed. Beirut, 1947.
103. ——— *Thimār al-Maqāṣid fī Dhikr al-Masājid*. Muḥammad 'Asad Ṭalas, ed. Beirut, 1943.
104. Ibn Duqmāq. *al-Intiṣār li-Wāsiṭat 'Iqd al-Amṣār*. 2 vols. Būlāq, 1309 A.H.
105. Ibn Kinnān. *al-Murūj al-Sundusiyya al-Fasīhiyya fī Talkhīṣ Ta'rīkh al-Ṣāliḥiyya*. Muḥammad Aḥmad Dahmān, ed. Damascus, 1947.
106. Ibn Shaddād. al-A'lāq al-Khaṭīra. ed. Dahān, Sāmī. *La Description de Damas d'Ibn Šaddād*. Damascus, 1956.
107. Dahān, Sāmī, ed. *Liban, Jordanie, Palestine Topographie Historique d'Ibn Šaddād*. Damascus, 1963.
108. Sourdel, Dominique, ed. *La Description d'Alep d'Ibn Šaddād*. Damascus, 1953.

109. Ibn al-Shiḥna. *al-Durr al-Muntakhab fī Ta'rīkh Mamlaka Ḥalab.* Beirut, 1919.

110. Sauvaget, Jean, tr. *Les Perles Choisies d'Ibn Ach-Chiḥna.* Beirut, 1933.

111. Ibn Ṭūlūn. *al-Qalā'id al-Jawhariyya fī Ta'rīkh al-Ṣāliḥiyya.* 2 vols. Damascus, 1949.

112. ——— ed. Taymūr, Aḥmad. "Waṣf Rabwat Dimashq," *RAAD,* II (1922), 147-52.

113. ——— ed. Zayāt, H. "Ḥārāt Dimashq al-Qadīma," *al-Mashriq.* Beirut, XXXV (1937), 33-36.

114. Kurd 'Alī. *Ghūṭa Dimashq.* Damascus, 1949.

115. ——— *Khiṭaṭ al-Shām,* vol. VI. Damascus, 1928.

116. al-Maqrīzī. *al-Mawā'iẓ wal-I'tibār bi-Dhikr al-Khiṭaṭ wal-Athār.* 2 vols. Būlāq, 1854.

117. Bourriant, U., tr. *Description Topographique et Historique de l'Égypte.* Mémoires Mission Archéologique Française au Caire, vol. XVII. Paris, 1900.

118. Mujīr al-Dīn al-'Ulaymī. al-Ins al-Jalīl bi-Ta'rīkh al-Quds wal-Khalīl. tr. Sauvaire, H. *Histoire de Jérusalem et d'Hébron.* Paris, 1876.

119. al-Nu'aymī. *al-Dāris fī Ta'rīkh al-Madāris.* 2 vols. Damascus, 1948–1951.

120. ——— *Dūr al-Qurān fī Dimashq.* S. Munajjid, ed. Damascus, 1942.

121. Sauvaire, Henry. "Description de Damas," *JA,* Ser. IX, vol. III (1894), 251-318, 385-501; vol. IV (1894), 242-331, 460-503; vol. V (1895), 269-315, 377-411; vol. VI (1895), 221-313, 409-84; vol. VII (1896); 185-285, 369-459.

122. Ouéchek, Emilie E. *Index Général de la "Description de Damas" de Sauvaire.* Damascus, 1954.

123. Sibṭ ibn al-'Ajamī. Kunūz al-Dhahab fī Ta'rīkh Ḥalab. tr. Sauvaget, Jean. *Les Tresors d'Or.* Beirut, 1950.

124. al-Suyūṭī. *Ḥusn al-Maḥāḍara fī Akhbār Miṣr wal-Qāhira.* 2 vols. Cairo, 1904.

125. al-Ṭabbākh. *A'lām al-Nubalā' bi-Ta'rīkh Ḥalab.* 7 vols. Aleppo, 1923–1926.

126. Zayāt, H. "Khānat Dimashq al-Qadīma," *al-Mashriq,* Beirut, XXXVI (1938), 66-70.

4. Economic and Social Texts

127. Ibn 'Abd al-Hādī. ed. Zayāt, H. "Kitāb al-Ḥisba," *al-Mashriq,* Beirut, XXXV (1937), 384-90.

128. Ibn Abī Rabī'. *Sulūk al-Mālik fī Tadbīr al-Mamālik.* Cairo, 1329 A.H.

129. Ibn al-Ukhuwwa. *al-Ma'ālim al-Qurba fī Aḥkām al-Ḥisba.* Ruben Levy, ed. and tr. E. J. W. Gibb Memorial Series, vol. XII. London, 1938.

130. al-Jay'ān. *al-Tuḥfa al-Sanīh bi-Ismā' al-Bilād al-Miṣriyya.* Cairo, 1898.

131. *Kitāb Waqf.* Damascus, 1929.

132. al-Maqrīzī. *Ighāthat al-Umma bi-Kashf al-Ghumma.* Cairo, 1940.

133. Wiet, Gaston, tr. "Le Traité des Famines de Maqrīzī," *JESHO,* IV (1962), 1-90.

134. ——— *Shudhūr al-'Uqūd.* L. A. Mayer, tr. Alexandria, 1933.

135. al-Subkī. *Kitāb Mu'īd al-Ni'am wa Mubīd an-Niqam*. David W. Myhrman, ed. London, 1908.

5. Geographies

136. Abū 'l-Fidā'. Kitāb Taqwīm al-Buldān. ed. Reinhard, J. F. and W. MacGucken de Slane. *Géographie d'Aboul-féda,* Texte Arabe. Paris, 1840.

137. al-Dimashqī. Nukhbat al-Dahr fī 'Ajā'ib al-Barr wal-Baḥr. ed. Froehn, M. and M. A. F. Mehren. *Cosmographie de Chems-ed-Din Abou Abdallah Mohammed ed-Dimichqui.* Saint Petersburg, 1866.

138. Mehren, A. F., tr. *Manuel de la Cosmographie du Moyen Âge.* Copenhagen, Paris, and Leipzig, 1874.

139. Ferrand, Gabriel. *Relations de Voyages et Textes Géographiques Arabes, Persans, et Turks Relatifs à l'Extrême-Orient,* vol. II. Paris, 1914.

140. Gaudefroy-Demombynes. *La Syrie à l'Époque des Mamelouks.* Paris, 1923.

141. Ibn Baṭṭūṭa. ed. and tr. Defrémery, C. and B. R. Sanguinetti. *Voyages.* 4 vols. Paris, 1853–1858.

142. Gibb, Sir Hamilton A. R. *The Travels of Ibn Battuta.* 2 vols. Cambridge, Eng., 1958–1961.

143. Le Strange, Guy. *Palestine under the Moslems.* Boston and New York, 1890.

144. Lewis, Bernard. "An Arabic Account of the Province of Safed," *BSOAS,* XV (1953), 477-86.

145. Marmardji, A. S. *Textes Géographiques Arabes sur la Palestine.* Paris, 1951.

146. al-Qazwīnī. Kitāb Athār al-Bilād. ed. Wüstenfeld, F. *El-Cozwinis Kosmographie.* 2 vols. Göttingen, 1847.

147. al-'Umarī. *Masālik al-Abṣār fī Mamālik al-Amṣār.* Cairo, 1924.

148. Hartmann, Richard. "Politische Geographie des Mamlukenreichs," *ZDMG,* LXX (1916), 1-40, 477-511.

6. Histories and Chronicles

149. Abū 'l-Fidā'. *al-Mukhtaṣar fī Ikhbār al-Bashar.* n.p., 1325 A.H. Continued by Ibn al-Wardī.

150. al-'Aynī. " 'Iqd al-Jumān," *Recueil des Historiens des Croisades,* vol. II, part 1. Paris, 1887.

151. ——— tr. and ed. LaMonte, John and M. M. Ziada. "Bedr ed Din al-Aini's Account of the Conquest of Cyprus, 1424–1426," *Annuaire de l'Institut de Philologie et d'Histoire Orientales et Slaves,* Brussels, VII (1939–1944), 241-64.

152. al-Dawādārī. al-Durr al-Fāḥir fī Sīrat al-Mālik al-Nāṣir. ed. Roemer, H. R. *Die Chronik des Ibn ad-Dawādārī.* Cairo, 1960.

153. al-Dhahabī. *Duwal al-Islām.* 2 vols. Hyderabad, 1337 A.H.

154. Somogye, Joseph. "Adh-Dhahabī's Record of the Destruction of Damascus by the Mongols in 699–700/1299–1301," *Ignace Goldziher Memorial Volume,* part 1. S. Löwinger and Joseph Somogye, ed. Budapest, 1948. pp. 353-86.

155. ——— "The Ta'rīkh al-Islām of adh-Dhahabī," *JRAS* (1932), 815-55.

156. al-Duwayhī. "Ta'rīkh al-Azminat," *al-Mashriq*. Beirut, XLIV (1950), 1-437.
157. Ernst, Hans, ed. and tr. *Die Mamlukischen Sultansurkunden des Sinai-Klosters*. Wiesbaden, 1960.
158. Ibn 'Abd al-Zāhir. al-Rawḍ al-Zāhir fī Sīrat al-Mālik al-Zāhir. ed. and tr. al-Khowaitir, Abdul Aziz. "A Critical Edition of an Unknown Source of the Life of al-Mālik al-Zāhir Baibars." 3 vols. Unpub. thesis in the School of Oriental and African Studies, University of London, 1960.
159. Sadeque, Syedah Fatima, ed. and tr. *Baybars I of Egypt*. Dacca, Pakistan, 1956.
160. ——— ed. and tr. Moberg, Axel. *Ibn 'Abd eẓ-Zāhir's al-Alṭāf al-Khafiyya*. Lund, 1902.
161. Ibn 'Arab Shāh. Kitāb 'Ajā'ib al-Maqdūr fī Akhbār Tīmūr. n.p., 1841.
162. Manger, Samuel Henricus, ed. and tr. *Ahmedis Arabsiadae Vitae et Rerum Gestarum Timur II*. Leovardiae, 1772.
163. Sanders, J. H. *Tamerlane, or Timur, the Great Amir*. London, 1936.
164. Vattier, Pierre, tr. *L'Histoire du Grand Tamerlan*. Paris, 1658.
165. ——— "Panegyric on Sultan Jaqmaq," *JRAS* (1907), 395-96. Arabic text, 27pp. Editor not named.
166. Ibn al-Furāt. *Ta'rīkh al-Duwal wal-Mulūk*, vols. VII-IX. Beirut, 1936–1942.
167. Ibn Ḥabīb. *Durrat al-Aslāk fī Dawlat al-Atrāk*. T. G. J. Juynboll, T. Roorda, and H. E. Weijers, ed. Orientalia, II. Amsterdam, 1846.
168. Ibn Ḥajja al-Ḥamwī. ed. Ṭarbayn, Aḥmad. "Yāqūt al-Kalām fī mā Nāba al-Shām," *RAAD*, XXXI (1956), 611-30.
169. Ibn Iyās. *Badā'i' al-Zuhūr fī Waqā'i' al-Duhūr*, 2 vols. Būlāq, 1311 A.H., vols. IV-V. Muḥammad Muṣṭafā, ed. 2nd ed. Cairo, 1960–1961.
170. Devonshire, R. L., tr. "Extrait de l'Histoire de l'Égypte," *BIFAO*, XXV (1925), 113-45; XXXIV (1934), 1-29.
171. Muṣṭafā, Muḥammad. *Unpublished Pages of the Chronicle of Ibn Iyas*. Cairo, 1959.
172. ——— "Unveröffentlichte Seite der Chronik des Ibn Iyās," *Proceedings of the Twenty-Second Congress of Orientalists*, vol. II. Leiden, 1957. pp. 202-06.
173. Salmon, W. H. *An Account of the Ottoman Conquest of Egypt*. London, 1924.
174. Wiet, Gaston. *Histoire des Mamlouks Circassiens*, vol. II. Paris, 1945.
175. ——— *Journal d'un Bourgeois du Caire, Chronique d'Ibn Iyās*. 2 vols. Paris, 1955, 1960.
176. Ibn Kathīr. *al-Bidāya wal-Nihāya fī al-Ta'rīkh*, vols. 13-14. Cairo, n.d.
177. Ibn Ṣaṣra. al-Durra al-Muḍī'a fī al-Dawla al-Zāhiriyya. ed. and tr. William M. Brinner. *A Chronicle of Damascus, 1389–1397*. 2 vols. Berkeley and Los Angeles, 1963.
178. Ibn Shaddād. ed. and tr. Sobernheim, M. "Darstellung der Geschichte Baalbeks in Mittelalter," *Centenario della Nascita di Michele Amari*, vol. II. Palermo, 1910. pp. 152-63.

179. Ibn Taghrī Birdī. *Ḥawādith al-Duhūr fī Madā al-Ayyām wal-Shuhūr.* William Popper, ed. University of California Publications in Semitic Philology, vol. VIII. Berkeley, 1930–1931.
180. ——— *al-Nujūm al-Zāhira fī Mulūk Miṣr wal-Qāhira.* William Popper, ed. and tr. University of California Publications in Semitic Philology, vols. V-VII, XIII, XIV, XVII-XIX, XXII. Berkeley, 1915–1960.
181. Ibn Ṭūlūn. *Mufākahat al-Khilān fī Ḥawādith al-Zamān,* vol. I. Cairo, 1962.
182. ——— *Rasā'il Ta'rīkhiyya.* 4 vols. Damascus, 1348 A.H.
183. ——— ed. Hartman, Richard. "Das Tübinger Fragment der Chronik des Ibn Ṭūlūn," *Schriften der Königsberger Gelehrten Gesellschaft,* Berlin, III (1926), 87-170.
184. ——— ed. Kurd 'Alī. "Darb al-Ḥūṭa 'ala Jamī' al-Ghūṭa," *RAAD,* V (1925), 216-22.
185. ——— tr. Laoust, Henri. *Les Gouverneurs de Damas sous les Mamlouks et les Premiers Ottomans.* Damascus, 1952.
186. al-Jazarī. tr. Sauvaget, J. *La Chronique de Damas d'al-Jazari.* Paris, 1949.
187. al-Maqrīzī. *al-Sulūk li-Ma'rifat Duwal al-Mulūk.* 2 vols. Cairo, 1936–1958.
188. Quatremère, Étienne Marc. *Histoire des Sultans Mamlouks de l'Égypte.* 4 vols. in 2. Paris, 1837–1845.
189. Mufaḍḍal ibn Abī al-Faḍā'il. al-Nahj al-Sadīd wal-Darr al-Farīd. ed. and tr. Blochet, Edgar. "Histoire des Sultans Mamlouks," *Patrologia Orientalis,* XII (1919), 345-550; XIV (1920), 375-672; XX (1929), 1-270.
190. Mujīr al-Dīn al-'Ulaymī. *al-Ins al-Jalīl bi Ta'rīkh al-Quds wal-Khalīl.* 2 vols. Cairo, 1866.
191. Mayer, L. A., tr. "A Sequel to Mujīr ad-Dīn's Chronicle," *Journal of the Palestine Oriental Society,* Jerusalem, XI (1931), 85-104.
192. Mukhliṣ, 'Abd-allāh. "Ṣafaḥāt Maṭwiyya," *RAAD,* XVI (1941), 241-47.
193. al-Munajjid, Ṣalāḥ al-Dīn. "Ḥarīq al-Jami' al-Umawī bi-Dimashq," *RAAD,* XXXI (1956), 35-47.
194. al-Nu'aymī. ed. al-'Ech. "Mudhakkarāt Yawmiyya Dawwana bi-Dimashq," *RAAD,* XVIII (1943), 142-54.
195. Petis de la Croix, F. *Histoire de Timur-Bec,* vol. III. Paris, 1722. From the text of Sharāf al-Dīn 'Alī Yazdī.
196. al-Ṣafadī. *Umarā' Dimashq fī al-Islām.* Damascus, 1955.
197. al-Sakhāwī. *al-Tibr al-Masbūk fī Dhayl al-Sulūk.* Būlāq, 1896.
198. Ṣāliḥ ibn Yaḥya. *Ta'rīkh Bayrūt.* P. Louis Cheikho, ed. 2nd ed. Beirut, 1927.
199. Sauvaget, Jean. "Corrections au Texte Imprimé de l'Histoire de Beyrouth de Ṣāliḥ b. Yaḥyā," *BEO,* VII-VIII (1937–1938), 65-82.
200. Sauvaget, Jean. *Historiens Arabes.* Paris, 1946.
201. Wiet, Gaston. *Grandeur de l'Islam.* Paris, 1961.
202. al-Yūnīnī. *Dhayl Mirāt al-Zamān.* 4 vols. Hyderabad, 1955.

203. al-'Aynī. *al-Rawḍ al-Zāhir fī Sīrat al-Mālik al-Zāhir Ṭaṭar*. Hans Ernst, ed. Cairo, 1962.
204. al-Zāhirī. tr. Devonshire, R. L. "Relations d'un Voyage du Sultan Qāitbāy en Palestine et en Syrie," *BIFAO,* XX (1921), 1-43.
205. Zetterstéen, K. V., ed. *Beiträge zur Geschichte der Mamlūken-sultāne in den Jahren 690–741 der Higra*. Leiden, 1919.

7. Inscriptions

206. Alūf, Michal M. *Ta'rīkh Ba'labakk* (Baalbek). 2nd Arabic edition. Beirut, 1904.
207. van Berchem, Max. "Arabische Inschrifte aus Syrien," *Mitteilungen und Nachrichten des Deutschen Palästina-Vereins,* Leipzig, XIX (1896), 105-113; XXVI (1903), 33-70.
208. ——— *Matériaux pour un Corpus Inscriptionum Arabicarum*. Syrie du Sud. Mémoires de l'Institut Français d'Archéologie Orientale, vol. XLIII, XLIV. Cairo, 1922, 1925–1927.
209. ——— and Edmond Fatio. *Voyage en Syrie*. Mémoires de l'Institut Français d'Archéologie Orientale, vol. XXXVII. Cairo, 1914.
210. Combe, E., Jean Sauvaget and Gaston Wiet. *Répertoire Chronologique d'Épigraphie Arabe*. Mémoires de l'Institut Français d'Archéologie Orientale, vol. XI-XV. Cairo, 1941–1956.
211. Herzfeld, Ernst. *Matériaux pour un Corpus Inscriptionum Arabicarum*. Mémoires de l'Institut Français d'Archéologie Orientale, vol. LXXVI, LXXVII. Cairo, 1955, 1956.
212. Jaussen, J. A. "Inscription Arabe du Khān al-Akmar à Beïsān (Palestine)," *BIFAO,* XXII (1922), 99-103.
213. ——— "Inscriptions Arabes à la Ville d'Hébron," *BIFAO,* XXV (1924), 1-45.
214. ——— "Inscriptions Arabes de Naplouse," *BIFAO,* XXVII (1927), 91-110.
215. Littman, Enno. *Semitic Inscriptions*. Princeton University, Archeological Expeditions to Syria. Leiden, 1949.
216. Mauss, C. and H. Sauvaire. *Voyage de Jérusalem à Karak et à Chaubak*. Voyage d'Exploration, vol. II. Le Duc de Luynes, ed. Paris, 1874.
217. Mayer, L. A. "Arabic Inscriptions of Gaza," *Journal of the Palestine Oriental Society,* Jerusalem, III (1923), 69-78; V (1925), 64-68; IX (1929), 219-25; X (1930), 59-63; XI (1931), 144-51.
218. ——— "Satura Epigraphica," *The Quarterly of the Department of Antiquities in Palestine,* Jerusalem, I (1931), 37-43; II (1932), 127-31; III (1933), 24-25.
219. ——— "Two Inscriptions of Baybars," *The Quarterly of the Department of Antiquities in Palestine,* Jerusalem, II (1932), 27-33.
220. Rihaoui, Abdul Kader. "Découverte de Deux Inscriptions Arabes," *Les Annales Archéologiques de Syrie,* Damascus, XI-XII (1961–1962), 207-11.
221. Sauvaget, Jean. "Caravansérails Syriens du Moyen Âge," *Ars Islamica,* VII (1940), 1-19.
222. ——— "Un Décret Mamelouk de Syrie," *Mémorial Jean Sauvaget*. Damascus, 1954. pp. 93-99.

223. ——— "Décrets Mamelouks de Syrie," *BEO,* II (1932), 1-52; III (1934), 1-29; XII (1947–1948), 1-60.
224. ——— "Un Monument Commémoratif d'Époque Mamelouks," *Mélanges Maspéro,* vol. III. Cairo, 1940. pp. 15-18.
225. ——— "Notes sur Quelques Inscriptions Arabes de Baalbekk et de Tripoli," *Bulletin du Musée de Beyrouth,* VII (1944–1945), 7-11.
226. Sobernheim, Moritz. "Die Arabischen Inschriften von Aleppo," *Der Islam,* XV (1926), 161-210.
227. ——— "Die Inschriften der Moschee von Hims," *Festschrift zu C. F. Lehmann-Haupts.* Vienna and Leipzig, 1921. pp. 225-239.
228. ——— "Die Inschriften der Zitadelle von Damaskus," *Der Islam,* XII (1922), 1-28.
229. ——— "Inschriftliche Wirtschafts- und Verwaltuns-Verordnungen der Mamluken-Sultane aus der Omajjaden-Moschee von Damaskus," *Festschrift Max Freiherrn von Oppenheim.* Archiv für Orientforschung, Beiband I. Berlin, 1933. pp. 108-26.
230. ——— *Matériaux pour un Corpus Inscriptionum Arabicarum.* Syrie du Nord. Mémoires de l'Institut Français d'Archéologie Orientale, vol. XXV. Cairo, 1909.
231. Sourdel-Thomine, Janine. "Deux Décrets Mamelouks de Marqab," *BEO,* XIV (1952–1954), 61-64.
232. ——— "Inscriptions Arabes de Karak Nuḥ," *BEO,* XIII (1949–1951), 71-84.
233. Sourdel, Janine and Dominique. "Notes d'Épigraphie et de Topographie sur la Syrie du Nord," *Les Annales Archéologiques de Syrie,* Damascus, III (1953), 81-105.
234. von Oppenheim, Max. "Inschriften aus Syrien, Mesopotamien und Kleine Asien," *Beiträge zur Assyriologie,* Leipzig, VII (1909), 1-156.
235. Wiet, Gaston. "Un Décret du Sultan Mamlouk Malik Ashraf Sha'ban à la Mecque," *Mélanges Louis Massignon,* vol. III. Damascus, 1957. pp. 383-410.
236. ——— "Une Inscription du Sultan Djaḥmaḥ," *BIE,* XXI (1938–1939), 79-88.
237. ——— "Notes d'Épigraphie Syro-Musulmane," *Syria,* Paris, V (1924), 216-56; VI (1925), 150-73; VII (1926), 46-66.
238. ——— "Répertoire des Décrets Mamlouks de Syrie," *Mélanges Syriens Offerts à Monsieur René Dussaud,* vol. II. Paris, 1939. pp. 521-37.

8. *Travelers' Accounts and Western Sources*

239. Adler, Elken Nathan, ed. *Jewish Travellers.* New York, 1931.
240. Annales Ragusini Anonymi, item Nicoli de Ragnena, *Monumenta Spectantia Historiam Slavorum Meridionalium,* vol. XIV. Zagreb, 1883.
241. Bellorini, Fr. Theophilus and Fr. Eugene Hoade, tr. *Visit to the Holy Places of Egypt, Sinai, Palestine and Syria.* Includes travels of Frescobaldi, Gucci, and Sigoli. Publications of the Studium Biblicum Franciscanum, vol. VI. Jerusalem, 1948.

242. de Breydenbach, Bernard. *Les Saintes Pérégrinations de Bernard de Breydenbach.* F. Larrivaz, tr. Cairo, 1904.
243. Broquière, Bertrandon de la. ed. Wright, Thomas. *Early Travels in Palestine.* London, 1848. pp. 283-382.
244. Carmoly, E. *Itinéraires de la Terre Sainte des XIV, XV, XVI & XVII Siècle.* Brussels, 1847. Tr. from the Hebrew.
245. Casolá, Pietro. *Pilgrimage to Jerusalem in the year 1494.* M. Margaret Newett, tr. Manchester, 1907.
246. de Clavijo, Ruy Gonzalez. *Embassy to Tamerlane.* Guy Le Strange, tr. London, 1928.
247. ——— *Narrative of the Embassy of Ruy Gonzalez de Clavijo to the Court of Timour at Samarcand, 1403–1406.* Clements R. Markham, tr. London, 1859.
248. Coste, E. de la. *Anselme Adorne, Sire de Corthnay.* Brussels, 1855.
249. Esposito, Mario, ed. *Itinerarium Symones Semeonis ab Hybernia ad Terram Sanctam.* Dublin, 1960.
250. Fabri, Felius. *Evagatorium in Terrae Sanctae.* C. D. Hassler, ed. 3 vols. Stuttgart, 1849.
251. Stewart, Aubrey, tr. *Felix Fabri.* 2 vols. London, 1892.
252. Fulin, Renaldo. *Diarii e Diaristi Veneziani.* Venice, 1881.
253. Grotefend, G. L. "Die Edelherren von Boldensele oder Boldensen," *Zeitschrift des Historischen Vereins für Niedersachsen,* Hanover (1852), 209-86.
254. Guglengensis, Pauli Waltheri. *Itinerarium in Terram Sanctam et ad Sanctam Cathorinam.* M. Sollwech, ed. Tübingen, 1892.
255. von Harff, Arnold. *The Pilgrimage of Arnold von Harff.* Malcolm Letts, tr. London, 1946.
256. Kahler, Charles. "Description de la Terre Sainte par un Franciscain Anonyme, 1463," *Revue de l'Orient Latin,* Paris, XII (1909), 1-67.
257. de Khitrowo, B. *Itinéraires Russes en Orient,* vol. I. Geneva, 1889.
258. de Lannoy, Ghuillebert. *Oeuvres de Ghuillebert de Lannoy.* Charles Potvin, ed. Louvain, 1878.
259. Legrand, Léon. "Relation du Pèlerinage à Jérusalem de Nicolas de Martoni," *Revue de l'Orient Latin,* Paris, III (1895), 566-669.
260. Lengherand, Georges. *Voyage, 1485–1486.* Charles Denys le Marquis de Godefroy-Ménilgaise, ed. Mons, 1861.
261. Makhairos, Leontios. ed. and tr. Dawkins, R. M. *Recital Concerning the Sweet Land of Cyprus.* 2 vols. Oxford, 1932.
262. de Mas Latrie, René. *Chroniques d'Amadi et de Strambaldi.* 2 vols. Paris, 1891–1893.
263. Mariano da Siena. *Del Viaggio in Terra Santa.* Domenico Morani, ed. Florence, 1822.
264. Maundeville, Sir John. ed. Wright, Thomas. *Early Travels in Palestine.* London, 1848. pp. 127-282.
265. Mignanelli, B. de. ed. and tr. Fischel, W. J. "Ascensus Barcoch—A Latin Biography of the Mamlūk Sultan Barqūq of Egypt," *Arabica,* VI (1959), 57-74, 152-72.
266. ——— Fischel, W. J. "Vita Tamerlane—a New Latin Source on Tamerlane's Conquest of Damascus," *Oriens,* Leiden, IX (1956), 201-32.

267. Pero Tafur. *Travels and Adventures.* Malcolm Letts, tr. London, 1926.
268. Piloti, Emmanuel. ed. Baron de Reiffenberg. "Traité d'Emmanuel Piloti d'Ile de Crète sur le passage dans la Terre Sainte," *Monuments pour Servir à l'Histoire des Provinces de Namur, de Hainaut et de Luxembourg,* IV (1846), 312-419.
269. Poggibonsi, Fra Nicolà da. *Libra d'Oltramare 1346–1350.* P. B. Bagatti, ed. Pubblicazioni dello Studium Biblicum Franciscanum, no. 2. Jerusalem, 1945.
270. Poloner, John. *Description of the Holy Land.* Aubrey Stewart, tr. Palestine Pilgrim's Text Society. London, 1894.
271. Rieter, Hans. *Das Reisebuch der Familie Rieter.* Reinhold Röhricht and Heinrich Meisner, ed. Tübingen, 1884.
272. Röhricht, Reinhold. *Deutsche Pilgerreisen nach dem Heiligen Lande.* Innsbruck, 1900.
273. ——— and Heinrich Meisner. *Deutsche Pilgerreisen nach dem Heiligen Lande.* Berlin, 1880.
274. da Sanseverino, Roberto. *Viaggio in Terra Santa.* Bologna, 1888.
275. Sanuto, Marino. *Secrets for True Crusaders.* Aubrey Stewart, tr. London, 1896.
276. Schefer, Charles, ed. *La Voyage de la Saincte Cyté de Hierusalem,* vol. II. Recueil de Voyages et de Documents pour Servir à l'Histoire de la Géographie. Charles Schefer and M. Cordier, ed. Paris, 1882.
277. ——— *La Voyage d'Outre-mer de Jean Thenaud suivi de la Relation de l'Ambassade de Domenico Trevisan auprès du Soudan d'Égypte.* Paris, 1884.
278. Suriano, Fra Francesco. *Treatise on the Holy Land.* Fra Theophilus Bellorini and Fra Eugene Hoade, tr. Publication of the Studium Biblicum Franciscanum, vol. VIII. Jerusalem, 1948.
279. von Suchem, Ludolph. *Description of the Holy Land, A.D. 1350.* Aubrey Stewart, tr. Palestine Pilgrim's Text Society. London, 1895.
280. Varthema, Ludovico de. *The Itinerary of Ludovico de Varthema of Bologna from 1502–1508.* R. C. Temple, ed. London, 1928.

9. Treaties

281. Alarcon Santón y Ramon Garcia de Linares, Maximiliano A. *Los Documentos Árabes Diplomáticos del Archivo de la Coroño de Aragon.* Madrid and Granda, 1940.
282. Amari, Michele. *I Diplomi Arabi de Reale Archivio Fiorentino.* Florence, 1863.
283. ——— "Nuovi Ricordi Arabici su la Storia di Genova," *Atti della Società Ligure di Storia Patria,* Genoa, V (1867), 606-14.
284. ——— "Trattato Spolata da Giacoma II di Aragona Col Sultano d'Egitto," *Reale Academia dei Lincei,* Rome, CCLXXX (1882–1883).
285. Atiya, Aziz S. *Egypt and Aragon, Embassies and Diplomatic Correspondence between 1300 and 1330.* Abhandlungen für die Kunde des Morgenlandes, Deutsche Morgenländischen Gesellschaft, XXIII. Leipzig, 1938.

286. ——— "An Unpublished XIV Century Fatwā on the Status of Foreigners in Mamluk Egypt and Syria," *Studien zur Geschichte und Kultur des Nahen und Fernen Ostens Paul Kahle*. Leiden, 1935. pp. 55-68.

287. Belgrano, L. T. "Trattato del Sultano d'Egitto Col Commune de Genova nel 1290," *Atti della Società Ligure di Storia Patria,* Genoa, XIX (1888), 111-75.

288. Blancard, Louis. *Documents Inédits sur le Commerce de Marseille au Moyen Âge,* vol. II. Marseilles, 1885.

289. Canard, Marius. "Le Traité de 1281 entre Michel Paléologue et le Sultan Qalā'ūn," *Byzantion,* X (1935), 669-80.

290. ——— "Une Lettre du Sultan Mālik Nāṣir Ḥasan à Jean VI Cantacuzene," *AIEO,* II (1937), 27-52.

291. ——— "Un Traité entre Byzance et l'Égypte au XIIIe Siècle et les Relations Dipomatiques de Michel VIII Paléologue avec les Sultans Mamlūks Baibars et Qalā'ūn," *Mélange Gaudefroy-Demombynes.* Cairo, 1935–1945. pp. 197-224.

292. Dölger, Franz. "Der Vertrag des Sultans Qalā'ūn von Ägypten mit der Kaiser Michael VIII Palaiologos," *Serta Monacensia Franz Babinger.* H. J. Kissling and A. Schmaus, ed. Leiden, 1952. pp. 60-79.

293. Jorga, Nicolas. *Notes et Extraits pour Servir à l'Histoire des Croisades au XVe Siècle,* vols. I-III. Paris, 1899–1902.

294. Lammens, Henri. "Correspondances Diplomatiques entre les Sultans Mamlouks d'Égypte et les Puissances Chrétiennes," *Revue de l'Orient Chrétien,* Paris, IX (1904), 151-87, 359-92.

295. Orsatti, Reginaldo Ruiz. "Tratado de Paz entre Alfonso V de Aragon y el Sultán de Egypto, al Mālik al-Ašraf Barsbāy," *Al Andalus,* Madrid-Granada, V (1939), 333-89.

296. Reinard, M. "Traités de Commerce entre la République de Venise et les Derniers Sultans Mameloucs d'Égypte," *JA,* Ser. I, vol. IV (1829), 22-51.

297. Thomas, Georg Martin. *Diplomatarium Veneto-Levantium 1330–1350.* Venice, 1880.

298. Wansbrough, John. "A Mamluk Letter of 877/1473," *BSOAS,* XXIV (1961), 200-13.

II. *Secondary Works*

A. ART HISTORY

299. Abdul-Hak, Selim. "Contribution à l'Étude de la Verrerie Musulmane du VIIIe au XVe Siècles," *Les Annales Archéologiques de Syrie,* Damascus, VIII-IX (1958–1959), 3-20.

300. van Berchem, Max. "Notes d'Archéologie Arabe. Étude sur les Cuivres Damasquinés et les Verres Émaillés," *JA,* Ser. X, vol. III (1904), 5-96.

301. Dimand, M. S. *A Handbook of Mohammedan Decorative Arts.* New York, 1930.

302. Hein, Wilhelm. "Eine Datierbare Moscheelampe aus der Mamlukenzeit," *Wiener Zeitschrift für die Kunde des Morgenlandes,* LIII (1957), 88-91.

303. Jungfleisch, Marcel. "À Propos d'une Publication du Musée de l'Art Arabe; Garbī et les Grands Faïenciers Égyptiens d'Époque Mamlouke par M. Armand Abel," *BIE*, XIV (1931–1932), 257-74.
304. Lamm, Carl Johan. *Cotton in Mediaeval Textiles of the Near East*. Paris, 1937.
305. ——— *Mittelalterliche Gläser und Steinschnittarbeiten aus dem Nahen Osten*. Berlin, 1930.
306. Mayer, L. A. *Islamic Astrolabists and Their Work*. Geneva, 1956.
307. ——— *Islamic Woodcarvers and Their Work*. Geneva, 1958.
308. ——— *Mamluk Costume*. Geneva, 1952.
309. Migeon, Gaston. *Manuel d'Art Musulman; Arts Plastiques et Industriels*. 2 vols. 2nd ed. Paris, 1927.
310. Reich, S. "Une Inscription Mamlouke sur un Dessin Italien du Quinzième Siècle," *BIE*, XXII (1939–1940), 123-31.
311. ——— and Gaston Wiet. "Un Astrolabe Syrien du XIV Siècle," *BIFAO*, XXXVIII (1939), 195-202.
312. Rice, D. S. "Studies on Islamic Metalwork," *BSOAS*, XIV (1952), 564-78.
313. Sauvaget, Jean. *Poteries Syro-Mésopotamiennes*. Documents des Études Orientales de l'Institut Français de Damas, vol. I. Damascus, 1932.
314. Schmidt, J. Heinrich. "Damaste der Mamlūkenzeit," *Ars Islamica*, I (1934), 99-109.
315. Wiet, Gaston. "Inscriptions Mobilières de l'Égypte Musulmane," *JA*, CCXLVI (1958), 237-85.
316. ——— "Lampes en Verre Émaillé," *BIE*, XIV (1931–1932), 117-26.
317. ——— *Objets en Cuivre*. Catalogue du Musée Arabe du Caire. Cairo, 1932.

B. ECONOMIC HISTORY

318. Ashtor, Eli. "Le Coût de la Vie dans la Syrie Médiévale," *Arabica*, VIII (1961), 59-72.
319. ——— "Le Coût de la Vie dans l'Égypte Médiévale," *JESHO*, III (1960), 56-77.
320. ——— "L'Évolution des Prix dans le Proche-Orient à la Basse-Époque," *JESHO*, IV (1961), 15-46.
321. ——— "The Karimi Merchants," *JRAS* (1956), 45-56.
322. ——— "Matériaux pour l'Histoire des Prix dans l'Égypte Médiévale," *JESHO*, VI (1963), 158-89.
323. ——— "Quelques Indications sur les Revenues dans l'Orient Musulman au Haut Moyen Âge," *JESHO*, II (1959), 262-80.
324. Balog, Paul. "Aperçus sur la Technique du Monnayage Musulman au Moyen-Âge," *BIE*, XXX (1948–1949), 95-105.
325. ——— *The Coinage of the Mamlūk Sultans of Egypt and Syria*. Numismatic Studies. American Numismatic Society, vol. XII. New York, 1964.
326. ——— "Études Numismatiques de l'Égypte Musulmane," *BIE*, XXXIV (1951–1952), 17-55.
327. ——— "History of the Dirhem," *Revue Numismatique*, Paris, Ser. III, vol. VI (1961), 109-46.

328. ——— "Quelques Dinars du Début de l'Ère Mamelouke Bahriite," *BIE,* XXXII (1949–1950), 229-52.

329. ——— "Un Quart de Dinar du Sultan Naser Mohammed Ben Qalaoun," *BIE,* XXXII (1949–1950), 255-56.

330. Becker, C. H. "Zur Kulturgeschichte Nord Syriens im Zeitalter der Mamlūken," *Der Islam,* I (1910), 93-100.

331. Boüard, Michel de. "Sur l'Évolution Monétaire de l'Égypte Médiévale," *L'Égypte Contemporaine,* Cairo, XXX (1939), 427-59.

332. Dunlop, D. M. "Sources of Gold and Silver in Islam according to Ibn al-Hamdānī," *Studia Islamica,* VIII (1957), 29-49.

333. Ehrenkreutz, A. S. "Contributions to the Knowledge of the Fiscal Administration of Egypt in the Middle Ages," *BSOAS,* XVI (1954), 502-14.

334. Fischel, Walter J. "The Spice Trade in Mamluk Egypt," *JESHO,* I (1958), 157-74.

335. ——— "Über die Gruppe der Kārìmī-Kaufleute," *Studia Arabica,* Rome, I (1937), 65-82.

336. Gaudefroy-Demombynes, M. "Sur Quelques Ouvrages de Hisba," *JA,* CCXXX (1938), 449-57.

337. Gennep, A. Rouge von. "Le Ducat Venitien en Égypte," *Revue Numismatique,* Paris, Ser. IV, vol. I (1897), 373-81, 494-508.

338. Goitein, S. D. "From the Mediterranean to India," *Speculum,* XXIX (1954), 181-97.

339. ——— "The Main Industries of the Mediterranean Area," *JESHO,* IV (1961), 168-97.

340. ——— "Slaves and Slave Girls in the Cairo Geniza Records," *Arabica,* IX (1962), 1-20.

341. Inalcik, H. "Bursa and the Commerce of the Levant," *JESHO,* III (1960), 131-47.

342. Jungfleisch, Marcel. "Tentative d'Identifier les Petits Bronzes Frappés par les Deux Mouayad," *BIE,* XIX (1946–1947), 45-50.

343. Labib, Subhi. "Geld und Kredit, Studien zur Wirtschaftsgeschichte Ägyptens im Mittelalter," *JESHO,* II (1959), 225-46.

344. Lewis, Bernard. "A Jewish Source on Damascus just after the Ottoman Conquest," *BSOAS,* X (1939), 179-84.

345. ——— *Notes and Documents from the Turkish Archives—A Contribution to the History of the Jews in the Ottoman Empire.* Oriental Notes and Studies published by the Israel Oriental Society, vol. III. Jerusalem, 1952.

346. ——— "Studies in the Ottoman Archives," *BSOAS,* XVI (1954), 469-501.

347. Lombard, M. "Le Bois dans la Méditerranée Musulmane, VIIe-XIe Siècles," *Annales. Économies, Sociétés, Civilisations,* XIV (1959), 234-54.

348. Michel, Bernard. "L'Organisation Financière de l'Égypt sous les Sultans Mamelouks d'après Qalqachande," *BIE,* VII (1924–1925), 127-47.

349. Minost, E. "Au Sujet de Traité des Monnaies Musulmanes de Makrizi," *BIE,* XIX (1936–1937), 45-61.

350. Moberg, Axel. "Zwei Ägyptische Wakf-Urkunden aus dem Jahre 591/1292," *Le Monde Oriental,* Uppsala, XII (1918), 1-64.

351. Sacy, Silvestre de. "Traité des Monnaies Musulmanes Traduit de l'Arabe de Makrizi," *Bibliothèque des Arabisants Français,* vol. I. Cairo, 1905. pp. 9-66.
352. ——— "Trois Mémoires sur la Nature et les Révolutions du Droit de Propriété Territoriale en Égypte," *Bibliothèque des Arabisants Français,* vol. II. Cairo, 1923.
353. Sauvaire, H. "Matériaux pour Servir à l'Histoire de la Numismatique et de la Métrologie Musulmanes," *JA,* Ser. VII, vol. XIV (1879), 455-533; vol. XV (1880), 228-77, 421-78; vol. XVIII (1881), 499-516; XIX (1882), 23-77, 281-327.
354. Sobernheim, M. "Das Zuckermonopol unter Sultan Barsbāī," *Zeitschrift für Assyriologie und Verwandte Gebiete,* Berlin, XXVII (1912), 75-84.
355. Strauss, Eli. "Prix et Salaires à l'Époque Mamlouke," *REI* (1949), 49-94.
356. Sublet, J. " 'Abd al-Laṭīf al-Takrītī et la Famille des Banu Kuwayk, Marchands Kārimī," *Arabica,* IX (1962), 193-96.
357. Ṭalbī, Muḥammad. "Les Courtiers en Vêtements en Ifriqiya au IXᵉ et au Xᵉ Siècle," *JESHO,* V (1962), 160-94.
358. ——— "Quelques Données sur la Vie Sociale en Occident Musulman d'après un Traité de Ḥisba du XV Siècle," *Arabica,* I (1954), 294-306.
359. Tomiche, N. "La Situation des Artisans et Petits Commerçants en Égypte de la Fin du XVIIIᵉ Siècle jusqu'au Milieu du XIXᵉ," *Studia Islamica,* XII (1960), 79-98.
360. Le Tourneau, R. and L. Page. "L'Industrie de la Tannerie à Fes," *Hesperis,* Paris, XXI (1935), 167-240.
361. Wickens, G. M. "al-Jarīfī on the Ḥisba," *Islamic Quarterly,* London, III (1956), 176-87.
362. Wiet, Gaston. "Les Marchands d'Épices sous les Sultans Mamlouks," *Cahiers d'Histoire Égyptienne,* Cairo, VII (1955), 81-147.
363. Zayāt, H. "Khaṣā'iṣ Ba'albak Qadīmā fī al-Sinā'a wal-Zirā'a," *al-Mashriq,* Beirut, XLI (April-June 1947), 13-17.

C. HISTORY OF SYRIA AND EGYPT

364. Abel, A. "Reflexions Comparatives sur la Sensibilité Médiévale autour de la Méditerranée aux XIII et XIV Siècles," *Studia Islamica,* XIII (1960), 23-41.
365. Aubin, Jean. "Comment Tamerlan Prenait Les Villes," *Studia Islamica,* XIX (1963), 83-122.
366. ——— "Les Princes d'Ormuz du XIII au XV Siècle," *JA,* CCXXXXI (1953), 77-137.
367. 'Awād, Ibrāhīm. "Lubnān fī 'Ahd al-Mamālīk," *al-Mashriq,* Beirut, XL (1942–1943), 1-28.
368. Ayalon, David. "Studies on the Transfer of the 'Abbāsid Caliphate from Bagdād to Cairo," *Arabica,* VII (1960), 41-59.
369. Cahen, Claude. "Contribution à l'Histoire du Diyār Bakr au Quatorzième Siècle," *JA,* CCXLIII (1955), 65-100.
370. ——— "La Chronique de Ḳirṭāy et les Francs de Syrie," *JA,* CCXXIX (1937), 140-45.

371. Cheikho, Père Louis. "Un Dernier Écho des Croisades," *Mélanges de la Faculté Orientale, Université Saint Joseph,* vol. I. Beirut, 1906. pp. 303-75.
372. ——— "Ta'rīkh Bayrūt fī 'Ahd Mamālīk Miṣr," *al-Mashriq,* Beirut, XXIII (1925), 944-48.
373. Combe, E. "Les Sultans Mamlouks Ashraf Sha'bān et Ghouri à Alexandrie," *Bulletin de la Société Royale d'Archéologie d'Alexandrie,* IX (1930), 33-48.
374. Darrag, Ahmad. *L'Égypte sous le Règne de Barsbay.* Damascus, 1961.
375. *Encyclopaedia of Islam.* 2nd ed. Leiden, 1954– .
376. Fischel, Walter J. *Ibn Khaldun and Tamerlane.* Berkeley and Los Angeles, 1952.
377. Grant, C. P. *The Syrian Desert,* London, 1937.
378. Heyd, Uriel. *Ottoman Documents on Palestine, 1552–1615.* Oxford, 1960.
379. Hitti, Philip K. *History of Syria.* London, 1957.
380. Hookham, Hilda. *Tamburlaine the Conqueror.* London, 1962.
381. Lammens, Henri. *La Syrie: Précis Historique.* 2 vols. Beirut, 1921.
382. Laoust, Henri. "Ibn Katīr, Historien," *Arabica,* II (1955), 42-88.
383. ——— "Remarques sur les Expeditions du Kasrawan sous les Premiers Mamluks," *Bulletin du Musée de Beyrouth,* IV (1940), 93-115.
384. Lewis, Bernard. "The Ismā'īlites and the Assassins," *A History of the Crusades.* Kenneth M. Setton, ed. vol. I. Philadelphia, 1958. pp. 99-132.
385. Minorsky, Vladimir. "La Perse au XVe Siècle," *Orientalia Romana,* Rome, XVII (1958), 99-117.
386. Mostafa, Mohamed. "Beiträge zur Geschichte Ägyptens," *ZDMG,* LXXXIX (1935), 194-224.
387. Muir, William. *The Mameluke or Slave Dynasty of Egypt 1260–1517.* London, 1896.
388. Reinaud, M. "Histoires des Guerres des Croisades sous la Règne de Baibars, Sultan d'Égypte, d'après les Auteurs Arabes," *JA,* XI (1827), 3-33, 65-94, 129-63.
389. Richard, Jean. "Un Partage de Seigneurie entre Francs et Mamelouks: 'les Casaux de Sur,'" *Syria,* Paris, XXX (1953), 72-82.
390. Runciman, S. *The Kingdom of Acre and the Later Crusades.* History of the Crusades, vol. III. Cambridge, Eng., 1954.
391. Salibi, K. S. "The Buḥturids of the Garb," *Arabica,* VIII (1961), 74-97.
392. ——— *Maronite Historians of Medieval Lebanon.* Beirut, 1959.
393. ——— "The Maronites of Lebanon under Frankish and Mamluk Rule (1099–1516)," *Arabica,* IV (1957), 288-303.
394. Sacy, Silvestre de. *Chrestomathie Arabe.* 4 vols. Paris, 1826.
395. "A Servian Embassy to Egypt in the 14th Century," *JRAS* (1913), 1047-48.
396. Surūr, Muḥammad Jamāl al-Dīn. *Dawlat Bani Qalāūn fī Miṣr.* Cairo, n.d.
397. Tritton, A. S. "The Tribes of Syria in the 14th and 15th Centuries," *BSOAS,* XII (1948), 567-73.

398. Wiet, Gaston. "Deux Princes Ottomanes à la Cour d'Égypte," *BIE*, XX (1937–1938), 137-50.
399. ——— *L'Égypte Arabe*. Histoire de la Nation Égyptienne, vol. IV. G. Hanotaux, ed. Paris, n.d.
400. ——— "Réfugiés Politiques Ottomans en Égypte," *Arabica*, I (1954), 258-71.
401. Ziada, Mustafa M. "The Mamluk Sultans to 1293," *A History of the Crusades*. Kenneth M. Setton, ed. vol. II. Philadelphia, 1962. pp. 735-58.

D. THE MAMLUK STATE

402. Ayalon, David. "The Circassians in the Mamluk Kingdom," *JAOS*, LXIX (1954), 135-47.
403. ——— *L'Esclavage du Mamelouk*. Oriental Notes and Studies, The Israel Oriental Society, no. 1. Jerusalem, 1951.
404. ——— *Gunpowder and Firearms in the Mamluk Kingdom*. London, 1956.
405. ——— "Notes on the Furūsiyya Exercises and Games in the Mamluk Sultanate," *Scripta Hierosolymitana*, vol. IX. Uriel Heyd, ed. Jerusalem, 1961. pp. 31-62.
406. ——— "Le régiment Bahriya dans l'Armé Mamelouke," *REI* (1951), 133-41.
407. ——— "Studies on the Structure of the Mamluk Army," *BSOAS*, XV (1953), 203-28, 448-76; XVI (1954), 57-90.
408. ——— "The System of Payment in Mamluk Military Society," *JESHO*, I (1957–1958), 37-65, 257-96.
409. ——— "The Wafidiya in the Mamluk Kingdom," *Islamic Culture*, XXV (1951), 89-104.
410. Becker, C. and Claude Cahen, ed. " 'Uthmān b. Ibrāhīm al-Nābulusī. Kitāb Luma' al-Qawānīn al-Muḍiyya fī Dawāwīn al-Diyār al-Miṣriyya," *BEO*, XVI (1958–1960), 119-34, Arabic text, 78pp.
411. Björkman, Walther. *Beiträge zur Geschichte der Staatskanzler im Islamischen Ägypten*. Hamburg, 1928.
412. Bosworth, C. E. "A Maqāma on Secretaryship: al-Qalqashandī's al-Kawākib al-Duriyya fī'l Manāqib al-Badriyya," *BSOAS*, XXVII (1964), 291-98.
413. ——— "Some Historical Gleanings from the Section on Symbolic Actions in Qalqašandī's Ṣubḥ al-a'šā," *Arabica*, X (1963), 148-53.
414. Cahen, Claude. "Contribution à l'Étude des Impôts dans l'Égypte Médiévale," *JESHO*, V (1962), 244-78.
415. ——— "L'évolution de l'Iqtā' de IXᵉ au XIIIᵉ Siècle," *Annales. Économies, Sociétés, Civilisations*, VIII (1953), 25-52.
416. ——— "Quelques Aspects de l'Administration Égyptienne Médiévale," *Bulletin de la Faculté des Lettres de Strasbourg*, XXVI (1948), 97-118.
417. ——— "Un Traité Financier Inédit d'Époque Fatimide-Ayyubide," *JESHO*, V (1962), 139-59.
418. Mayer, L. A. *Saracenic Heraldry*. Oxford, 1933.
419. Neustadt, David. "The Plague and Its Effects upon the Mamlūk Army," *JRAS* (1946), 67-73.

420. Pevzner, S. B. "Ikta' v Egipte v Kontse XIII-XIV Vekakh," (The Iqtā' in Egypt at the End of the 13th and the 14th Centuries), *Pamiati Akademika Ignatiia Iulianovicha Krachkovskogo*. I. A. Orbeli, ed. Leningrad, 1958. pp. 176-91.
421. Poliak, A. N. "La Féodalité Islamique," *REI*, X (1936), 247-65.
422. ——— *Feudalism in Egypt, Syria, Palestine and the Lebanon, 1250–1900*. London, 1939.
423. ——— "The Influence of Chingiz-Khan's Yāsa upon the General Organization of the Mamluk State," *BSOAS*, X (1942), 862-76.
424. ——— "Some Notes on the Feudal System of the Mamluks," *JRAS* (1937), 97-107.
425. Popper, William. *Egypt and Syria under the Circassian Sultans, 1382–1468* A.D. University of California Publications in Semitic Philology, vols. XV, XVI. Berkeley, 1955, 1957.
426. Sauvaget, Jean. "Noms et Surnoms de Mamelouks," *JA*, CCXXXVIII (1950), 31-58.
427. ——— *La Poste aux Chevaux dans l'Empire des Mamelouks*. Paris, 1941.
428. ——— "Un Relais du Barīd Mamelouk," *Mélanges Gaudefroy-Demombynes*. Cairo, 1935–1945. pp. 41-45.
429. Schimmel, Annemarie. "Kalif und Kadi im Spätmittelalterlichen Ägypten," *Die Welt des Islams*, Leiden, XXIV (1943), 1-128.
430. Toussoun, Prince Omar. *Mémoire sur les Finances de l'Égypte depuis les Pharaons jusqu'à nos Jours*. Mémoires Présentés à l'Institut d'Égypte, vol. VI. Cairo, 1924.
431. Tyan, E. *Histoire de l'Organisation Judiciaire en Pays d'Islam*. 2nd ed. Leiden, 1960.
432. Zappoth, Gerhard. "Muhammad ibn Mängli Ein Ägyptischer Offizier und Schriftsteller des 14. Jhs.," *Wiener Zeitschrift für die Kunde des Morgenlandes*, LIII (1957), 288-99.

E. Mediterranean cities and trade

433. Andréadès, A. "Byzance, Paradis du Monopole et du Privilège," *Byzantion*, IX (1934), 171-81.
434. Atiya, Aziz S. *Crusade, Commerce and Culture*. Bloomington, Indiana, 1962.
435. ——— *The Crusade in the Later Middle Ages*. London, 1938.
436. Baratier, Édouard and Félix Reynard. *Histoire du Commerce de Marseille*, vol. II. Paris, 1951.
437. Berchet, G. *Del Commercio dei Veneti Nell'Asia*. Venice, 1864.
438. Bragadin, H. *Histoire des Républiques Maritimes Italiennes*. R. Juffé and R. Jouan, tr. Paris, 1955.
439. Canard, M. "Les Relations entre les Mérinides et les Mamelouks au XIVe Siècle," *AIEO*, V (1939–1941), 41-81.
440. Capmany, Antonio de. *Memorias Historicas sobre la Marina Commercio y Artes de la Antigua Ciudad de Barcelona*. 3 vols. Madrid, 1779.
441. Carrere, Claude. "Le Droit d'Ancrage et le Mouvement du Port de Barcelone au Milieu du XVe Siècle," *Estudios de Historia Moderna*, Barcelona, III (1953), 65-156.

442. Colin, G. S. "Contribution à l'Étude des Relations Diplomatiques entre les Musulmans d'Occident et l'Égypte aux XV Siècle," *Mélanges Maspéro,* vol. III. Cairo, 1940. pp. 197-206.
443. Collier, Raymond. *Histoire du Commerce de Marseille,* vol. III. Paris, 1951.
444. Darrag, Aḥmad. *Al-Mamālīk wal-Franj.* Cairo, 1961.
445. Day, John. "Prix Agricoles en Méditerranée à la Fin du XIVe Siècle," *Annales. Économies, Sociétés, Civilisations,* XVI (1961), 629-56.
446. Delaville de Roulx, J. *La France en Orient au XIV Siècle,* vol. I. Paris, 1886.
447. ——— *Les Hospitaliers à Rhodes, 1310–1421.* Paris, 1913.
448. Desimoni, A. "Actes Passés à Famagouste de 1299 à 1301," *Archives de l'Orient Latin,* Paris, I (1893), 58-139, 274-312, 321-53; II (1884), 3-120.
449. Dulaurier, Édouard. *Étude sur l'Organisation Politique, Réligieuse et Administrative du Royaume de la Petite-Arménie à l'Époque des Croisades.* Paris, 1862.
450. Germain, A. *Histoire du Commerce de Montpellier.* Montpellier, 1861.
451. Grierson, Philip. "La Moneta Veneziana Nell' Economia Mediterranea del Trecento e Quattrocento," *La Civiltà Veneziana del Quattrocento.* Venice, 1958.
452. Guiraud, L. *Sur le Prétendu Rôle de Jacques Coeur.* Paris, 1900.
453. Hazlitt, W. Carew. *The Venetian Republic: Its Rise, Its Growth, and Its Fall.* 2 vols. London, 1945.
454. Heers, Jacques. *Gênes au XV Siècle.* Paris, 1961.
455. ——— "Il Commercio nel Mediterraneo alla Fina del Secolo XIV," *Archivio Storico Italiano,* Florence, LXIII (1955), 151-209.
456. ——— "La Sahara et le Commerce Méditerranéen à la Fin du Moyen Âge," *AIEO,* XVI (1958), 247-55.
457. Heyd, W. *Histoire du Commerce du Levant au Moyen Âge.* 2 vols. F. Raynaud, tr. Leipzig, 1885.
458. ——— "Les Consulats Établis en Terre Sainte au Moyen Âge pour la Protection des Pèlerin," *Archives de l'Orient Latin,* vol. II. Paris, 1884. pp. 355-63, 512.
459. Hill, Sir George. *A History of Cyprus.* 3 vols. Cambridge, Eng., 1948.
460. Jorga, N. *Brève Histoire de la Petite Arménie.* Paris, 1930.
461. Julia, N. Coll. "Aspectos del Corso Catalan y del Comercio Internacional en el Siglo XV," *Estudios de Historia Moderna,* IV (1954), 157-87.
462. Kovacevic, D. "Dans la Serbie et la Bosnie Médiévales: Les Mines d'Or et d'Argent," *Annales. Économies, Sociétés, Civilisations,* XV (1960), 248-58.
463. Krekić, B. *Dubrovnik (Raguse) et le Levant au Moyen Âge.* Paris, 1961.
464. Labib, S. Y. *Handelsgeschichte Ägyptens im Spätmittelalter.* Wiesbaden, 1964.
465. LaMonte, John L. "The Communal Movement in Syria in the Thirteenth Century," *Anniversary Essays on Medieval History by Students of Charles Homer Haskins.* Boston, 1929. pp. 117-31.

466. Lane, Frederic C. *Andrea Barbarago, Merchant of Venice, 1418–1449.* Baltimore, 1944.

467. ——— "Cargaison de Coton et Réglementations Médiévales contre la Surcharge des Navires-Venise," *Revue d'Histoire Économique et Sociale,* XL (1962), 21-31.

468. ——— "Fleets and Fairs, the Functions of the Venetian Muda," *Studi in Onori di Armando Sapori.* 2 vols. Milan, 1957. pp. 649-63.

469. Lavergne, G. "La Pêche et le Commerce de Corail à Marseille aux XIV et XV Siècles," *Annales du Midi,* Toulouse, LXIV (1952), 199-211.

470. Lombard, M. "L'Évolution Urbaine Pendant le Haut Moyen Âge," *Annales. Économies, Sociétés, Civilisations,* XII (1957), 7-28.

471. Lopez, Roberto S. *Storia Delli Colonie Genovesi nel Mediterraneo.* Bologna, 1938.

472. ——— "The Trade of Medieval Europe: The South," *Cambridge Economic History of Europe,* vol. II. Cambridge, Eng., 1952.

473. ——— and Irving W. Raymond. *Medieval Trade in the Mediterranean World.* New York, 1955.

474. Marin, Carlo Antonio. *Storia Civile e Politica del Commercio di Veneziani,* vol. VII. Venice, 1800.

475. Marinescu, Contantin. *Notes sur les Corsaires au Service d'Alfonse V d'Aragon.* Mélanges d'Histoire Générale. Cluj, 1927.

476. Meneses, Amada López de. "Los Consulados Catalanes de Alejandria y Damasco en el Reinado de Pedro el Ceremonioso," *Estudios de Edad Media de la Coroña de Aragon,* Saragosa, VI (1956), 82-183.

477. Nicolau d'Olwer, Luis. *L'Expansio de Catalunya en la Mediterrania Oriental.* Barcelona, 1926.

478. Pegolotti, Francesco B. *La Pratica della Mercatura.* Allen Evans, ed. Cambridge, Mass., 1936.

479. Pernaud, R. *Histoire du Commerce de Marseille,* vol. I. Paris, 1949.

480. Pomés, Madelena Sacez. "Los Aragoneses en la Conquista Sagueo de Alejandria," *Estudios de Edad Media de la Coroña de Aragon,* Saragosa, V (1952), 360-405.

481. Port, Célestin. *Essai sur l'Histoire du Commerce Maritime de Narbonne.* Paris, 1854.

482. Sattos, Jules. *Les Messageries Maritimes de Venise aux XIVe au XVe Siècles.* Paris, 1938.

483. Sauvaget, Jean. "Une Ancienne Représentation de Damas au Musée du Louvre," *BEO,* XI (1945–1946), 5-12.

484. Schwarzfuchs, Simon. "Dans la Méditerranée Oriental au XVIe Siècle, Les Marchands Juifs," *Annales. Économies, Sociétés, Civilisations,* XII (1957), 112-18.

485. Spont, Alfred. "La France et l'Égypte au Début du XVIe Siècle," *Revue de l'Orient Latin,* Paris, I (1893), 445-51.

486. Tenenti, Alberto and Corrado Vivanti. "Les Galères Marchandes Vénetiennes, XIV–XVI Siècles," *Annales. Économies, Sociétés, Civilisations,* XVI (1961), 83-86.

487. Uzzano, Giovanni di Antonio da. *La Practica della Mercatura,* vol. IV.

Giovanni Franceso Pagnini della Ventura, ed. Lisbon and Lucia, 1766.

488. Wansbrough, John. "A Mamluk Ambassador to Venice in 913/1507," *BSOAS,* XXVI (1963), 501-30.

F. MUSLIM AND MAMLUK CITIES

489. Adler, E. N. "Aleppo," *Gedenkbuch zur Erinnerung an David Kaufman.* M. Brann and F. Rosenthal, ed. Breslau, 1900. pp. 128-37.

490. Alouf, Michel M. *Histoire de Baalbek.* Beirut, 1890.

491. ——— *History of Baalbek.* 9th English ed. Beirut, 1953.

492. Ashtor, Eli. "L'Urbanisme Syrien à la Basse-Époque," *Revista degli Studia Orientalia,* XXXIII (1958), 181-209.

493. Barkan, Ömer Lutfi. "Essai sur les Données Statistiques des Registres de Recensement dans l'Empire Ottoman aux XVe et XVIe Siècles," *JESHO,* I (1957), 9-36.

494. ——— "Quelques Observations sur l'Organisation Économique et Sociale des Villes Ottomanes," *La Ville,* vol. VII. Société Jean Bodin. Brussels, 1955. pp. 289-311.

495. Bergsträsser, G. "Das Islamische Damaskus," *Orientalistische Literaturzeitung,* Berlin, XXIX (1926), 317-24.

496. Brunschvig, R. "Urbanisme Médiéval et Droit Musulman," *REI* (1947), 127-55.

497. Cahen, Claude. "Mouvements et Organisations Populaires dans les Villes de l'Asie Musulmane au Moyen Âge: Milices et Associations de Foutouwwa," *La Ville,* vol. VII. Société Jean Bodin. Brussels, 1955. pp. 273-88.

498. ——— "Mouvements Populaires et Autonomisme Urbain dans l'Asie Musulmane de Moyen Âge," *Arabica,* V (1958), 225-50; VI (1959), 25-56, 223-65.

499. ——— "Zur Geschichte des Städtischen Gesellschaft im Islamischen Orient des Mittelalters," *Speculum,* Freiburg-Munich, IX (1958), 59-76.

500. Dussaud, René. *Topographie Historique de la Syrie Antique et Médiévale.* Paris, 1927.

501. Écochard, Michel and Claude Le Coeur. *Les Bains de Damas.* Beirut, 1943.

502. von Grunebaum, G. E. "The Structure of the Muslim Town," *Islam: Essays on the Nature and Growth of a Cultural Tradition.* 2nd ed. London, 1961. pp. 141-58.

503. Issa Bey, Ahmed. *Histoire des Bimaristans (Hôpitaux) à l 'Époque Islamique.* Cairo, 1928.

504. Kahle, Paul. "Die Katostrophe des Mittelalterlichen Alexandria," *Mélanges Maspéro,* vol. III. Cairo, 1940. pp. 137-54.

505. Kremer, Alfred von. *Mittelsyrien und Damascus.* Vienna, 1853.

506. Lane-Poole, S. *The Story of Cairo.* London, 1924.

507. Mantran, Robert. *Istanbul dans la Seconde Moitié du XVIIe Siècle.* Paris, 1962.

508. Marçais, G. "Considerations sur les Villes Musulmanes et Notamment sur le Rôle du Mohtasib," *La Ville,* vol. VI. Société Jean Bodin. Brussels, 1955. pp. 248-62.

509. ——— "La Conception des Villes dans l'Islam," *Revue d'Alger,* II (1945), 517-33.
510. Marçais, W. "L'Islamisme et la Vie Urbaine," *Comptes Rendus, Académie des Inscriptions et Belles Lettres* (1928), 86-100.
511. Mazloum, S. *L'Ancienne Canalisation d'Eau d'Alep.* Documents d'Études Orientales de l'Institut Français de Damas, vol. V. Damascus, 1936.
512. Mehren, A. F. *Syrien og Palestina Studie efter en Aribisk Geograph.* Copenhagen, 1862.
513. Mesnil du Buisson, Le Comte du. "Les Anciens Défenses de Beyrouth," *Syria,* Paris, II (1921), 235-57.
514. Meyer, Martin A. *History of the City of Gaza.* New York, 1907.
515. al-Munajjid, Ṣalāḥ al-Dīn. "Ḥammāmāt Dimashq," *al-Mashriq,* Beirut, XLI (1947), 401-25.
516. ——— "Khiṭaṭ Dimashq," *al-Mashriq,* Beirut, XLII (1948), 39-65, 242-88.
517. Pauty, Edmond. "Villes Spontanées et Villes Créées en Islam," *AIEO,* IX (1951), 52-75.
518. de Planhol, X. *Le Monde Islamique.* Paris, 1957.
519. Richmond, Ernest. "The Significance of Cairo," *JRAS* (1913), 23-40.
520. Sauvaget, Jean. *Alep.* Paris, 1941.
521. ——— "Deux Sanctuaires Chiites d'Alep," *Syria,* Paris, IX (1928), 224-37, 320-27.
522. ——— "Esquisses d'une Histoire de la Ville de Damas," *REI,* VIII (1934), 421-80.
523. ——— "Inventaire des Monuments Musulmans de la Ville d'Alep," *REI,* V (1931), 59-114.
524. ——— "La Citadelle de Damas," *Syria,* Paris, XI (1930), 56-90, 216-41.
525. ——— *Les Monuments Historiques de Damas.* Beirut, 1932.
526. ——— "Notes sur les Défenses de la Marine de Tripoli," *Bulletin du Musée de Beyrouth,* II (1938), 1-25.
527. Sourdel-Thomine, Janine. "Le Peuplement de la Région des 'Villes Mortes' à l'Époque Ayyubide," *Arabica,* I (1954), 187-200.
528. Thoumin, R. *Géographie Humaine de la Syrie Centrale.* Tours, 1936.
529. Tolkawsky, S. "New Light on the History of Jaffa," *Journal of the Palestine Oriental Society,* Jerusalem, II (1925), 82-85.
530. Weulersse, J. "La Primauté des Cités dans l'Économie Syrienne," *Géographie Humaine.* Comptes Rendus du Congrès International de Géographie, vol. II, Leiden, 1938. pp. 233-39.
531. Wiet, Gaston. "La Madrasa Khaidarīya, à Damas," *Mélanges Gaudefroy-Demombynes.* Cairo, 1935–1945. pp. 18-23.
532. Wultzinger, Karl and Carl Watzinger. *Damaskus, Die Islamische Stadt.* 2 vols. Berlin and Leipzig, 1924.
533. Zayāt, H. "Nuzhat al-Rifāq 'an Shar' Ḥāl al-Aswāq," *al-Mashriq,* Beirut, XXXVII (1939), 18-28.
534. Ziadeh, Nicola A. *Damascus Under the Mamlūks.* Norman, Oklahoma, 1964.
535. ——— "Town Administration in Syria under the Early Mamluks,"

Proceedings of the Twenty-Second Congress of Orientalists, vol. II. Leiden, 1957. pp. 206-27.

536. ——— *Urban Life in Syria under the Early Mamluks*. Beirut, 1953.

G. SOCIAL HISTORY

537. Behrnauer, W. "Mémoire sur les Institutions de Police chez les Arabs, les Persans et les Turcs," *JA*, Ser. V, vol. XV (1860), 461-508; vol. XVI (1860), 114-90, 347-92; vol. XVII (1861), 5-76.

538. Belin, M. "Fetoua Rélatif à la Condition des Zimmis," *JA*, Ser. IV, vol. XVIII (1851), 417-516; vol. XIX (1852), 97-140.

539. Brinner, William M. "The Murder of Ibn an-Našū: Social Tensions in Fourteenth Century Damascus," *JAOS*, LXXVII (1957), 207-10.

540. Brunschvig, R. "Métiers Vils en Islam," *Studia Islamica*, XVI (1962), 41-60.

541. Eckmann, János. "The Mamluk-Kipchak Literature," *Central Asiatic Journal*, The Hague, VIII (1963), 304-19.

542. Gaulmier, J. "Pèlerinages Populaires à Hama," *BEO*, I (1931), 137-52.

543. Gottheil, Richard J. H. "Dhimmis and Moslems in Egypt," *Old Testament and Semitic Studies in Memory of William Rainey Harper*, vol. II. R. F. Harper, F. Brown, and G. F. Moore, ed. Chicago, 1908. pp. 351-414.

544. Kahle, Paul. "The Arabic Shadow Play in Egypt," *JRAS* (1940), 21-34.

545. ——— "The Arabic Shadow Play in Medieval Egypt," *Journal of the Pakistan Historical Society*, Karachi, II (1954), 85-115.

546. ——— "A Gypsy Woman in Egypt in the Thirteenth Century A.D.," *Journal of the Gypsy Lore Society*, Edinburgh, XXIX (1950), 11-15.

547. Labib, Subhi. "The Problem of the Bid'a in the Light of an Arabic Manuscript of the 14th Century," *JESHO*, VII (1964), 191-96.

548. Laoust, Henri. *Essai sur les Doctrines Sociales et Politiques de Taḳī-d-dīn Aḥmad b. Taimīya, 661/1262–728/1328*. Cairo, 1939.

549. ——— "Le Hanbalisme Sous les Mamlouks Bahrides (658–784/1260–1382)," *REI*, XXVIII (1960), 1-77.

550. Lecerf, J. "Les 'Arāda de Damas," *BEO*, VII-VIII (1937–1938), 237-64.

551. Lewis, Bernard. "The Islamic Guilds," *Economic History Review*, VIII (1937), 20-37.

552. Marguet, Yves. "La Place du Travail dans l'Hiérarchie Ismā'īlienne d'après l'Encyclopédie des Frères de la Purité," *Arabica*, VIII (1961), 225-37.

553. Massignon, Louis. "La 'Futuwwa' ou 'Pacte d'Honneur Artisanal' entre les Travailleurs Musulmans au Moyen Âge," *La Nouvelle Clio*, Brussels, IV (1952), 171-98.

554. ——— "Les Corps de Métier et la Cité Islamique," *Revue Internationale de Sociologie*, XXVIII (1920), 473-89.

555. Perlmann, Moshe. "Asnawi's Tract Against Christian Officials," *Ignace Goldziher Memorial Volume*, part II. Samuel Löwinger,

Alexander Schreiber, Joseph Somogyi, ed. Jerusalem, 1958. pp. 172-208.
556. ——— "Notes on Anti-Christian Propaganda in the Mamlūk Empire," *BSOAS,* X (1942), 843-61.
557. Poliak, A. N. "Les Révoltes Populaires en Égypte à l'Époque des Mamelouks et Leurs Causes Économiques," *REI,* VIII (1934), 251-73.
558. Raymond, André. "Essai de Géographie des Quartiers de Residence Aristocratique au Caire aux XVIIIe Siècle," *JESHO,* VI (1963), 58-103.
559. Salibi, Kamal S. "The Banū Jamā'a, A Dynasty of Shāfiite Jurists in the Mamluk Period," *Studia Islamica,* IX (1958), 97-109.
560. ——— "Listes Chronologiques des Grandes Cadis de l'Égypte sous les Mamelouks," *REI* (1957), 81-125.
561. Strauss, Eli. "The Social Isolation of Ahl adh-Dhimma," *Études Orientales à la Mémoire de Paul Hirschler.* O. Komlos, ed. Budapest, 1950. pp. 73-94.
562. Taeschner, F. "Futuwwa, eine Gemeinschaftbildende Idee im Mittelalterlicher Orient und ihre Verschiedene Erscheinungsforme," *Schweizerisches Archiv für Volkskunde,* Basel, LII (1956), pp. 122-58.
563. Tritton, Arthur Stanley. *The Caliphs and their Non-Muslim Subjects.* London, 1930.
564. Wangelin, Helmut. *Das Arabische Volksbuch vom König aẓ-Ẓāhir Baibars.* Bonner Orientalistische Studien, vol. XVII. Stuttgart, 1936.

III. *Bibliographies*

565. Ashtor, Eli. "Some Unpublished Sources for the Baḥrī Period," *Scripta Hierosolymitana,* vol. IX. Uriel Heyd, ed. Jerusalem, 1961. pp. 11-30.
566. Brockelmann, Carl. *Geschichte der Arabischen Litteratur.* 2 vols. 2nd ed. Leiden, 1945–1949; Supplements. 3 vols. Leiden, 1937–1942.
567. Cahen, Claude. "Les Chroniques Arabes Concernant la Syrie, l'Égypte et la Mésopotamie, de la Conquête Arabe à la Conquête Ottomane, dans les Bibliothèques d'Istanbul," *REI,* X (1936), 333-62.
568. Laoust, Henri and Sami Dahan. "L'Oeuvre de l'Académie Arabe de Damas 1921–1950," *BEO,* XIII (1949–1951), 161-219.
569. Lewis, Bernard and P. M. Holt, ed. *Historians of the Middle East.* London, 1962.
570. Mayer, L. A. *Bibliography of Moslem Numismatics.* London, 1954.
571. *Revue de l'Institut des Manuscrits Arabs.* Cairo.
572. Rosenthal, Franz. *A History of Muslim Historiography.* Leiden, 1952.
573. Sauvaget, Jean and Claude Cahen. *Introduction à l'Histoire de L'Orient Musulman.* Paris, 1961.

NOTES

INTRODUCTION

1. The literature on European cities is vast. Among the useful introductions are Henri Pirenne, *Medieval Cities* (Princeton, 1925); and *La Ville,* vols. VI-VIII, Société Jean Bodin (Brussels, 1954–55), which contain extensive bibliographies. Max Weber, *The City* (Glencoe, 1958) gives an influential sociological appraisal of Roman and medieval cities.
2. General discussion of Muslim cities: **470**; **496**; **497**; **498**; **499**; **502**; **507**; **508**; **509**; **510**; **517**; **518**; **530**; **554**.
3. Gideon Sjoberg, *The Preindustrial City* (Glencoe, 1960); studies by Claude Cahen: **497**; **498**; **499**.
4. A. H. M. Jones, *The Greek City from Alexander to Justinian* (Oxford, 1940); M. Rostovtzeff, *The Social and Economic History of the Roman Empire,* 2 vols. 2nd ed. (Oxford, 1957); F. F. Abbott and A. C. Johnson, *Municipal Administration in the Roman Empire* (Princeton, 1926).

CHAPTER I. A HISTORY OF CITIES IN THE MAMLUK EMPIRE

1. General histories of the Mamluk period: **379**; **387**; **399**. Histories of the crusades in the Mamluk period: **388**; **390**; **401**. Important Arabic sources in print include: **149**; **150**; **166**; **180**; **188**; **189**.
2. Administration: Syrie **140**, pp. 48, 79, 173-83; Sulūk **187**, II, 137; Iyās **169**, I, 157-58; **425**, XV, 14-15. Postal system: **427**, pp. 68-76; **425**, XV, 45-53; **148**, p. 481; **399**, p. 435.
3. Kathīr **176**, XIII, 320, 344-46; Yūnīnī **80**, IV, 17a, 216a; Dhahabī **14**, p. 113a; Jazarī **47**, pp. 67b-68a; **186**, pp. 18, 20, 21, 48. Among the more exciting Mamluk displays was the famous game of polo. (Kathīr **176**, XIII, 344-46.) Other games: **405**.
4. Volunteers: see above, p. 164. Shi'ites: **379**, pp. 622-24. Ismā'īlites: **384**, pp. 130-32. Forced assimilation of the Nuṣayrīs of the Lebanon: Sulūk **187**, II, 174-75, 178, 935-52; **536**, p. 47; **383**, pp. 113-14.
5. The rebellion of Sinjar al-Ḥalabī in 659: Dhahabī **153**, II, 127; Yūnīnī **202**, I, 438; Kathīr **176**, XIII, 230; **149**, III, 208-10; **390**, p. 315. Sanqar al-Ashqar in 678-79: **399**, pp. 414, 444, 446; Furāt **166**, VII, 162, 167, 170-72, 208-09; Dhahabī **153**, II, 139; **189**, II, 473-82; **397**, pp. 567-70. Tensions in Damascus over a disputed succession in 696: Dhahabī **153**, II, 154; **205**, p. 42; Furāt **166**, VIII, 225-27; Jazarī **186**, pp. 57-59; **399**, p. 465; Quatremère **188**, II_2, 43-46. The victory of Sultan Nāṣir Muḥammad at Damascus in the civil war of 709: Dawādārī **152**, pp. 158-59, 172-75; **189**, XX, 148-56; Sulūk **187**, II, 61-62, 67-68; Kathīr **176**, XIV, 51-52; **205**, pp. 138-46.
6. Yūnīnī **202**, I, 349-51; Quatremère **188**, II_2, 99; Kathīr **176**, XIII, 218-19; **237**, VII, 53; **121**, III, 482 appraise the damage.

7. The basic accounts are in fundamental agreement about the events of 699 although they differ in detail and completeness. (**189**, XIV, 635-70, XX, 24; **205**, pp. 58-79; Sulūk **187**, I, 889-96; Quatremère **188**, II_2, 150-63; Dhahabī **153**, II, 157; Kathīr **176**, XIV, 6-11; Dawādārī **152**, pp. 18-40; **149**, IV, 43; Ṭūlūn **182**, IV, 71-72; Yūnīnī **80**, III, 154a-167b; **64**, pp. 189b-190a; Shuhba **34**, yr. 699; Dhahabī **14**, pp. 125a-138a; Nuwayrī **61**, I, 66a-68b, III, 187a-191a; Birzālī **10**, II, 6b-19b; **8**, p. 225b; **505**, pp. 82-83; Kutubī **39**, pp. 81b-86b.)
8. In 666 Damascus was taxed one million dirhems with 400,000 to be paid immediately and the rest in three installments. (Yūnīnī **202**, II, 386-87; Quatremère **188**, I_2, 58-59.) The taxes on Damascus gardens were removed after Baybars' death (**189**, XIV, 446-47; Furāt **166**, VII, 117), but in its place 50,000 dinars or about one million dirhems (at an average of twenty to one), the equivalent of two months rent, were taken anyway. (Kathīr **176**, XIII, 280.) In 680 a tax farm called *al-jihat al-mufrada* was auctioned for two million dirhems. (Sulūk **187**, I, 688; Quatremère **188**, II_1, 31.) In 689 new taxes were levied on wheat imported to Damascus (Iyās **169**, I, 122), but they were abolished in 693. (Furāt **166**, VIII, 166.) Other taxes and arrears were canceled in 691 to celebrate the victory of Acre. (Jazarī **186**, p. 17.) Harsh exactions followed in 695 (**132**, p. 38; **133**, p. 40), and in 700 properties were assessed the equivalent of four months rent on the basis of the values of 698, an exceptionally good year, even though the damage done by the Mongols in 699 made the assessments impossibly difficult. People fled or destroyed taxable property rather than meet the demand for cash. (Sulūk **187**, I, 907; Quatremère **188**, II_2, 174-75; **205**, pp. 82-83; Dawādārī **152**, p. 44; **189**, XX, 31-32.) Ibn Hajar adds that supplementary fees were taken from brokers, merchants, and shopkeepers. Jurists suffered confiscations and loans were taken from the spice merchants. (**90**, II, 77-78.) Finally in 714 with the passing of the Mongol threat numerous taxes and fees were abandoned. (Sulūk **187**, II, 136-37.)
9. Mosul glass makers migrated to Cairo and Syria. (**299**, pp. 19-20; Khiṭaṭ **116**, II, 22.) The influences of Mesopotamian styles on copper and pottery also indicate that refugees from the east settled in Syria. (**312**, passim; **313**, pp. 5-6; **509**, II, 69-84.) In 720, famine atop Mongol exploitation and bedouin raiding drove large numbers of people from Mosul, Diyārbakr, and Jazīrat Ibn 'Umar into Syria. ('Aynī **3**, I, 5a; **369**, p. 71.)
10. Movement of markets: Décrets **223**, II, 34-40; **522**, pp. 464-65. Damascus silks and other fine cloths: Dawādārī **152**, p. 248; Quatremère **188**, II_2, 72. Glass: **305**, pp. 256, 349-82; **309**, II, 125. Luxuries made by order of the Sultans included cross bows with silk strings for a gift to Khan Berke of the Golden Horde (**159**, pp. 82, 189), royal pavilions (Jazarī **186**, p. 76; Dhahabī **14**, p. 114b), and the one hundred inlaid brass candlesticks, fifty gold and fifty silver ones inlaid with the titles of the Sultan, a thousand garments, one hundred and fifty inlaid and fifty brocaded saddles, plus other garments and furnishings made for Sultan al-Ashrāf Khalīl in 692. (Khiṭaṭ **116**, II, 112; variant accounts are given in Jazarī **186**, p. 28; Yūnīnī **80**, III, 29a; **312**, p. 573.)

11. See Appendix B.
12. Year 658: Sulūk **187**, I, 422; Quatremère **188**, I_1, 90; **149**, III, 201, 203, 209; Kathīr **176**, XIII, 218-19; Yūnīnī **202**, I, 435-36; **189**, XII, 418; **125**, II, 286-87, 298-300; **8**, p. 169b; Dhahabī **153**, II, 124; **101**, III, 160.

    Year 679: Sulūk **187**, I, 682; Quatremère **188**, II_1, 25-26; Furāt **166**, VII, 186; Dhahabī **153**, II, 140-41. Years 699–700: Baṭṭūṭa **142**, I, 95; **189**, XX, 36; Dawādārī **152**, p. 46; **205**, p. 84; **149**, IV, 45.
13. The citadel was rebuilt between 681 and 691. Inscriptions: **226**, pp. 177-78; **211**, p. 91; **210**, XIII, 107-09; **209**, p. 213. Literary notices: **149**, IV, 26; Ḥabīb **23**, p. 75b; Jazarī **186**, p. 10; Furāt **166**, VIII, 129; **125**, II, 336-37; **110**, pp. 27-30; **520**, pp. 167-68. The reconstruction of the walls: **211**, I, 26-27.
14. Mamluk strategy in 659: Yūnīnī **202**, I, 435; Dhahabī **153**, II, 127; Sulūk **187**, I, 442; Quatremère **188**, I_1, 132-33. Year 670: Kathīr **176**, XIII, 261; Yūnīnī **202**, II, 468; **189**, XII, 545; Sulūk **187**, I, 601-02; Quatremère **188**, I_2, 100-01. Year 679: Furāt **166**, VII, 186; Dhahabī **153**, II, 140-41; Sulūk **187**, I, 682; Quatremère **188**, II_1, 25-26. Year 680: Furāt **166**, VII, 212-13; Dhahabī **153**, II, 140-41; **149**, p. 332. Year 698: **149**, IV, 41; **125**, II, 346. Ibn Iyās refers to a defeat inflicted on the Mongols by the governor of Aleppo in 700 (**169**, I, 144), but no other source reports this skirmish. Year 712: **125**, II, 368.
15. Constructions: Appendix C. Water works: See above, pp. 70-71.
16. Ascalon destroyed in 669: **189**, XII, 526; Sulūk **187**, I, 590; Quatremère **188**, I_2, 84. Tripoli in 688: Furāt **166**, VIII, 80-81; Sulūk **187**, I, 747. Acre in 690: Sulūk **187**, I, 763-67; **149**, IV, 25-26; **205**, p. 18. Other towns: **536**, p. 56; Furāt **166**, VIII, 113.
17. Tripoli and the role of Governor Sayf al-dīn Asandamūr: Baṭṭūṭa **142**, I, 88; Syrie **140**, pp. 110-14; Furāt **166**, VIII, 81; **230**, pp. 43-46, 83-85; **210**, XIII, 53-54, 122-23, 178, 263; **90**, I, 113; Nuwayrī **61**, III, 24b-25a. Beirut: **198**; **372**; **381**; **391**; **392**; **393**.
18. **425**, XVI, 108-09; **422**, p. 24. Cadastre of Damascus: Sulūk **187**, II, 127. Tripoli: Sulūk **187**, II, 935-52. Beirut and the Lebanon: **391**, p. 90; **198**, pp. 91-92. The last survey made, that of Aleppo, marked its re-emergence as a military center. (Iyās **169**, I, 164; **125**, II, 374.)
19. The gold-silver ratio applies to the standard dirhem which was about two-thirds silver, and of course only approximates the average of fluctuating values. Coinage: **324**; **325**; **326**; **327**; **328**; **329**; **331**; **333**; **348**; **349**; **351**; **353**; **134**; **425**, XVI, 41-79; Qalqashandī **84**, III, 440-45, 465-68. Food prices: **318**; **319**; **320**; **322**; **323**; **355**.
20. Note 19, above, and see above, pp. 144-45 for coinage strikes.
21. The observations of Ibn Baṭṭūṭa are the most fruitful source of information on the imports of Damascus. (Baṭṭūṭa **141**, I, 128, 145, 186; **142**, I, 82, 93, 117.) Other sources: **536**, p. 144. Grain imports: Kathīr **176**, XIV, 224; **539**, p. 208; Décrets **223**, II, 20; **137**, p. 200. Pilgrims reported Jaffa as a local market for olive oil, cotton thread, soap, earthenware, cloth, and fruit. (**244**, p. 247.) Safad and Nablus were also regional market centers in Palestine. (**144**, p. 483; **536**, p. 68.) A fifteenth century visitor reported that Jerusalem imported grapes and grain from Ramla and Gaza, and figs, apples, pears, and walnuts

from Damascus. (**278**, pp. 39-40.) Aleppo imported fruits and salt from her local region and other products from Qārā. (Syrie **140**, pp. 81-82, 91; Décrets **223**, III, 16-17.) Homs and Hama traded with Baalbek. (Syrie **140**, p. 76; Yūnīnī **202**, I, 399.)

22. Syrian exports of apricots, raisins, figs, pistachios, candles, oil, soap, and animals: **145**, pp. 199-200; **136**, pp. 25, 247; Baṭṭūṭa **141**, I, 128, 131-32, 145-46; **142**, I, 82, 84, 93-94; **536**, pp. 67, 140; **143**, p. 347; Sulūk **187**, II, 409, 463, 525-26, 855. Manufactures exported from Syria: **304**, p. 230; **522**, p. 466; **305**, p. 493; **249**, p. 75; **504**, pp. 148-49. Other trade: Yūnīnī **80**, III, 47b, 69b; **202**, I, 408; **205**, p. 74; Furāt **166**, IX, 33, 380. Qaṭyā customs station: Baṭṭūṭa **141**, I, 112; **142**, I, 72; Sulūk **56**, II, 87b; Qalqashandī **84**, III, 470. Syrian bazaars in Cairo: Khiṭaṭ **116**, II, 94; Sulūk **187**, II, 226.

23. Bridge constructions: In 664, over the Jordan River at Dāmiya (Nuwayrī **61**, II, 31b); 668, three bridges over the Nile to Alexandria (Birzālī **10**, I, 18b); 671, two bridges on the Syrian coast (Birzālī **10**, I, 35a); 672, the Sultan built two bridges near Ramla (Nuwayrī **61**, II, 53a; Furāt **166**, VII, 6); 687, emir of Jerusalem rebuilt bridge of Dāmiya (Ṣaqā'ī **65**, p. 9b); A.D. 1291, bridge over Nahr al-Kalb near Beirut (**209**, p. 101); A.D. 1340–45, bridge over River Damūr near Beirut rebuilt (**209**, p. 101; **198**, pp. 107-08); 777, death of emir who built bridges (Ḥabīb **25**, pp. 71-72); 781, bridge in Syria (Iyās **169**, I, 254); 782, Jordan bridged between Damascus and Baysān by Sultan Barqūq (Bāsiṭ **1**, I, 126a; 'Aynī **3**, I, 120a; Nujūm **180**, V, 421, 600; Sulūk **56**, II, 70b, 104b).

Khans and caravansaries: **221**; 427, pp. 31, 58-63; **212**, pp. 100-03; **218**, I, 42-43; **428**, pp. 45, 48.

24. I am grateful to Avram Udovitch for pointing out how likely it is that Damascus and Cairo served as regional markets, importing goods which were then redistributed. This is a very probable explanation for the apparent tendency for regional produce to be concentrated in the largest cities, but unfortunately the sources give no evidence of subsequent redistributions.

Peasants: Note 21, above. Ibn Baṭṭūṭa reports cloth exports from Egypt to Syria. (**141**, I, 54.) Damascus silks were taken to Bāniyās. (**90**, II, 387-88.) Egyptian grain exports: Sulūk, **56**, II, 96a, 143b, 189a; **187**, II, 254, 869; **198**, p. 183; Furāt **166**, IX, 25, 366, 382. Grain shipments from Syria to Egypt: Jazarī **186**, p. 48; **536**, p. 148; Sulūk **187**, II, 394.

25. Examples: Furāt **166**, VIII, 121-22; Sulūk **56**, III, 63b; **187**, II, 443; **144**, p. 483.

26. Most information on the Bagdad-Damascus trade is found in notices mentioning news brought by merchants rather than in direct discussion of trading activities. (Yūnīnī **80**, III, 69b, 79a, 145a, IV, 137a; Jazarī **48**, p. 13, 631; **186**, p. 48; Furāt **166**, IX, 7.) Al-Dimashqī and al-Qazwīnī, the geographers, mention Bagdad-Damascus exchanges but their sources may refer to the Ayyūbid period. (**137**, p. 93; **146**, II, 137.) Bagdad paper, horses, and fruits were imported to Syria. (Quatremère **188**, I, 212; Sulūk **187**, II, 525-26; Syrie **140**, pp. 81-82.) Damascus and Aleppo glass was exported to Iraq, Persia, and China. (**305**, pp. 259, 493.) There is but one explicit reference

to a trade caravan coming from Bagdad to Syria through al-Raḥba. (Sulūk **187**, II, 651.)

27. Merchants coming from the Black Sea and Iyās: Jazarī **48**, p. 458; **186**, pp. 36, 84; Yūnīnī **80**, III, 50b, 146a; Dawādārī **152**, p. 12; **189**, XIV, 629; Duqmāq **20**, p. 74b. Slave trade: See above, pp. 122-23. Exchange of protocols between the Byzantine Empire and the Mamluks on the protection of the traffic in slaves and horses: Furāt **166**, VII, 229-33; **289**; **291**; **292**. For a diplomatic imbroglio over the delivery of slaves: **297**, pp. 23-29. Also: **405**, pp. 1-4; **423**.

Greek merchants also came to Egypt by sea and in 787 a treaty with Constantinople established a consul in Alexandria. (Baṭṭūṭa **141**, I, 45; Sulūk **56**, II, 89a.)

28. Aleppo: Sibṭ **123**, pp. 18-19, 40-41, 101; **520**, pp. 165-70; **536**, p. 133; **137**, pp. 251-52. Aleppo glass: **305**, pp. 249, 291-348; **309**, II, 125-26; **146**, II, 123. Baalbek cloth: Iyās **169**, I, 120; Baṭṭūṭa **142**, I, 12, 116; **206**, p. 68; Nujūm **180**, VII, 760; **304**, pp. 229-30; **237**, VI, 172; Sulūk **56**, II, 64b; **187**, II, 524. Baalbek glass: **305**, pp. 38, 87-89. Tripoli's silk industry: Sulūk **187**, I, 748; Quatremère **188**, II_1, 103. Sugar cane: **136**, p. 253; **137**, p. 207; Syrie **140**, p. 112; **536**, p. 132. The noteworthy products of other towns included Jerusalem cloth and enameled silver. (**304**, p. 233; **145**, p. 35.) Hama sold silks, drugs, and perfumes. (Jazarī **48**, p. 460.)

Studies of surviving art masterpieces are an important source of the history of Damascus crafts. (**301**; **305**; **309**.) Damascus ceramics are on display at the National Museum, Damascus. Gold and silver smithing: **305**, p. 493; Furāt **166**, IX, 307; **241**, p. 143; **266**, p. 226. Copper and brass wares: **241**, pp. 143, 182; Furāt **166**, IX, 307; **266**, p. 226; Syrie **140**, pp. 44-45; Qalqashandī **84**, IV, 188. Glass: Baṭṭūṭa **141**, I, 208; **142**, I, 130; **266**, p. 226; **241**, p. 143; Furāt **166**, IX, 307; Syrie **140**, pp. 44-45; Qalqashandī **84**, IV, 188; **492**, p. 205. Silk, cotton, wool, and linen: **305**, p. 493; Baṭṭūṭa **141**, I, 208; **241**, pp. 143, 182; Furāt **166**, IX, 307; **132**, pp. 270-71; **266**, p. 226; **304**, p. 231. Fine instruments: Kathīr **176**, XIV, 207-08; Furāt **166**, IX, 307; Syrie **140**, pp. 44-45, 140; **306**, pp. 40-41, 44, 61. Paper: **305**, p. 493; Baṭṭūṭa **141**, I, 208; **143**, pp. 270-71; Furāt **166**, IX, 307; **473**, pp. 109-10. Confectionary, dried fruits, and rose water: Sulūk **187**, II, 196; **241**, p. 86; **266**, p. 226; **536**, p. 132; Qalqashandī **84**, IV, 188. Iron utensils: **143**, pp. 270-71; **266**, p. 226; **492**, p. 205; Qalqashandī **84**, IV, 188. Leather: Furāt **166**, IX, 307; **492**, p. 205; Syrie **140**, pp. 44-45.

Ibn Ṭūlūn and Ibn Ṣaṣra describe the fabulous gold and silver building materials, brocades, embroideries, horse-trappings, robes, saddle cloths and saddle bags manufactured in Damascus for the Sultan in 775. Governor Sayf al-dīn Baydamur brought all the workers to his palace where the precious materials could be better accounted for. (Ṭūlūn **185**, p. 14; Ṣaṣra **177**, pp. 187b-188b.) Royal pavilions made in Damascus were sent as a gift to the Merinids of North Africa in 741. (**439**, p. 64.) Also: Sulūk **187**, II, 346; Nujūm **180**, V, 569.

29. The campaigns between 713 and 722 in which Damascus took the leading role: Iyās **169**, I, 159; Shuhba **34**, yr. 714; **59**, p. 233; Kathīr **176**, XIV, 73; Duqmāq **21**, I, 130a; Sulūk **187**, II, 203, 229, 236-37; **149**,

IV, 88. The capture of Iyās: Dawādārī **152**, p. 309; **262**, II, 400-01; **459**, III, 277-78; **447**, pp. 79-84. The period of Aleppo leadership from 735: Dawādārī **152**, p. 397; Dhahabī **153**, II, 187-89; Iyās **169**, I, 168; Kathīr **176**, XIV, 170, 178, 271; **125**, II, 387, 407, 417, 442-43; Shuḥba **34**, yr. 735; Ḥabīb **23**, p. 209a; **59**, p. 269; Jazarī **48**, pp. 503, 574; Sulūk **56**, II, 4b, 22b; **187**, II, 417-18, 420-21, 428-30, 650, 694-95, 726; 'Aynī **4**, pp. 113-16; **149**, IV, 135, 139, 147. In 776 the definitive conquest of Cilician Armenia: **125**, II, 453; Nujūm **180**, V, 224; Iyās **169**, I, 229-30; **399**, p. 508; **460**, pp. 144-45.

30. Successive stages marked the growing administrative importance of Aleppo. In 692/1293 Bahasna was put under her control. (Dhahabī **153**, II, 150.) In 737 new estates in Armenia were assigned the emirs of Aleppo. (**125**, II, 396.) In 768 protocol honors were given Aleppo and her new governor brought an enlarged garrison to the city. (Bāsiṭ **1**, I, 80b; Iyās **169**, I, 217; Nujūm **180**, V, 199.) Wiet remarks on the enlargement of Aleppo's administrative zone in Armenia. (**399**, p. 508.)

31. Wiet and Muir review the political history. (**399**; **387**.) The political and social chaos is treated from the point of view of mob rioting and street fighting in Chapter V.

32. Rebellion of 741: Ṭūlūn **185**, pp. 9-10; **382**, pp. 51-52; Kathīr **176**, XIV, 193-97; Sulūk **187**, II, 566, 573, 577, 580-93; Shuḥba **35**, I, 18a; Kutubī **39**, p. 69b. Fighting at Kerak from 741 to 745: **399**, pp. 500-01; Dhahabī **153**, II, 194; Kathīr **176**, XIV, 204-05, 212-13, Sulūk **187**, II, 573, 615, 628-29, 653, 657, 661-62; **391**, p. 93. Damascus rebellion of 747: Nujūm **180**, V, 13-18; Kathīr **176**, XIV, 218-20; Sulūk **187**, II, 708-09; Kutubī **37**, II, 8-9. Rebellion threatened in Damascus in 748: Sulūk **187**, II, 733; Nujūm **180**, V, 33-35; Kathīr **176**, XIV, 223. In 750 the governor of Damascus forcibly removed from his post: Kathīr **176**, XIV, 230-31; Nujūm **180**, V, 76-79. In 751 rebellion in Safad: Nujūm **180**, V, 86; Sulūk **187**, II, 826; Kathīr **176**, XIV, 237-38. In the following year Aleppo: **125**, II, 431-34; Sulūk **187**, II, 868-73; Kathīr **176**, XIV, 245, 247; Iyās **169**, I, 196-97; Nujūm **180**, V, 120-24; **382**, p. 54; **399**, p. 504; Ḥabīb **23**, p. 275a. Aleppo rebellion of 759: Kathīr **176**, XIV, 258-59; **382**, p. 56; Kutubī **39**, pp. 145a-b. Damascus in 762: Nujūm **180**, V, 175-76; **382**, p. 58; Kathīr **176**, XIV, 280-81, 283-87; Iyās **169**, I, 211; Sulūk **56**, II, 3a-b. There is one mention of a Damascus rebellion in 781 in conjunction with fighting in Cairo. (Iyās **169**, I, 248.)

33. Bedouin difficulties after the death of Sultan Nāṣir Muḥammad in 1341: Sulūk **187**, II, 407, 445, 563, 623, 627-29, 651, 657, 666-69, 684, 692, 698-99, 771, 905; **149**, IV, 138, 142, 144, 147, 154; Kathīr **176**, XIV, 266-67, 270, 272, 288, 301-02, 321; **397**.

    Turkomans: **125**, II, 396, 407, 411-13, 434-35, 449-50, 455; Sulūk **187**, II, 430-31, 459, 469, 494, 665, 691, 705, 820, 891, 894-96, 898, 917; Nujūm **180**, V, 126, 133, 334.

34. Appendix B and see above, pp. 59-60, 70, 72.

35. Constructions: Appendix C. Water works: **511**. Quarters: **520**, pp. 173-76.

36. See bibliography sections IB-9 and IIE.

37. Alexandria's fortifications remained intact in the fifteenth century, but

the city was underpopulated and partly in ruins. Houses were often demolished to carry off the materials for use in new Cairo palaces. (**504**; **255**, p. 93; **250**, III, 149; **278**, p. 198; **254**, p. 241; **374**, p. 87.)

Other towns were in ruins: Acre: **375**, I, 341; **278**, p. 163; **279**, p. 49. Jaffa: **251**, I, 238; **245**, p. 235; **278**, p. 38; **243**, p. 286; **270**, p. 29; **529**, pp. 82-84. Tyre: Baṭṭūṭa **142**, I, 83; **264**, p. 141; **279**, p. 49; **278**, p. 163. Sidon: **278**, p. 164; **270**, p. 30; **279**, p. 49. Al-Ẓāhirī, however, reports the port of Sidon as silted but still in use in the fifteenth century. (**88**, p. 70.) Latakia: **278**, p. 179; **88**, p. 71; Iyās **170**, XXXIV, 10.

Tripoli's active history: **230**, pp. 53-54, 86, 114, 122-23; **210**, XV, 59, 83-84; **209**, p. 124; **526**, pp. 24-25. Tripoli in Mamluk protocol ranked as the third town in Syria after Damascus and Aleppo. (**86**, pp. 68-72; Kathīr **176**, XIV, 241, 252-53, 258; Dawādārī **152**, pp. 344, 352, 380-81.) Beirut, by contrast, received little attention. Some houses for emirs, stables, halls, a mosque, and upper floors in the markets were built in 734 and a khan and some water works in 1365 when Beirut was required to build two ships to prepare a Mamluk fleet in retaliation for the Cypriote crusade. (**198**, pp. 110, 113, 168-69, 180; **391**, pp. 94-96; **392**, p. 123; **19**, pp. 153a-b.) Beirut was chosen as a supplementary site for construction because of the availability of wood in the region. It was scarcely a shipbuilding port, however, for carpenters had to be sent from Damascus and naval supplies such as tar, pitch, iron, oars, and nails seem normally to have been stored in Tortosa. Also, the works had to be carried out at some distance inland for fear of sudden Christian attacks against which the Muslims were still helpless. In all, only two boats were actually put to sea from Beirut, and both were lost. (Kathīr **176**, XIV, 320; **198**, pp. 34-35; **73**, p. 258a; Nujūm **180**, V, 195; **536**, p. 67; **381**, II, 7; **435**, pp. 372-74; **261**, I, 193.) After the revival of trade, defensive towers were repaired, but the town was never completely walled. (**198**, p. 41; **241**, pp. 88, 184; **513**, pp. 229-30, 245.)

38. For full accounts of the civil wars: Nujūm **180**; Iyās **169**; **399**; **125**, II, III. Important manuscripts include: 'Ayni **4**; Jawharī **46**; Duqmāq **20**; **21**; **22**; Sulūk **56**.

39. The first encounters of Tamerlane with the Mamluks in 790: Furāt **166**, IX, 24-31; Iyās **169**, I, 268; Nujūm **180**, V, 389-90; Ḥabīb **24**, pp. 228a-b, 229a. Skirmish in 796: Furāt **166**, IX, 370; **125**, II, 486; 'Ayni **3**, I, 207b. Sack of Aleppo in 803: Nujūm **180**, VI, 50-52; Iyās **169**, I, 326-27; **161**, pp. 185-93; **125**, II, 494-98, 501-03; **195**, pp. 287-304, 349-51; **164**, pp. 132-41; Shiḥna **40**, II, 150b, 152b; Jawharī **46**, pp. 63b-65b; Inbā' **26**, III, 172a-b; Duqmāq **22**, p. 175; Sulūk **56**, II, 183a-b. Sack of Damascus: **161**, pp. 216-40; Iyās **169**, I, 332-35; **195**, pp. 337-47; **164**, pp. 158-59; Nujūm **180**, VI, 61-72; **266**, pp. 219-31; Inbā' **26**, III, 173b; Jawharī **46**, pp. 65a-66a; **19**, pp. 164a-b, 166b-167a; Duqmāq **21**, I, 215a-b; **22**, p. 180; **73**, pp. 328b-331a; Sulūk **56**, II, 186a-187b, 194a; **365**, pp. 99-100.

40. For Mamluk accounts of the Ak Koyunlu and the Kara Koyunlu in 806 and 809: Nujūm **180**, VI, 109; **125**, II, 510-11. Invasion of 820 in which Aintab, the first important city north of Aleppo, was burned:

Nujūm **180**, VI, 47-49, 57-58; **101**, III, 225-26; **125**, II, 518-19; Jawharī **46**, p. 98a.

41. The assaults of Cypriote fleets between 767 and 772 on both Egypt and Syria: **399**, pp. 506-508; **262**, I, 70-74, 89-92, II, 419, 428-29; **434**, pp. 366, 370-71; **457**, II, 52-53, 55-57, 63; **447**, pp. 154-56, 158, 161, 165-66; **459**, II, 343, 345, 353-54, 373; **261**, I, 169, 283; Iyās **169**, I, 217. Sporadic piracy between 770 and 780: Iyās **169**, I, 229; Sulūk **56**, II, 22b-23a, 24a, 42a; 'Aynī **3**, I, 112b; Bāsiṭ **1**, I, 117a. After 784 almost every year brought new assaults: **198**, pp. 35-36; Inbā' **26**, III, 72a-b, 79b, 92b, 106b, 138b, 187b, 195b; **513**, pp. 229-30; Bāsiṭ **1**, I, 132b, 134a; Jawharī **46**, pp. 5a-b, 7a, 11b, 35b, 73a; Sulūk **56**, II, 48b-49a, 80b-81a, 82b-83a, 85a, 94a, 97b, 125b, 138a, 143b, 189a, 198a; 'Aynī **3**, I, 142b; Furāt **166**, IX, 7, 33, 38, 341-42, 466. Crusade of Boucicaut in 806 which struck Alexandria, Tripoli, Beirut, Sidon, and Latakia: **198**, pp. 37-39; **321**, p. 53; **446**, pp. 437-47; **447**, pp. 294-300; Jawharī **46**, p. 74a; Inbā' **26**, III, 201b; Duqmāq **22**, pp. 192-93; Sulūk **56**, II, 199b. Attacks continued unabated until 1425 when the Muslim counterattacks on Cyprus began: **457**, II, 472-73; **447**, p. 327; **293**, I, 177-79, 272, 279, 327, 375-76; **294**, pp. 366-67; **392**, pp. 228-29; **399**, pp. 552-53; **262**, I, 249, 264-68, II, 498; **374**, pp. 334, 336; Inbā' **26**, II, 63b-64a, 76b, 130b; Jawharī **46**, pp. 93a-b; Sakhāwī **66**, I, yr. 819; **72**, pp. 101b, 104b; Sulūk **56**, III, 64b-65a, 67b, 100b; **198**, p. 219; **459**, II, 471; Nujūm **180**, VI, 561, 578-79.

42. Year 791: **168**; Ṣaṣra **177**, pp. 27 (39)b, 35 (5)a-b, 36 (6)a-b, 41 (11)a, 55a; Jawharī **46**, p. 29a. Ayalon discusses the use of cannon. (**403**, pp. 27-28.) In the fighting of 793 bombardment and fire did comparably severe damage on the western side of the city when the Dār al-Biṭṭīkh (Melon Market), the Mosque of Tankiz, and other buildings were damaged. (Ṣaṣra **177**, pp. 83b-84a, 86b; 'Aynī **3**, I, 192a.) In the following year severe fires ravaged the rich business districts around the Umayyad Mosque. (Ṣaṣra **177**, pp. 116b-118a; Jawharī **46**, p. 39b; Inbā' **26**, III, 115a; Furāt **166**, IX, 307; Quatremère **188**, I_1, 179.) Other conflagrations are reported for 798 and in 800 a great fire raged from the Umayyad Mosque to al-Nūriyya Madrasa in which the silk, bowmakers, swordsmiths, and money changers markets burned down. (Inbā' **26**, III, 154b; Sulūk **56**, II, 159a; Ṣaṣra **177**, pp. 172b-173b.)

The fires set by the Tatars in 803 also did considerable damage, but, the hyperbole of the chroniclers to the contrary notwithstanding, did not totally destroy the city. Serious damage was done to the Umayyad Mosque, and to the area between it and the citadel and as far as al-Qilījiyya Madrasa to the south. Rubbish fires spread easily because the upper floors of dwellings were made of wood. (**376**, pp. 39, 95, 97; Quatremère **188**, II_1, 286; **121**, IV, 276.) The citadel was damaged on the north and west sides, the sides facing outside the city. (**98**, pp. 60-61; **376**, pp. 38-39.)

In 815 canals were cut and markets burned in the civil war fighting. (Inbā' **26**, II, 29b; Sulūk **56**, III, 40a-b.) Fires in the markets in 818 from Bāb al-Sa'āda to the hospital caused losses of 30,000 dinars. Seven madrasas between the citadel and al-'Ādaliyya were lost in the same year as well as important markets in fires ordered set by the governor of the citadel to clear the surrounding areas and bridges of squatters' stalls and shops. In 823 shops in al-Shāghūr district burned. For other fires in 823, 824, and 825: Ṭūlūn **182**, IV, 31-33. Bertrandon de la Broquière remarked on his visit to Damascus in 1432 A.D. that the Bāb Kaysān area was still in ruins. (**243**, p. 294.) Darrag has misunderstood the passage in the travels of Lannoy which describes the ruin of the city. Lannoy does not say that only the walls, the citadel, and the Umayyad Mosque were spared the ravages of Tamerlane, but the contrary, that these were destroyed by him. (**374**, p. 90.)

Severe damage was done to Aleppo by Mamluk efforts to reconstruct the fortifications. (Sibṭ **123**, pp. 161-66.)

43. See Chapter V.

44. Bedouin unrest in Egypt goes back to the middle of the fourteenth century. Risings in al-Ṣa'īd (Upper Egypt) are noted frequently between 744 and 756. (Bāsiṭ **1**, I, 5a, 13b, 17b, 22a, 37b, 39a-b, 47a-b, 56a; 'Aynī **3**, I, 64a; Kutubī **39**, p. 125b; Duqmāq **21**, I, 160b-161a; Sulūk **56**, I, 232a; Nujūm **180**, V, 93.) Between 780, however, and 807 risings in both al-Baḥrī (Lower Egypt) and Upper Egypt became virtually annual occurrences. (Bāsiṭ **1**, I, 118a-b, 122a, 124b; Sulūk **56**, II, 59a, 60a, 68a, 69b, 71a, 74a, 75b, 77b, 82b, 89a, 125b, 127b-128a, 129b, 142b, 143b, 151b, 164a, 177b-178a, 197b; Duqmāq **21**, I, 186b; Inbā' **26**, III, yrs. 782, 783, 785; Jawharī **46**, pp. 7a, 11b, 16b, 30a, 35b, 49b; 'Aynī **3**, I, 135a; Nujūm **180**, V, 406; Furāt **166**, IX, 248, 251; Duqmāq **22**, pp. 200, 202-03.) Serious troubles resumed again in 813 as plundering and rebellious bedouins were met with counter-raids by the government forces. This round of fighting persisted until 825. (**399**, p. 543; Nujūm **180**, VI, 335, 560; Inbā' **26**, II, 57b-58a, 63b, 76b, 94a, 96a, 108b, 122a; Duqmāq **20**, pp. 103b-104a; Jawharī **46**, p. 98a; Sulūk **56**, III, 53a.)

Most of the damage done by Arab and Turkoman nomads in Syria in the period of civil wars was in conjunction with the battles of Mamluk factions, but Arab bedouins did not lose the opportunity to plunder on their own. In 793 villages around Damascus and Ramla were sacked. (**397**, pp. 560-63; Sulūk **56**, II, 124b.) Between 803 and 806 villages around Aleppo, Damascus, and Gaza and between Damascus and al-Raḥba were plundered. (**101**, III, 217; Inbā' **26**, III, 188b; Sulūk **56**, II, 190b, 193b, 200a.) Further Arab risings occurred in 819 at Gaza, Ramla, and Jerusalem. (Inbā' **26**, II, 63a.)

Turkoman participation in the civil wars and plundering raids cost Aleppo heavily. Apart from sporadic attacks (Inbā' **26**, III, 196a, 232b-233a, 236a-b; **52**, pp. 26a, 30a-b; **101**, III, 219, 222-23) great damage was done when a Turkoman confederation led by Ibn Ṣāḥib al-Bāz occupied northern Syria between 806 and 808. (**101**, III, 219; **52**, pp. 27a-b, 29b; Inbā' **26**, III, 218b-219a; Nujūm **180**, VI, 127.) They were finally stopped at Hama in 808 and were set back in 811 and 814. But not until 824 were they definitely defeated. (**125**, II, 507-10, III, 18-19; Sulūk **56**, II, 209b, 214b-215a, III, 15a, 25a.)

The decline of agriculture in Egypt: **374**, pp. 59-66. Syria: Nujūm **180**, VI, 195, 271; Sulūk **56**, II, 203a, 206b, 208b, III, 43b. Al-Maqrīzī asserts that the plague carried off one-third of the population. The

Hama province was notably reduced although Bertrandon de la Broquière saw the villages being restored in 1432. (**88**, p. 221; **243**, p. 310.)

45. See Appendices B and C. Notes 42 and 44, above.
46. The art historians are generally agreed on 1400 as a turning point in the quality of Mamluk crafts. (**304**, p. 290; **299**; **316**; **317**; **301**, p. 116.) For example the silk industry of Alexandria declined radically. Before the civil wars there were 14,000 looms of which a census of 837 showed that only eight hundred remained. (Nujūm **180**, VI, 714; also **268**, p. 351; **442**, p. 199; **374**, pp. 66-73.)
47. Our most sensitive index for the incidence of taxation is the frequency with which illegal taxes were denounced and abolished. (**223**, passim; **238**, pp. 522-24; **206**, pp. 148-49; **227**, pp. 230-31; **230**, p. 56.) Confiscations: Jawharī **46**, pp. 30a, 66a; Inbā' **26**, II, 2a, III, 172a, 174a, 209b, 234b; 'Aynī **3**, I, 181a, 193a; Sulūk **56**, II, 205b, 206b-207a, 208b, 215a, 219b. Also see **408**, p. 290.
48. Tamerlane took weavers, tailors, masons, architects, carpenters, hatmakers, veterinarians, painters, bowmakers, apothecaries, engravers, coppersmiths, silk weavers, glass and earthenware makers, armorers, etc. (**164**, p. 172; **161**, pp. 236-39; **247**, p .171; **246**, p. 288; **266**, p. 229; **399**, p. 532.)
49. Decline of communications: **427**, pp. 80-84. Revenues of Qaṭyā: Jawharī **48**, p. 48b; Sulūk **56**, II, 128a, 150b. Cairo bazaars or *qayṣariyyas*: Khiṭaṭ **116**, II, 89; **374**, p. 72; **104**, I, 38. Caravan movements: **268**, p. 348; Jawharī **48**, p. 73a; Sulūk **56**, II, 139a, 177a, 216a, III, 29a.
50. **425**, XVI, 41-79; **325**; **327**; **337**; **348**; **349**; **351**; Maqrīzī **132**; **133**; **134**.
51. **425**, XVI, 80-106; **355**.
52. **132**, pp. 72-75; **133**, pp. 71-75; **425**, XVI, 107-23. The peculiar advantages of artisans were due to manpower shortages ascribed to massive extermination by plague. (**355**, pp. 76, 90-93; Kathīr **176**, XIV, 276; **128**, p. 75; **132**, p. 75; **133**, p. 75; Sulūk **56**, II, 217a.)
53. Cloth: Sulūk **56**, II, 197a, 200b, 205a; Jawharī **48**, pp. 72a, 75b; Duqmāq **21**, I, 224a; **22**, pp. 199-200; **132**, p. 78; Inbā' **26**, II, 34b; **308**, p. 74. See also **319**, p. 75; **320**, pp. 41-44; **339**.
54. **374**, pp. 352, 363-409.
55. Cyprus: Iyās **170**, XXV, 132-35, 138; Nujūm **180**, VI, 19-28, 32-38, 44-45, 50-51, 143; **262**, II, 499-504; **399**, pp. 556-58; **88**, pp. 237-43; **374**, pp. 244-67; **198**, pp. 220-29; **435**, p. 471; **44**, p. 171a; **72**, pp. 46b-48a, 53b; Inbā' **26**, II, 138a-142b; **19**, p. 171b; **151**; **371**. Rhodes: **399**, pp. 582-83; Nujūm **180**, VII, 112-14, 131-36; Sakhāwī **197**, pp. 6, 15, 87-89.
56. **425**, XVI, 80-106.
57. **121**, III, 258, 265, 276, 277, 315, 395, 431, 438, 439, IV, 256, 274, 297, 486, V, 291, VI, 409-22, 426, 429-40, 445, 451, 453, 468, 478, 562, VII, 226-27, 381, 395, 410, 430; **98**, pp. 62-63, 362-63; Décrets **223**, II, 32-41; Ṭūlūn **185**, p. 107.
58. Aleppo: Shiḥna **110**, pp. 157-59, 186-87, 193-96; Sibṭ **123**, pp. 42, 45, 53, 69, 91, 92, 153, passim; **520**, p. 174; **125**, V, 477; **238**, pp. 531, 533, 534, 536; Décrets **223**, III, 23. Baalbek cottons: Jawharī **46**, p. 128a; Sakhāwī **197**, pp. 43, 346; Ḥawādith **179**, p. 7; Jawharī **45**, pp. 109b, 171b; Iyās **169**, IV, 81, 456. Tripoli silks and cottons: **230**, pp. 46, 66-

67, 80, 105, 110, 116-17. Tripoli tanning: **230**, pp. 131-32; **217**, p. 46; **330**, p. 99. Hama: **243**, p. 311; Décrets **223**, III, 2, 5; **280**, p. 8. Jerusalem: **276**, p. xxxvi; 'Ulaymī **190**, II, 686; **239**, p. 238. Ramla: 'Ulaymī **190**, II, 686; **457**, II, 466-67. Safad: **355**, pp. 488, 494. Nablus: **355**, p. 494; **537**, XVII, 27. Tiberias: **243**, p. 299. Kerak: Iyās **169**, IV, 204. Hebron: **305**, p. 492. Gaza: **514**, pp. 93-94; **304**, p. 233. Sarmīn: **457**, II, 612; Décrets **223**, XII, 41-42.

59. Damascus copper: **317**, pp. 99-100, 134-36, 142-43; **239**, pp. 145, 152, 161, 199, 230, 246. Fifteenth century copper is on display at the National Museum in Damascus. Glass: **316**, p. 123; **299**, pp. 9-11; **305**, pp. 494-95; **309**, II, 139-40; Sibṭ **123**, p. 43; **238**, p. 528; Décrets **223**, II, 32-33. Cloths: **98**, pp. 362-63; **243**, p. 304; **443**, p. 97; **454**, pp. 239, 378; **484**, p. 114; **344**, p. 181; **238**, pp. 527-28; Décrets **223**, II, 31. Jewelry: **98**, pp. 362-63; **454**, p. 64; **239**, p. 199. Lead working: 'Ulaymī **190**, II, 653, 660; Ḥimṣī **29**, pp. 79a-b, 83a, 84a-b.

60. Woolen cloths: Shiḥna **110**, p. 199; Ḥawādith **179**, p. 481; **343**, p. 326; Khiṭaṭ **116**, II, 98; **276**, pp. 100-01; **262**, II, 374; **520**, pp. 164-65; **268**, pp. 373, 376-77; **459**, II, 489-90; Nujūm **180**, VI, 681. Heer notes that by mid-century compensating Syrian wool exports had ceased. (**454**, p. 230.) Chinese ceramics: **303**, p. 265. To conclude, however, that imports of glass and silk into Syria meant the total demise of local industry fails to take the evidence of continued production into account. (**457**, II, 469; **305**, p. 494; **276**, p. xxxv; **309**, II, 142.)

61. Syrian food exports: Sibṭ **123**, p. 26; Shiḥna **110**, pp. 196-97; **98**, p. 364; Ṭūlūn **111**, I, 52-53; **355**, p. 488; Iyās **169**, IV, 102; **174**, p. 490; **121**, VII, 441. Cloth exports: **374**, p. 155; Ḥawādith **179**, pp. 229-30. Baalbek cloth: Note 56, above. Egyptian grain exports to Syria: Ḥawādith **179**, pp. 251-52, 700; **268**, p. 323; Iyās **169**, IV, 302. Damascus imports: **88**, p. 69; Décrets **223**, XII, 26-27; Ṭūlūn **185**, p. 112. Aleppo imports: Décrets **223**, III, 16-17; Sibṭ **123**, pp. 115, 154; **238**, pp. 531, 534; **101**, III, 238. Palestinian trade: **355**, p. 488.

62. Military tensions between 853 and 870: Ḥawādith **179**, pp. 46, 79, 95, 103, 117, 127, 221, 256-69, 275-80, 292, 303, 305, 466, 473-74, 490-94, 500, 510, 513, 699; Nujūm **180**, VII, passim for corresponding years; Sakhāwī **197**, pp. 262, 307-08, 323, 345, 384; Iyās **171**, pp. 23, 39-47, 55, 150-54, 157, 161.

63. Pirate assaults: **374**, pp. 32, 344; **526**, pp. 24-25; Jawharī **45**, pp. 175b, 176b-177a, 192b; **46**, pp. 130a-b, 134a, 146a, 151b-152a, 163b, 188b; Inbā' **26**, II, 166a-b, 196b, 218a, 252b, 256a-b, 257a; **52**, p. 72a; Nujūm **180**, VI, 644, VII, 106; Sakhāwī **66**, I, yrs. 840, 845, II, 60b; **197**, pp. 9, 323-24, 351; **461**, pp. 159-60; Ḥawādith **179**, pp. 96, 109, 273, 298-99; **236**, pp. 82-83; Iyās **171**, p. 64; **174**, pp. 83, 87, 99; **54**, pp. 12a, 73a, 102b, 111b, 120a, 122a; **239**, p. 179. Coastal defenses: Nujūm **180**, VII, 106; Ḥawādith **179**, pp. 68, 105, 107, 129, 181; Sakhāwī **197**, p. 388; Iyās **174**, pp. 167, 172; **404**, p. 112. The Tyre to Acre road in Syria was also improved, probably to facilitate troop movements. (**236**, pp. 79-82.)

Occupation of Cyprus: Nujūm **180**, VII, 520-21, 537, 543, 551-52; Iyās **171**, pp. 65-66, 72, 75-77, 79-80, 82-83, 89, 104, 107-09, 124, 148; Ḥawādith **179**, pp. 329, 340, 342-43, 345-48, 409, 413-14, 435, 455-71, 477-78, 571-73, 755, 770-71, 779.

64. Tax abolitions: **208**; Décrets **223**; **227**; **229**; **230**; **238**; **101**, III, 228-38. *Muhtasib*'s and other taxes: see above, pp. 99-100.
65. Monopolies and forced sales: see above, pp. 126-27.
66. See above, pp. 50-51; **408**.
67. Year 842: Nujūm **180**, VII, 80, 91-93; **399**, p. 582; Iyās **170**, XXXIV, 11-12. Year 866: Ḥawādith **179**, pp. 425-27; **125**, III, 58; Iyās **171**, p. 117. Bedouins: Inbā' **26**, II, 207b, 213a, 225a, 245b-246a; Nujūm **180**, VI, 662; Ḥawādith **179**, pp. 51, 407. Severe damage was done at Aleppo in 853. (**63**, p. 36.)
68. Cairo riots: Inbā' **26**, II, 166a, 168b, 184b, 202a, 218b, 219a; Ḥawādith **179**, pp. 19, 221, 232-33; Sakhāwī **66**, I, yr. 859, II, 12b, 113a; **197**, pp. 123-24, 314, 429-31; Iyās **171**, pp. 13, 23, 42-43, 65, 106, 125-32, 174; **174**, pp. 105, 263, 382, 496-97; Nujūm **180**, VII, 468-69; **62**, p. 67a; Jawharī **45**, p. 128b; **46**, p. 133b. Mamluk abuses at Aleppo and Damascus at the very end of the period turned the populations to the Ottomans. (Iyās **169**, IV, 400, 432; Ṭūlūn **181**, pp. 317, 349, 382; **183**, p. 163.)
69. Appendices B and C. Khans and water works in Aleppo: **211**; **511**; **523**; **520**, pp. 181-82. Damascus: Ṭūlūn **112**; **184**.
70. Dulghādir wars: Ḥawādith **179**; Iyās **171**; **174**; **399**, pp. 590-91; **375**, II, 239-40; **125**, III, 59-71. Ottoman-Mamluk war of 889-895: **399**, pp. 599-603; **375**, II, 240; Iyās **174**; **125**.
71. Upper Egypt throughout the 870's: **54**, pp. 15b, 22a, 52a, 59a, 65a, 68b, 91a; Ḥawādith **179**, pp. 695-96; Jawharī **45**, p. 19a; **73**, p. 378a. Syria around 875: Iyās **174**, p. 49; **54**, pp. 63a, 81b-82a; **71**, p. 37. In the 880's Hama was troubled by the bedouins. (Iyās **174**, pp. 162, 181-82, 188-89; **125**, III, 82-87.) In the following decade Palestine was in turmoil. (**239**, p. 241; Sakhāwī **66**, II, 96b-97a; 'Ulaymī **57**, p. 216b; **117**, p. 294; **190**, II, 669, 703. After 900, damage in the Damascus area became massive. (Ḥimṣī **30**, yr. 903 reports the loss of two hundred villages; also yrs. 904, 916, 917; Sakhāwī **66**, II, 144a; Ṭūlūn **185**, pp. 43, 52, 87-88, 93-94, 123-31, 133-34, 139.) Villages lost in Syria: **115**, pp. 20-21; **378**, pp. 54-55; Iyās **174**, p. 450; **125**, III, 114; **81**, pp. 77-80. Total revenue losses: **130**, pp. 2-3; **430**, pp. 149, 153.
72. Revenues of Qaṭyā: **54**, pp. 76a, 85b; Jawharī **45**, p. 86a; **72**, pp. 11b-12a. Caravans: Jawharī **45**, p. 106b, 112a, 116b; **514**, pp. 92-93, 95; Ṭūlūn **181**, pp. 119, 268; **183**, p. 146; **255**, p. 181; **54**, pp. 59a, 61a, 98b; Ḥawādith **179**, p. 638; **255**, p. 181. Waqfs: **54**, p. 153a. Pilgrimage after 900: 'Ulaymī **57**, p. 219b; **191**, pp. 3-4, 11-12; Ḥimṣī **29**, p. 178b; **52**, pp. 213b, 217b-218a; Ṭūlūn **185**, pp. 82, 111, 131-32; Iyās **169**, IV, 99, 117; **174**, pp. 344-45, 472.
73. See above, pp. 56-59, 77, 92-93, 99-100. Taxes on property: Sakhāwī **66**, II, 140a-b; Iyās **31**, pp. 234b, 235b, 241b; Ḥimṣī **30**, yr. 903. Thefts and extortions: Iyās **169**, IV, 166, 176-79, 364, 427-28, 431; **174**, pp. 217, 223, 245-46, 300.
74. Copper coin: **425**, XVI, 72-73, 78-79; Iyās **174**, pp. 137-38, 184, 249, 359, 429, 436; **175**, I, 18, 22, 84, 233-34, 251, 276, 305, 316, II, 51, 57. Price disturbances: **425**, XVI, 88-89; Ṭūlūn **185**, pp. 65, 95, 97-98, 107-08, 110, 112, 125, 132, 138.
75. Traffic in common goods such as donkeys and linen and more valuable

spices and slaves between Syria and Egypt on the one hand and Anatolia on the other: Jawharī **46**, pp. 103b, 148b; **268**, pp. 351, 356; **243**, pp. 230, 309; **72**, p. 56b; **454**, pp. 369, 382, 384; Sakhāwī **197**, p. 265; **271**, p. 107; Ṭūlūn **181**, p. 119. The Dulghādir wars interrupted the trade and in 873 Shāh Suwār sent a circular to Aleppo, Tripoli, and Damascus guaranteeing the security of merchants. (Ḥawādith **179**, pp. 686-87; Sakhāwī **66**, I, yr. 873; **71**, p. 31.) Sea traffic between Egypt and Turkey: **250**, III, 164; Iyās **174**, p. 77; **341**, pp. 143-44. Aleppo trade in soap and carpets: **125**, V, 477; Sibṭ **123**, pp. 78, 154; Shiḥna **110**, pp. 196-97. Spice trade: **454**; **341**. Persia: **268**, pp. 329-30; Sibṭ **123**, p. 154; **520**, p. 165; **271**, p. 107; **280**, p. 8; **536**, p. 140; **139**, pp. 473-74.

76. See bibliography section IIE, and especially **455**.

77. Piracy: Tripoli attacked in 901 and 917: Ṭūlūn **183**, pp. 141, 159. Ṭīna in 914: Iyās **169**, IV, 146. Rumors: **255**, p. 103; Ḥimṣī **30**, p. 11. Indian Ocean and Red Sea fleets: Iyās **169**, IV, 109, 142-43, 182-83, 286-87; **383**; **278**, p. 8; **277**, pp. xlv-xlvi.

78. Rebellions at Damascus in 903: Iyās **174**, pp. 430, 434, 450, 459-60; **125**, III, 106, 108-10; **101**, III, 238-39; **399**, p. 610; Ṭūlūn **181**, pp. 182-200; **185**, pp. 40-42. Revolt of 905: Iyās **174**, pp. 466, 472-74, 488, 490, 493-94; Ṭūlūn **181**, pp. 221-30; **185**, pp. 53-67, 72-73, 77-78. Rebellion of 910: **125**, III, 114; Ṭūlūn **181**, p. 283; **183**, p. 144; **185**, pp. 102-03. Chapter V, passim, for the social difficulties of Damascus and Cairo.

CHAPTER II. THE MAMLUK REGIME IN THE LIFE OF THE CITIES

1. Ayalon, Popper, and Poliak in bibliography, section IID. Mamluk games: **405**.

2. Administrative manuals in bibliography sections IB-1 and IID, especially articles by Cahen, Popper, Ayalon, and Poliak. Also Syrie **140**. For military encroachments on the civil services: **425**, XV, 96; **407**, XVI, 61; Syrie **140**, p. lxviii. In the fifteenth century *muḥtasibs,* public treasurers, and administrative commissioners (*shādds*) tended to be Mamluks. Similarly the office of the civil *wazīr* declined in favor of the powers of the Mamluk *ustādār* in taxation.

3. **408**; **415**; **420**; **421**; **422**; **424**; **425**.

4. References to the scribes, *wakīls, nāẓirs,* and *dīwāns* of emirs: Ṣaqāʿī **65**, pp. 11b, 15a-b, 17a-18b, 44a, 56a-58a, 71b, 72b, 81a-b, 82b-83a, 84a-b, 88b; **90**, I, 77, 82, IV, 46; **91**, II, 527-31; **92**, p. 299; **95**, VIII, 47, XI, 33-34; Furāt **166**, IX, 354, 357; Sulūk **56**, II, 75a, III, 40b; Ṭūlūn **181**, p. 236. The retinue of emirs: Sulūk **56**, II, 36a, 53a-b, 180a.

5. Ashtor (**492**) considers the government of towns as part of regular Mamluk administration. The actual duties of the governors and the motives for their behavior must be more closely examined.

6. The blending of public and private powers was a common ancient and medieval phenomenon. Rostovtzeff remarks that "no sharp line can be drawn between private and public life in the Hellenistic monarchies in general." (M. Rostovtzeff, *A Large Estate in Egypt in the Third*

Century B.C., University of Wisconsin Studies in the Social Sciences and History, VI [1922], p. 35.)

In Europe the collapse of the Roman Empire confided state jurisdictions to the hands of landlords, and the merger was the basis of the feudal system. Max Weber characterizes this type of government as "patrimonial," but to stress how little the emirs were regulated in the use of their fortunes, and how free they were to neglect administrative functions not in their interests, the term "private" is employed here. (Max Weber, *The Theory of Social and Economic Organization,* A. M. Henderson and T. Parsons, tr. [Glencoe, 1947], pp. 346-54.)

In discussing the privatization of economic power the role of the Sultan himself is omitted. The activities of the Sultan ought to be considered as private household activities like those of the Mamluks, but by discussing the lesser lords it is easier to avoid confusion of household and state activities. The emirs, moreover, were much closer to the daily life of the cities, and their roles are more revealing.

7. Mamluk consumption: Quatremère **188**, I_1, 238, 243, I_2, 135; Furāt **166**, IX, 73; **159**, pp. 215-16. Movement of markets: Décrets **223**, II, 34-40.

8. Wages of workers: **425**, XVI, 117, 121. A daily wage of one and a half dirhems plus a bread ration paid to laborers on Egyptian canal works in the middle of the fourteenth century was equivalent to the two dirhems a day wage of a laborer at the beginning of the fifteenth century. (Khiṭaṭ **116**, II, 168; Nu'aymī **119**, II, 404-05.) Records of waqfs' provisions for the wages of servants and workers indicate wages ranging from twenty to sixty dirhems a month, or about three to seven hundred dirhems a year. (Nu'aymī **119**, I, 9-10, 32-34; Ṭūlūn **111**, p. 72; **121**, III, 260-61; **210**, XIII, 100; 'Aynī **3**, I, 138a; **351**, pp. 49-50; **355**, pp. 77-86; **75**.)

9. Salaries of emirs: **425**, XVI, 107-16; **424**; **408**. Tankiz: **91**, I, 179-81; Nu'aymī **119**, I, 123-28; **64**, p. 204a; Sulūk **187**, II, 507-08. Other fortunes: Sulūk **56**, II, 45b; **187**, II, 481-82; Ṣaqā'ī **65**, p. 45a; Nujūm **180**, VI, 378; Shuhba **35**, I, 14a, 25a; Duqmāq **20**, p. 74a. Gifts: Furāt **166**, IX, 454; Nujūm **180**, V, 569; Sulūk **56**, II, 28a, 114b. A gift from the Emir Taghrī Birdī of Aleppo to the Sultan in 800/1397 was considered all the more wonderful because "despite . . . excellent administration and his avoidance of tyranny in his government of Aleppo, and despite the large number of servitors and Mamluks which he maintained, he had been able to offer this remarkable gift." (Nujūm **180**, V, 576; tr. by Popper. Nujūm **180**, XIV, 156.)

Fifteenth century fortunes: **374**, p. 54; Jawharī **45**, pp. 78b, 85a; **72**, p. 31b. A list of salaries of emirs in 818/1415 shows the top rank paid only 6,000 dinars. (**72**, p. 31b.)

10. Cahen points out that the Ayyūbid *dīnār jaysh* (military dinar) in which salaries were stated was an accounting unit. It was worth half a dinar in cash and one *irdabb* of grain of two-thirds wheat and one-third barley. (**415**, p. 46.) In Mamluk times salaries continued to be paid in kind. (**408**, pp. 274-77.) Only Wiet, however, has noted the

importance of these payments for the urban grain market, and no study of the subject has yet been attempted. (**399**, p. 451.)

By contrast with the loose methods adopted by the Mamluks for passing rural supplies into the urban market, the Byzantine and Ottoman empires adopted strict controls to assure the provisioning of the capital. Whereas the Mamluks were willing to give the emirs an opportunity for speculative profits, the other empires refused to permit this. (**507**, pp. 179-94; G. J. Bratianu, "Nouvelles Contributions à l'Étude de l'Approvisionnement de Constantinople sous les Paléologues et les Empereurs Ottomans," *Byzantion,* VI [1931], pp. 641-56; G. J. Bratianu, "La Question de l'Approvisionnement de Constantinople à l'Époque Byzantine et Ottomane," *Byzantion,* V [1929], pp. 83-107; L. Güçer, "Le Commerce Intérieur des Céréales dans l'Empire Ottoman pendant la Seconde Moitié du XVIème Siècle," *Revue de la Faculté des Sciences Économiques Université d'Istanbul,* II [1949-50], pp. 163-88; L. Güçer, "Le Probleme de l'Approvisionnement d'Istanbul en Céréales vers le Milieu du XVIIIème Siècle," *Revue de la Faculté des Sciences Économiques Université d'Istanbul,* II [1949-50], pp. 153-62.

11. Grain stores: Birzālī **10**, II, 157a; Sulūk **56**, II, 106b; **187**, II, 97-98, 357, 565, 700, 880-81; Jawharī **46**, pp. 41b, 61a; Duqmāq **20**, p. 133a; Kathīr **176**, XIII, 235. Imports: Sulūk **56**, III, 62b; Duqmāq **20**, p. 109b. Plunder of the stocks of a defeated emir once put so much grain on the market that the price fell from twenty dirhems per *irdabb* to six. (Sulūk **187**, II, 592.) In a fifteenth century episode emirs transferred stocks of grain from warehouses to their own residences to protect it against pillage. (Iyās **168**, II, 31.) Further evidence of the importance of emirs as grain owners will be cited below.

12. Jazarī **48**, p. 545; Shuḥba **35**, I, 40b; Ṣaqā'ī **65**, p. 14a. Waqfs were also grain owners. An example comes from Medina. (Sulūk **56**, II, 14b.)

13. Employees: **59**, p. 269; Jawharī **46**, p. 45a; 'Aynī **4**, pp. 100b, 101b; Sulūk **187**, II, 823. In 658/1260 Mamluks and officials in Damascus sold grain variously estimated as worth 100,000 and 600,000 dirhems. (Ṣaqā'ī **65**, p. 20a; Kutubī **37**, I, 368.) Emirs sometimes sold grain to raise cash to meet fines or to finance rebellions. (Ṣaqā'ī **65**, pp. 13b-14a; Kathīr **176**, XIV, 219; Kutubī **39**, p. 86.)

14. Sulūk **187**, II, 254; **198**, p. 183; Ṭūlūn **111**, I, 52-53; Nu'aymī **119**, II, 50-52.

15. Sultan Barsbāy: **88**, p. 206; **374**, p. 152; Jawharī **46**, p. 145a; Inbā' **26**, II, 172a. Ibn al-Nashū: See above, p. 146 and note 5. Others: Inbā' **26**, II, 246a; Iyās **169**, II, 115; **54**, p. 5a.

16. Sulūk **56**, II, 79b, 92a-b, 125b, 199a; **187**, II, 409, 414, 438, 444; 'Aynī **3**, I, 167b; **4**, pp. 107b, 108b; Kutubī **38**, p. 142a; Furāt **166**, IX, 144, 219, 427-30, 439; Inbā' **26**, II, 14a, III, 84a; **230**, p. 56; **374**, p. 152; Jawharī **46**, pp. 14a, 154b; **2**, yr. 798; Ḥimṣī **29**, p. 66b; **30**, yr. 882; Ṭūlūn **181**, pp. 65, 119.

17. Quatremère **188**, II_1, 65; Sulūk **187**, II, 206. Year 736: Sulūk **187**, II, 394-96; Duqmāq **21**, I, 146b; 'Aynī **4**, pp. 101a-b; **59**, p. 269; Jazarī **48**, p. 497. Year 796: Jawharī **46**, p. 45a; Furāt **166**, IX, 387; Sulūk

56, II, 144a. Other: Sulūk **56**, II, 75a, III, 58a, 63a, 87b; Duqmāq **22**, pp. 197-98; Sakhāwī **66**, I, yr. 818; **197**, p. 346; Inbā' **26**, II, 62a; Ḥawādith **179**, p. 617.

18. Year 662: Yūnīnī **202**, I, 555, II, 232; Quatremère **188**, I_1, 232-33; Sulūk **187**, I, 507-08; Ḥabīb **23**, p. 23a; Kutubī **37**, I, 235; **158**, pp. 500-01, 1012-13; Duqmāq **21**, I, 100a; Iyās **169**, I, 103. Year 694: Quatremère **188**, II_2, 26. Year 749: **59**, p. 296. Years 775-76: **70**, p. 406b; Duqmāq **20**, p. 54b; **21**, I, 174b; **9**, p. 86b; **18**, p. 173a; 'Aynī **3**, I, 98a; Inbā' **26**, III, 16b; Bāsiṭ **1**, I, 104b. Year 798: Furāt **166**, IX, 432. Year 808: Inbā' **26**, III, 218b.

19. Expeditions for grain and animals: Sulūk **56**, III, 62b, 63b, 65b, 73a; **187**, II, 408, 676; Nujūm **180**, VI, 357; **54**, p. 153a. In one case Sultan Jaqmaq sent to Cyprus for grain in return for which he excused the island from the annual tribute. (Sakhāwī **197**, p. 312; Ḥawādith **179**, pp. 91-92.) Price fixing: Sulūk **187**, II, 679; **56**, II, 35b; Inbā' **26**, II, 57b-58a, III, 135a; Furāt **166**, IX, 439; Nujūm **180**, VI, 355-56; Ḥawādith **179**, pp. 230-31; Jawharī **45**, p. 6a; **54**, pp. 59a, 62a; Ṭūlūn **185**, pp. 95, 107-08.

20. See above, pp. 29, 35, 40. Direct collection of salaries: **83**, VIII, 246.

21. Before 733: Furāt **166**, VIII, 82; Kutubī **37**, I, 6; **132**, pp. 34, 39. Al-Nashū: 'Aynī **3**, II, 193b; **4**, pp. 107b-108b, 124b-125a, 138b; **59**, pp. 271, 280; Sulūk **187**, II, 360, 390, 412-14, 420, 435, 439, 460, 488, 552. Civil war period: Sulūk **56**, II, 47a, 140a, III, 35a, 43b, 63a, 67a-b; Nujūm **180**, VI, 13, 151, 272; Duqmāq **20**, pp. 113b, 122a.

22. Barsbāy: **374**, p. 147; Ṭūlūn **182**, III, 3; Jawharī **46**, pp. 132a, 133b, 137b. Others: Sakhāwī **66**, I, yr. 859; Ḥawādith **179**, pp. 406, 409; Jawharī **45**, p. 161a; Ḥimṣī **29**, p. 98a; **239**, p. 165; Décrets **223**, XII, 30; **230**, pp. 76-79.

23. Nablus oil: 'Ulaymī **57**, pp. 216a, 221a-b; **58**, p. 144a; **190**, II, 686-87, 694-95, 702; **208**, XLIII, 375-76. Damascus sugar: Ṭūlūn **181**, pp. 41-42, 44-46, 48. Other: Ṭūlūn **181**, pp. 119, 213, 292; **185**, pp. 47, 83, 112; Décrets **223**, II, 51-52; **230**, p. 60; Iyās **169**, IV, 242-43, 442-43. Other usages of *rimāya* and *ṭarḥ* refer to simple taxes or fees. (See above, pp. 92-93.) French *gabelles*: George T. Matthews, *The Royal General Farms in Eighteenth Century France* (New York, 1958).

24. See Appendix A.

25. Damascus baths: Birzālī **10**, I, 176b, 181b, 225b; Dhahabī **14**, pp. 111a, 117a; **26**, I, 4b; Ḥimṣī **29**, p. 111a; Shuhba **34**, yrs. 694, 720, 721, 722, 726, 728; Kutubī **37**, I, 47-48; **38**, p. 133a; Jazarī **48**, pp. 453-54; **64**, p. 184b; **106**, p. 40; Nu'aymī **119**, II, 240; **121**, VI, 281; Kathīr **176**, XIII, 339, XIV, 98, 122, 133, 170; Ṭūlūn **181**, pp. 88, 253, 259; **187**, IV, 43; **185**, pp. 35, 119; **208**, XLIV, 323-24; **501**, pp. 58, 73; **525**, pp. 76-78. Markets: Dhahabī **14**, p. 117a; Duqmāq **22**, p. 196; **7**, pp. 46a-47b; Ḥimṣī **29**, pp. 74b, 88a-b; Ḥabīb **23**, p. 223b; Shuhba **34**, yrs. 694, 736; Kutubī **39**, p. 99a; **59**, p. 276; Sakhāwī **66**, II, 144b; **67**, p. 58a; Nu'aymī **119**, II, 400; **126**, p. 66; Furāt **166**, VIII, 64-65; Kathīr **176**, XIII, 311, XIV, 167, 174, 218; Ṭūlūn **182**, IV, 54-55; **505**, p. 89. Khans: Shuhba 34, yr. 732; Nu'aymī **119**, II, 244, 290; **121**, VI, 236; Kathīr **176**, XIV, 104, 157; Ṣaṣra **177**, p. 168b; **516**, p. 54. *Qayṣariyyas:* **8**, pp. 235b, 244a, 245b; Birzālī **10**, II, 234a; Ḥabīb **23**, p. 223b; Ḥimṣī **29**, p. 111a; Shuhba **34**, yr. 715; Kutubī **39**, pp. 6b,

140a; Jazarī **48**, pp. 196, 276; **59**, p. 276; **126**, p. 66; Dhahabī **153**, II, 172, 182; Kathīr **176**, XIV, 74, 157, 218, 313; Ṭūlūn **182**, IV, 55; **185**, p. 35.

Aleppo khans: **210**, XIV, 141, 222; **125**, II, 451, III, 81; **211**, II, 347, 403; **69**, p. 37; **101**, II, 84; **523**, pp. 94, 96-97, 107. Baths: **125**, II, 451, III, 81, V, 179; **211**, II, 352, 402; **523**, pp. 91-92, 108, 111; **69**, p. 37; **101**, II, 84; Sibṭ **123**, p. 137. Markets: **125**, II, 451; **69**, p. 37; **101**, II, 84; **523**, p. 111.

26. Year 691: Décrets **223**, XII, 30; Jazarī **186**, p. 20; Kutubī **37**, I, 72; Yūnīnī **80**, III, 17b; Birzālī **10**, I, 185b, 209a-b; Dhahabī **14**, p. 116a. Year 726: Kathīr **176**, XIV, 122. Year 829: **121**, VII, 222-23; Nu'aymī **119**, II, 406-07. Others: Dhahabī **12**, pp. 60b-61a; Nu'aymī **119**, II, 400; Ḥimṣī **29**, p. 187b; **30**, yr. 903; **106**, p. 80.

27. Purchases: **149**, IV, 115-16; Furāt **166**, VII, 97; Quatremère **188**, I_2, 162; Sulūk **56**, I, 237b, II, 38a, 128a; **187**, II, 320, 634; Jazarī **48**, pp. 202, 245; **59**, p. 268; Kutubī **39**, p. 99a; Ḥawādith **179**, p. 255; Ṭūlūn **111**, I, 53; Nu'aymī **119**, I, 501. One famous instance was the purchase of a house by Governor Tankiz of Damascus. He paid 40,000 dirhems for a house which he converted into his palatial *Dār al-Dhahab,* worth a half million dirhems, and the most valuable single property in Damascus in his time. (Nu'aymī **119**, I, 123; Jazarī **48**, p. 110; Shuhba **34**, yr. 728; Kutubī **38**, p. 196a; **91**, I, 179-81; **121**, III, 316-17; **379**, p. 637.) Even water canals could be privately owned and purchased. In 720/1320 a canal was purchased for 45,000 dirhems to bring water to a new mosque in al-Qubaybāt. ('Aynī **3**, I, 4a; Kutubī **38**, p. 118b; **97**, p. 238; **121**, VII, 231; Sulūk **187**, II, 184; Nu'aymī **119**, II, 416; Ḥabīb **23**, pp. 155a-b; Shuhba **34**, yr. 720.)

28. Treasury sales of *qayṣariyyas,* markets, houses, and land: **74**, p. 111a; Birzālī **10**, I, 174b, 185b, 247a; Yūnīnī **80**, III, 17b; Kutubī **37**, I, 72; **39**, p. 6b; **125**, III, 41; Shuhba **34**, yr. 732. *Al-khizānat al-bunūd:* Sulūk **187**, II, 640-42; Bāsiṭ **1**, I, 2a-b, 3a; 'Aynī **4**, p. 180b; **59**, p. 289.

29. Legitimate purchases: Jazarī **48**, pp. 278, 463; Sulūk **56**, III, 33a-b, 34b; **187**, II, 362; Kutubī **39**, p. 30a; Ṭūlūn **181**, p. 346. Frauds: Sulūk **187**, II, 321; 'Aynī **3**, II, 137a. Witnesses who were specialists in property assessments: Jazarī **47**, p. 299a; **48**, pp. 2, 11, 19, 49, 63; **121**, III, 310.

30. Reconstruction of Damascus: Inbā' **26**, III, 187b, 238a, 240a. Seizures: Ṭūlūn **181**, p. 216; Sulūk **56**, II, 38a.

Direct evidence for seizures is lacking, for rarely are the fortunes of emirs described as including real estate. Tankiz's arrest, however, may nonetheless be typical of what happened to other emirs who had neglected to convert their holdings into waqfs. (Note 9, above.) Property seizures may be inferred from the histories of civil wars of Mamluks in which mobs of the common people were sent to plunder the losing side. Having taken this liberty with the houses of defeated emirs, it seems likely that there was little compunction about seizing the remains.

31. Streets were widened, hovels and shacks taken down or burned out, bridges cleared of shops which clogged the passages, access to waterfronts improved, and illegal shops, houses, balconies, and benches re-

moved. ('Aynī **3**, II, 138b, 248a; Jazarī **48**, p. 373; Inbā' **26**, I, 5a; Sakhāwī **197**, p. 211; Ḥimṣī **29**, p. 148b; Nu'aymī **119**, II, 403-04; Nujūm **180**, VII, 499; Ṭūlūn **181**, pp. 20-21, 24, 48-50, 77-78, 102; Sulūk **56**, III, 56b, 64b.) Qadis' approval: Ḥimṣī **29**, p. 98b; Kathīr **176**, XIV, 261; **56**, p. 88b; Ṭūlūn **181**, pp. 57, 319; Iyās **169**, II, 171, 177; Sulūk **56**, II, 33a-b. Compensations: Jazarī **48**, pp. 278, 492; **44**, pp. 91b-92a.

32. Year 690: Yūnīnī **80**, III, 5b; Kutubī **37**, I, 47-48; Birzālī **10**, I, 181b; Furāt **166**, VIII, 128; Jazarī **186**, pp. 9-10; Kathīr **176**, XIV, 322-23. Other: 'Aynī **3**, II, 34b; Sibṭ **123**, pp. 161, 166; Shiḥna **110**, p. 29.

33. Sulūk **56**, I, 232a; **187**, II, 385; Kathīr **176**, XIV, 221; **121**, VII, 239; Iyās **169**, V, 53; Sibṭ **123**, p. 116.

34. **374**, pp. 134-35; Inbā' **26**, II, 119b, 122a; Jawharī **45**, p. 75a; Ṭūlūn **185**, p. 48; **121**, VII, 271; Sulūk **56**, III, 67b.

More grandiose schemes than the mere seizure of a few adjacent houses or lots for personal gain might be imagined. In 687/1288 agents of the Sultan inspecting properties in Damascus wished to have the qadis declare their owners legally incompetent so that they could purchase the assets without consent and confiscate previous yields. The qadis refused, but in the following year estates owned by Bint Mālik Ashraf were turned over to the Sultan, and the back yields from the time she acquired them until the time of seizure, a half-million dirhems were demanded. About 80,000 were paid. Evidently the Sultan's purpose was to capture back lands, once given in return for military service. (Kutubī **37**, I, 7; Furāt **166**, VIII, 64-65.)

35. **121**, VII, 239; Nu'aymī **119**, II, 429; Inbā' **26**, II, 63a.

36. Sulūk **187**, II, 385.

37. *Maḥākir* were ground rents: Ṭūlūn **111**, I, 61, 101; Nu'aymī **119**, I, 223-24, 340, 412; Nuwayrī **61**, III, 46a.

38. Fortifications: Quatremère **188**, I_2, 41; Shiḥna **110**, pp. 23-24, 48. Dams, canals, and bridges: Sulūk **56**, II, 73a, 77a-b, III, 99b; **187**, II, 48-49, 261-62, 387; 'Aynī **3**, II, 34b; Ḥabīb **23**, p. 191b; Iyās **169**, II, 17. Use of clienteles: Sulūk **56**, III, 56b-58a; Nujūm **180**, VI, 345-46.

39. Kutubī **37**, I, 268; **38**, p. 142b; Sulūk **56**, II, 54a; **187**, II, 818; **70**, p. 423a; Nujūm **180**, VII, 502-06, 510.

40. Sulūk **56**, III, 56b-57a; **187**, II, 447, 450, 472, 765; Khiṭaṭ **116**, II, 166, 167, 169; Quatremère **188**, I_2, 19; Inbā' **26**, II, 53a; Nujūm **180**, VI, 345-46; Jawharī **46**, p. 91b; 'Aynī **4**, p. 154a. Canals in the Damascus area were built in 713/1313 by conscripted labor. (Kutubī **38**, p. 85a; **19**, p. 123b.)

41. Damascus: **237**, VII, 53-54; **149**, III, 208; Quatremère **188**, I_1, 121; Inbā' **26**, III, 196a, 227a. Aleppo: Sibṭ **123**, p. 171; Furāt **166**, IX, 215; Nujūm **180**, V, 527; 'Aynī **3**, I, 180b; Sulūk **56**, II, 124b-125a. Ja'bar: **101**, III, 178-79; Ḥabīb **23**, p. 208b; **125**, II, 387-88; **149**, IV, p. 116; Jazarī **48**, p. 461; Dawādārī **152**, p. 400. In 690/1291, out of fear of the governor, the common people of Damascus worked for two days on the enlargement of the hippodrome. (Jazarī **186**, p. 10; **47**, p. 32b; Kutubī **37**, I, 47-48; Birzālī **10**, I, 181b; **17**, p. 71a.)

42. Sulūk **187**, II, 320, 486, 641-42; 'Aynī **4**, pp. 128a, 155b; **249**, pp. 16, 91; **279**, p. 117; Ṭūlūn **181**, p. 150. Shipyards and foundries: **404**, passim.

43. Fourteenth century Syrian constructions: Quatremère **188**, I_1, 205, I_2,

26; Ḥabīb **23**, p. 28b; **74**, p. 364b; Yūnīnī **80**, III, 29b; **159**, pp. 28, 113; **192**, p. 244. Mecca and Medina constructions: Quatremère **188**, I_1, 223; **237**, VII, 57; Yūnīnī **202**, I, 534-35; Ḥabīb **23**, pp. 26a-b; **90**, I, 469-70, for the biography of a carpenter who worked in Medina. Fifteenth century Syria: 'Ulaymī **190**, II, 651; Sibṭ **123**, p. 42; Ṭūlūn **181**, p. 324. Mecca and Medina: **374**, p. 191; Ḥawādith **179**, p. 93; Sakhāwī **197**, pp. 320-21; Ḥimṣī **29**, p. 92a; Iyās **31**, p. 230a; **169**, IV, 163; **73**, p. 391a; Ṭūlūn **181**, p. 51. Other: 'Aynī **4**, p. 121a; Kathīr **176**, XIV, 315, 320.

Payment: Inbā' **26**, II, 63a; Ṭūlūn **185**, p. 42; Sulūk **56**, III, 63a.

44. Birzālī **10**, I, 166b, 170b; **62**, p. 110b; **404**, p. 75; **266**, p. 227; Iyās **169**, V, 34; **241**, p. 173; Quatremère **188**, II_2, 144; Yūnīnī **80**, IV, 160b; **64**, p. 199b. Otherwise the troops carried biscuits or assembled local markets from towns en route. (Dhahabī **13**, II, 60b; Duqmāq **20**, p. 121b.)

45. Public works: Jawharī **46**, pp. 145b, 180b; Nujūm **180**, V, 29, VI, 676; Sakhāwī **197**, p. 36; Sulūk **187**, II, 449; Iyās **169**, IV, 59, 63, 211, V, 13; **70**, p. 360a; Duqmāq **22**, p. 201. Minor ordinances: Kathīr **176**, XIV, 123, 158; Sulūk **56**, II, 109b-110a, 131b, 132b, 180a; **187**, II, 222, 275; Nujūm **180**, V, 317-18; 'Aynī **3**, I, 115a; Yūnīnī **202**, II, 433; **19**, pp. 134b-135a; Iyās **31**, p. 254b; **169**, IV, 346, V, 47; Jawharī **46**, p. 145b; Ḥimṣī **30**, yr. 904; Ṣaṣra **177**, pp. 100b-101a.

46. Forests of the Sultan: **229**, pp. 116-17; **238**, p. 535; Ṭūlūn **181**, p. 12. Controls: **158**, p. 374; **159**, pp. 30, 117; Iyās **169**, IV, 355. *Dīwān* controls of imports: **416**, pp. 109-10; Sulūk **187**, II, 486; note 1; Khiṭaṭ **116**, I, 109; **88**, pp. 205-06. Especially see Claude Cahen, "Douanes et Commerce dans les Ports Méditerranéens de l'Égypte Médiévale d'après le Minhādj d'al Makhzūmī," *JESHO*, VII (1964), pp. 218-314. Expeditions to the Gulf of Alexandretta: Ḥawādith **179**, pp. 255-56, 317, 379; Nujūm **180**, VII, 487, 492, 522, 572, 627; Iyās **169**, II, 59, 182, IV, 163, 183-85, 189, 191-92; **171**, p. 46; Ḥimṣī **30**, yr. 916; **277**, pp. lvi-lviii. Ottoman assistance: Iyās **169**, IV, 196, 201, 285; **277**, pp. lii-liv.

Allocation of supplies by the Sultan: Quatremère **188**, I_1, 205, 223; **237**, VII, 57; **74**, pp. 159a-b, 160a; Dhahabī **12**, p. 67a; Sulūk **187**, II, 385; Ḥimṣī **29**, p. 78a; **70**, p. 375a; **67**, p. 54a. Reuse of existing materials: Sulūk **187**, II, 334; 'Aynī **3**, I, 29a; Inbā' **26**, II, 25a; Ḥimṣī **29**, pp. 78a, 171a.

47. *Dīwān* controls: See note 46, above. Foundries and the *shādd al-masābik* (superintendant of metals): Shuhba **34**, yr. 732; Kutubī **39**, p. 6b; **404**, passim; Qalqashandī **84**, IV, 11-12, 188; **425**, XV, 119; **536**, p. 112; Syrie **140**, p. 151.

48. Quarries: Sulūk **187**, II, 633, 765; Kathīr **176**, XIV, 221; Sibṭ **123**, p. 26; Shiḥna **110**, p. 69. Reuse of stone: Shiḥna **110**, pp. 35, 48, 128-29; Sibṭ **123**, pp. 130, 161, 166; Dhahabī **14**, p. 11a; **121**, VII, 204-05; **211**, p. 80; Nujūm **180**, VI, 584; **19**, p. 41b; Kathīr **176**, XIV, 221, 261; Nu'aymī **119**, II, 426; Ḥimṣī **29**, pp. 147b-148b. The Damascus madrasa: **121**, VI, 227, 262-63.

Marble: Jazarī **48**, pp. 71, 453; Sulūk, **187**, II, 632; **213**, pp. 7-9. House to house searches were sometimes made to confiscate marble.

(Inbā' **26**, II, 21a-b; Nujūm **180**, VI, 359; Iyās **169**, II, 116-17, IV, 53, 68, 80, V, 90; Sulūk **56**, III, 65a.)

49. Khiṭaṭ **116**, II, 213-14; **403**, p. 14.

50. Uses of water: **239**, p. 168; **255**, p. 111. *Al-sharāb khānā* juxtaposed the duties of supervisor of canal constructions and inspector of the purity of beverages. How could the drinks be guaranteed and not the canals? (Décrets **223**, XII, 8-14.)

51. Syrie **140**, pp. 34, 38, 47; **137**, pp. 193-94. Tankiz's project: Sulūk **187**, II, 289; 'Aynī **3**, II, 101a. Other canalizations: **54**, p. 208a; Ṭūlūn **181**, pp. 16, 22, 107, 138, 339, 345. Fountains: **210**, XIII, 207, XIV, 166; **374**, p. 419; Ṭūlūn **185**, p. 127.

52. Aleppo aqueduct: Sulūk **187**, II, 131; Kutubī **38**, p. 85a; **19**, p. 123b; Shuḥba **34**, yr. 731; Kathīr **176**, XIV, 69; **189**, XX, 235; **125**, II, 382; Jazarī **48**, p. 242; **511**, pp. 8-9; **101**, III, 238. Cisterns: Syrie **140**, p. 82; Shiḥna **110**, p. 61; **520**, p. 181. Fourteenth century fountains: Shiḥna **110**, pp. 150-62; **210**, XIII, 250, XIV, 119-29; **211**, II, 324, 327-31, 339, 343-44; **523**, pp. 76, 90. New canals were laid to provide water for a hospital built in 755/1354. (**15**, p. 171a.) Fifteenth century water works, canals, and fountains: Shiḥna **110**, p. 160; Sibṭ **123**, p. 139; **101**, III, 230; **211**, II, 369, 382, 387, 393-95, 397, 403; **520**, p. 182; **523**, passim; **511**, passim.

53. Other towns: **536**, pp. 91-93; **216**, pp. 187, 196; **144**, pp. 487-88; **209**, pp. 286-87; **198**, pp. 112, 139; **230**, pp. 122-24; **204**, pp. 7, 29. Jerusalem and Hebron: Quatremère **188**, I_2, 249; **59**, p. 232; **208**, XLIII, 242, 339, 343; Sulūk **187**, II, 302; Ḥabīb **24**, p. 194b; Nujūm **180**, V, 600; **213**, pp. 35-37.

54. Waqfs: **101**, III, 238; Décrets **223**, III, 7. Supervision: **135**, p. 93; Décrets **223**, XII, 9-10. Sometimes the chamberlain, as a leading Mamluk officer, took charge of regulating the water supply. (Ṣaṣra **177**, p. 199b.) Note 50, above, for *al-sharāb khānā*.

55. In 728/1328, Tankiz widened Bāb al-Barīd, and all the houses obstructing access to the river in al-Ṣāliḥiyya were destroyed. (Jazarī **48**, pp. 116, 121; Kutubī **38**, p. 197b.) In the following year Tankiz tackled Sūq al-Qaṣb outside Bāb al-Salāma, and removed the outside benches in the bowmaker's suq to add a few cubits to the width of the street. In addition, all the shops from Bāb al-Jābiya to Bāb al-Naṣr were knocked down to create a new wide avenue. (Jazarī **48**, pp. 159, 161; Shuḥba **34**, yr. 729; Kutubī **38**, p. 203a.) Thus the ancient straight street of Damascus was restored. In 730/1330, the horse market, an open area outside the citadel which was the center of markets serving the Mamluks, was widened by tearing out twenty shops. Benches were removed in another suq while a still larger project involved tearing out the shops outside the Bāb al-Naṣr to widen the street. ('Aynī **3**, II, 138b; Shuḥba **34**, yr. 730; Kutubī **38**, p. 210b; Jazarī **48**, pp. 201, 204, 206.) Even the foundations were dug out to prevent reconstruction on the site. In 731/1331 Tankiz cleared the area from Bāb al-Jābiya through various suqs outside the city. (Kutubī **39**, p. 2a; Shuḥba **34**, yr. 731; Jazarī **48**, pp. 243, 248, 250.) At this point the governor's efforts slackened, and only in 733/1333 did he tear out a few benches to widen a market (Jazarī **48**, p. 329), but in 735/1335 he returned to the project with a vengeance,

clearing the way through the city from Bāb al-Jābiya to Bāb al-Naṣr. Shops and even a mosque were torn down, and the benches of all the suqs in that area of the city were removed. (Shuḥba **34**, yr. 735; 'Aynī **3**, II, 248a; Kutubī **39**, p. 30a; Jazarī **48**, pp. 262-63, 492; **59**, p. 268.) Tankiz also widened the street from the bridge of Bāb al-Ḥadīd to Bāb al-Farādis, from the east exit of the citadel to a gate in the north wall. (**90**, I, 522.)

Other sporadic street repairs: Notes 31 and 45, above.

56. Kathīr **176**, XIV, 123, 215, 336; Jazarī **48**, pp. 6, 163, 286, 329; **186**, p. 37; Sulūk **187**, II, 275, 313; **19**, pp. 132a-b; Kutubī **38**, p. 203b; Shuḥba **34**, yrs. 729, 732; Sakhāwī **66**, I, yr. 745; Nujūm **180**, V, 317-18; 'Aynī **3**, I, 115a; Ṭūlūn **185**, p. 11. Other: Yūnīnī **202**, II, 433.
57. **536**, p. 90; Ḥabīb **23**, pp. 170b-171a; **19**, p. 146a; **258**, p. 149; Ṭūlūn **182**, IV, 60; Jawharī **45**, p. 188b; Iyās **174**, pp. 131-33. Tripoli: **230**, pp. 43, 45-46.
58. Appendix B.
59. Appendix A.
60. Appendix C.
61. A waqf scroll in the National Museum in Damascus and another in al-Ẓāhiriyya Library name the founders and their heirs in perpetuity as administrators. Other instances: **210**, XIII, 71; **54**, pp. 192b, 193b, 205b, passim; Ṭūlūn **181**, pp. 148-49; Décrets **223**, XII, 36-37; Sulūk **56**, II, 155a. Family control of waqfs led to abuses. In times of lax supervision, families might usurp the property and convert it to private use or change the terms of the waqf in their favor. (Sibṭ **123**, pp. 101-04, 159.) See also **330**.
62. Sibṭ **123**, pp. 42-43; **69**, pp. 64-65, 76-77; **54**, p. 24a; Ṭūlūn **181**, pp. 202, 364, 386.
63. Before Tankiz: Kutubī **37**, I, 324, II, 374-75; **38**, p. 167a. Tankiz: Sulūk **187**, II, 289; Jazarī **48**, 70, 155, 194; Kutubī **38**, pp. 189b-190a, 209b; Shuḥba **34**, yrs. 727, 730; 'Aynī **3**, I, 25b, II, 116a-b; **121**, VII, 218; Décrets **223**, XII, 36-37. Also: Sulūk **56**, II, 147a for the efforts of an emir to restore discipline in a *khānaqā*.
64. Nu'aymī **119**, I, 448, II, 404-05; **121**, IV, 266-67, 276-78; **374**, p. 136.
65. Décrets **223**, III, 14-17; **238**, p. 524-25; **208**, XLIV, 322-28; **374**, pp. 137-38; 'Ulaymī **118**, p. 252; Kutubī **38**, pp. 203a-b; Ḥimṣī **29**, p. 77b.
66. Illegal seizures: Jawharī **46**, p. 206b; 'Ulaymī **190**, II, 669; **57**, p. 215b; **54**, p. 213b; Décrets **223**, II, 25; Shiḥna **110**, pp. 10-11; Sibṭ **123**, pp. 44-45; Ṭūlūn **181**, pp. 87, 113, 250, 277, 319.

Civil war period taxes: Décrets **223**, II, 5, 33, XII, 7; **238**, pp. 522, 526; **121**, VII, 274; **234**, pp. 52-53. Late fifteenth, early sixteenth century: **238**, pp. 531, 533; Décrets **223**, III, 7, 11, 20-21; **101**, III, 238; **54**, p. 221b; **230**, p. 82; Iyās **169**, IV, 15; **206**, pp. 140, 146; **491**, p. 147; Ṭūlūn **181**, p. 86.

CHAPTER III. THE URBAN SOCIETY

1. **243**, p. 294; **536**, p. 96; **266**, p. 226; **493**, p. 27; **494**, pp. 292-93.

Comparison with other contemporary cities is suggestive. Istanbul in 1478 had a population of about 98,000. Bursa between 1520 and 1530 had about 35,000 and Adrianople about 22,000. (**493**; **494**.) According to Braudel's estimates, Venice in 1500 had a population of 100,000, Naples 150,000, Palermo 50,000, and Messina 35,000. (Ferdinand Braudel, *La Mer Méditerranée à l'Époque de Phillippe II* [Paris, 1949], p. 269.) However, in the sixteenth century, these cities grew substantially while Damascus and Aleppo declined.

2. Damascus region: Baṭṭūṭa **141**, I, 229-37; **114**, passim; **184**; Nuʿaymī **119**, II, 431-40.

Agriculture and urban living were not so completely separated as we now tend to think. See Syrie **140**, p. 106 for Hama and above, p. 13 and note 8 for taxes levied on Damascus gardens.

3. The phrase *al-khāṣṣa wal-ʿāmma* (nobles and commoners) appears in contexts describing official decrees, the reaction of the populace to new taxes, changes of officials, and other public events. (Jawharī **45**, p. 152b; **46**, pp. 20b, 39a; Sulūk **56**, II, 4a, 114a; Sakhāwī **66**, II, 34a; ʿUlaymī **58**, p. 144a; **190**, II, 628; Ṭūlūn **181**, pp. 10, 360; Ṣaṣra **177**, p. 68a.) One variation links *al-nās* and *al-khāṣṣa* in opposition to *al-ʿāmma*. (Furāt **166**, IX, 142.)

The phrase *al-khāṣṣa wal-ʿāmma* applied to distinctions within the military elites: Yūnīnī **79**, p. 146b; Dhahabī **14**, II, 64a. Officeholders: Sulūk **56**, II, 1b; **72**, p. 77b. Descendants of the prophet: Ṭūlūn **181**, p. 25; **9**, p. 65a. Ulama: ʿUlaymī **57**, p. 216a; Ṭūlūn **181**, p. 38. Distinctions were made within *al-khāṣṣa* of men of sword, pen, and religion who were entitled to different robes of honor. (Qalqashandī **84**, IV, 14-39; Quatremère **188**, I_1, 70, 72; **64**, p. 227a; **43**, p. 239.)

Professor Cahen has kindly pointed out to me that the original meaning of *al-khāṣṣa* was "personal servants of the ruler." While this use was evidently still in force in the Mamluk period, these instances show, I believe, that the word had taken on a broader meaning and applied to members of the regime more generally.

Neither important dignitaries who were not part of the ruling elite nor peasants were included among the subjects, as in *al-khawāṣṣ min al-raʿāyā wal-ʿawāmm* (dignitaries and commoners of the subjects). (Ḥabīb **23**, pp. 39a-b; **55**, p. 72b.) More commonly, however, the term *raʿiyya* was restricted to the lower classes who were the mass of the subjects. Contexts which mention qadis, jurists, notables, and other ulama distinguished them from the *raʿāyā* (pl.) or the *ʿāmmat al-raʿāyā* (common subjects). (Yūnīnī **80**, III, 156b; Nuwayrī **61**, III, 189b; Jazarī **48**, p. 8; Iyās **169**, I, 150, 279; **52**, p. 33b; Sulūk **56**, II, 168a-b.) Later Ottoman usage, confirming this drift of meaning, confined the term to the taxpaying subjects alone. The *raʿāyā* were the peasants. (H. A. R. Gibb and H. Bowen, *Islamic Society and the West*, vol. I [London, 1950], pp. 207, 237.)

4. *Aʿyān* of witnesses: Yūnīnī **79**, p. 44a. Qadis: Birzālī **10**, I, 18b. Soldiers: Dawādārī **152**, pp. 65, 318. Ulama: Iyās **169**, I, 263; Ṭūlūn **181**, p. 144. Scribes: Sulūk **56**, II, 154b. Emirs: Ḥabīb **23**, p. 45b;

Sulūk **187**, II, 724; **64**, p. 180b. Mamluks: Sakhāwī **197**, p. 237. Eunuchs: Sulūk **56**, II, 47a. Merchants: **18**, p. 144a; **8**, p. 242b; **104**, I, 39; 'Ulaymī **57**, p. 220a; Iyās **169**, IV, 433. *A'yān al-nās* referred to ulama and officials. (Yūnīnī **79**, p. 146a; Iyās **169**, I, 119, 163.) *A'yān al-bilād* (notables of the towns) applied to qadis, sheikhs, ulama, officials, witnesses, and *muḥtasibs*. (Dawādārī **152**, p. 19; Yūnīnī **79**, p. 215a; Jawharī **46**, p. 37a.) This term was once used to include merchants as well. (Iyās **169**, I, 334.)

A'yān referred collectively to the ulama on public ceremonial occasions. (Kathīr **176**, XIII, 89, XIV, 181, 183; Furāt **166**, IX, 321; Ḥabīb **23**, p. 172b; Kutubī **38**, pp. 189b-190a; Iyās **169**, II, 31; 'Aynī **3**, I, 165a; 'Ulaymī **190**, II, 618.) Used as a title for sheikhs, preachers, scholars, jurists, accountants, and others: Ṣaqā'ī **65**, pp. 45b, 46a, 47a, 49b; Ḥabīb **23**, p. 151; Sulūk **187**, II, 258, 613, 636, 658; Ṭūlūn **181**, pp. 51, 146. The word also diffused to other notables such as emirs. (Furāt **166**, IX, 478; **90**, II, 182.)

5. Examples of *al-nās* and *al-'āmma* used in conjunction to mean the populace as a whole, notables and commoners: **19**, p. 77a; Shiḥna **40**, I, 73a; Yūnīnī **80**, III, 97a; Jazarī **48**, p. 60; Furāt **166**, IX, 195; Jawharī **46**, p. 124b; **54**, p. 37a. In some contexts *al-nās* referred to people of prominence and high status though no particular class was indicated. *Al-nās* were wealthy people, often with influence in the regime. (Furāt **166**, VIII, 63, 68, IX, 162; Jawharī **46**, p. 174a; 'Ulaymī **190**, II, 647-48.) Sauvaget translated *al-nās* as "gens de bien." (Jazarī **186**, p. 58.)

Al-nās also meant the Mamluks, and *awlād al-nās*, the children of Mamluks enrolled in an auxiliary military corps. (Ḥawādith **179**, glossary, p. xix; **407**, XV, 456; **54**, pp. 68a, 71a, 206b; Iyās **31**, p. 258b.) Ayalon believes that *al-nās* in this sense occurred as often as *al-nās* meaning "people," but did not see that it also designated notables.

Contexts in which *al-nās* applied to all notables, officials, and men of sword, pen, and learning: **74**, p. 37b. To ulama, qadis, preachers, Koran readers, Sufis, *a'yān*, teachers, jurists, and officials: Furāt **166**, VIII, 135, IX, 182; **189**, XIV, 636; Kathīr **176**, XIV, 92; Jazarī **48**, p. 106; **63**, p. 226a; Ḥawādith **179**, p. 622; **95**, XI, 23. Notices which mention all classes of the population including *al-'āmma* imply that all those enumerated separately were *al-nās:* emirs, ulama, and officials. (Duqmāq **21**, II, 100a-b; Yūnīnī **79**, p. 192b; **80**, III, 49a, 155b; Nuwayrī **61**, III, 98b; Kutubī **37**, I, 103; Kathīr **176**, XIV, 210; Jazarī **48**, pp. 284, 489; **9**, p. 82a; Inbā' **26**, II, 95b; Sakhāwī **197**, p. 211; Sulūk **56**, III, 81b.) Merchants included among the ulama as *al-nās:* Kathīr **176**, XIV, 7; Sakhāwī **66**, II, 183b. An eighteenth century text explains this sense of *al-nās* when it lists prominent Damascus families of merchants, ulama, and qadis by name and adds: "There are countless groups of *al-'awāmm*." (**105**, pp. 61-64.) *Al-nās* are distinguished from the nameless, faceless multitude.

Merchants as *al-nās:* Sulūk **187**, I, 449, 506, II, 361, 414; Furāt **166**, IX, 15; **17**, p. 389b; Iyās **169**, I, 267, 330, IV, 29, 235; **31**, pp. 235b, 256b; Jawharī **45**, pp. 112b-113a; **46**, p. 83b; 'Ulaymī **190**, II,

686-87; Ḥawādith **179**, pp. 270-71; Yūnīnī **202**, I, 451; 'Aynī **3**, I, 183a; Sakhāwī **66**, II, 192b; Ḥimṣī **30**, yr. 907.

Status distinctions: the high ranking men of the army, the administration, and religion were entitled to gifts of the Sultan's robes of honor. (See note 3, above.) The scribes and the ulama were entitled to wear distinctive turbans. (Quatremère **188**, II_2, 21; Syrie **140**, p. xciii.) The descendants of the prophet wore distinctive green turbans. (Ḥabīb **25**, p. 463.) A qadi who did not wear a turban was likely to be taken for a merchant. (Ḥawādith **179**, p. 724.)

The privilege of riding was also accorded to the higher ranks. A European traveler remarked that some 30,000 donkeys were available in Cairo for the hire of merchants, but that nobles rode horses. (**249**, p. 75.) Sometimes religious notables, scribes, and merchants were expressly forbidden to ride horses, which were reserved for the Mamluks. (Sulūk **56**, II, 116a, 127b, III, 15b; Ḥawādith **179**, p. 534.) For *al-'āmma* to ride at all was indeed exceptional. (Sakhāwī **66**, II, 198b.)

Another more general classification of Muslim society comes from earlier sources and is described in G. E. von Grunebaum, *Medieval Islam* (Chicago, 1953), pp. 211-20. The Abbasid literati, under Sassanian influence, valued highly cultivated men of state affairs, the intimates of the Caliphs, and the great families of administrators and bureaucrats. They despised the merchant and artisan, be he rich or poor. Muslim ulama, however, often came to the defense of the dignity of trade and the qualities of the merchant. (S. D. Goitein, "The Rise of the Near-Eastern Bourgeoisie in Early Islamic Times," *Journal of World History,* III [1957], pp. 583-604.)

6. These class distinctions are evident in the uses of the sources, but how much class consciousness or class feeling was present is impossible to assess. A good deal of tension was manifested in the celebrations of the holiday of Nawrūz in Cairo, the Coptic New Year's day adopted from the ancient Persian festival. On Nawrūz, the social universe was turned topsy-turvy by horseplay in which the poor had their chance to tax the rich, students the opportunity to insult their teachers, and the rabble a moment to abuse the notables. They forced the markets to close and peppered whatever notables they caught with water and eggs. Damascus did not have this custom and resented the harm caused by the Mamluk troops celebrating the holiday there. Sultan Barqūq tried to end or limit the practice, but without much success. (G. E. von Grunebaum, *Muhammadan Festivals* [London, New York, 1958], p. 55; D. S. Margoliouth, *Cairo, Jerusalem and Damascus* [New York, 1907], p. 172; Khiṭaṭ **116**, I, 266, 269; Iyās **169**, I, 263; Inbā' **26**, III, 55b; Kutubī **37**, I, 69-70; Jazarī **47**, p. 66a.) A similar but less appreciated license was given the Mamluks at the time of the leaving of the pilgrimage procession, but these activities became occasions for plain assault and theft and pillage, and did not have the same social feeling as the Nawrūz holiday. (**374**, pp. 185-86; Sakhāwī **66**, I, yr. 831, II, 48b-49a.)
7. In some contexts the phrase *'āmmat al-nās* meant lesser *nās* or notables, as in *'āmmat al-nās min al-tujjār wal-ghilmān* (the lesser *nās* of merchants and servants), who were low ranking officials of the Sultan

and entitled to certain honorific names. (Qalqashandī **84**, III, 388-90.) Generally, however, the term cannot be said to signify more than *al-ʿāmma.* Of two texts which described orders given professional witnesses to wear turbans as a way of distinguishing them from the common people, one uses the term *ʿawāmm al-nās* and the other simply al-ʿāmma. (Kathīr **176**, XIV, 140; Shuhba **34**, yr. 728.) *ʿĀmmat al-nās* and *al-ʿāmma* seem to be equivalent. (Birzālī **10**, II, 37a, 96b; Yūnīnī **80**, IV, 26a, 45b; Kutubī **39**, pp. 130a-b; **33**, p. 101b.)

Al-ʿāmma meaning shopkeepers and common people of the markets: Kathīr **176**, XIV, 123; Sulūk **187**, II, 275, 392; Bāsiṭ **1**, I, 119b; Inbāʾ **26**, III, 92b; Furāt **166**, IX, 25; Jawharī **46**, pp. 175b, 176b; Sakhāwī **197**, p. 218; **62**, p. 116b. A decree suppressing the taxes on weavers and wine growers of a village near Tripoli was addressed to *al-ʿawāmm.* (**230**, p. 67.)

Al-sūqa meaning food retailers and other shopkeepers: **133**, pp. 37-38; **394**, I, 67; **225**, p. 9; Birzālī **10**, I, 97b, II, 278b; **192**, p. 246; **205**, p. 132; Dawādārī **152**, p. 172. *Al-sūqa* were subject to economic measures affecting the markets such as extortionate taxes and price controls. (Jawharī **45**, p. 161b; Iyās **169**, II, 258, IV, 242, 305, 465.) The term *ahl al-aswāq* (people of the markets) was not the equivalent of *al-sūqa.* The latter referred to small shopkeepers while the former included merchants and craftsmen, the whole of the business population of the suqs. (Furāt **166**, IX, 12-13, 25.)

Al-bāʿa were the retailers as distinct from *al-tujjār* or wholesalers, the middle level of traders between *al-tujjār* and the smallest of *al-sūqa.* (**132**, p. 36.) They were sufficiently important to be made responsible with merchants for forced sales and monetary regulations. (Duqmāq **20**, p. 113b; Jawharī **46**, p. 97b; Inbāʾ **26**, III, 234b; Nujūm **180**, VII, 469; **62**, p. 68b; Ḥawādith **179**, p. 324.) Once the term was applied to bread dealers. (**54**, p. 70b.)

Wiet defined *al-mutaʿayyishūn* to mean the food retailers, as a synonym for *al-sūqa.* (**133**, pp. 71-72.) Other contexts distinguish them from *al-tujjār* and craftsmen. (Furāt **166**, IX, 25; Sulūk **187**, II, 520; Qalqashandī **84**, IV, 37.) A more precise identification is found in a decree which forbad *al-mutaʿayyishūn* to sit in the streets. They may have been the peddlers with a bit of foodstuffs set out between their legs whom one so often sees in the East today. (Ṭūlūn **182**, IV, 63.) The importance of the peddlers in the economy of Muslim towns can scarcely be overestimated. Even today how incredible are the numbers of people selling fruit and vegetables, people without skill or capital beyond day-to-day needs! Other references: Jazarī **186**, pp. 37-38; Kutubī **38**, p. 203a; Sulūk **187**, II, 592, 763-64; Yūnīnī **80**, III, 139b. Another usage is *al-mutaʿayyishūn bil-ṣanāʾiʿ*—those who eke out a living in craftwork. (Kathīr **176**, XIV, 195.) Also *al-ṭuruqiyya*—those who sell wares in the public thoroughfare: Ṣaṣra **177**, I, 24, note 147.

The class called the *arbāb al-maʿāyish* were also defined by Wiet as food peddlers like *al-mutaʿayyishūn* and *al-sūqa.* (**133**, p. 71.) Other texts suggest a different interpretation, and identify the *arbāb al-maʿāyish* with a wealthier element of the population. They were *al-*

nās who lived in the suqs. (Kutubī **39**, p. 99a.) Along with merchants and property owners they were subject to taxes on real estate and rents levied in Damascus. (Shuḥba **34**, yr. 700.) Moreover, they were subjected to the same confiscations as officials and rich merchants. ('Aynī **4**, p. 131a; Inbā' **26**, III, 234b; Ṭūlūn **181**, p. 316.) In the company of merchants and money changers they received the Sultan's instructions on handling new silver coins. ('Aynī **4**, p. 155b; Duqmāq **20**, p. 123.) Perhaps the sense of the distinction between *arbāb al-ma'āyish* and *al-muta'ayyishūn* may best be captured from the linguistic value of the terms—those who possess a living and those who eke out their livelihood.

Al-mutasabbibūn, the poorest of the small peddlers and retailers: **229**, pp. 121-22; **367**, p. 131; Iyās **169**, IV, 430; 'Ulaymī **190**, II, 647.

The craftsmen, *arbāb al-ṣanā'i'* or *aṣḥāb al-sanā'i': **133***, pp. 38, 44, 75; 'Aynī **4**, p. 145a; Furāt **166**, IX, 12, 25. Skilled workmen might, like rich merchants, be subject to confiscations. (Jawharī **45**, p. 266b; Iyās **169**, I, 159, II, 7; **31**, p. 257a.)

8. **533**; **553**.

Brunschvig in a more recent study also points out how estimates of religious value created invidious distinctions. While the cloth, soap, paper, iron, and weapons trades were highly regarded, speculators such as money changers, grain speculators, and goldsmiths; coffin makers and butchers, who dealt with the dead; and professional musicians, entertainers, and bath servants were despised on moral grounds. Tanners and weavers were despised, Brunschvig speculates, because they were associated with slave's work or women's work, but more probably because these were trades of a miserably poor and unruly part of the population. Similar notions of occupational pollution are evident in Mālikī law school restrictions on suitable marriages. Not only tanners and weavers, but barbers, bath boys, veterinarians, and waste removers were ostracized. (**540.**)

A classification of trades by the Encyclopedia of the Pure Brethren regards the cultivator, weaver, and mason as essential; and the blacksmith, spinner, carder, tailor, embroiderer, and miller as subordinate to the necessary trades. Silk and perfume selling is regarded as aesthetically desirable. In this mystical context, no account is taken of the truly menial trades. (**552.**)

Such distinctions commonly formed the basis of social stratification in Islamic and other societies. The brokers' profession in North Africa was held in low esteem. (**357.**) The tanners of Fez were among the unruly part of the population. In the nineteenth century they were organized as a paramilitary group and had regular ties to the Berber tribes of the area. (**360.**)

The concept of dangerously tempting or immoral trades was found in another Semitic society, the ancient Israelite. Among first-century Jews the goldsmiths, tanners, silkweavers, tailors, fullers, and hairdressers were regarded as open to moral suspicion, while pottery and dyeing crafts which soiled the hands were not respected. (F. M. Heichelheim, *Roman Syria* [Paterson, 1959], p. 197.) The Indian caste system was based in part on the distinction of ritually worthy from morally defiling occupations. Outcaste systems also existed in

China. (S. N. Eisenstadt, *The Political Systems of Empires* [New York, 1963], p. 76.) In the Roman Empire to qualify for a magistracy one had to be free from the taint of an ignoble trade. (F. F. Abbott and A. C. Johnson, *Municipal Administration in the Roman Empire* [Princeton, 1926], p. 59.)

9. **127.**

Confirmation of the continued existence of this viewpoint in the Mamluk period can also be found in the fourteenth century tract of al-Subkī, *Kitāb al-Mu'īd al-Ni'am . . .* (**135**). This was a tract of moral advice to all classes of the population, and while al-Subkī did not directly distinguish the menial, filthy, and vicious from the acceptable trades, his sequence of presentation was itself based on notions of social hierarchy. Al-Subkī began with advice to the Sultan, high officials, and the ulama and eventually came to the artisans, merchants, and the rich. He continued on to builders, architects, and masons (artisans important to the projects of the Sultan and the ulama whom we occasionally see endowed with the Sultan's robes of honor) to the auxiliary intelligentsia of teachers, copyists, paper sellers, and bookbinders. Then follow such professionals or semi-professionals as barbers, physicians, and oculists; and a sequence of more modest trades—weavers, bath managers, house painters, tailors, and dyers. From the producing trades we enter the realm of menials: the bath watchmen, valets, servants, water pourers, money changers (here obviously because of usury), camel drivers, washers of the dead, jailors, butchers, torch bearers, and brokers (probably because of a reputation for dishonesty). At the bottom of the list we find doorkeepers, grooms, dog handlers, guards, night patrollers, sweepers, shoemakers, shooters, and inevitably beggars.

10. *Arādhil* meant "lowest." (Jawharī **45**, p. 199a; **46**, p. 101b; Sulūk **56**, II, 180b.) Sailors and dog handlers were put in the company of *arādhil al-'āmma.* (Sulūk **187**, II, 225.) *Ra'ā'* (rabble) was applied to the followers of a Turkoman sheikh, and to a mob which slept in the mosques. (Kathīr **176**, XIV, 46, 72.)

The term *ghawghā'* meant troublemakers, but had no specific reference to any particular class. In the fourteenth century the *ghawghā'* were the mob of the city streets. (Shuḥba **35**, I, 41b; Kathīr **176**, XIII, 298, XIV, 46; Sulūk **56**, II, 66b; **91**, II, 14; Quatremère **188**, I_2, 195.) In the fifteenth century, however, the term applied to mobs of plunderers in time of civil war, food shortages, or tension with Christians and foreigners. (Inbā' **26**, III, 13a, 30b, II, 159a; Sakhāwī **197**, pp. 97, 254, 303, 390; **66**, II, 87a; **62**, p. 143b; 'Ulaymī **190**, II, 670.)

Awbāsh meant people of the lowest or meanest sort and referred to the cooks' apprentices or kitchen boys of the Sultan involved in rioting and plundering attendant on fighting among the Mamluks. (Sulūk **187**, II, 603.) The *awbāsh* were also servants, gatekeepers, water boys of the bath (Nujūm **180**, V, 10, 41-42; Bāsiṭ **1**, I, 19b, 24a), prostitutes (Sulūk **187**, II, 152), and the servants and attendants in army camps (Dhahabī **153**, II, 171; Nujūm **180**, VII, 487; Ḥawādith **179**, p. 538). Some of them lived in the rubbish heaps outside Cairo. (Sulūk **187**, II, 649.) In other contexts they were merely the crowd or unruly city mobs. (Sulūk **187**, II, 769, 818; Bāsiṭ **1**, I, 53a; Ḥawādith **179**, pp. 302, 425-27; Jawharī **45**, p. 150a; Iyās **169**, II, 318; Furāt **166**, IX, 89; Inbā' **26**, III, 163a-b; Ṣaṣra **177**, pp. 25a, 155a.)

Al-sūqa was also used as a term of contempt. (Ṭūlūn **181**, pp. 10, 88; Sulūk **187**, II, 396.)

Menials: Nujūm **180**, VII, glossary, p. xix; **98**, p. 63; Baṭṭūṭa **142**, I, 61. Door boys responsible for removing dogs from Damascus: Quatremère **188**, I_1, 195; Dhahabī **14**, p. 116b; Jazarī **45**, p. 124b; Birzālī **10**, I, 217b. Scavengers: **277**, p. 48. Prostitutes and singing girls: Ṣaṣra **177**, pp. 63a, 74a, 102a, 114a, 128a, 135b, 161a, 165b.

For an exotic picture of the entertainers, gypsies, prostitutes, and the characters of Cairo low life at the end of the thirteenth century Egyptian shadow plays are an invaluable source. (**544**; **545**; **546**.) Gypsies in Damascus: Ṣaṣra **177**, p. 54a.

11. *Al-mashā'iliyya:* Iyās **175**, II, 17 has a partial list of references. Also: Sulūk **56**, III, 43a; **208**, XLIV, 317-21; Iyās **169**, IV, 430; Ṭūlūn **181**, pp. 16, 192, 213; **185**, pp. 47, 57; Ṣaṣra **177**, pp. 5 (17)b, 10 (22)a, 19 (31)a, 63b, 68a, 71b, 82b, 140a; Décrets **223**, XII, 6; Quatremère **188**, I_2, 4-6. *Al-ḥurrās:* Kutubī **38**, p. 177a; Sulūk **56**, II, 116b; Furāt **166**, VIII, 205; Birzālī **10**, I, 235a; Jazarī **45**, p. 173b; 'Aynī **3**, I, 123b. *Al-khufarā':* Jawharī **46**, p. 27b; Ṭūlūn **185**, p. 71; Iyās **169**, IV, 39-40, 279-80. *Aṣḥāb al-arbā':* **535**, p. 211; **536**, p. 109; Sulūk **187**, II, 54. Cairo also had a police force called *al-shurṭa,* but there is only one mention of this in the Mamluk period to my knowledge. (Sakhāwī **197**, p. 36.)

Criminals called *al-mansīr* and *al-ḥarāmiyya:* See above, p. 171. *Ahl-fasād* or *mufsidūn,* meaning plunderers and highwaymen: Ḥimṣī **30**, yr. 903; **54**, pp. 13b, 97b-98a; Furāt **166**, IX, 66, 80, 89, 92-93, 102, 124; Jawharī **46**, pp. 20a-b, 159b; Nujūm **180**, V, 401, VI, 642; Iyās **169**, II, 362. *Ahl-du''ār* meaning immoral and licentious people, thieves: Quatremère **188**, II_2, 215; Furāt **166**, IX, 65, 80, 84. Thieves called *al-surrāq:* Jawharī **46**, pp. 144b, 159a; **54**, p. 186b; Ṭūlūn **181**, pp. 27, 49, 132. Thieves called *al-laṣūṣ:* Iyās **169**, II, 214. *Al-'ayāq* referred to the dissolute adherents of a rebellious emir: Iyās **169**, I, 240. *Quṭṭā' al-ṭarīq,* highwaymen: Sulūk **56**, II, 39a, 75b, 203b, III, 58a; **54**, p. 205b; Ṭūlūn **181**, p. 385. Other criminal and illegal activities included gambling, which was one of the entertainments available beneath the citadel of Damascus. (Ṭūlūn **182**, IV, 63.) Wine selling and prostitution: Note 10, above.

'Abīd, black slaves: See above, pp. 171-72. Other menials in the Mamluk service: Sulūk **187**, II, 225; Quatremère **188**, I_1, 122-23, 129; Kathīr **176**, XIV, 257; 'Aynī **3**, I, 140b-141a.

12. Rootless masses: Shuhba **34**, yr. 695; Iyās **169**, I, 134; Jawharī **45**, p. 101b; 'Aynī **3**, I, 152a; Birzālī **10**, II, 93b; Ḥimṣi **30**, yr. 905; **69**, p. 35. Strangers: Ḥawādith **179**, pp. 247, 313-17; Sulūk **56**, II, 119a, 140b; **187**, II, 208-09; Jazarī **186**, pp. 82-83; Nujūm **180**, VI, 73; Inbā' **26**, II, 206b; Ṭūlūn **181**, p. 123.

Al-ṭarḥī and *al-khasharī:* 'Aynī **3**, I, 98a; Ḥawādith **179**, glossary, p. xliii; Nujūm **180**, VII, 528, 534, glossary, xxxvii; Sulūk **56**, II, 27a, 35a, 97a, 111a, III, 63b; Qalqashandī **84**, IV, 188; Furāt **166**,

IX, 450; Sakhāwī **197**, p. 254; Ṭūlūn **185**, p. 101; Quatremère **188**, I_2, 151-52. A western visitor reported that 100,000 homeless people slept in the streets of Cairo. (**241**, p. 49.)

Mantran describes a similar populace in seventeenth century Istanbul composed of ruined peasants, agricultural workers, peddlers, tripe sellers, gypsies, washers, street workers, and entertainers—all those outside of the normal guild and family cadres of the city. (**507**, p. 105.)

Beggars called *ḥarāfīsh* and *ju'aydī:* See above, pp. 177-83. *Al-sā'il* and *al-ṣa'ālīk:* Ṣaqā'ī **65**, p. 64a; Birzālī **10**, I, 235a; Yūnīnī **202**, I, 555, II, 232; Kutubī **37**, I, 257; **59**, p. 296; Sulūk **56**, II, 34b, 151a. *Al-fuqarā'* or poor Sufis: 177, I, 272; Baṭṭūṭa **142**, I, 37, note 106; Sulūk **56**, II, 135a, 150b; **187**, I, 507-08; Ḥabīb **23**, p. 23a; Quatremère **188**, I_1, 232-33; **158**, pp. 94-95, 204-05; **159**, pp. 500-01, 1012-13; Kutubī **37**, I, 247; Bāsiṭ **1**, I, 51a, 104a; Duqmāq **21**, I, 143b; **20**, p. 74a; Iyās **169**, I, 306, II, 6; Furāt **166**, IX, 432-33; **73**, p. 309a.

13. Fugitives from the Mongols: **125**, II, 319; **189**, XIV, 483-84; Quatremère **188**, I_2, 34; Yūnīnī **79**, p. 168b. Refugees from Syria in Egypt: Khiṭaṭ **116**, II, 20-22; Jawharī **46**, p. 66a; Yūnīnī **202**, I, 489; Quatremère **188**, I_1, 85, 178; **189**, XX, 31. Rural refugees inside walled towns: **189**, XIV, 663, XX, 222-25; Dawādārī **152**, pp. 33, 169, 256-57; Kathīr **176**, XIV, 66; Kutubī **37**, I, 80; Ṣaṣra **177**, pp. 42 (12)b, 50 (16)b. Other: Kutubī **39**, p. 119b; Kathīr **176**, XIV, 243, 281-82; **19**, p. 149a; Ṭūlūn **181**, pp. 118, 123; **185**, p. 138; Jazarī **48**, p. 151.

14. The phenomenon of classes beyond the pale of society is of course not unique to the Muslim world. It is a phenomenon of modern metropolises and of western medieval cities, too. Hazlitt, in his description of medieval Venice, notes the *bravi*—men of the night, without employ, ready to lend themselves to any patron for any job, men skirting and darting in and about the curtain of violence. (**453**, II, 585.)

15. The names for a quarter were *ḥāra, khuṭṭ,* and *maḥalla. Darb, sikak,* and *aziqqa* meant streets and narrow lanes. Lists of quarters, Cairo: Khiṭaṭ **116**, II, 2-46; Duqmāq **104**, I, 12-29, II, 35-42. Damascus: **113**, pp. 33-36; **103**, pp. 147-58. Aleppo: Shiḥna **110**, pp. 185-87. Jerusalem: 'Ulaymī **118**, pp. 174-82, 220. Other references to these terms: Sulūk **56**, II, 23a, 103b, 104a, 187a-b; Ṣaṣra **177**, p. 101b, and passim; **73**, p. 330a-b; Duqmāq **22**, p. 179; Ṭūlūn **181** and **185**, passim. Quṭr (pl. aqṭār), districts, has a less definite signification. (Ṭūlūn **181**, p. 16; Sulūk **56**, II, 103b.)

16. **375**, I, 230; **561**, pp. 86-89. Cairo: **255**, p. 113; Jawharī **46**, p. 207a. Damascus: Kathīr **176**, XIV, 301; Ṣaṣra **177**, p. 37 (7)a and note 355; **344**, pp. 180, 182-83. Aleppo: Sibṭ **123**, pp. 157-58; **520**, pp. 174, 178-79. Jerusalem: 'Ulaymī **118**, pp. 32, 175-80, 190; Homs: **257**, p. 247.

Jews also lived in Ajlūn, Safad, Gaza, Nablus, Hebron, Ramla, and Tripoli, but whether or not they had separate quarters in these cities is not explicit. ('Aynī **3**, I, 211a; **244**, pp. 242-43, 247, 333-34; **239**, pp. 133, 135, 138, 158, 180, 186, 234, 250; **514**, pp. 93-94; **345**, passim.) Damascus, Nablus, and Gaza also had Samaritan communities. (Iyās **169**, V, 84; **239**, p. 180; **137**, p. 201.)

17. Aleppo: **520**, pp. 174-76; Shiḥna **110**, p. 187; Sibṭ **123**, pp. 157-58. Kurdish quarters in Hebron, Gaza, Safad, Damascus, and Jerusalem: **355**, p. 479; Ṭūlūn **183**, p. 132; 'Ulaymī **118**, pp. 174, 230. Turkomans lived in Gaza, Ramla, and probably Aleppo. There were quarters of Bashkīr and Egyptians in Ramla and refugees from Granada in Damascus at the end of the fifteenth century. (**355**, p. 479; Ṭūlūn **181**, p. 143.)
18. Ḥarrānī in Damascus: Kutubī **37**, II, 309; **39**, p. 59b; Ṣaqā'ī **65**, 58a; Shuhba **34**, yr. 740. Aleppo: Shiḥna **110**, p. 186; Sibṭ **69**, p. 36. Villagers from Bayt Jibrīn had a quarter in Hebron. ('Ulaymī **118**, p. 220.) Damascus had a street named Ibn Bāniyās which suggests a common village origin for at least the original inhabitants of the quarter, and a community (ṭā'ifa) from al-Biqā' living near al-Ṣābūniyya Madrasa. (Jazarī **48**, p. 154; Ṭūlūn **181**, p. 21.) In Jerusalem there were quarters of people from Salt and Toreh and sedentarized bedouin communities called the Banu Zayd, Hārit, and Sa'd. ('Ulaymī **118**, pp. 175, 180-81, 185.) In Hama migrants from Bārīn were obliged to live together and were taxed collectively until a decree of 902/1496-97 abolished the dues and permitted them to live where they pleased. Fiscal coercion may have kept collectivities from being dispersed and assimilated into the cities. (Décrets **223**, III, 7-8.) Al-Qubaybāt: **121**, VII, 231; Décrets **223**, II, 20; **522**, p. 457. Camps of Turkomans and Arabs on the outskirts of Aleppo: Shiḥna **110**, p. 52.
19. **103**, p. 159; Kutubī **39**, p. 132a. At Aleppo Sufi convents were concentrated to the east of the city, and some of the cohesion of Bānaqūsā may have come from the leaven of sheikhs and devotees. (**520**, p. 178.)
20. Aleppo: Shiḥna **110**, pp. 52, 186-87; Sibṭ **123**, pp. 46-47, 59; **125**, III, 46. Damascus: Décrets **223**, II, 20. Jerusalem had a quarter for leather workers and Hebron for glass makers. ('Ulaymī **118**, pp. 179, 220.) Quarters in villages of both Upper and Lower Egypt were known for their singing women and prostitutes. (Sulūk **56**, II, 40b-41a.)
21. We have no precise information on the composition of quarters in Damascus and Aleppo. A study of Cairo in the Ottoman period indicates that some quarters were favored, but that there were no exclusively aristocratic neighborhoods. (**558**.)
22. **54**, pp. 130b, 134b; 'Ulaymī **57**, pp. 139b, 142b; **190**, II, 632, 656; **276**, pp. xvi, xviii-xix. The word *'aṣab* is used in Arabic for kin or allies.
23. Year 791: Ṣaṣra **177**, pp. 34 (46)a, 49 (15)b, 63b. Late Mamluk period: Ṭūlūn **181**, pp. 27-28, 92-93, 132, 180, 232, 250; **183**, pp. 156-57; Ḥimṣī **29**, pp. 109a-110a; **54**, p. 178b. See above, pp. 159-61 for the part of the *zu'ar*.
24. *Shalāq:* **146**, II, 123. The games imply that Aleppo may have been divided into gymnastic factions similar to the circus parties of ancient cities and Constantinople. Iranian towns had sporting clubs, and hunting associations called *shuṭṭār* are known for the Mamluk period. (**547**, pp. 191-96; **498**, VI, 29-30; A. K. S. Lambton, *Islamic Society in Persia* (London, 1954); **498**, V, 29-30.

The civil war of 791: see above, pp. 165-67. Later events: Sibṭ **69**, p. 50; **125**, III, 50-51, 81, V, 397; **520**, pp. 162-63.

Cairo quarters manifested little of the sort of hostility found in the Syrian towns. This may be due to the weakness of communal ties, although a certain amount of common feeling in the defense of districts against outsiders was evident. For example, in 869/1464-65 the people of the island of Ṣābūn murdered a Mamluk who had killed one of their nightwatchmen. The Mamluks returned to the fray, pillaging the island's markets and quarters. (Ḥawādith **179**, pp. 494-95; Iyās **171**, p. 151.) In a more curious episode of 875/1470-71, one of the Sultan's slaves married a woman from Būlāq, but then divorced her. People of the quarter protested this insult to the Sultan's executive secretary. (Jawharī **47**, p. 90a.)

25. Quatremère **188**, I_2, 231; Birzālī **10**, II, 237b; Sulūk **187**, II, 669, 771; **149**, IV, 147; Bāsiṭ **1**, I, 26a-27a; **101**, III, 189; Kathīr **176**, XIV, 290; Furāt **166**, IX, 264; Inbā' **26**, II, 5b; Sakhāwī **66**, I, 51b; **197**, p. 116; Iyās **169**, II, 234; **54**, p. 143b.

26. Fourteenth century: Kathīr **176**, XIV, 55, 289; Birzālī **10**, II, 149b; Kutubī **39**, p. 145a. Sixteenth century: Ṭūlūn **181**, p. 380; **183**, p. 132; **185**, p. 136.

Similar struggles occurred under the Ottomans. For example, the Nablus region was divided into the Red and White Banner factions. In 979/1571-72, the Red Banner alliance attacked Ḥiṭṭīn near Safad. (**378**, pp. 83-86, 92-93.)

27. Joseph Schacht, *An Introduction to Islamic Law* (Oxford, 1964); see in particular his bibliographies.

28. Ibn Naḥḥās: Dhahabī **153**, II, 124-25; Jibrīnī **51**, II, 141a; Yūnīnī **202**, II, 413-14; Ṣaqā'ī **65**, p. 31b; Kutubī **37**, II, 313; **101**, III, 160; **149**, III, 201; **125**, II, 286-87, IV, 514-15; **8**, p. 169b. Cairo: Furāt **166**, IX, 80, 83-84, 124; Iyās **169**, V, 16. A Jerusalem quarter was named after an emir, a prominent notable who died and was buried there in 802/1399. (**208**, XLIII, 312-16.)

Hazlitt describes a clientele pattern of residence in Venice where clusters of blind allies and courts were occupied by "dependents of the master of the *casa* or *palazzo* . . . who lived thus surrounded by his clan." (**453**, II, 331.)

29. Sheikhs and *'arīfs:* Ṭūlūn **181**, pp. 89, 213, 274, 278, 282, 289, 309, 330, 332, 374; Décrets **223**, III, 13. See also notes 30-32, below. Another name for the leading notable of a quarter was *mustashār* (adviser). (Ṭūlūn **181**, p. 21.) Honors: Sibṭ **123**, p. 44; Ḥimṣī **30**, yrs. 903, 917; Ṭūlūn **183**, p. 132; **492**, pp. 207-08.

In Damascus the family of Khawājā Muḥammad ibn Yūsuf endowed the Ḥāra Masjid al-Bī' with a madrasa, baths, khans, and houses. (**113**, pp. 33-34.) Also: Sibṭ **123**, p. 42.

Villages and tribal groups were similarly headed by a sheikh. (Ṭūlūn **181**, pp. 96-97, 183, 194, 196, 200, 276, 360; **185**, pp. 43-44; Sulūk **56**, II, 204a, III, 23b, 68a. Village leaders are sometimes called *ra'īs* (headman). (**378**, pp. 83-86, 92-93.) Village headmen probably had the same functions as the sheikhs of urban quarters, supervising internal affairs and mediating relations with the state.

30. Thirteenth century: Birzālī **10**, I, 201b. Other: Ṭūlūn **181**, pp. 228, 247,

254, 258, 282, 292-93, 309, 311, 314-17, 321, 330, 332, 335, 340, 348-49, 373, 376; Ṭūlūn **183**, pp. 139, 142, 146; Ṭūlūn **185**, pp. 35-36, 38, 44-49, 85-87, 91-93, 99-100, 110, 117-18, 137; Iyās **169**, IV, 17, 408, 448, V, 9; **174**, p. 316; Ḥimṣī **29**, p. 145a; **30**, yr. 907; **54**, p. 202a; Décrets **223**, III, 10.

In Cairo taxes were levied on markets, waqfs, land, and rents rather than by quarters. Since the quarters of the Syrian towns were stronger solidarities they could be better expected to raise the money.

31. **492**, pp. 207-08; Kutubī **37**, I, 47; **38**, p. 203b; Jazarī **47**, pp. 31b-32a; **48**, p. 163; **186**, p. 8; Birzālī **10**, I, 198b.

32. Ṭūlūn **181**, pp. 160, 227, 234, 249, 267, 287, 309, 330, 363, 366, 377; Ṭūlūn **185**, pp. 52, 63, 69, 107, 112, 116; Décrets **223**, II, 44-47; **238**, p. 535. The quarter was responsible in law for blood money. (Joseph Schacht, *An Introduction to Islamic Law* [Oxford, 1964], p. 184.)

33. Cf. J. Weulersse, "Antioche, un Type de Cité d'Islam," *Comptes Rendus du Congrès International de Géographie*, vol. III, Géographie Humaine (Leiden, 1938), pp. 258-60; H. A. R. Gibb and H. Bowen, *Islamic Society and the West*, vol. I (London, 1950), p. 279.

Active defenses: Furāt **166**, IX, 80, 83-84, 124; Ṭūlūn **181**, pp. 174, 191; Ḥawādith **179**, pp. 251, 332-33. Gates, Damascus: Kutubī **37**, I, 131; Yūnīnī **80**, III, 79a; Dhahabī **14**, pp. 118a, 127a. Cairo: 'Aynī **3**, I, 100b; Sulūk **187**, II, 300-01; Ḥimṣī **30**, yr. 902; Iyās **169**, II, 336, V, 49, 54-55.

34. Syrie **140**, p. 167; **407**, XVI, 59, 69; **492**, p. 202; Qalqashandī **84**, V, 467. Biographies: Ṭūlūn **181**, p. 56; Ṣaqā'ī **65**, pp. 12a-13b, 22a-b; **90**, I, 75; **92**, p. 124; **96**, p. 174.

35. *Ra'īses* of the *kārimī:* Appendix D, al-Takrītī, Ibn Kuwayk, al-Kharrūbī, al-Maḥallī. The *ra's al-tujjār*, Ibn al-Muzallaq: see above, p. 128 and note 25. Others: Kutubī **37**, I, 241; Saqā'ī **65**, pp. 15b-16a; Kathīr **176**, XIV, 43; **95**, II, 45, VI, 30; **41**, IV, **157b**; Nujūm **180**, VI, 824; Ḥawādith **179**, p. 314; **374**, pp. 147, 149; Sakhāwī **66**, II, 186b; **92**, p. 111; Khiṭaṭ **116**, II, 98; Inbā' **26**, III, 90a.

36. Jazarī **48**, pp. 200-01; Birzālī **10**, I, 23b, II, 248b; Ṣaqā'ī **65**, 86a; Ḥimṣī **30**, yr. 917; **211**, II, 398; Décrets **223**, III, 21-23; Ṭūlūn **181**, pp. 78, 100, 113, 126, 162; **28**, pp. 14a-b; **125**, V, 378-79. There was also an *'arīf* of a *qayṣariyya.* (Sulūk **56**, II, 76a.) In 844, an inscription abolished the jurisdiction of an officer called the *shaykh al-mashāyikh* in the markets of Damascus and referred disputes to other officials. (**229**, pp. 115-16; **238**, p. 526.)

37. Inbā' **26**, III, 75a; Duqmāq **20**, p. 123a; **95**, III, 127; **367**, p. 126; **62**, p. 115b; Iyās **168**, II, 245; Sakhāwī **66**, II, 110a-b.

Al-a'yān and *kabīrs* of the *kārimī:* Appendix D. *Khawājās* called *al-a'yān* or *kabīr* of the merchants: Appendix E. Other *al-a'yān* and *kabīrs:* Dhahabī **13**, II, 30a, 88a, 89b; **153**, II, 130; Yūnīnī **79**, pp. 94a-b, 181b-182a; **202**, II, 348-49; Ṣaqā'ī **65**, pp. 48b, 67a-b; **54**, p. 165a; Birzālī **10**, I, 95b, II, 199b; Kutubī **37**, I, 37-38; **95**, III, 103, 149, 178, VI, 159, VII, 126; Jazarī **186**, p. 3; Inbā' **26**, II, 47b, 99a, III, 20b, 75b, 95a, 117a, 157b, 170a-b; **90**, I, 336-39, III, 340, 438, 443-44, IV, 152; Shuhba **34**, yr. 733; **367**, p. 114.

38. **498**; **551**; **553**; **562**.

39. Sylvia L. Thrupp, "The Gilds," *Cambridge Economic History of*

Europe, vol. III (Cambridge, Eng., 1963), pp. 230-80; and George Ostrogorsky, *History of the Byzantine State,* tr. Joan Hussey (Oxford, 1956), pp. 224-25.

40. **86**, pp. 116-26; **129**; **336**; **358**; **361**; **431**; **496**; **537**. The jurisdiction of the governor impinged on that of the *muḥtasib* in the control of the grain markets. (Jazarī **47**, p. 201; **186**, p. 58; Furāt **166**, VII, 98.)

41. Biographies: Ṣaqā'ī **65**, pp. 14a, 15a-b, 17a-b, 54a, 69a-b, 70b-71b, 73a-74a, 81a-b, 87b; **90**, I, 18, 27, 41, 58, 67, 103, IV, 7-8, 46; Sulūk **56**, II, 70a, 94b, 130a, 145a, 153b, 214a, 218b, 221a, III, 24a, 32a-b, 48b, 55a; **92**, pp. 32, 34, 158, 358, 394; **95**, VIII, 73, XI, 25; **96**, pp. 132, 143, 174-75; Furāt **166**, VIII, 106-08, IX, 47, 292-93, 477; Ṭūlūn **181**, pp. 31, 121. Iyās **169**, I, 122-23; Shuhba **34**, yr. 693; Dhahabī **13**, II, 212a-b; **42**, III, 460b; Inbā' **26**, II, 99a, III, 182a; Nujūm **180**, VII, 164-65.

The office also became venal. For example in 789 50,000 dirhems were paid for the post and a decade later about 250,000 dirhems. Fees of five hundred or a thousand dinars plus a payment of a hundred dinars per month are also mentioned for this period. (Sulūk **56**, II, 94b, 153b, III, 24a, 48b.) In 921 an emir paid 15,000 dinars for the post. (Iyās **169**, V, 27.)

42. *'Arīfs:* **536**, pp. 17, 123-24; **492**, pp. 201-02; **537**, XVI, 349. Biographies: Birzālī **10**, I, 82b, II, 48b-49a. Military duties: See above, p. 163. Ceremonials: Dhahabī **14**, p. 113a; Yūnīnī **80**, IV, 17a; Jazarī **186**, pp. 18-20; **47**, pp. 67b-68a. Liturgies: **19**, p. 132; Kutubī **38**, p. 203b. Tax: **208**, XLIV, 317.

Decoration of the markets by order of the government and other ceremonials: Yūnīnī **80**, IV, 216a; Bāsiṭ **1**, I, 4b; Jawharī **45**, p. 123a; **54**, p. 18b; Sulūk **56**, II, 125b, 155b, 160b, 210a; Ṭūlūn **181**, pp. 9, 138-39, 165, 167, 230, 262, 267, 303; **185**, p. 91.

43. Fourteenth century: Kathīr **176**, XIV, 280. Fifteenth century: Décrets **223**, II, 42, XII, 32-33; **230**, pp. 105, 107; **208**, XLIV, 144-45, 153-54; **238**, pp. 524-25, 529; **229**, pp. 121-26; 'Ulaymī **190**, II, 647; Jawharī **45**, p. 108b; **206**, p. 150; Ṭūlūn **181**, p. 84. Sixteenth century: Ḥimṣī **30**, yr. 904, 907; Iyās **169**, IV, 24-25, 446-49, V, 17-18, 89; **175**, II, 4, note 3; Ṭūlūn **185**, p. 106; **81**, pp. 50-51.

44. *Taḥkīr:* Décrets **223**, XII, 26-27, 30-31; **81**, p. 22; **374**, p. 150. Property interests of emirs in the markets; Chapter II, notes 24-26. In 750 one shop in Alexandria was singled out to have a monopoly of perfumes and another for drinks. The benefits went to a Sufi's convent for which the shops had been made waqfs. (Sulūk **187**, II, 809.)

45. *Nāẓir al-aswāq* and *shādd* of the camel market: 'Aynī **4**, p. 128a; Sulūk **56**, II, 52b, 113a, 124a. *Ḍamān:* Birzālī **10**, II, 209a; Kutubī **38**, p. 160a; Jazarī **48**, p. 505; Furāt **166**, IX, 71. Quotation from Jawharī **48**, p. 20b; cf. Sulūk **56**, II, 102a.

Brokers and criers: **90**, II, 177-78; Sulūk **187**, II, 150; **238**, pp. 523-24, 526-27; **208**, XLIII, 334; **237**, VI, 167-68; **81**, pp. 12-13; Quatremère **188**, II_2, 167.

46. Furāt **166**, IX, 12-13, 71; Sulūk **56**, II, 94b. There is no indication that the tax was levied by trade or craft but simply on the merchants represented by their *a'yān.* (Iyās **169**, II, 245; Sakhāwī **66**, II, 110a-b.)

An instance of collective tax payments comes not from the Mamluk world but from North Africa. Merchants contributed a dirhem at each purchase of cloth to a common treasury to meet taxes, but the arrangement was of uncertain legality. (**358**, p. 294.)

47. Several indications have been taken by scholars to imply corporate organization of economic life in Mamluk times. Blochet translates the *ḍamān shādd al-zaʿīm* to be "l'impot que versaient les corporations et corps de métiers à l'occasion de l'élection de leur chef." (**189**, XX, 264.) A *shādd,* however, was a commissioner of the Sultan. Sauvaget considered the *muʿallim* of the weavers of Sarmīn the chief of the corporation. He was more probably a master weaver or owner of the looms. (Décrets **223**, XII, 41-42.) Neither is the opinion of Tomiche that protests and closures in the markets were inspired by guilds borne out by the citations. (**359**, p. 84.)

Further indirect evidence on the question of market organization comes from a Jewish traveler to Damascus in 1520 who remarked on the lively business activity in the city. Anyone, he said, could borrow money and go into the business of selling cloth. This trade, though subject to taxation and supervision, was evidently not organized as a corporation. (**344**, p. 181.)

Another indication that guilds did not exist in the European sense was that luxury copper works, astrolabes, wood carvings, and pottery were engraved or embossed with the name of the maker, a sign of pride and individuality out of keeping with the guild spirit as we know it for the West. (**306**, passim; **307**, passim; **311**; **313**.)

48. A master workman was called a *muʿallim.* (Note 47, above.) A North African author, ʿAlī al-Ḥakīm, *Al-Dawḥa al-Mashtabika fī Ḍawabiṭ Dār al-Sikka,* ed. Ḥussain Monés (Madrid, 1960), p. 57 refers to the workers of the mint as *muʿallimūn* (master artisans), *ʿammālūn* (journeymen), and *mutaʿallimūn* (apprentices).

49. Iyās **169**, IV, 122-23; **175**, I, 118-19.

50. Sufis: Birzālī **10**, I, 14a, 42b, 276b, 279b; **121**, V, 404; Dhahabī **13**, II, 232a; Kathīr **176**, XIV, 12, 313; Sulūk **56**, II, 29b. *Ḥarīrī* expressly identified as silk workers: Birzālī **10**, II, 75a, 83b; **90**, III, 376, IV, 9; Nujūm **180**, VI, 788-89; **95**, I, 10-11, IV, 157, 256, VII, 245. Others: Birzālī **10**, I, 42b, 80b, 85b, 242b, II, 51b, 66a; Kathīr **176**, XIII, 283, 351; **90**, I, 171, 445, II, 338-39, III, 374, IV, 39, 42, 66; Nujūm **180**, V, 242; Inbā' **26**, II, 18a; **95**, I, 36, 83-84, 234, II, 202, IV, 156, 163, 278, VI, 77, VII, 238; Ṭūlūn **181**, p. 131; Furāt **166**, IX, 424.

Worker fraternities, however, are known for other times and for other parts of the Muslim world. They were strong in the Ottoman Empire, until quite recently in Fez. The tanners of Fez had a chief who was the arbiter of disputes among the workers, and collected money for an annual gift to the Sultan. His activities, however, did not extend to the regulation of economic life. Even mutual aid seems to have been arranged by the personal assistance of other workers rather than through the fraternity itself. The bonds may have been strong in a personal sense, but they were organizationally and collectively very weak. (**360**, pp. 235-38.)

51. Ṭūlūn **181**, p. 146; **194**, p. 152.

52. Herzfeld (**211**, II, 397) holds the view that mosques did not belong to

individual crafts. Prayers and instruction in the markets: Dhahabī **13**, I, 257b; Sulūk **56**, II, 96a; **187**, II, 651; Bāsiṭ **1**, I, 3b; Inbā' **26**, III, 92b; Furāt **166**, IX, 25.

53. The religious mentality of the working classes: Massignon **553**; L. Massignon, *Salman Pâk et les Prémices Spirituelles de l'Islam Iranien,* Société des Études Iraniennes et de l'Art Persan, vol. VII (Paris, 1934). For animism and saint worship: H. A. R. Gibb, "The Structure of Religious Thought in Islam," *Muslim World,* XXVIII (1948), pp. 17-28, 113-23, 185-97, 280-91; F. W. Hasluck, *Christianity and Islam under the Sultans,* 2 vols. (Oxford, 1929). Also H. A. R. Gibb and H. Bowen, *Islamic Society and the West,* vol. II (Oxford, 1957), pp. 179-207.

    Opposition to popular preachers and cults: Kathīr **176**, XIII, 298; Inbā' **26**, II, 257b-258a, III, 7b; **548**, pp. 251-52. In Cairo in 744 a buried mosque was found in the rubbish heaps outside the city and soon became the shrine of a popular cult of dubious orthodoxy. Great crowds gathered there until the qadis asked the governor to disperse them. (Sulūk **187**, II, 649-50.) Anti-ulama feeling: **54**, p. 134b.

54. Nuwayrī **83**, VIII, 248; **548**, pp. 457, 461.

    A similar feeling is expressed in a decree of the Roman Emperor Trajan forbidding plebeian clubs and assemblies of any kind on the grounds that "whatever title, or whatever pretext, we grant to those who form unions, they will become highly noxious political clubs." (A. H. M. Jones, *The Greek City* [Oxford, 1940], p. 134.) Also S. N. Eisenstadt, *The Political Systems of Empires* (New York, 1963), p. 146.

55. **125**, II, 225; Kathīr **176**, XIV, 222-23; Sulūk **187**, II, 751; Nujūm **180**, VII, 394.
56. Criminal and slave gangs: See above, pp. 171-72.
57. Chapter V, passim.
58. For a list of the active Sufi orders: **536**, pp. 162-63. Also: Baṭṭūṭa **141**, I, 61, 71-75. Indications of the Sufi groups marching with their banners may be found in Furāt **166**, IX, 199; Sibṭ **123**, pp. 33-34; Ṭūlūn **181**, pp. 65, 91. For the chief sheikhs of the Sufis: See above, pp. 105-06, 137 and note 44; Baṭṭūṭa **141**, I, 71-75.
59. Sufis, year 758: Kathīr **176**, XIV, 257; Kutubī **39**, pp. 140b-141a. Year 899: 'Ulaymī **57**, pp. 218b-219a. Other: Dhahabī **153**, II, 132; Sulūk **187**, II, 656; Ṭūlūn **181**, pp. 8-9, 32, 65, 84, 128.
60. *Ḥarāfish:* See above, pp. 177-83.
61. A general study of the ulama in Islamic society is found in H. A. R. Gibb and H. Bowen, *Islamic Society and the West,* vol. II, pp. 70-114. For the legal corps: **429**; **431**.
62. For qadis and witnesses: **431**. *Muḥtasib:* Notes 54 and 55, above. A symbol of the economic functions of the ulama is the fact that witnesses, deputy judges, and *muḥtasibs'* agents had shops in the suqs for their regulatory and administrative duties. For examples: Jawharī **46**, p. 151b; Sakhāwī **197**, pp. 248, 274; **95**, II, 310, III, 92, 172, VI, 66, 317-18, VII, 110, XI, 21; Furāt **166**, IX, 291, 353, 421, 426, 474, 476-77. Also: **554**, for a discussion of the place of administrative organs in the markets.

    Witnesses employed by *dīwāns* and institutions: Sulūk **56**, II, 73b;

Ṣaqā'ī **65**, pp. 18b, 68b-69a; **91**, II, 173-78; **95**, VIII, 64; **425**, XV, 119.

One little-known ulama economic function was to hold deposits. Ulama acted as bankers for safekeeping of money and goods for both merchants and emirs. (See above, pp. 120-21.) A less seemly instance of such assistance was the case of a sheikh who harbored a cloth-dealer and his wares in his *khānaqā* (monastery) to enable the dealer to evade taxes. (Furāt **166**, IX, 309.)

Ulama administered religious institutions in the posts of *nāẓir* (controllers) of madrasas, mosques, *khānaqās*, *zāwiyas*, and so on. For illustrations see: **90**, I, 37, 42, 77, IV, 9-10; **91**, I, 21-23, II, 8-15; **92**, pp. 312, 367-68; Ṣaqā'ī **65**, pp. 11b, 18b, 57b-58a; **425**, XV, 108. *Nāẓir* of waqfs: **92**, p. 310; Ṣaqā'ī **65**, pp. 23b, 69b, 74a, 80a-b, 85b; Sulūk **56**, II, 81a. *Mubāshir* (functionaries) of waqfs: **92**, pp. 193, 336; **95**, VIII, 39; **91**, II, 458-69; Furāt **166**, IX, 417; **90**, I, 72. *Mubāshir* of institutions: Furāt **166**, IX, 327; **95**, VIII, 70, 79, 84; Ṭūlūn **181**, p. 113. Other administrators: **90**, IV, 38, 60; Furāt **166**, IX, 393; Ṣaqā'ī **65**, p. 59b; Ṭūlūn **181**, pp. 113, 148, 336. *Nāẓir awqāf al-ashrāf* (controller of the waqfs of the descendants of the prophet): Sulūk **56**, II, 8b, 55a, 75a, 80b, 153a.

63. Some contemporary authors such as al-Maqrīzī were aware of the situation. Stratifying the society according to wealth, al-Maqrīzī distinguished seven classes: officers of the regime, rich merchants, middling merchants, peasant landowners, rentiers including professors, students, and soldiers, workers and artisans, and the miserable poor. In this categorization, the ulama are implicitly divided into at least two groups, those associated with state office, and the more humble teachers and students who received meager stipends from waqfs. Al-Subkī too, in a tract of moral advice to all classes of the population, basing his sequence of presentation on implicit notions of the ordering of society, separated the prominent ulama and the auxiliary intelligentsia of teachers and copyists. (**132**, pp. 72-76; **133**, pp. 71-75; **135**.)

    Functionaries educated as ulama: **90**, I, 71, 73, 76, 96, 99, 104, 111-12, IV, 20, 24-25, 62; **91**, II, 315-18, 564-76; **92**, pp. 84, 120, 158, 318; **95**, VIII, 36, 39, 55, 77, XI, 5-6, 33-34; **96**, p. 118; Ṣaqā'ī **65**, pp. 55b, 79b-80a. For ulama employed in bureaucratic posts: See above, pp. 137-38.

64. For lists of merchants with references see the author's dissertation, "The Muslim City in Mamluk Times" (Harvard University, 1964), Appendices D, E, and F.

65. Carpenter-ulama: Birzālī **10**, II, 107b, 219b; **90**, I, 469, IV, 181, 273; **95**, I, 116, II, 59, IV, 332, V, 280, VI, 90, 124, 147, 286, VII, 95. Coppersmiths: **90**, II, 307, III, 444; Ṣaqā'ī **65**, p. 72b; Kutubī **37**, I, 339-40; Jibrīnī **51**, II, 22b. Perfumer-druggists: Birzālī **10**, I, 34a, 60b, II, 159b, 247b, 249b-50a, 303b; Dhahabī **13**, II, 89b, 92a, 129a, 151b-152a, 165b, 231b; Jibrīnī **51**, II, 45a, 56b, 111a, 198b; **90**, I, 52, 181, 227, II, 136, III, 210, 235, IV, 57-58, 153; **95**, I, 34, 125, 170, 182, 326-27, II, 43-44, 159, 209, IV, 121, 142, 162, 317, V, 203, 216, 274, VI, 54, 195, VII, 174. Tailors: **92**, pp. 70, 108, 284, 295; **91**, II, 370; Dhahabī **13**, II, 243a; **95**, VI, 308; **375**, I, 107. Others: Birzālī **10**, I, 164a, II,

194b-195a; **90**, I, 70-71, 101, 142, 437; Nujūm **180**, V, 270, 510-11; **95**, I, 47-48, 185, II, 163, IV, 254, 270, V, 289.

Perfumer-druggists might better be considered professionals, but they are included here as one of the specifically designated trades.

66. Examples of soldier-ulama: Sulūk **56**, II, 44b; Furāt **166**, IX, 324-25, 444-45, 451. Ibn Taghrī Birdī, the chronicler, was the son of a Mamluk.

67. Note 65, above.

68. *Kārimī* families: **321**; **367**; Appendix D. Family of al-Muzallaq: See above, p. 128 and note 25. Biographies of sheikhs, teachers, jurists, qadis, and Sufis whose fathers were merchants: **95**, I, 182, 186-87, 331-32, 358, 515, II, 44, 167, V, 271, VII, 195-96; Sakhāwī **197**, pp. 137-38; Ḥawādith **179**, p. 540; **125**, V, 278; Duqmāq **104**, V, 82, 91; **54**, p. 22b; Birzālī **10**, II, 298a; Kutubī **37**, I, 256; **50**, II, 330; **90**, III, 151-52; **211**, II, 343. For merchants in the famous ulama families of Ibn Taymiyya and Ibn Ṭūlūn: Ṭūlūn **185**, p. x; **548**, p. 11. Sons of craftsmen were often sheikhs, prayer leaders, professors, members of the law schools, scholars, and officials. Sons of perfumer-pharmacists: **95**, I, 130, II, 115-17; Sakhāwī **197**, p. 90; Nujūm **180**, V, 209; Kathīr **176**, XIV, 305; **51**, II, 173b. Sons of coppersmiths: Yūnīnī **202**, I, 410; Ṣaqā'ī **65**, p. 71b; Ḥabīb **23**, p. 244a; **178**, p. 208; **50**, II, 50b. Sons of soap makers: Dhahabī **13**, II, 201b; **51**, II, 75b; Ḥabīb **23**, pp. 211b-212a; **28**, p. 172a; **125**, V, 444. Sons of carpenters: **95**, I, 349, II, 46, VII, 35, 129. Sons of other craftsmen: **50**, II, 361-62; Birzālī **10**, II, 191b-192a; Inbā' **26**, II, 20a; **95**, VII, 95; **125**, V, 295.

Biographies of bureaucrats from ulama families: Furāt **166**, IX, 46, 288, 323-24, 353, 419, 445, 449; Ṣaqā'ī **65**, pp. 18b-19b, 21b, 47b-48b, 58b-59a, 81b; **92**, pp. 84, 93, 96, 158; **91**, I, 376-78, 477-78, II, 154-59, 564-76; **95**, VIII, 39, XI, 33-34.

69. *Jamā'a:* Ṭūlūn **181**, pp. 22, 57, 108, 165; **90**, IV, 17. *Waẓā'if dīniyya:* Furāt **166**, IX, 175.

70. **425**, XVI, 100-01. Innumerable qadis' *nā'ibs* (deputies) are mentioned in the biographical dictionaries. Clerks: **90**, I, 16; Furāt **166**, IX, 447, 449. *Wakīl* (agent): Furāt **166**, IX, 450; Ḥabīb **24**, pp. 27b-28a. *Naqībs* (orderlies): Sulūk **56**, II, 80b; Ṣaṣra **177**, p. 5 (17)b. *A'wān* (aides): Sulūk **56**, II, 63b, III, 80b. See al-Subkī **135**, pp. 85-88 for descriptions of the duties of the scribes, chamberlains, orderlies, and assistants of the qadis.

71. *Ra'īs* of muezzins: Ṭūlūn **181**, pp. 22, 52, 62, 145, 338; **90**, I, 56, 79, IV, 44, 180; Sulūk **56**, II, 29b, 96b; **95**, VIII, 82; Furāt **166**, IX, 45, 390, 445, 447-48. *Shaykh al-qurrā'* (Koran readers): Furāt **166**, IX, 328, 448; **91**, I, 527-29; **90**, I, 44, 53; **96**, pp. 122-23; **549**, p. 47. *Naqīb al-Ashrāf* (syndic of the descendants of the prophet): Ṣaqā'ī **65**, pp. 31b-32a, 49a, 66b; **90**, I, 41, IV, 47, 64; Furāt **166**, IX, 322; **92**, p. 383; Yūnīnī **80**, III, 167a. *Imāms* (prayer leaders) of the law schools: Ṭūlūn **181**, p. 253; Furāt **166**, IX, 326; **92**, p. 378; **96**, pp. 120, 150; **90**, I, 101. Other ulama chiefs: *Muftī al-Shām* (jurisconsult for Syria): Sulūk **56**, II, 37a; Ṭūlūn **181**, p. 19. *Khaṭīb al-khuṭabā'* (chief preacher); Furāt **166**, IX, 39. *Naqīb* or *ra'īs al-muta'ammimīn* (syndic of the turbaned [ulama]): Baṭṭūṭa **142**, I, 33; Ṭūlūn **181**, p. 299, *Imām al-muḥaddithīn* (doyen of the traditionalists): Baṭṭūṭa **142**, I,

36. *Nāẓir al-fuqahā'* (syndic of the jurists): **91**, II, 523-24. *Ra'īs al-'ulamā'* (chief of the ulama): **90**, I, 38. *Naqīb al-Ashrāf al-'Ajamī* (syndic of the Persian descendants of the prophet): Ṭūlūn **181**, p. 383. *Ra'īs al-qawm* (head of the group, in various madrasas): Furāt **166**, IX, 321-33; **90**, IV, 55. *Imām al-Ashrāf:* **96**, p. 159, *Muftī al-Ḥanbalī:* Ṭūlūn **181**, p. 19.

72. Ḥanbalī school: **548**; **549**. The lists of madrasas compiled by Ibn Shaddād in the middle of the thirteenth century and al-Nu'aymī at the beginning of the sixteenth show the superior size of the Shāfi'ī and Ḥanafī schools in the two cities. (**106**; **108**; **118**.)

73. *Ra'īs al-madhhab:* Furāt **166**, IX, 423-24; **90**, I, 34, 84; **91**, I, 522-24, 546-47; **95**, XI, 21-24; **96**, pp. 31-35, 94, 115-16, 177-78. *Shaykh al-madhhab:* Ṭūlūn **181**, p. 279; Ṣaqā'ī **65**, p. 50a; **91**, I, 368; **96**, pp. 110, 143, 166. *Imām* of law school (with implication that the term attaches to the school and not to any particular mosque or madrasa): Ṭūlūn **181**, p. 253; **95**, XI, 14-15; **96**, p. 119. Qadis: See above, pp. 136-38. *Ṭā'ifa:* **549**, p. 51.

74. Year 693: Dhahabī **14**, p. 116b. Year 707: Kutubī **39**, p. 146a; **37**, I, 247-48; Yūnīnī **80**, IV, 139a-b. Year 743: Sulūk **187**, II, 628; Kathīr **176**, XIV, 206; Shuḥba **35**, I, 41a; Kutubī **39**, p. 74a. Year 822: Jawharī **46**, p. 102a; Sulūk **56**, III, 83b. Year 874: **54**, pp. 81a-b; 'Ulaymī **190**, II, 623; **58**, p. 139a; Jawharī **45**, p. 102b. Year 880: Ḥimṣī **29**, pp. 66b-67a. Also note 65, above.

CHAPTER IV. THE POLITICAL SYSTEM: THE MAMLUK STATE AND THE URBAN NOTABLES

1. Palaces: Inbā' **26**, II, 119b, 122a, 192a; **374**, pp. 134-35. Luxuries: Khiṭaṭ **116**, II, 105.

2. Wealth: **132**, p. 74; **425**, XVI, 116; **408**, pp. 290-91; **255**, p. 114; **277**, p. 48. Confiscations: Sulūk **187**, II, 412, 452. Biographies: Birzālī **10**, I, 29a-b, 105b, II, 78a-b, 119b, 246a, 266b; Dhahabī **13**, II, 30a, 54a-b, 89b; **153**, II, 130, 133; Shuḥba **34**, yrs. 713, 723, 731; Kutubī **37**, I, 241, II, 353-54; Jibrīnī **50**, II, 291-92; **51**, II, 14a; **54**, pp. 19b, 123b; Sulūk **56**, II, 23a, III, 17b; **187**, II, 132, 340; Ṣaqā'ī **65**, pp. 15b-16a, 69a, 87a; Yūnīnī **78**, pp. 182a-b, 183a; **79**, pp. 94a-b, 173b-174a; **202**, II, 126, 348-49, 487-89; **92**, p. 304; **93**, pp. 24, 207, 233; **41**, I, 63b, IV, 70a, 132a; Ḥawādith **179**, p. 156; Nujūm **180**, V, 281, VI, 812-13; **90**, II, 383-84, III, 429, 493, IV, 257; Sakhāwī **197**, p. 328; **95**, III, 133, V, 240, VII, 125, 129-30, 217; Nu'aymī **119**, I, 232-33, 272-73, II, 246; **121**, V, 379, VI, 253, 259, VII, 249; Inbā' **26**, III, 169b-170a; Kathīr **176**, XIII, 262, XIV, 43, 107, 156, 171; Khiṭaṭ **116**, II, 401; Iyās **169**, I, 340; **367**, pp. 108, 111-12, 116.

3. Land: **492**, p. 192; **356**, p. 493. Urban property: Appendix A. Brokers: Birzālī **10**, I, 57a, 158b; Ḥimṣī **29**, p. 96b; Ṭūlūn **181**, p. 55; For witnesses specializing in property transactions: See above, pp. 61-62.

4. **340**, pp. 3-5; **405**, pp. 1-4; Nujūm **180**, V, 372, VI, 144; Iyās **169**, I, 168, IV, 126; 'Aynī **4**, p. 131b; Kathīr **176**, XIV, 96; **28**, p. 97b; **239**, p. 259; **90**, IV, 148. Ibn Rawāḥa: Baṭṭūṭa **141**, I, 46-47.

5. *Simsār* (pl. *samāsira*), brokers or wholesalers of grain and spices: Birzālī **10**, I, 75a, II, 201b, 297a; Dhahabī **13**, II, 31a; Inbā' **26**, III,

197a, 218a; Shuḥba **34**, yr. 717; **51**, II, 41a; Ṣaqāʿī **65**, pp. 82b, 84b; Furāt **166**, IX, 387, 439; Ṣaṣra **177**, pp. 141b, 207a, I, 55; Sulūk **187**, II, 96, 150, 394-95, 398, 408, 420, 669; Ṭūlūn **181**, p. 44; **282**, passim. The *simsār* who dealt with European merchants who had come to Egypt to buy spices was an official of the state who certified the value of the goods and assessed a tax of 1/200th for his services. (Claude Cahen, "Douanes et Commerce dans les Ports Méditerranéens de l'Égypte Médiévale d'après le Minhādj d'al Makhzūmī," *JESHO*, VII [1964], p. 239.)

Jallāba: Brinner defines the term to mean an importing merchant bringing goods from one town to another. (Ṣaṣra **177**, pp. 18 (30)a, 112b.) Other contexts establish the term to mean "grain importer." (Kutubī **38**, p. 160b, *tujjār al-jallāba* ordered to bring wheat to Damascus; Furāt **166**, IX, 439, *jalaba*—to import grain; Jawharī **48**, p. 49a; **539**, p. 208; Inbāʾ **26**, II, 58b.)

Tājir saffār, merchant traveling in international trade: Birzālī **10**, I, 274b, II, 73b, 110a, 199b, 226a, 244a, 310a, 314b; Dhahabī **13**, II, 161a, 207a, 232b, 234b, 248b; Ḥabīb **23**, p. 67a; Inbāʾ **26**, II, 99a; Shuḥba **34**, yr. 693; Kutubī **37**, I, 241; **39**, p. 49b; **41**, V, 124a; **93**, p. 317; Saqāʿī **65**, pp. 15b-16a, 70a, 85b; **90**, II, 169, 270-72, 496, III, 443, IV, 10; **95**, II, 88, 126, III, 267, IV, 292, V, 185-86, 285, VI, 191, VIII, 73; Nuʿaymī **119**, II, 8, 254; **121**, IV, 460; Furāt **166**, VIII, 186-87, IX, 7; Kathīr **176**, XIV, 43, 104, 181, 227; Jazarī **186**, pp. 3, 22, 38; Yūnīnī **202**, I, 364; **50**, I, 394, II, 95; **51**, I, 56b-57a, II, 146a, 179a-b.

Kārimī spice merchants: Appendix D.

6. See above, pp. 50-51 on the military households as consumers. Butchers: **407**, XVI, 61; **408**, pp. 280-81; Nujūm **180**, VII, 718; Iyās **169**, II, 286, IV, 320, 339. Jewelers: Sulūk **187**, II, 536. Purchases: Jawharī **46**, p. 125a; **45**, p. 54a; Kathīr **176**, XIV, 282-83; Nujūm **180**, VI, 616.

Dealing with the *dīwāns*, however, was not necessarily the road to riches. Merchants were subjected to abuse. For example, a Cairo cloth dealer who had a claim of 90,000 dirhems against the Sultan's treasury was imprisoned for his pleas and finally set free only after renouncing the claim. (Sulūk **187**, II, 372.) Also: Ṣaqāʿī **65**, p. 76a; Sulūk **187**, II, 829; **54**, p. 63a.

7. Sulūk **187**, II, 184, 361, 366, 400-01, 439, 833; Ṣaqāʿī **65**, pp. 13b-14a; ʿAynī **3**, II, 215b-216a; Jazarī **48**, p. 382; Kutubī **39**, p. 21b; **466**, p. 30.

8. Deposit banking: Shuḥba **34**, yrs. 698, 717; Ṣaqāʿī **65**, pp. 82b, 84b; **50**, II, 41a; Yūnīnī **78**, p. 175b; **202**, II, 470; Dhahabī **13**, II, 10a; Birzālī **10**, I, 28a; Jazarī **49**, p. 106b; **186**, pp. 85-86; Kutubī **37**, II, 287; Inbāʾ **26**, III, 140b-141a. *Ṣayrafīs*: **425**, XV, 100; Jazarī **48**, pp. 200-01; Sulūk **56**, II, 170a, 187b, 203a, III, 98a; **91**, II, 11; **95**, VIII, 43, XI, 12, 20; Jawharī **46**, pp. 142a-b; Duqmāq **20**, p. 106a; Kathīr **176**, XIV, 127. Al-Arminī: Nujūm **180**, VI, 279; Sulūk **56**, II, 163b. If the deposited funds were used for business investments, then *fāʾida* (interest) might be due the depositor. (**158**, pp. 305, 908.) For the legal status of a deposit see Joseph Schacht, *An Introduction to Islamic Law* (Oxford, 1964), p. 157.

9. This type of transaction is called the *ḥawāla* in Islamic law. (Richard Grasshoff, *Das Wechselrecht der Araber* [Berlin, 1899], pp. **8**-15.)
10. Year 687: Kutubī **37**, II, 372; Furāt **166**, VIII, 62; Quatremère **188**, II_1, 92-93. Year 711: **90**, I, 402; Sulūk **187**, II, 103-04; **335**, p. 70; **367**, pp. 103-04. Loans to Sultan: Quatremère **188**, II_2, 167; Iyās **169**, I, 302; Jawharī **46**, p. 44b; Inbā' **26**, III, 123b; **362**, p. 116. Foreign loans to Mali: **362**, p. 110; Dhahabī **153**, II, 187; **90**, II, 405; Baṭṭūṭa **142**, II, 356. Yemen: Nujūm **180**, V, 89-90, 117; Bāsiṭ **1**, I, 35a, 42a; Sulūk **187**, II, 852, 867; **90**, III, 50; **321**, p. 53; **335**, pp. 76-77.

 Other merchant lenders: 'Aynī **4**, pp. 108b, 118a, 123b, 126b, 155b; Sulūk **187**, II, 419, 452, 488, 852, 869; Nujūm **180**, V, 121, VI, 69; Bāsiṭ **1**, I, 42b; Kathīr **176**, XIV, 269; Inbā' **26**, II, 113b, 236b, III, 75b; Jawharī **45**, p. 156a; Iyās **169**, I, 130. *Ṣayrafis,* money lenders: Jazarī **48**, pp. 200-01; Jawharī **46**, pp. 142a-b; Duqmāq **20**, p. 106b.

 The chronicles say little about business and banking practices. *Awrāq,* commercial paper, receipts, and notes were in use. ('Aynī **4**, p. 155b; Dhahabī **13**, II, 3a-b.) Security (*rahn*) was given for loans. (Jawharī **45**, p. 75a.) Treaties between the Mamluks and the European trading cities give some information on the terms of credit in the spice trade, but nothing on internal practices. (Bibliography section IB-9 on Treaties; see especially: **343**.)
11. The various titles in use were *tājir al-Sulṭān* (merchant of the Sultan), *tājir al-khāṣṣ al-Sulṭāniyya* (merchant of the Sultan's privy purse), *tājir al-khāṣṣ al-sharīf* (merchant of the noble privy purse), *tājir al-matjar* (merchant of the trading bureau), *'āmil al-matjar* (controller of the trading bureau), and the rank or title of *khawājā.*

 The Sultan's merchants: Sulūk **56**, II, 81b, 91b, 148a, 150a; **187**, II, 116, 486, note 1; Dhahabī **13**, II, 185a; Furāt **166**, IX, 49, 411, 458; Jawharī **46**, p. 51a; **321**, pp. 47-48; Inbā' **26**, III, 83b, 134b; 'Aynī **3**, I, 142a; **90**, II, 402; Khiṭaṭ **116**, II, 396; Ṣaqā'ī **65**, p. 88a.
12. Slave dealers: **405**, pp. 1-4; **90**, II, 206; **93**, p. 375; Nujūm **180**, VI, 322. Title *khawājā:* Nu'aymī **119**, I, 124; **121**, III, 313; Bāsiṭ **1**, I, 31a; Sulūk **187**, II, 906. The most renowned slave merchant—*khawājā* of the fourteenth century was the importer of Sultan Barqūq, 'Uthmān ibn Musāfir. 'Uthmān imported Barqūq's father and brother as well, was very wealthy, and owned a *qayṣariyya* in Damascus. He was highly respected by the Sultan and was able to assist his city, Damascus, by obtaining the abolition of taxes on pomegranates. (Nujūm **180**, V, 325, 361, 364; Bāsiṭ **1**, I, 127b-128a; Inbā' **26**, III, 64a; Sulūk **56**, II, 78b.) Ties were so close that slaves took the name of their merchant as a sign of subjugation, and more practically, to assist the merchants to whom all the original names of the slaves sounded alike. (Dawādārī **152**, pp. 71-72.)

 Ambassadors: Sulūk **187**, II, 423, 524-25, 554; Dawādārī **152**, p. 303; Kutubī **38**, p. 133a; Birzālī **10**, II, 339a; Furāt **166**, IX, 342; Sakhāwī **197**, p. 67; **54**, p. 68b.
13. Byzantine Empire: **289**; **290**; **291**; **292**; Qalqashandī **84**, XIV, 72ff.; Furāt **166**, VII, 229-33. Tyre and Armenia: **74**, pp. 184b-206a, 209b-229b; Quatremère **188**, II_1, 166-76, 201-23. Acre: Furāt **166**, VII,

262-69; Quatremère **188**, II_1, 179-85, 224-32. For European treaties: Bibliography section IB-9.

14. Circular of 687: Furāt **166**, VIII, 65; Qalqashandī **84**, XIII, 339-42; Quatremère **188**, II_1, 98; **362**, pp. 90-92; Sulūk **187**, I, 742; **411**, p. 171. Ceylon: Furāt **166**, VII, 261; Quatremère **188**, II_1, 59-60; **74**, pp. 101b-105a. India: Jazarī **48**, p. 205; Sulūk **187**, II, 322, 333, 645; **86**, p. 49; Bāsiṭ **1**, I, 2b; Iyās **169**, II, 131, 152-53, 190, 225; Sakhāwī **66**, II, 87a.

    Anatolian principalities made similar efforts in the wake of disrupting wars in order to assure the flow of trade. For example, during the Mamluk-Dulghādir wars, Shāh Suwār sent a circular to Aleppo, Tripoli, and Damascus guaranteeing the security of merchants. This wartime effort was denounced as a deception. (Ḥawādith **179**, pp. 686-87. Also: Bāsiṭ **1**, I, 40b-41a; Sakhāwī **66**, I, yr. 836; Inbā' **26**, II, 191a.)

15. Piracy: See above, pp. 27, 35; **374**, pp. 239-362; **293**, passim. For extensive negotiations to recover slaves and merchants taken as prisoners to Crete: **297**, pp. 23-29. Land frontiers: Yūnīnī **78**, p. 183b; Ḥabīb **23**, p. 37a; Inbā' **26**, II, 227a; **74**, pp. 184a, 207b; **159**, pp. 93, 203; 'Aynī **3**, II, 42b; **125**, III, 100; Iyās **169**, II, 260.

    War between the Mongols and the Mamluks in the late thirteenth and early fourteenth centuries made caravan traffic in Northern Syria and Anatolia unsafe and subject to plunder. Peace was the only defense possible in these circumstances. (Furāt **166**, VII, 2; **74**, p. 8a; Birzālī **10**, II, 270a-b; Shuhba **34**, yrs. 717, 723.)

16. Tributes: Dawādārī **152**, pp. 114-15; **265**, p. 154. For bedouin risings and interference with trade see Chapter I, passim.

17. Sulūk **187**, II, 516; **374**, pp. 89-90; **427**, pp. 54-55; **221**, pp. 1-19; **54**, p. 153a.

18. Taxes and abuses: See above, pp. 29, 35-36, 40, 56-59, 92-93, 99-100. Appeals sometimes even went to the Sultan's harem. (Sulūk **187**, II, 412; Inbā' **26**, III, 60b; Nujūm **180**, V, 372; Ḥawādith **179**, pp. 129-30; Ḥimṣī **29**, pp. 101b-102a; **125**, V, 375.)

19. The *kārimī* and their trade is perhaps the only thoroughly covered topic in Mamluk social and economic history: **321**; **334**; **335**; **338**; **362**. The most important sources are: **41**; **42**; **84**; **90**; **95**; **187**. For a résumé of the biographies of the known *kārimī* see Appendix D. These notes contain but a few supplementary details hitherto unpublished. A *kārimī* not hitherto identified is Ḥasan ibn Dā'ūd. His biography in **90**, II, 55, and **50**, I, 391-92 gives no indication that he was one of the *kārimī,* but in another text (**51**, I, 145a) he is so identified.

    Relations with emirs and the *dīwāns*: Ṣaqā'ī **65**, 13a-14a, 88a. Taxes and tax supervisors: Sulūk **56**, II, 8a, 70a, 72b, 159a; Furāt **166**, IX, 445.

20. The spice monopoly: **282**, passim; **293**, passim; **296**; **374**, pp. 194-239, 293-363; **457**, passim. 'Alī al-Kīlānī: Inbā' **26**, II, 34b; **95**, V, 313, VI, 229; **362**, p. 124; **374**, pp. 207, 222. Other merchant members of his family: Inbā' **26**, II, 91a, 203a; **95**, II, 32, VI, 38. Other merchants: **95**, III, 3. For the *commenda* in the Islamic world: A. L. Udovitch, "At the Origins of the Western Commenda: Islam, Israel, Byzantium?" *Speculum,* XXXVII (1962), pp. 198-207.

An episode of 855/1451 indicates that it was common for merchants to deal in spices on behalf of the Sultan. An official who had embezzled the Sultan's funds in Jidda fled to Abyssinia, and when forced away by the complaints of merchants who feared that association with him would lead to the confiscation of their goods, went to Calcutta where he presented himself as the agent of the Sultan to buy spices. It was a plausible story and he encountered no trouble there so far as we learn. (Sakhāwī **197**, pp. 347-48; Nujūm **180**, VI, 208-11.)

The Sultan's merchants and the Alexandria trading services: **282**, pp. 212, 275-76; **440**, I_2, 264; Sakhāwī **66**, II, 101a, 115a, 124a, 195a; **95**, III, 133, VI, 63-64; **197**, p. 345; Jawharī **45**, p. 191a; Ṭūlūn **181**, p. 132. The offices of *tājir al-Sulṭān* and *tājir* of Alexandria were the same. (**95**, IV, 259-60; **362**, p. 127; Iyās **169**, II, 162, 166, 222, 231.) *Mālik al-tujjār:* **95**, III, 137, V, 116, 177, VI, 38; **367**, pp. 127-28; Sakhāwī **66**, II, 94a. An official in charge of trade in Jidda was called the *Shāh-bandar*. (**95**, II, 43; **367**, p. 124.) The *tājir al-khāṣṣ* (merchant of the privy purse) also handled spices. (**293**, I, 375-76; **457**, II, 474-76; **343**, pp. 324-25.)

Some fifteenth century merchants were titled *kārimī* or were said to deal in the *kārim,* but the term had simply been carried over to mean "spices," and there is no evidence for the continued existence of the *kārimī* in the old sense. For example, the *khawājā* Shams al-dīn Muḥammad was called *al-tājir fil-kārim* (merchant in the *kārim*), but is also referred to in the same text as *al-tājir al-khawājā fil-bahār* (merchant *khawājā* in spices). He was simply an official of the Sultan trading in spices. (Jawharī **45**, pp. 83b-84a, 120b-121a.)

21. Sugar: **354**. Natron: Qalqashandī **84**, I, 455-56; Nujūm **180**, VII, 433; **348**, pp. 134-35; **398**, p. 329; Ḥawādith **179**, p. 53. Silk: **208**, XLIII, 334. Salt: Décrets **223**, XII, 47; Iyās **169**, II, 243, IV, 355, V, 90; **54**, p. 106b.
22. Slave dealers: **243**, p. 307; **268**, p. 339. Khawājās: **403**, pp. 1-4; **95**, II, 270, III, 40, VI, 201; **72**, p. 35a; Sibṭ **123**, p. 167; **54**, p. 36b; **73**, p. 366b; Iyās **169**, II, 3, 39; **171**, pp. 4, 96. *Tājir al-mamālīk al-Sulṭāniyya* (the Sultan's merchant of Mamluks) and the *mu'allim tujjār al-Mamālīk* (supervisor of the slave merchants). This supervisor was also chief of the brokers, which was probably a means of increasing his income by giving him tax collecting duties. (**374**, p. 321; Iyās **169**, II, 249; **88**, p. 115; **211**, II, 395-96; Sakhāwī **66**, II, 183a; Ḥawādith **179**, p. 229; Nujūm **180**, VII, 216.) Slave merchants related to the families of emirs: **95**, I, 118; Iyās **169**, V, 3. Slave merchants holding offices or ambassadorships: Inbā' **26**, II, 66; **54**, p. 70a; Nujūm **180**, VII, 216.

    The attrition of Mamluks through war, plague, and political retirement made efforts to keep up the supply of manpower a matter of desperate urgency. (**419**.)
23. *Tājir al-Sulṭān* or *tājir al-khāṣṣ:* See note 20, above, for spice trade. Others are: Ḥawādith **179**, p. 97; **95**, II, 358, VI, 175, 193-94, and Ibn al-Muzallaq, note 25, below. *Al-matājir:* **95**, VI, 50-51. The *nāẓir al-khāṣṣ* supervised the *matājir khawāṣṣ* (royal trading

bureaus) and was ordered to deal justly with the merchants. (Qalqashandī **84**, XI, 318-20.)

24. Trevisan, a Venetian ambassador at the beginning of the sixteenth century defined *khawājā* to mean "great merchants trading for the account of the Sultan." (**277**, p. 193.) Other definitions and discussions of rank: **121**, III, 261-63, 268; **208**, XLIII, 345-50; Qalqashandī **84**, VI, 165-68. See notes 20-23, above, for the employment of *khawājās* and Appendix E.

The rank of ṣāḥib rather than *khawājā* was sometimes applied to merchants of the Sultan. (Jawharī **45**, p. 62b; **54**, pp. 96b, 107b.)

25. *Kārimī* merchants holding offices: Appendix D.

Khawājās described as merchants but holding other official positions: **95**, II, 257; Jawharī **45**, p. 195b; **362**, p. 127. The al-Muzallaq family were merchant *khawājās* and held other official posts for generations. Shams al-dīn Muḥammad was *tājir al-khāṣṣ* (merchant of the privy purse), *ra'īs* of the *khawājās,* and manager of the Yalbugha mosque in Damascus. He died in 848. (Ṭūlūn **111**, I, 74-75; Nu'aymī **119**, II, 290-91; **121**, III, 279, VI, 261-63; Sakhāwī **197**, pp. 112-13; **95**, III, 85; **374**, pp. 150, 192-93, 208, 235-36; **125**, V, 146; Ḥawādith **179**, p. 24; Jawharī **46**, p. 187a; Sulūk **56**, III, 13b.) His son, *al-Khawājā* Badr al-dīn Ḥasan, was a tax collector in Jidda and *nāẓir al-jaysh* (army controller) in Damascus. (Ḥawādith **179**, p. 24; Sakhāwī **197**, p. 113; **374**, pp. 208, 236; Ḥimṣī **30**, yr. 857.) Another son Shams al-dīn was a *ra'īs,* qadi, and *kātib al-sirr* in Damascus. (Ḥimṣī **30**, yr. 878; Sakhāwī **66**, II, 91a; Ṭūlūn **181**, pp. 54-55, 64, 70-71.) A grandson, Ibrāhīm ibn Badr al-dīn succeeded his father as *nāẓir al-jaysh* after buying the post for 10,000 dinars. (**54**, p. 13b.) Yet another descendant was a *khawājā* and *nāẓir* of the waqfs of the original Shams al-dīn. (Ḥimṣī **30**, yr. 916.) *Khawājās* not designated as merchants but involved in merchants' affairs: Sakhāwī **197**, p. 328; Inbā' **26**, II, 238a.

For a tabular listing of merchants and officials who bore the title *khawājā* see Appendix E and the author's dissertation, "The Muslim City in Mamluk Times" (Harvard University, 1964), Appendices G and H.

Other merchants employed as scribes, *nāẓirs* (controllers), *wālīs* (governors), *wakīls* (agents), and viziers of the bureaucracy: Birzālī **10**, I, 29a-b; Dhahabī **13**, II, 20a, 54a-b, 212a-b; **153**, II, 133; Inbā' **26**, II, 242b, III, 122a, 170a, 182a, 218a; Shuhba **34**, yrs. 693, 723; Kutubī **37**, I, 196-97, II, 313, 353-54; **41**, II, 168b-169a; Jibrīnī **50**, II, 291-92; **51**, II, 141a; **54**, p. 206b; Ṣaqā'ī **65**, pp. 31b, 69a, 70b, 87a; Yūnīnī **78**, pp. 182a-183a; **202**, II, 413-14, 487-89; **90**, I, 456-57, II, 372, III, 143; **91**, I, 184-85; **95**, I, 268, II, 206, III, 127, 149, 319, VI, 314, VII, 147; Nu'aymī **119**, I, 272-73; **121**, V, 379, VI, 253, 259; **125**, IV, 514-15; Furāt **166**, VIII, 106-08, IX, 354; Iyās **169**, I, 122-23, IV, 481; Kathīr **176**, XIII, 262, XIV, 107; Ḥawādith **179**, pp. 162, 464, 540; Sakhāwī **197**, p. 80. Merchants employed as *muḥtasibs:* See above, p. 98 and note 41. For other examples of merchant-officials and merchants bearing official titles such as *ṣadr, ṣāḥib, amīn* but not expressly designated as employed in official posts: See "The Muslim City in Mamluk Times," Appendix E.

26. Purchases of fiefs: **374**, p. 54; **407**, XV, 353-54; **408**, p. 45; **362**, p. 108; Sulūk **187**, II, 643, 840; Bāsiṭ **1**, I, 23a, 128a; Jawharī **45**, p. 15b. Patronage: Birzālī **10**, I, 29a-b, 105b; Dhahabī **13**, II, 54a-b, 89b, 106b, 212a-b, 227a; Shuhba **34**, yr. 693; Kutubī **37**, I, 196-97, II, 313, 353-54; **41**, II, 168b-169a; Jibrīnī **50**, II, 291-92; **51**, II, 141a; Ṣaqā'ī **65**, pp. 31b, 48b, 69b, 70b; Yūnīnī **78**, pp. 182a-183a, 202b; **79**, pp. 94a-b, 173b-174a; **90**, II, 420; **91**, I, 184-85; **121**, V, 379; **125**, IV, 514-15; Furāt **166**, VII, 119, VIII, 106-08; Iyās **169**, I, 122-23; Kathīr **176**, XIII, 243, 262; Ḥawādith **179**, pp. 40, 71; Nujūm **180**, VI, 139-40, VII, 164-65; Sakhāwī **95**, III, 149; **197**, pp. 80, 221, 333; Yūnīnī **202**, II, 413-14, 487-89. Merchants employed in the service of emirs: See above, p. 48.
27. Craftsmen rose to high office. A coppersmith became a *wakīl, wazīr,* and *nāẓir* of the Cairo hospital. (Iyās **169**, II, 29, 31, 36, 46, 64, 70; **42**, III, 492b; **93**, p. 421; Nujūm **180**, VII, 150-53, 630-32; Ḥawādith **179**, pp. 35, 329, 392; Sakhāwī **197**, p. 215.) Furriers became viziers, army controllers, or managers of waqfs. (**95**, II, 313; Iyās **169**, II, 212; Inbā' **26**, II, 17b.) A tailor rose to be a vizier (Sulūk **187**, II, 14), and another was elected to the post of *dawādār*. (**121**, VI, 233, 280-81.)

    Even men of the very lowest classes and origins became officials. (Ḥawādith **179**, p. 146; Nujūm **180**, VII, 222, 464; Dawādārī **152**, p. 350; Iyās **169**, IV, 372-73, 389; **95**, V, 207.) The most curious case was that of a bath attendant who became *muḥtasib* of Cairo. An exceptionally menial and disreputable profession was a stepping stone to one of the high ulama offices. (**93**, p. 108.)
28. See above, p. 13 and note 7.
29. Reaction of the ulama: Nujūm **180**, VI, 62-63; **161**, pp. 208, 215-16; Iyās **169**, I, 331-32; **195**, p. 332; Duqmāq **22**, pp. 178-79.
30. **429**, p. 118; Iyās **169**, V, 70; Ṭūlūn **183**, p. 132.
31. See above, p. 13 and note 7.
32. Duqmāq **22**, pp. 178-79.
33. Ṭūlūn **183**, pp. 132, 134; **185**, p. 46; Iyās **169**, V, 84; **557**, pp. 270-71.
34. Muslim political theory: E. I. J. Rosenthal, *Political Thought in Medieval Islam* (Cambridge, Eng., 1958); H. A. R. Gibb, "Constitutional Organization," *Law in the Middle East,* M. Khadduri and H. J. Liebesney, ed. (Washington, 1955), pp. 3-27; H. A. R. Gibb, "Some Considerations on the Sunni Theory of the Caliphate," *Archives d'Histoire du Droit Oriental,* III (1948), pp. 401-10; L. Binder, "Al-Ghazali's Theory of Islamic Government," *Muslim World,* XLV (1955), pp. 229-41; **548**.

    Ceremonial welcome of new governors: Shiḥna **110**, pp. 203-06; 'Ulaymī **57**, p. 217b.
35. Military volunteers: See above, p. 164. Year 699: Dhahabī **14**, p. 132a; Shuhba **34**, yr. 699; Sulūk **187**, I ,903; Kutubī **39**, p. 86a; Birzālī **10**, II, 30a-b; Ḥabīb **23**, pp. 106a-b; Yūnīnī **80**, III, 167a; Kathīr **176**, XIV, 12. Preaching holy wars: Kathīr **176**, XIV, 10-12, 14-16, 322; **154**, p. 386; **383**, p. 103; **393**, p. 299; **549**, p. 15; Dhahabī **14**, p. 32b; Jawharī **46**, p. 184a; Sulūk **56**, II, 184a; Ṣaṣra **177**, p. 149a.
36. Ulama support: Furāt **166**, IX, 274-75, 290; Sulūk **56**, II, 115a, 127b,

173b, III, 21b, 43a, 48a; Nujūm **180**, VI, 253-54; Ṣaṣra **177**, pp. 37 (7)b, 74b. Merchants sometimes assisted fugitive emirs by hiding them. (**374**, p. 25; Iyās **169**, IV, 42-43.)

37. *Fatwā* of 666: Dhahabī **13**, II, 6a-b; Yūnīnī **202**, II, 386-87; Ṣaqā'ī **65**, p. 18b. Councils: Sulūk **56**, II, 60b, 72b, 94a, 115a, 117a, 147b, 183b, III, 40a.
38. *Muḥtasib:* See above, pp. 99-100. Qadis: Furāt **166**, IX, 12-13. Sheikhs: Ṭūlūn **185**, pp. 84-85, 102, 117; Ṭūlūn **183**, p. 146; Iyās **169**, II, 258.
39. Qalqashandī **84**, VII, 165, XII, 174-270, 370-77, XIII, 38-85, 338-83, 417; **425**, XV, 100-01, 108-09; Syrie **140**, pp. lxxvi-lxxviii, 160-66, 209-10; **88**, pp. 145-49, 193; **417**. Consultation: Ṭūlūn **181**, pp. 25, 39.
40. Venality: Furāt **166**, VII, 175; Décrets **223**, XII, 46; **399**, pp. 569-71; Sulūk **56**, II, 126b, 219a; Ṭūlūn **181**, pp. 30, 37, 63, 77, 140.
41. Cairo qadis: Quatremère **188**, I_1, 223. Damascus: Ḥabīb **23**, p. 26b; Kathīr **176**, XIII, 246; Aleppo: Syrie **140**, p. 209; Baṭṭūṭa **142**, I, 156; Fidā' **149**, IV, 147-48; **101**, III, 184; **125**, II, 421; Nujūm **180**, V, 58; Sulūk **187**, II, 753. Jerusalem and Ramla: Inbā' **26**, III, 239a.

    Qadis as managers of waqfs: **90**, IV, 4-6; **92**, p. 193, 310; **96**, p. 151. Authority in management of religious institutions: Sibṭ **123**, pp. 20-21, 32-33; Décrets **223**, II, 6-9; **238**, p. 525.
42. Year 731: **59**, p. 263. Year 782: Bāsiṭ **1**, I, 125b. Year 819: Inbā' **26**, II, 63b; Duqmāq **20**, p. 108b; Sulūk **56**, III, 63b. In this case, al-Maqrīzī states that there were 136 deputies and the Ḥanafī were reduced to five rather than ten and the Mālikī to four. Year 842: Jawharī **46**, p. 177b. Other: Ṭūlūn **181**, pp. 96, 309.
43. Witnesses: Inbā' **26**, I, 9b; Sulūk **56**, II, 28a, 69b, 165b, III, 75a. For other assistants see above, p. 111 and note 70.
44. *Shaykh al-Shuyūkh:* Sulūk **56**, II, 114a; Ṭūlūn **181**, pp. 99, 114, 134; **91**, I, 113-15; **96**, pp. 45-53. *Khaṭībs:* Furāt **166**, IX, 39-40, 423, 476; **91**, I, 132-33, 367, 594-96, II, 353-54; **92**, pp. 78, 224, 305; **95**, IV, 36; **96**, pp. 90, 166-68. Professors and teachers: Ṣaqā'ī **65**, pp. 3b-4a, 36a-b, 58a, 84b; Furāt **166**, IX, 177-78, 281-83; **91**, I, 555-57, II, 368-69, 484-92; **92**, pp. 12, 15, 52, 64, 91, 94, 110, 170, 173, 188, 197, 218, 249, 268, 293, 312, 379; **95**, IV, 11-12, 30-31, 38, 44, 47, VIII, 41, 62, XI, 17-18, 28-31; **96**, pp. 23-24, 29, 35, 92-93, 106, 113, 124, 125, 139, 140, 142, 153. Also **431**.
45. Illustrations of qadis holding official posts as *kātib al-sirr* (private secretary to the Sultans), *nāẓir al-khāṣṣ* (controller of the privy purse), *nāẓir al-jaysh* (army controller), and other posts as scribes in the *dīwāns:* Ṣaqā'ī **65**, pp. 4a-b, 33a, 58a-b, 59a, 78a, 84a, 86b; **95**, XI, 6; **92**, pp. 130, 180, 271, 302, 315, 336, 383; **96**, pp. 26-27, 95-96, 162, 168, 171-72, 178-79; **91**, I, 451-63, 534-37, II, 8-15, 39-40, 46-49. Also: **429**, pp. 44-53, 99-122. Sheikhs and *imāms* holding posts as scribes and officials: Ṣaqā'ī 65, pp. 52a-b, 53a, 54a-b, 87a; **91**, I, 115-18, 567, II, 154, 376-78. Religious administrators who were also scribes of the *dīwāns:* **90**, I, 77, 82, IV, 7, 10, 50, 77; **91**, I, 21-23, 362-66, II, 203-05; **96**, p. 153; Ṣaqā'ī **65**, pp. 4b, 21b, 35a-b, 57b-58a, 64b, 74b; Furāt **166**, IX, 357.
46. Year 725: Jazarī **48**, p. 542. Waqf stipends: Furāt **166**, VII, 272, VIII, 10; Nujūm **180**, V, 119; Nu'aymī **119**, I, 9-10, 413, 427-28, II, 420; **230**, p. 11; **330**, pp. 93-100; **355**, pp. 86-87, 90-93; **425**, XVI, 118-23.

Gifts and waqfs from merchants: Birzālī **10**, II, 78a-b, 322a; Inbā' **26**, III, 20b, 75a; Shuḥba **34**, yrs. 720, 731; Kutubī **37**, I, 241; **39**, p. 49b; **41**, IV, 157b; **93**, p. 244; Jibrīnī **50**, I, 632; **51**, II, 14a, 232b-233a; Ṣaqā'ī **65**, pp. 15b-16a; **90**, I, 391, II, 33-34, 353, III, 128-29, 437, IV, 152; **95**, I, 188, 281, II, 18-19, 80, III, 90-91, 127, IV, 247, 259-60, V, 191-92, 245, 307, VI, 30; Ṭūlūn **111**, I, 60, 199, 230; Nu'aymī **119**, I, 232-33, II, 8, 246, 254, 439; **121**, III, 266-67, 286, 389, IV, 460, 478, VI, 222, 225, 237, 268, 311, VII, 245, 249, 277-78; Sibṭ **123**, pp. 52-53, 55; **125**, V, 92, 378-79, 395-96; Furāt **166**, IX, 354; Kathīr **176**, XIII, 347, XIV, 43, 142-43, 167, 171, 181, 227; Nujūm **180**, VI, 118, 824; **367**, pp. 106, 114; **374**, pp. 147, 149. Also Appendix D.

Poverty: **132**, p. 75; See above, pp. 177-83.

47. Ulama-craftsmen: See above, p. 109.

48. Defense of property: Sulūk **187**, II, 888-89. See above, pp. 62-63. Year 803: Nujūm **180**, VI, 47. Year 827: Inbā' **26**, II, 136b. Other: Nujūm **180**, V, 30; Kutubī **39**, pp. 98b-99a; Inbā' **26**, II, 160b; Sakhāwī **197**, p. 175; Jawharī **45**, pp. 111b-113a; Ṭūlūn **181**, pp. 180-81; Sulūk **56**, II, 63a.

49. Fourteenth century: Furāt **166**, VII, 75; Birzālī **10**, I, 164b, 201b, II, 172a; Kathīr **176**, XIV, 62; **189**, XX, 202, 212; **59**, p. 229; Shuḥba **34**, yr. 711; Kutubī **38**, pp. 64a-b, 65a; Yūnīnī **80**, IV, 219b. Fifteenth century: Note 37, above; Ṭūlūn **183**, p. 146; **185**, pp. 38, 102. Witnesses: Nuwayrī **61**, II, 209b.

The Jewish and Christian leaders similarly represented their communities in tax matters. For example, in 791/1389 the *ra'is* of the Jews compromised with the rebel emir Minṭāsh by paying him half of his 100,000 dirhems demand. The Jacobite bishop did the same. ('Aynī **3**, I, 169b.)

50. Protests of abuses: Iyās **169**, I, 116; **69**, p. 89; Ḥawādith **179**, p. 278. Settling Mamluk disputes: Jawharī **46**, p. 32a; Sakhāwī **66**, II, 184a; Ṭūlūn **185**, pp. 62-63; Ṣaṣra **177**, pp. 8 (20)b-9 (21)a.

CHAPTER V. THE POLITICAL SYSTEM: THE COMMON PEOPLE BETWEEN VIOLENCE AND IMPOTENCE

1. Closures for protection: Kutubī **37**, I, 242; **39**, p. 119b; Bāsiṭ **1**, I, 8b, 111b, 119b, 123b; Nujūm **180**, V, 385, 594, VI, 642, VII, 190, 507-08, 516; Iyās **169**, II, 279, IV, 235, 430; **171**, p. 181; **54**, pp. 194b, 213b; Sulūk **56**, II, 59a, 65a, 106b-107a, 109a-b, 162a, 166a, 209a, III, 51a; **69**, p. 72; Dawādārī **152**, p. 148; Furāt **166**, IX, 77; Kathīr **176**, XIV, 195-97; Ḥawādith **179**, p. 410; Ṭūlūn **183**, pp. 135, 140; **205**, pp. 65-66; Ṣaṣra **177**, p. 113a.

Strikes: Sulūk **56**, II, 74b, 170a, 189a, 203a, III, 37a; **187**, II, 392, 414; Iyās **169**, IV, 16, 243, 305, 327; Ḥimṣī **30**, yr. 907; 'Aynī **3**, I, 100a; **4**, p. 108b; **59**, p. 248; **69**, p. 90; Ṭūlūn **181**, pp. 30, 84.

An example of how common action could spread in the suqs without guilds occurred in the 880's/1475–85. To celebrate removal of a tax, some craftsmen decorated their shops and gradually the rest of the markets followed suit until the Sultan ordered the decorations removed. (**54**, p. 85b.)

Initiative of the governor: **125**, II, 433; Kathīr **176**, XIV, 243-44; Iyās **169**, I, 195-96.

2. Sulūk **56**, II, 150b-151a, III, 60a-62b; **73**, p. 362a; Iyās **169**, II, 31; Ḥawādith **179**, pp. 47, 88-89; Sakhāwī **197**, pp. 259-61; Nujūm **180**, VII, 175-79, 195; **42**, II, 494b; Inbā' **26**, II, 57b-68a; Duqmāq **20**, p. 99b; Ṣaṣra **177**, p. 15a.
3. Iyās **169**, I, 150; Inbā' **26**, II, 211a, III, 14a; Jawharī **46**, p. 159a; Bāsiṭ **1**, I, 99a; Sulūk **56**, II, 32b, 63b; Furāt **166**, IX, 387, 439.
4. Kutubī **39**, pp. 74b, 116b; **54**, pp. 7a, 67a, 71a; **73**, p. 310a; **125**, III, 55; Ḥawādith **179**, p. 685; Jawharī **45**, pp. 12a, 190a-b; **46**, p. 51b; Sulūk **56**, II, 151a, 154a, III, 60a; **187**, II, 758; Furāt **166**, IX, 459; Nujūm **180**, VI, 594; Ṭūlūn **181**, p. 84.
5. Ibn al-Nashū: Iyās **169**, I, 307; **2**, yr. 798; Duqmāq **20**, pp. 72a-b; **21**, I, 142a-b; Inbā' **26**, III, 142a; Furāt **166**, IX, 462; Ṣaṣra **177**, pp. 207a-209b; **539**. Year 843: Jawharī **46**, pp. 190a-b; **53**, pp. 94b-95a. Others: Ḥimṣī **29**, pp. 66b, 108b, 145b; Sulūk **187**, II, 5-6.
6. Furāt **166**, IX, 387, 439.
7. Tax protests: Sulūk **187**, II, 420; 'Aynī **4**, p. 124a; Bāsiṭ **1**, I, 37b; Inbā' **26**, III, 49a; Ḥawādith **179**, pp. 531-32.
8. Year 770: Iyās **169**, I, 226; Bāsiṭ **1**, I, 88b; 'Aynī **3**, I, 88b; **9**, p. 51b; **43**, p. 105. Year 800: Iyās **169**, I, 308. Other: Inbā' **26**, II, 225b; Jawharī **45**, p. 144a; **46**, p. 192b.
9. Bāsiṭ **1**, I, 19a, 62b; **9**, p. 3b; Duqmāq **20**, p. 53a; **69**, p. 75; **70**, pp. 356b, 392b; Iyās **169**, I, 187-88, 218, II, 210, 258; Sibṭ **123**, p. 34; Ḥawādith **179**, pp. 166, 231; Sakhāwī **197**, p. 428.
10. Inbā' **26**, II, 249b; **69**, p. 64; Iyās **169**, II, 160; Ḥimṣī **29**, 88a, 104b, 109a; Ṭūlūn **181**, pp. 62, 70, 82, 95, 126-27, 154, 178.
11. Year 852: **125**, III, 46; **69**, p. 35; Ḥawādith **179**, p. 28; Sakhāwī **197**, p. 200. Year 860: Ḥawādith **179**, p. 275; **69**, p. 88. Year 885: Ṭūlūn **181**, p. 24; **183**, p. 169; Ḥimṣī **29**, p. 84a; **125**, III, 86.
12. Tripoli: Duqmāq **20**, pp. 123a-b; Inbā' **26**, II, 82a; Jawharī **46**, p. 97b. Aleppo: Ḥimṣī **29**, p. 173a; 'Ulaymī **57**, p. 219a.
13. Damascus: Ṭūlūn **181**, pp. 41, 71, 124-25, 147; Ḥimṣī **29**, pp. 103b, 107a, 108b, 150a, 151b, 161b-162a, 168a, 171b-173a, 174a-b; **194**, p. 154.
14. Tripoli: Inbā' **26**, III, 162b-163a; Nujūm **180**, VI, 21-22; Duqmāq **21**, I, 206b; **68**, p. 89b; Sulūk **56**, II, 174b.
15. Kerak: Furāt **166**, IX, 462. Damascus: Nujūm **180**, VI, 92; Iyās **169**, I, 341. Hama: **192**. Aleppo: Jawharī **46**, p. 89a. Hama in 848: Jawharī **46**, p. 204b.
16. Year 882: Iyās **169**, II, 174. Year 896: Ṭūlūn **181**, p. 141, 143, 151; Iyās **169**, II, 272; **125**, III, 104. Year 898: Iyās **169**, II, 279. Year 900: 'Ulaymī **57**, pp. 220a-b; Ḥimṣī **29**, p. 187a. Kerak: Iyās **169**, IV, 94. Aleppo in 921: Iyās **169**, V, 73-74. For further discussion of rebellions see notes 18-30 on *zu'ar* below.
17. Kutubī **38**, pp. 187b-188b; 'Aynī **3**, I, 20b, II, 75a-76b; Jazarī **48**, pp. 62-64; **59**, p. 256; Shuhba **34**, yr. 727; Baṭṭūṭa **141**, I, pp. 45-46; Dawādārī **152**, p. 342; **464**, pp. 229-32.

Similarly in 843/1439–40 a rebellion occurred in Damietta when the common people, outraged at the satisfaction of local Christians with the loss of Muslim raiding ships, attacked and plundered the local church. The Sultan promptly held the notables and merchants responsible for the payment of fines. Most of the people fled, and the Sultan was later persuaded to relent. (Jawharī **46**, p. 189a.)

18. **497**; **498**.

At the very beginning of the Mamluk period the breakdown of order in Aleppo in the wake of the Mongol occupation gave the *ahdāth* and *shuṭṭār* an opportunity to plunder the city. (Yūnīnī **202**, I, 440; Kathīr **176**, XIII, 230-31; **125**, II, 302; **189**, XII, 422.) The *shuṭṭār* are identified elsewhere as young men's hunting associations of the *futuwwa* type. (**547**.)

19. Ṭūlūn **181**, pp. 166, 186, 191, 195, 204, 238-39, 251-52, 268, 270, 283, 293, 316; Ṭūlūn **183**, pp. 153-57; Ṭūlūn **185**, pp. 85, 95, 113, 121.
20. Ṭūlūn **181**, pp. 121, 204, 316. For other names of quarters see other references to *zu'ar*. Al-Suwayqa as given in Ibn Ṭūlūn should be al-Shuwayka. (Ṣaṣra **177**, p. 34(46)b.)
21. Ṭūlūn **181**, pp. 180, 196, 219, 225, 251-52, 259, 262, 280, 283, 295, 315; Ṭūlūn **185**, pp. 51-52, 89-91, 108, 110, 114, 116.
22. Ṭūlūn **181**, pp. 204, 332.
23. Ṭūlūn **181**, pp. 160, 168, 176, 181-82, 221, 279-80, 283; Murders of *bal-lāsiyya* (tax collectors) not specifically attributed to the *zu'ar* are mentioned: Ṭūlūn **185**, passim.
24. Ṭūlūn **181**, pp. 250-52, 259-61, 283; Ṭūlūn **185**, pp. 82, 84-85, 89-91; **19**, p. 214a; Iyās **169**, IV, 23.
25. Ṭūlūn **181**, pp. 92-93, 179-80, 182-84, 232, 238.
26. Ṭūlūn **181**, pp. 153, 177, 186, 191, 195, 204, 238-39, 265, 280-81, 287; Ṭūlūn **183**, pp. 132, 134, 153-57; Ṭūlūn **185**, pp. 34, 43-44, 107-08, 110, 146; Iyās **169**, V, 84.
27. Ṭūlūn **181**, pp. 280, 293, 316; Ṭūlūn **185**, pp. 113, 121.
28. Ṭūlūn **181**, pp. 92, 120-21, 123, 141, 185, 212, 225, 235, 250-51, 262, 268, 277-78, 283-84, 286, 316, 330; Ṭūlūn **183**, pp. 119, 147; Ṭūlūn **185**, pp. 51-52, 64-65, 172.
29. Ṭūlūn **181**, pp. 185-86, 189, 191, 194-95, 199-200, 283-86; Ṭūlūn **183**, pp. 145, 153-57; Ṭūlūn **185**, pp. 39-42, 103-04.
30. Ṭūlūn **181**, pp. 204, 207, 232, 252, 269, 278-79, 295; Ṭūlūn **185**, pp. 85, 96, 113-14, 116.
31. Repression: Ṭūlūn **181**, pp. 196-97, 202, 204, 213, 219-20, 233, 259, 268, 284, 298-300, 314, 315, 331; Ṭūlūn **183**, pp. 142-43; Ṭūlūn **185**, pp. 39-42, 56, 104, 115-16, 119-20.
32. Thirteenth century: **64**, p. 173b; **101**, III, 158-59; **8**, p. 200a; **19**, p. 99a; Dhahabī **13**, II, 65b; Furāt **166**, VII, 216; Yūnīnī **80**, III, 194a; Dawādārī **152**, p. 35; Kathīr **176**, XIV, 6, 15, 22-23; **189**, XIV, 664-65; Birzālī **10**, II, 93a-b; **154**, p. 381. Organization: Kutubī **37**, II, 243; **38**, p. 36a; Quatremère **188**, II_2, **171**; 'Aynī **4**, p. 171b; Yūnīnī **80**, III, 167a; Birzālī **10**, II, 30b; Kathīr **176**, XIV, 12; Sulūk **187**, I, 903; **536**, p. 109. Alexandria: Sulūk **56**, II, 9b. Year 803: Duqmāq **20**, p. 85b; **21**, I, 212a-b; **22**, p. 174b-175a; **73**, p. 325a; **101**, III, 208; Nujūm **180**, VI, 50, 54; **195**, p. 314.
33. Sulūk **56**, II, 85a-b, 218a; Ṭūlūn **181**, pp. 94, 96-97, 344. Infantry taxes: See above, pp. 92-93; notes 18-31, above. Also **425**, XVI, 16-18.
34. Quatremère **188**, I_2, 9; Jazarī **186**, p. 1; **64**, p. 192a; **205**, p. 81; Kathīr **176**, XIV, 102; Inbā' **26**, II, 244a, 266b, III, 72a; Jawharī **46**, p. 189a; Sakhāwī **197**, pp. 63, 88. Volunteers were called *mutaṭawwi'ūn*.

35. Civil wars: Sulūk **56**, II, 15b, 18b, 19a, 30a, 66a, 75b; **187**, II, 588-89; Shuhba **35**, I, 17a; 'Aynī **3**, I, 51b, 84b; **4**, p. 179a; Bāsiṭ **1**, I, 81b-82a; **70**, pp. 395b, 398a-b; **9**, pp. 37b-38a; **73**, p. 262a; Inbā' **26**, III, 50b.
36. Cairo in 791–92: Sulūk **56**, II, 103b, 106b, 109b-110b, 115a, 120b-121a, 125a; 'Aynī **3**, I, 150b-151a, 158b, 174b-175a; Jawharī **46**, pp. 22a, 26b, 33a; Inbā' **26**, III, 104a; Furāt **166**, IX, 82, 88, 116, 191-92; Nujūm **180**, V, 461-66. The populace of Kerak also assisted Sultan Barqūq. (Ṣaṣra **177**, p. 25 (37)b; Sulūk **56**, II, 114b, 167b.)
37. Damascus: Ṣaṣra **177**, pp. 8(20)b, 24(36)b, 27(39)a-28(40)a, 30(42) b, 32(44)b, 33(45)b, 35(5)a, 42(12)a, 49(15)b, 51b, 63b, 76b, 77a, 78b, 82b-83a, 84b, 87a, 89a, 91a, 100a-b, 131a-b, 143a, 157a; 'Aynī **3**, I, 164a-b, 176a, 184b, 191b-192a; Iyās **169**, I, 282-83, 287, 292-94; Jawharī **46**, pp. 32b, 35b; Ḥabīb **24**, p. 264a; **25**, pp. 127, 133, 137; Inbā' **26**, III, 99a; Duqmāq **21**, I, 197a; **73**, p. 293b; Nujūm **180**, V, 483; Furāt **166**, IX, 218, 255; **265**, pp. 155-56.

Aleppo: Furāt **166**, IX, 170-71, 215; 'Aynī **3**, I, 165a, 180a-b; Jawharī **46**, pp. 18b, 28b; Sulūk **56**, II, 113b-114a, 118a, 124b-125a; Sibṭ **123**, pp. 170-71; **125**, II, 469-70; Nujūm **180**, V, 479, 507-08, 526-27.
38. Nujūm **180**, VI, 181, 207-08, 305-06, VII, 66-68, 95-96; Jawharī **46**, p. 83a, 173a, 183b; Inbā' **26**, II, 235b-236a; **72**, p. 65a; **125**, III, 35-38; Sulūk **56**, III, 92b.
39. Bribes: Yūnīnī **80**, III, 80a; Nujūm **180**, VII, 46-48; Ṭūlūn **185**, p. 59. Agitation: 'Aynī **4**, p. 100a; Iyās **169**, I, 150; **59**, p. 223; Sulūk **187**, II, 71; Bāsiṭ **1**, I, 116a; Inbā' **26**, I, 14b, II, 102b; Jawharī **46**, p. 176b; **54**, p. 43a; Nujūm **180**, V, 10.
40. Tax remissions: Nujūm **180**, V, 42; Furāt **166**, IX, 60, 71-72, 85; Inbā' **26**, II, 29b, III, 96a; Jawharī **46**, pp. 19b, 22a-b. Good will: Sibṭ **123**, pp. 33-34; Sulūk **56**, III, 49a; Ḥawādith **179**, p. 404.
41. Thirteenth century: Birzālī **10**, I, 46a. Year 742: 'Aynī **3**, I, 40b; **59**, pp. 385-86; Shuhba **35**, I, 22a; Sulūk **187**, II, 591-95, 598-99; **70**, p. 346b; Iyās **169**, I, 178. Other fourteenth century: Kutubī **39**, p. 89b; **70**, pp. 368b-369a, 380a, 399b; Sulūk **56**, I, 235b, II, 16a, 17a, 65b; Iyās **169**, I, 208, 224, 246; **18**, pp. 170b, 171b, 176b; Bāsiṭ **1**, I, 83b, 84b, 121a; Inbā' **26**, III, 53b; Duqmāq **21**, I, 184b; **73**, pp. 275a-b; Nujūm **180**, V, 319. Post 790 civil wars: Iyās **169**, I, 286, 311, 320, 338; Inbā' **26**, III, 145b; Jawharī **46**, p. 67b; **73**, p. 335b; Sulūk **56**, II, 122a, 160a; Ṣaṣra **177**, pp. 13(25)a, 117a. Fifteenth century; Nujūm **180**, VII, 139, 845; **73**, p. 378b; Iyās **31**, pp. 239b, 252b.
42. In 658/1260, in Damascus, Muslims took revenge on the Christian community for insults and abuse against Islam during the Mongol occupation. The Christians had paraded the cross and defiled Muslim holy places, and in retaliation their churches were burned. The Jews, who were at first subject to looting, were later protected because they had not in fact betrayed the Muslims. This deep suspiciousness and Muslim fear that the Christians meant to betray them to the enemy was the cause of many similar reactions. (Dhahabī **153**, II, 125; Kutubī **37**, II, 183-84; **8**, p. 173b; Kathīr **176**, XIII, 219, 221-22; Quatremère **188**, I_1, 98-99, 106-07; Yūnīnī **202**, I, 362-63; **149**, III, 204-05; 'Aynī **150**, pp. 215-16.)

The mere existence of churches and synagogues often offended Muslim sensibilities. In 718/1318, in Cairo, despite permission given by the Sultan to build a church, neighborhood Muslims protested and tore it down. (Sulūk **187**, II, 182-83.) In 721/1321 one of the most extensive outbursts of communal violence in the Mamluk period took place. Construction workers in Cairo were obliged to stop at a church. Resentment over the obstruction led a mob to tear it down, and word then went round for a general attack on churches. The assaults spread to all of Egypt. Soon after, large fires broke out in Cairo for which the Christians were responsible, and the mobs demanded action against them. The government sought to disperse the crowds and executed a few rioters as an example, but popular insistence forced the Sultan to yield and declare it lawful for the crowds to kill or rob Christians. The usual discriminatory measures about dress, riding, and employment were revived. The Christians had no recourse but to hide, convert, or pass as Jews. (Sulūk **187**, II, 215-227; Ḥabīb **23**, p. 163b; **59**, p. 248.) Other episodes of this sort: Sulūk **187**, II, 900, 925-26; Bāsiṭ **1**, I, 48b; Dhahabī **13**, II, 8b-9a; Yūnīnī **78**, p. 185a; Kutubī **37**, II, 5. Quarrels resulting in violence: Jazarī **47**, p. 120b; **186**, pp. 34-35; **54**, p. 100b-101a; Jawharī **45**, p. 168b. Attacks on foreigners: Sulūk **56**, II, 84a; Nujūm **180**, VII, 139-40.

43. Year 753: Sulūk **187**, II, 873-74; Nujūm **180**, V, 124-25; Kutubī **39**, p. 120a. Aleppo: **52**, p. 31a; note 37, above. Damascus: Nujūm **180**, VII, 93-94.

44. *Al-mansīr* and *al-ḥarāmiyya,* organization: Jazarī **186**, p. 51; Yūnīnī **80**, III, 82a; Kutubī **37**, I, 133; Sulūk **56**, II, 90b, III, 73a; **187**, II, 644; 'Aynī **3**, I, 136a; Inbā' **26**, III, 83b; Duqmāq **20**, pp. 120b-121a; **2**, p. 6; Ṭūlūn **181**, pp. 35, 66, 126-27, 344; Iyās **169**, IV, 108-09.

At the end of the thirteenth century, Damascus suffered from thefts, assaults, and murders attributed to *al-ḥarāmiyya.* (Birzālī **10**, I, 137b, 149b, 235b, 248a-b; Jazarī **186**, pp. 24-25; **47**, p. 173b.) *Al-mansīr* and *al-ḥarāmiyya* again came to the fore in the civil wars after 790. (Jawharī **46**, p. 21b; Furāt **166**, IX, 124, 131; 'Aynī **3**, I, 160a; Iyās **166**, I, 324; **73**, p. 321a.) References to *al-ḥarāmiyya* for most of the fifteenth century are sporadic. (Jawharī **46**, pp. 144b, 180b; Ḥawādith **179**, p. 334; **62**, p. 51b.) A great outburst of banditry came after 890/1485. For almost three decades Cairo was at the mercy of *al-mansīr.* (Iyās **169**, II, 229, 236, 287, 294, 316, 320, 336, IV, 20, 51, 86, 126, 279-80; **31**, p. 249a; **54**, p. 210a; **73**, p. 412b; Ḥimṣī **30**, yrs. 905, 907.) Damascus was equally plagued by *al-ḥarāmiyya* and other thieves. (Ṭūlūn **181**, pp. 27, 49, 66, 68, 84, 105, 115, 126, 132, 134, 161, 174, 232, 255, 281, 284, 288, 314, 344, 348, 350, 374, 385, 389; Ṭūlūn **185**, pp. 34, 68, 102, 119.)

Al-ḥarāmiyya also meant pirates. ('Aynī **4**, p. 150a; **371**, pp. 315, 348.)

45. Slaves in 1260: Quatremère **188**, I_1, 122-23, 129; **557**, p. 272. Slave state: Iyās **169**, II, 28; Sakhāwī **66**, I, yr. 849; **197**, p. 126; Jawharī **46**, pp. 207a-b; Ḥawādith **179**, pp. 19-20. Other slave gangs: Iyās **169**, II, 265.

46. Slave riots: Fourteenth century: Jazarī **46**, pp. 240-41; Bāsiṭ **1**, I, 52b; Inbā' **26**, III, 80a; Iyās **169**, I, 278. Fifteenth century: Nujūm **180**,

VI, 594; Sakhāwī **66**, I, yrs. 848, 860, II, 9b, 111b; **197**, p. 220; Ḥawādith **179**, pp. 251, 253, 330, 650; **62**, p. 69b; **54**, p. 43a; Iyās **169**, II, 220, 230, IV, 17; **171**, p. 32; Ḥimṣī **30**, yr. 903; **52**, p. 182a; Jawharī **46**, p. 167b; Bāsiṭ **1**, II, 4a; **557**, p. 272.

47. 'Aynī **3**, II, 100a-b; Sulūk **187**, II, 392; Nujūm **180**, VII, 526-27.

48. Tax farms before 775: Duqmāq **21**, I, 100b-101a; Quatremère **188**, I_2, 4-6, II_1, 8; Dhahabī **13**, II, 9a; Furāt **166**, VII, 158-59; Nuwayrī **61**, III, 34b; Birzālī **10**, I, 94b, 176a, II, 140b, 268a; Jazarī **47**, pp. 31b-32a; **186**, p. 9; Kathīr **176**, XIV, 10; **8**, p. 236b; Sulūk **187**, II, 211, 622, 640-42; **59**, p. 248, 289; 'Aynī **4**, pp. 150a, 180b; Bāsiṭ **1**, I, 2a-b. A spate of abolitions came in 775, 782, and 791. (**73**, pp. 235a, 265b; **70**, pp. 343b, 407b-408a; Inbā' **26**, III, 13b, 56a; Bāsiṭ **1**, I, 98b, 110a, 126a; Duqmāq **20**, p. 55a; **21**, I, 175a; **18**, p. 173b; 'Aynī **3**, I, 102b, 120a; Furāt **166**, IX, 85; Sulūk **56**, II, 40b-41a.) Fifteenth century: Qalqashandī **84**, XIII, 117; Khiṭaṭ **116**, I, 89; Inbā' **26**, II, 129b, 159a; **54**, p. 89b, 94b; Décrets **223**, XII, 23-24. Singing girls used to receive the governor of Damascus. (See above, p. 83 and note 10.)

49. Nujūm **180**, V, 7; Iyās **169**, I, 286, II, 244, IV, 96; Inbā' **26**, III, 175b; Sulūk **56**, II, 191a.

50. Before 791: Sulūk **56**, II, 22b, 109a; **70**, pp. 380a, 395b, 398a-b; Iyās **169**, I, 220-21, 223, 230, 247; **73**, p. 262a; Inbā' **26**, III, 48b, 53b. Events of 791-92: Sulūk **56**, II, 101a, 102a, 103a-105b, 110b, 111b-112a; Furāt **166**, IX, 66, 80, 83-84, 89-93, 102, 118, 124, 131, 134, 193; Jawharī **46**, pp. 20a-b, 21b-22b, 25b, 27a-b, 33a; Nujūm **180**, V, 401, 405, 410, 417; 'Aynī **3**, I, 152a, 160a; Iyās **169**, I, 278, 286; Inbā' **26**, III, 98a-b.

51. Until 842: Jawharī **46**, pp. 56a, 176a, 180b; **73**, p. 321a; Iyās **169**, I, 320; Nujūm **180**, VI, 19-20, 235, 238, 642, VII, 46, 48; Inbā' **26**, II, 233a. Late fifteenth century: Ḥawādith **179**, p. 277; Sakhāwī **197**, p. 322; **54**, p. 43a; Iyās **169**, II, 220, 230, 244, IV, 17, 96.

52. Al-Ḥusayniyya: Khiṭaṭ **116**, II, 20-22; Nujūm **180**, VII, 534. Al-Ṣalībiyya: 'Aynī **3**, I, 69a.

53. Furāt **166**, IX, 213; Nujūm **180**, VII, glossary, xxx.

54. Sulūk **56**, II, 22b.

55. **8**, p. 251a; 'Aynī **4**, p. 121a; Khiṭaṭ **116**, II, 32, 167; 'Ulaymī **190**, II, 637. Professor Brinner's study of the *ḥarāfīsh* is the basis of this discussion. (**539**.)

56. Iyās **169**, I, 99, 103-04, 229, II, 262, IV, 141; Duqmāq **20**, p. 54b; **21**, I, 100a, 174b; Baṭṭūṭa **141**, I, 86, IV, 318; Dawādārī **152**, p. 361; Fidā' **149**, IV, 151; Kutubī **39**, p. 91a; **64**, p. 216a; Subkī **135**, p. 212; **18**, p. 173a; **70**, p. 406b; **9**, p. 86b; 'Aynī **3**, I, 98a; **73**, p. 265b; Sulūk **56**, II, 34b; Nujūm **180**, VI, 763-64; Jawharī **46**, p. 168b; Sakhāwī **197**, pp. 183-84.

57. Iyās **169**, I, 92; 'Aynī **3**, II, 116b; **4**, pp. 114b, 121a; Yūnīnī **80**, II, 78b; Khiṭaṭ **116**, II, 149, 166-69; Sulūk **187**, II, 396; Sakhāwī **197**, p. 349; **95**, V, 20; Ṭūlūn **181**, p. 88.

58. Kutubī **37**, II, 291; **39**, pp. 84a-b, 91a; Yūnīnī **79**, p. 110b; **80**, III, 160b, 161b; Birzālī **10**, I, 98a, II, 6b, 8b; **64**, p. 216a; **205**, p. 74; Kathīr **176**, XIV, 7, 24; Dhahabī **14**, p. 129a; Jazarī **48**, pp. 639-40; **49**, p. 103a; Fidā' **149**, IV, 151; Baṭṭūṭa **141**, IV, 318.

59. Kathīr **176**, XIV, 98-99; Shuhba **34**, yr. 721; Kutubī **38**, p. 142a; Sulūk **187**, II, 396; Khiṭaṭ **116**, II, 32.
60. Yūnīnī **80**, III, 129a; Kathīr **176**, XIV, 260; **205**, p. 44; Dawādārī **152**, pp. 187-88; Duqmāq **21**, I, 126b; Baṭṭūṭa **141**, I, 86; 'Aynī **4**, p. 151a.
61. Yūnīnī **202**, I, 491; **79**, p. 110a; Jazarī **49**, p. 103a; Birzālī **10**, I, 98a; Quatremère **188**, I_2, 196; Kutubī **37**, II, 291; 'Aynī **4**, p. 114b; **64**, p. 211a; Duqmāq **21**, I, 150a; Fidā' **149**, IV, 136; Sulūk **187**, II, 577; Shuhba **35**, I, 21b; **8**, p. 251a.
62. Baṭṭūṭa **141**, I, 86; Furāt **166**, IX, 240; Ṣaṣra **177**, p. 7(19)a; **95**, V, 20; Sakhāwī **197**, pp. 146, 349; Nujūm **180**, VI, 763-64, VII, 813-14; Jawharī **46**, p. 168b; Ḥimṣī **29**, p. 103a-b; Iyās **169**, IV, 43-44; Ṭūlūn **181**, p. 114.
63. 'Ulaymī **190**, II, 624; Tūlūn **181**, p. 114. Cf. **547** on women dervishes.
64. Kathīr **176**, XIII, 314; **95**, V, 20; Sakhāwī **197**, p. 349.
65. Sakhāwī **197**, p. 349; Nujūm **180**, VII, 813-14; 'Ulaymī **190**, II, 624; Ḥimṣī **29**, pp. 103a-b.
66. **95**, XI, 3; Ṭūlūn **181**, p. 200; Sulūk **56**, II, 8b, 10b; **539**, p. 206; Birzālī **10**, II, 216a.
67. Ṣaṣra **177**, p. 7(19)a; Nujūm **180**, VII, 763-64; Jawharī **46**, p. 168b; Ṭūlūn **181**, pp. 15, 207, 211; Iyās **169**, IV, 43-44.
68. **242**, p. 51; **245**, p. 124; Quatremère **188**, I_2, 194.

INDEX

Abbasid Empire, 5-6, 266
'Abd-allāh (sheikh), 102, 180-81
'Abīd, 171-72, 270. *See also* Slaves
Abū Bakr, *kabīr* of *zu'ar,* 173
Abū Bakr ibn al-Mubārak, 155, 157
Abū Ṭāqiyya, 155, 157, 161
Abyssinia, 212, 284
Acre, 11, 16, 24, 41, 65, 123, 244, 249, 282
Al-'Ādaliyya Madrasa, 75, 250
Adana, 32, 38, 159
Aden, 121, 127
Administration, *see* Governor; Mamluk emirs; Mamluk Empire; Sultan
Aegean Islands, 27, 35, 41
Africa, North, 41, 247, 268, 276
Agriculture, *see* Egypt; Syria
Aḥdāth, 154, 290
Ahl al-aswāq, 267
Ahl al-za'āra, 154
Ahl-du' 'ār, 270
Ahl-fasād, 270
Ain Jalut, 11
Aintab, 32, 249-50
Ajlūn, 271
Akhṭāṭ, see Khuṭṭ
Ak Koyunlu, 27, 32, 34, 36, 249
Akrād, 197
Albistān, 21, 32
Aleppo: administrative center, 28-29, 248; Arab and Turkoman quarters, 86, 272; Armenians, 86; bedouin damage, 21, 39, 251, 254; bridges, 260; communal feuds, 88-89; construction, 15, 22, 29, 60, 62, 207-10, 259; defense, 32, 34, 36, 38, 91; destruction of villages, 251; fortifications, 14-15, 38, 62-64, 71, 167, 251, 260; governor, 89, 152, 245; grand mosque, 71, 168; *ḥarāfīsh,* 177, 179; *ḥarrānī,* 272; hospital, 22, 76, 196, 208-10; Jewish quarter, 89-90; khans, 38, 197, 254; Kurds, 272; madrasas, 196-98, 207-10; Mālikī qadi, 104; Mamluk tax abuses, 40, 152, 254; Mamluk civil wars, 21, 26, 28, 36, 42, 89, 141, 151, 166-67, 169, 251, 291-92; Mamluk protocol, 20, 249; marble source, 68; merchants, 42, 89, 211, 214-16; military auxiliaries, 163-64; military base, 12, 15, 20-21, 70, 248; mob violence in civil wars, 28, 42; Mongol invasions, 14-15, 26, 91, 163-64, 290; mosques, 14, 22, 196-98, 207-10, 215; notables, 15; populace intercedes for emir, 168; population size, 79, 264; products, 19, 33, 41, 57, 86, 246-47, 252; qadis, 133, 136, 287; *qayṣariyyas,* 197-98; quarters, 22, 38, 71, 85-89, 92, 150, 152, 271-72; rebellions, 152, 248, 289; refugees, 84, 91, 132; *shalāq,* 89, 176-77, 272; Sufi convents, 15, 22, 37, 197-98, 207, 209-10; Tatar invasion, 9, 249; taxation, 93, 96, 100; trade, 18, 25, 33-34, 41, 246, 253-55, 283; Turkoman attacks, 28, 32, 36, 249; waqf endowments, 29, 37-38, 74, 76, 195-98; water works, 15, 38, 70-71, 260, 262. *See also* Bānaqūsā; al-Ḥawrānī
Alexandretta, Gulf of, 261
Alexandria: bridge, 246; condition of city, 248-49; confiscations, 118, 122; crusade against, 24, 250; defense, 35, 164, 248-49; European merchants, 23, 152; governor, 152-53; Greek consul, 247; international trade, 23-24, 27, 41, 127, 172; *kārimī,* 122, 125, 211; merchants, 119, 216; monopolies, 275; rebellion, 152-53; silk industry, 153, 252; Sultan's trading, 122, 284; *zu'ar,* 173
'Alī al-Kīlānī, 127, 283
'Alī al-Ḥarīrī, 102
'Alī ibn Sharbāsh, 161
Ambassadors, 123, 169, 213, 216, 282
'Āmil al-matjar, 282
Amīn, 160, 285
Amīr 'Alī, 180
al-'Āmma, 80, 82-84, 174-75, 264-67
'Ammālūn, 276
Anatolia, 11, 19, 21, 27, 33-35, 38, 41-42, 67, 124, 255, 283
Antioch, 28, 167, 179
Aqbirdī, Emir, 88, 160

Arabia, 25
Arabs, 88, 90, 272. *See also* Bedouins
'Arāḍa, 159
Arādhil al-'āmma, 83, 269, 299
Arbāb al-ma'āyish, 267-68
Arbāb al-sanā'i', 268
Arghūn Shāh, 122
'Arīfs, see Markets; Quarters; Working people
Arikmās, Emir, 160-61
Armenia, 11-12, 15, 19-20, 23-24, 123, 134, 164, 248, 282
al-Arminī, Tāj al-dīn, 121, 281
Army, *see* Mamluk Empire
Arsenals, 42, 65
Arsūf, 16
Artisans, *see* Working people
'Aṣab, 272
Asandamūr, Sayf al-dīn, 73, 245
Ascalon, 16, 245
Aṣḥāb al-arbā', 83-84, 270
Aṣḥāb al-sanā'i', 268
Ashrafiyya, 91
al-Ashrāf Khalīl, Sultan, 244
'Athlīth, 16
Auxiliaries, military, 164-70, 173-75, 251, 292. *See also* Mamluk Empire, army
al-'Awāmm, see al-'Āmma
A'wān, 279
Awbāsh, 83, 154, 175, 181, 269-70
Awlād al-nās, 69, 116, 265. *See also* Mamluk emirs, families
Awrāq, 282
al-A'yān, 80-81, 97, 212, 214-16, 264-65, 274-75. *See also* Notables
al-'Ayāq, 270
Ayyūbids, 9, 11, 13, 20, 128, 136, 246, 256
al-Azhar, 213

al-Bā'a, 82, 267
Ba'ādhīn, 68
Baalbek, 17, 19, 34, 84, 90, 99-100, 246-47, 252
Bāb al-Barīd, 262
Bāb al-Farādis, 263
Bāb al-Ḥadīd, 263
Bāb al-Jābiya, 28, 154-55, 262-63
Bāb al-Lūq, 95, 176
Bāb al-Muṣallā, 154
Bāb al-Naṣr, 176, 262-63
Bāb al-Sa'āda, 250
Bāb al-Salāma, 28, 262
Bāb al-Shāqhūr, 28, 157
Bāb Kaysān, 251
Badr al-dīn Ḥasan, 97, 285
Bagdad, 6, 134, 211-12, 246-47
Bahasna, 248
al-Baḥrī, 251
Balaṭūnūs, 71
Ballāsiyya, 290
Banāqisa, 89, 167. *See also* Bānaqūsā
Bānaqūsā, 85, 88-89, 152, 166-67, 169, 272
Bāniyās River, 62, 70, 246
Banking, 120-22, 281-82. *See also Ṣayrafī*
Banū Bābiyya, 91
Banū Hārit, 272
Banū Sa'd, 272
Banū Zayd, 87, 272
Baradā River, 62, 70
Bardbak, 71
Bārīn, 272
Barqūq, Sultan, 26, 71, 88-89, 121, 151, 165-67, 174, 176, 212-13, 246, 266, 282, 291
Barsbāy, Sultan, 9, 32, 36-37, 52-53, 57, 96, 126, 257-58
Bashkīr, 87, 272
Baybars, Sultan, 13-14, 32, 55, 71, 140, 168, 178, 244
Baybars II, 180
Baysān, 246
Bayt Jibrīn, 272
Bedouins: attacked by Mamluk forces, 58, 93, 159, 164; chiefs fear *zu'ar,* 158; factions, 89; hostilities with townspeople, 169-70; Mamluk army auxiliaries, 169; migrants to cities, 84; quarters in cities, 86-87, 272; raiding, 21, 25, 28, 32, 36, 39, 60, 88, 90, 244, 248, 251, 254; taxation, 39; trade, 100, 124, 214. *See also* Egypt; Syria
Beggars, 55, 64, 106, 164, 167, 169, 178, 182, 190, 271. *See also Ḥarāfīsh*
Beirut: bridges, 246; constructions, 249; crusade against, 250; defense, 16, 35; fortifications, 25; grain trade, 52; khan, 249; palaces of emirs, 73; postal route, 12; property of Tankiz, 50; quarters, 73; taxation, 99; trade, 18, 24, 27, 41; water works, 71, 249
Berke, Khan, 244
Bint Mālik Ashraf, 260
al-Biqā', 39, 272
Black Sea, 19, 23-24, 41, 247
Boucicaut, 27, 250

Bridges, 18, 65, 72, 246, 260
Brokers, 36, 52, 58, 82, 100, 117-19, 154, 212, 244, 268, 275, 280-81, 284
Broquière, Bertrandon de la, 29, 251-52
Būlāq, 101, 273
Bureaucracy, *see* Mamluk Empire, administration
Bursa, 41-42, 264
Byzantine Empire, 5, 98, 123, 247, 257, 282

Cadastre, 16, 245
Caesarea, 16
Cairo: beggars, 164; butchers, 58; canals, 62, 178-79; churches, 292; citadel, 61, 145-46, 148, 176; communal feuds, 101; constructions, 60, 65; criminal gangs, 171, 292; governor, 148, 172-74; grain, 16-17, 28, 39-40, 53-54, 101, 179; *ḥarāfīsh,* 177-79, 181; hospital, 286; labor pool, 65, 74; lumpenproletarians, 270-71; madrasa, 195; Mamluk army, 37, 44, 149, 153, 179, 183; Mamluk civil wars, 20-21, 26, 28, 37, 94, 165, 167-68, 248, 291; Mamluk plundering, 37, 273; markets, 18, 34; merchants, 42, 118, 125; mob violence, 20-21, 28, 168, 173-75; palaces, 73, 249; police, 83-84, 270; population characteristics, 79, 150; products, 30; qadis, 113, 136-37, 287; *qayṣariyyas,* 195, 252; quarters, 73, 85, 87, 91-92, 94-95, 174-76, 271-74; refugees, 244; riots and protests, 91, 113, 145-49, 172, 175, 254; *shalāq,* 176-77; slave gangs, 171-72; Syrian towns compared, 150, 153; taxation, 53, 56, 58, 97, 99-100, 118, 172; trade, 18-19, 24, 28, 30, 39, 53, 246; waqfs, 76, 195; *zu'ar,* 173-77
Calcutta, 215, 284
Caliph, 5, 134, 266
Canals, *see* Water works
Caravansaries, 18, 124, 246. *See also* Khans
Catalans, 23-24, 27, 41
Caucasus, 41, 44, 122-23
Central Asia, 6, 23-24
Ceramics, 20, 33-34, 247, 253
Ceylon, 123, 283
China, 23, 96, 123, 126, 211, 246, 268-69
Christians: churches, 169, 179, 200, 288-89, 291-92; disputes with Muslims, 269, 289-92; officials, 46, 121; persecution, 124, 169, 292; quarters, 85-86; taxation, 288. *See also* Crusades; Europeans
Churches, *see* Christians
Cilician Armenia, *see* Armenia
Circassian Mamluks, 26, 44, 166, 187
Citadels, 13-15, 27, 50, 61-62, 64, 71-72, 87, 95, 132, 145-46, 148, 152, 158, 167, 176, 181, 199, 202, 204, 245, 250-51, 262, 270
Civil wars, *see* Mamluk emirs, civil wars
Clienteles, 89-92, 104-05, 107, 111, 113-14, 186-87, 260, 286. *See also* Mamluk emirs; Sultan; Ulama
Coinage, 17, 30-31, 40, 54, 118, 144-45, 150, 245, 254. *See also* Copper; Gold; Money; Silver
Commenda, 127, 283
Commissioners, administrative, *see Shādd*
Common people, *see al-'Āmma*; Mamluk Empire, army auxiliaries; Mob violence; Protests; Rebellions; Working people
Communes, vii, 1-4, 184, 187
Confiscations, 29, 61, 66, 74, 118, 122, 125, 140, 215-16, 244, 252, 259-60, 263, 268, 280
Conjuratio, 105
Constantinople, 272
Controller of Privy Purse, *see Nāẓir al-Khāṣṣ*
Copts, 213, 266
Corporations, 96. *See also* Guilds
Corvée, 64, 178-79, 260
Craftsmen, *see* Working people
Crete, 283
Crimea, 122-23
Criminals, 36, 83-84, 94, 105, 133, 158, 161, 169-72, 190, 254, 270, 292. *See also Zu'ar*
Crusades, 1, 9, 11-12, 16, 20, 23, 26-27, 249-50
Cyprus, 24, 27, 32, 34-35, 134, 164, 249-50, 252-53, 258

Dallāl, 212. *See also* Brokers
Ḍamān, 275-76
Damascus: administrative capital, 12; bedouin raids, 254; bridge, 246; citadel, 13, 27, 50, 64, 72, 132, 167, 181, 199, 202, 204, 245, 250-51, 262, 270; communal feuds, 39, 87-88, 151; construction, 14, 22, 29, 59-60, 73, 199-206, 258-59; criminal gangs, 161, 171, 292; damages in warfare, 9, 26-

28, 30, 249-51, 254; defenses, 15, 36, 163-64; gardens, 244; gates, 28, 154-55, 157, 250-51, 262-63; Ghūṭa, 39, 79, 91; governors, 50, 58, 61, 74, 76, 93, 118, 122, 132, 135-36, 140-41, 146, 151-52, 156, 159, 161, 166, 168, 173, 248, 250-51, 259, 293; grain, 53, 87, 195, 244-45, 257, 281; gypsies, 270; *ḥarāfīsh,* 177-82; hippodrome, 62, 260; hospital, 13, 96, 199, 250; Jews, 291; *kārimī,* 125, 211-13; khans, 50, 195, 258, 273; labor pool, 65; madrasas, 13, 67, 75, 181, 195-206, 214, 250, 261, 273; Mamluk abuses, 254; Mamluk civil wars, 12, 21, 26-28, 42, 141, 151, 165-70, 243, 291-92; Mamluk protocol, 249; markets, 14, 28, 50, 96, 163, 244, 250, 256, 274; merchants, 42, 119, 146; military auxiliaries, 134, 160, 163-64; military base, 12, 15, 20, 50, 91, 247; mob violence, 28, 42, 53, 146, 158, 168, 179; Mongol invasions, 13, 26-27, 131-33, 163-64, 179, 291; mosques, 13-14, 27, 38, 67, 151, 196-206, 250; *Nawrūz* holiday, 266; notables, 131; Ottoman invasion, 133, 159; peasants, 86-87; population size, 79, 264; products, 14, 17-20, 33, 60, 96, 246-47, 253, 258; public works, 29, 62; qadis, 136, 182, 287; Qays-Kalb disputes, 165; *qayṣariyyas,* 60, 195-98, 258-59, 282; quarters, 40, 70, 85-88, 92-94, 133, 150-51, 154-63, 271-72, 274 (*see also* al-Ṣāliḥiyya; al-Shāghūr; *etc.*); rebellions and protests, 36, 39, 42, 58, 113, 140, 146-49, 151-52, 156, 162, 166-67, 248, 255, 289; refugees, 13-14, 84, 86-87, 132-33; religious traditions, 14, 38; sanitation, 73, 270; sheikhs, 103, 133; street works, 22, 72, 259-60, 262-63; suburbs, 79; Sufi convents, 195, 197-206; Tamerlane's invasions, 9, 26-27, 30, 249; taxation, 13, 26-27, 40, 52, 56-58, 92-93, 96, 99-100, 140, 149, 244, 268; textiles, 14, 18-19, 33-34, 60, 102, 244, 247, 250, 253, 276; trade, 17-19, 24-25, 33, 39, 41, 52, 126, 136, 146, 244-46, 253, 255, 283; Umayyad Mosque, 27, 33, 60, 62, 74-76, 102-03, 113, 151, 203, 205, 250-51; waqfs, 29, 37, 73-76, 195-98, 273; water works, 19, 22, 27, 64, 70, 250, 259-60, 262; Yalbugha Mosque, 285; *zu'ar,* 42, 105, 143, 153-64, 173, 177

Damietta, 27, 35, 289-90
Ḍāmin, 100
Dāmiya, 246
Damūr River, 246
Dār al-Biṭṭīkh, 250
Dār al-Dhahab, 259
Dārayyā, 13, 79, 91, 132
Dārayyā Kubrā, 91
Darb, 271
Dāriya, 87
Dawādār, 215, 286
Dervishes, 105, 180-81, 294. *See also* Sufis
Dīnār, Ashrāfī, 32
Dīnār jaysh, 256
Dinars, 20-21, 30, 32, 50, 58, 64, 118, 172, 175, 199, 211-14, 216, 244, 256, 275
Dirhems, 30, 32, 50, 52, 54, 58, 64, 70, 76, 138-40, 151, 174, 179, 183, 199, 201, 211-12, 214, 244-45, 256, 259, 275-76, 281, 288
Dīwāns, see Mamluk Empire, administration
Diyār Kush, 28
Diyārbakr, 32-33, 244
Ducat, Venetian, 32
Dulghādir, 21, 32, 34, 38, 92, 169, 254-55, 283

Egypt: agriculture, 251; bedouins, 21, 28, 39, 251, 254; Christians, 292; grain, 18, 30-31, 34, 52, 246, 253; *kārimī,* 125, 211-13; Mamluk army, 158, 160-61, 163; Mamluk civil wars, 42, 151; pirate attacks, 35, 250; refugees, 84, 128, 271; slaves, 23, 123; taxation, 36, 39, 41; textiles, 18, 29, 42, 246; trade, 18, 23-24, 30, 33-35, 39, 41-42, 52, 67, 96, 123, 246-47, 254-55, 281. *See also* Alexandria; Cairo; Mamluk Empire
Eminent domain, 62, 140
Emirs, *see* Mamluk emirs
Endowments, *see* Waqfs
Euphrates, 32
Europe, Europeans: ambassadors, 169; artisans, 186; banking, 120; church, 186; cities, 1-3, 8, 25, 185-91; communes, 1-4, 190-91; conflicts with Muslims, 152; guilds, 97, 186; merchants, 3, 23-24, 41, 120-21, 123, 151-52, 186, 247, 281; nobility, 186; trade, 23, 35, 67, 119-20, 123, 126, 153, 188. *See also* Christians; Cru-

sades; Genoese; Italians; Mediterranean; Piracy; Venetians

Fā'ida, 281
Famagusta, 24
Faraj, Sultan, 26, 167
Faqīr al-Ḥarīriyya, 102
Fatwā, 134, 287
al-Fayyūm, 28
Fez, 268, 276
Fiefs, 286. *See also* Iqṭā'
Fire protection, 66
Florence, 34, 216
Forced labor, *see* Corvée
Forced purchases, 36, 40, 53, 56-59, 62, 118, 120, 125, 127, 146-47, 244, 258, 267
Forests, 67, 127, 261
Fortifications, *see* Aleppo; Cairo; Damascus
Foundries, 65, 260
Franks, 12, 152, 164. *See also* Europeans
Fraternal associations, *see Ḥarāfīsh*; Sufis; *Zu'ar*
Funduq, 42, 212
al-Fuqarā', 271. *See also* Beggars; *Ḥarāfīsh*; Sufis
al-Fusqār, 87
Fuṭaym al-Akbā'ī, 155, 161
Futuwwa, 290

Gaza, 12, 39, 58, 90, 197, 245, 251, 253, 271-72
Genoa, Genoese, 23-24, 27, 33, 41, 127, 214
Gharb, emirs of, 16, 71
Ghawghā', 83, 154, 157-58, 175-76, 269
al-Ghazāliyya, 75
Ghāzān, Sultan, 13, 132, 179
Ghāzī, 63
Ghūṭa, 39, 79, 91
Glass, 19-20, 33, 244, 246-47
Gold, 30, 33, 51, 83, 96, 121, 150, 245. *See also* Dinar
Goldsmiths, 83, 247, 268
Golden Horde, 244
Governors: ceremonies, 134, 286; fiscal abuses, 56-57, 94, 102, 149, 172; fortunes, 62, 172; local administration, 46, 48, 92, 96, 99, 159; market controls, 60, 275; public works, 61, 71-72, 77-78; waqf administration, 74-77; waqf endowments, 73, 195-203, 205-10. *See also* Aleppo; Cairo; Damascus; Mamluk emirs; Sultan
Grain: brokers and importers, 280-81; markets, 16-18, 51-55, 256-58; official control, 147, 275; prices, 16-17, 40, 53-54, 147; property of emirs, 51-55, 119, 129, 145; speculation and hoarding, 51-55, 120, 145-46, 179, 268. *See also* Cairo; Damascus; Egypt; Syria
Granada, 272
Greco-Roman cities, 3-4
Greeks, 247
Guilds, 4, 96-102, 145, 276, 288
Gulf of Alexandretta, 67

Ḥadīth, 211-13
Haifa, 16
Ḥalqa, 116. *See also Awlād al-nās*
Hama, 15, 34, 39, 75, 84, 132, 151-52, 177, 179, 246-47, 251-52, 272, 289
Ḥanafī, 112, 137, 280, 287
Ḥanbalī, 86, 112, 132, 137, 280
Ḥāra (plural, *ḥārāt*), 85, 94, 114, 271. *See also* Quarters
Ḥāra Masjid al-Bī', 273
Ḥarāfīsh, 106, 177-83, 271, 277, 293
Ḥaram of Mecca, 212-15
Ḥarāmī, 172
al-Ḥarāmiyya, 170-71, 174, 270, 292
Ḥārāt al-'Abīd, 158
Ḥārāt al-Kilāb, 88
von Harff, Arnold, 118
Ḥārfūsh, see Ḥarāfīsh
Ḥārim, 28
Ḥarīrī, 102, 276
Ḥarran, Ḥarrānī, 86, 112, 214, 272
Ḥās, 89
Hashish, 83-84, 106, 170, 179, 181
Hauran, 17-18, 39, 90-91, 159
Ḥawāla, 282
al-Ḥawrānī, 89, 150
Ḥaww, 89
Hebron, 57-58, 71, 87, 195, 253, 262, 271-72
Hejaz, 67
Herat, 213
Hippodrome, 62, 146, 160, 162, 260. *See also Maydān*
Ḥiṣn al-Akrād, 196
Ḥiṭṭīn, 273
Holy War, 12, 164, 243, 286
Homs, 12, 15, 50, 84, 132, 163, 177, 179, 246, 271
Hormuz, 96, 213, 215-16
Hospitals, 13, 22, 46, 73, 76, 96, 135, 196, 199, 208-10, 250, 286
Hula, 17

Hūlūgū, 91
Humayl, 155
al-Ḥurrās, 83, 270
al-Ḥusayniyya, 91, 174, 176, 293

Ibn 'Abd al-Hādī, 82
Ibn al-Nashū, 53, 146-47, 257, 289
Ibn al-Sayyid Aḥmad al-Ṣawwāf, 158
Ibn al-Shiḥna, 71
Ibn al-Tabbākh, 154-55, 157
Ibn Baṭṭūṭa, 119, 179-80
Ibn Fa'alātī, 181
Ibn Kasār, 155
Ibn Kuwayk, 121, 211-12, 274
Ibn Muflih, 132
Ibn Musallam, 121, 212
Ibn Naḥḥās, 91, 273
Ibn Rawāḥa, 119, 280
Ibn Ṣāḥib al-Bāz, 251
Ibn Sha'bān, 181
Ibn Taghrī Birdī, 132
Ibn Taymiyya, 104, 110, 113, 279
Ibn Ṭūlūn, 93, 102, 136, 183, 279
Ibn al-Ustādh, 155, 157
Imām, 111-12, 212, 279-80, 287
India, 23, 96, 123, 125-27, 211-12, 215-16, 268, 283
Indian Ocean, 42, 255
International trade, 17-19, 23-25, 40-42, 119-27, 211-13, 283-85; between Mamluk Empire and Anatolia and North, 19, 23, 41, 67, 123, 247, 255, Bagdad, 19, 246-47, Europe, 23-25, 34, 41-42, 67, 120, 125-26, India and Far East, 23, 34, 42, 96, 123, 125-27, Yemen, 23, 120-21, 123-26; Egypt-Syria trade, 17-19, 30, 34, 39, 52, 246, 253-55
Iqṭā', 46
Iran, 27, 119, 272. *See also* Persia
Iraq, 13, 33, 88, 246
Irdabb, 16, 51-52, 54, 256
Iron, 20, 33, 42, 56, 58, 67, 247
Irrigation, 28, 68-69. *See also* Water works
Islam: converts, 89, 121, 128; law, 7, 94, 109, 111, 282; Mamluk conversions, 44, 68; property rights, 140; ulama and, 107-08, 111-12, 135
Ismā'īl ibn al-Qarawānī, 155
Ismā'īl ibn Muḥammad, 122
Ismā'īlites, 243
Istanbul, 41, 67, 264, 271
Italy, Italians, 23, 34, 41, 125. *See also* Genoa; Venice
Iyās, 24, 247-48

Jabala, 57
Ja'bar, 64
Jaffa, 16, 24, 41, 245, 249
Jallāba, 281
Jamā'a, 111, 279
Jāmi', 68
al-Jāmūs, 155-56
Janab, 89
Jānam, Governor, 168
Jaqmaq, Sultan, 175, 258
Jawābir, 101
Jazīrat ibn 'Umar, 244
Jericho, 65
Jerusalem: bedouins, 87, 251, 272; grain, 245; *ḥarāfīsh,* 177-78, 181; Kurds, 272; madrasa, 195; products, 33, 247, 253; public works, 65; qadis, 113, 136, 287; quarters, 85-87, 271-73; Sufi convents, 195; taxation, 40, 57-58, 99; trade, 17; ulama, 113; waqfs, 76, 195, 197; water works, 71, 262
Jews, 5, 58, 85-86, 89-90, 174, 182, 211, 268, 271, 288, 291-92
Jidda, 97, 213-14, 284-85
Jihād, see Holy War
al-Jihat al-mufrada, 244
Jordan River, 246
Ju'aydiyya, 180, 271. *See also Ḥarāfīsh*
Judges, *see* Qadis

Kabīr, 81, 97, 154-56, 171, 173, 212-13, 215, 274
Kaffa, 127
Kalb, 165
Kara Koyunlu, 27, 32, 249
Karamān, 32, 34
Kārimī, 96, 118, 121-22, 125-26, 128, 211-13, 274, 279, 283-84. *See also* Merchants
Kasrawān, 164
Kātib al-Sirr, 137, 285, 287
Kerak, 12, 65, 73, 90, 151-52, 248, 253, 289, 291
Khānaqā, 105, 113, 195, 197-200, 202-05, 207, 209-10, 214-15, 263, 278
Khans, 38, 50, 59-60, 62, 195-98, 214, 246, 249, 254, 258, 273
al-Kharrūbī, 121, 212-13, 274
al-Khasharī, 84, 270-71
al-Khāṣṣa, 80-82, 264
al-Khaṭīb, 155, 279, 287
Khawājā, 122-23, 127-29, 197-98, 202-05, 209-10, 214-16, 274, 282, 284-85
Khizānat al-bunūd, 60, 173, 259

al-Khufarā', 83, 270
Khuṭṭ (plural, *akhṭāṭ*), 85, 271
Kitbughā, Sultan, 146
Koran, 7, 103
Koran readers, 76, 109, 111, 139, 213
Kūrānī, 171
Kurds, 12, 86-87, 90, 96, 272
Kurtbāy, Governor, 160-61

Labor, *see* Working people
al-Laṣūṣ, 270
Latakia, 41, 249-50
Law schools, 7, 111-12, 114, 117, 136-37, 186, 280
Lebanon, 16, 67, 71, 164, 243
Lumpenproletarians, 79, 82-85, 105-07, 109-10, 169-87, 268-71, 277, 292-94. *See also Awbāsh*; Beggars; Criminals; *Ghawghā'*; *Ḥarāfīsh*; *al-Ḥarāmiyya*; Slaves; Sufi; *Zu'ar*

Madhhab, *see* Law schools
Madrasa, 11-13, 25, 67, 75, 134, 139, 181, 195-214, 250, 261, 273, 278, 280
Maḥākir, 260
Maḥalla, 85, 271. *See also* Quarters
Maḥalla Jāmi' Ḥasan, 154
Maḥalla al-Qaṭā'i', 158
al-Maḥallī, 118, 121-22, 212-13, 274
Mali, 121, 212, 282
Mālik al-tujjār, 127, 284
Mālikī, 62, 104, 112, 137, 213, 287
Mamluk emirs: administrative posts, 46, 48, 98, 255, 275; assaulted, 106, 151, 174, 182; civil wars, 9, 12-13, 20-21, 25-29, 32, 36-39, 42, 56, 68, 88-89, 94, 105, 134-35, 141, 145, 151, 160-70, 173-75, 180, 183-84, 190, 243, 248-49, 251-52, 259, 269, 291-92 (*see also* Auxiliaries); clienteles, 48, 50, 64, 92, 117, 129, 159-62, 165, 167, 184, 255; commercial interests, 51-55, 58, 77, 119-122, 125, 147; control of materials, 66-68; families, 69, 74, 110, 116-17, 265; fortunes and income, 16, 36, 50-51, 62, 118, 256; grain, 51-52, 54-55, 129, 147, 188, 257; households, 46, 48, 50-51, 54, 59, 77, 84, 95, 107, 119-20, 129, 188-89, 256, 281; influence on economy, 14, 22, 50, 58-59; patronage of economy, 14, 19, 29-30, 50-51, 65, 68-69, 74, 77-78, 129, 286; plundering, 94-95, 141, 144, 149, 168-70, 190, 273; property, 54-55, 59-60, 68, 77, 100-01, 118-19, 127, 141, 275; public works, 20, 37, 48, 59-61, 63-65, 69, 73, 77-78, 189, 246; relations with common people, 144, 146, 156, 167-69, 173, 184, *ḥarāfīsh*, 178-80, 183, merchants, 129, 283-84, 286-87, ulama, 11-12, 109-110, 112, 130-31, 134-35, 138, 185, 189-91, *zu'ar*, 154-161, 173-75, 177; slave system, 6, 74, 119, 123, 187; status, 68, 80-81, 265; tax abuses, 29, 35, 40, 53, 57, 77, 126, 148-49; waqf endowment and management, 22, 48, 73-74, 77, 195-210. *See also* Governors; Sultan
Mamluk Empire: economic decline, 28-31, 33; foreign affairs, *see* Ak Koyunlu, Armenia, Anatolia, Byzantine Empire, Crusades, Cyprus, Dulghādir, Europe, India, Kara Koyunlu, Mongols, Ottomans, Rhodes, Tamerlane, Tatars, Turkoman; legitimacy, 134; navy, 35, 42, 249, 255
  Administration, 44, 46, 48, 121, 187, 243, 255; *dīwāns*, 255, 261, 277-78, 281, 283, 287; finances, 16, 245; judicial organization, *see* Qadis; postal communications, 12, 30, 124, 243; protocol, 20, 249; public treasury, 60, 65, 135, 255. *See also* Taxation
  Officials: *dawādār*, 100, 215, 286; *nāẓir al-jaysh*, 215, 285, 287; *nāẓir al-khāṣṣ*, 53, 56, 284-85, 287; scribes, 40, 44, 46, 50, 95, 121, 132, 266, 285; *shādd*, 72, 255, 261, 275-76; vizier, 52, 121, 137, 211, 255, 285-86; *wakīl*, 122, 137, 149, 215, 255, 279, 285-86. *See also* Governors; Mamluk emirs; *Muḥtasib*; Qadis; Sultan
  Personnel: *kārimī*, 128, 211-13; merchants, 98, 119, 122, 127-29, 215-16, 284-85; ulama, 46, 98, 108, 134-35, 137-38, 279, 287
  Army, 44, 46, 48; auxiliary forces, 28, 40, 92-93, 99, 116, 149, 159-64, 175, 180, 265, 290; campaigns, 149, 153, 159, 247-48; labor, 63, 66; payment, 16, 36, 46, 51, 129, 140, 149, 256-58, 286; supplies, 18, 66, 261; training, 68-69; volunteers, 12, 243, 286, 290. *See also* Aleppo; Cairo; Damascus
al-Mansīr, 170-71, 270, 292
Maqām Gate, 71, 89
al-Maqrīzī, 31, 34, 68, 85, 139, 176
Marble, 68, 75, 199, 261

Mardin, 149
Market inspectors, *see Muḥtasib*
Markets, 17, 59-60, 66, 95-96, 151-52, 167, 259, 261, 275; *'arīf* of, 163-64, 274; closures, 95, 144, 157, 266, 288; mosques and prayers in, 103, 277; ownership, 119, 195-98, 259; physical form, 114; plunder of, 169, 171, 174; taxation of, 60, 93, 98, 101, 120, 275. *See also* Aleppo; Cairo; Damascus; Merchants
Maronites, 86
Mashā'iliyya, 83, 270
Matjar (plural, *matājir*), *see* Sultan, merchants in bureaucracy
al-Maydān al-Akhḍar, 62, 88
Maydān al-Ḥaṣā, 88, 154-58, 160, 165-66
al-Mazābil, 88, 154, 157-58
Mecca, 38, 65, 76, 96, 126-27, 177, 211-15, 261
Medina, 38, 65, 76, 261
Mediterranean, 2-3, 9, 24, 35, 40-42, 97, 101, 125, 127
Merchants (*tājir,* plural *tujjār*), 117-30; *a'yān* of, 80-81, 97, 212, 214-16, 267; banking, 120-22, 244, 282; bureaucratic posts, 98, 119, 122, 127-29, 215-16, 284-85; family ties, 117; forced purchases, 36, 56, 58, 146; fortunes, 118-19; guilds, 96-97; *ra'īs* of, 96, 125-26, 211, 274; relations with common people, 55, 91-92, 113, 153, 158, Mamluks, 48, 50, 141-42, 189-90, 255, 286-87, ulama, 108-10, 122, 279; security in trade, 37, 124-25, 174, 255, 281, 283; slave trade, 122-23; status, 80-81, 128-30, 265; taxation of, 56, 97, 101, 125, 140, 244, 275; waqf endowments, 22, 37, 59-60, 196-206, 208-10, 288. *See also Kārimī*; *Khawājā*
Tājir: al-jallāba, 281; *kabīr,* 81, 97, 212-13, 215, 274; *al-khāṣṣ,* 213-14, 282, 284-85; *khawājā,* 24, 214-16, 284; *al-mamālīk al-Sulṭāniyya,* 284; al-matjar, 282; saffār, 281; *al-Sulṭān,* 122, 127, 213, 216, 282, 284
Merinids, 247
Mesopotamia, 112, 176, 244
Metals, 17, 19, 23, 67, 127
Mint, 46
Minṭāsh, Emir, 88-89, 134, 165-67, 174-75, 177, 288
al-Mizza, 13, 79, 91, 132, 151
Mob violence, 20-21, 28, 37, 42, 53, 143-44, 173-75. *See also* Protests; Rebellions
Money, 16-17, 30, 32, 58, 120-22, 150. *See also* Coinage; Copper; Gold; Silver
Money-changers, *see Ṣayrafī*
Mongols, 9, 11-12, 14-15, 20, 23-24, 26, 70, 84, 91, 110, 112, 131-33, 163-64, 176, 179, 244-45, 271, 283, 286, 290
Monopoly, 36, 52-53, 56-58, 66-67, 126-27, 275, 283-84; spice, 36, 126-27, 283-84; sugar, 57-58, 96, 127, 284; wood, 58, 66-67
Mosques: construction, 25, 61-63, 65, 73, 199-210, 216, 249, 259; law schools and, 111-12; military training in, 134; relation to crafts, 103, 276-77; residence of the homeless, 64, 84, 177-78, 181, 269; in villages, 79, 86, 151; ulama administration of, 108, 138-39, 278
Mosul, 244
Mu'allim, 276
Mu'allim tujjār al-mamālīk, 127, 284
Mu'allimūn, 276
al-Mu'ayyad Sheikh, Sultan, 26, 32, 61, 135
Mubārak, Sheikh, 106
Mubāshir, 278
Muezzins, 76, 103, 111, 139, 279
Mufsidūn, 270
Muftī al-Ḥanbalī, 280
Muftī al-Shām, 279
Muḥaddith, 211-12, 214
Muḥammad, prophet, 7, 82, 109, 111
Muḥammad Sha'bān, Sheikh, 181
al-Muhtadī, 155
Muḥtasib, 98-100; agents, 277; attacked, 182; control of grain market, 51-54, 145-46, 275, prices, 101, 144, religious practices, 103, workers, 104; dispute over appointment, 113; fined, 118; merchants as, 98, 128, 212, 215; protection of public lands, 63; supervision of water supply, 72; taxation, 35, 40, 97, 99-100, 135, 156, 254; ulama as, 46, 108-09, 135, 138; venality, 147, 275
al-Muṣallā, 28, 155, 157
Mustashār, 273
Muta'allimūn, 276
Muta'ayyishūn, 82, 267-68
Mutasabbibūn, 82, 268
Mutaṭawwi'ūn, 290. *See also* Mamluk Empire, army, volunteers
al-Muzallaq family, 214-15, 274, 285

Nablus, 17, 39, 57, 90, 164, 245, 253, 258, 271, 273
Nafar, 101
Nahr al-Kalb, 246
Nā'ibs, 279
Naqīb al-Ashrāf, 134, 136, 279-80
al-Nās, 61, 80-82, 264-65, 267-68
al-Nashū, 56, 180, 258
al-Nāṣirī, Governor, 166
Nāṣir Muḥammad, Sultan, 20, 57, 121-22, 165, 180, 243, 248
Natron, 127, 147, 284
Nawrūz, Governor, 135, 152, 167
Nawrūz holiday, 266
Nāẓir, administrators, 125, 213, 275, 278, 280, 285-87
Nāẓir al-Jaysh, 215, 285, 287
Nāẓir al-Khāṣṣ, controller of the privy purse, 53, 56, 284-85, 287
Nile, 57, 246
Notables: common people and, 4, 7, 15, 71, 87, 159, 174, 184; families, 117; Mamluks and, 69, 116, 131, 141-42, 189; rebellions, 151, 153; status, 79-80; taxation, roles in, 58, 93, 139-40. *See also* Merchants; Ulama
Nubia, 124
Nūr al-Dīn, 136
al-Nūriyya Madrasa, 250
Nuṣayrīs, 243
al-Nuwayrī, 104

Officials, *see* Mamluk Empire, administration
Ottoman Empire: beggars, 183; census, 39, 79; conflicts with Mamluks, 9, 11, 34-35, 38, 41, 43, 92, 124, 133, 152, 159, 164, 175, 254, 261; grain trade, 257; guilds, 276; imports, 42; monopolies, 100

Palermo, 264
Palestine, 12, 21, 34-35, 39, 245, 253
Papacy, 23
Paper, 33-34, 70, 246
Patronage, *see* Clienteles; Mamluk Empire; Ulama
Peasants, 18, 28, 31, 84, 86-87, 91, 100
Peddlers, 82, 267-68
Peloponnesus, 41
Persia, Persians, 5, 19, 42, 86, 93, 169, 177, 246, 255, 280. *See also* Iran
Peter I of Cyprus, 24
Piracy, 9, 23, 26-27, 34-35, 42, 124, 134, 250, 253, 255, 283, 292
Police, 48, 83-84, 93-95, 156, 172, 270
Portuguese, 9, 40, 42
Prices, 16-17, 30-32, 40, 53-54, 58, 84, 258
Prisoners, 65, 178, 183
Prophet, descendants of, 264, 266
Prostitution, 82-83, 170, 173
Protests, 37, 42, 58, 102, 113, 140, 143-53, 254, 289. *See also* Mob violence; Rebellion
Provençals, 41
Public treasury, 60, 65, 135, 255, 259
Public works, 20, 29, 37-38, 48, 61-62, 65-66, 71-72, 77-78, 189, 259-63. See also Aleppo; Cairo; Damascus; Jerusalem; Water works

al-Qābūn, 93, 151
Qadis: bureaucratic offices, 136-37, 214-16, 285; common people and, 71, 89, 106, 113, 155, 166-67, 277; corruption, 77, 136; judicial organization, 108, 111, 137, 287; law schools and, 112, 136; Mamluks and, 117, 134-35, 166-67; mediators in popular feuds, 88, 146, 156; merchants and, 109, 128, 213-16; property rights, 62-63, 66, 260; rebellions, 151-53; religious authority, 137; salaries, 51, 76, 138-39; tax collecting, 101, 135; taxation, resisting, 140-41, 173; waqf administration, 60-61, 75, 287; waqf endowments, 37, 59, 74, 196, 198, 200-01, 203-07, 209-10
Qalāūn, Sultan, 54
Qanawāt River, 70
Qārā, 18, 246
Qar'ānī, 154
Qaṣr al-Hajjāj, 28
Qassābīn, 89
Qaṭyā, 18, 39, 121, 246, 252, 254
Qawsūn, Emir, 61, 168
Qāyitbāy, 57, 71
Qays, 88-91, 154, 165
Qayṣariyyas, 59-60, 81, 95-96, 119, 174, 195-98, 216, 252, 258-59, 282
al-Qazwīnī, 89
al-Qilījiyya Madrasa, 250
Qinṭār, 57-58
Quarries, 67, 127, 261
Quarters, 85-95, 271-74; *'arīf* of, 92, 171, 174, 273; criminal attacks, 171; defense, 94-95, 156-57, 161, 166, 273-74; developed by emirs, 73; economic specialization, 101; feuds, 39, 43, 87-89, 101, 151, 157-58, 161; Jewish, 85-86, 89-90; law schools,

112; physical form, 114; responsibility for blood money, 157, 274; sheikh of, 73, 86, 92-93, 133, 135, 141, 152, 155-56, 273; streets, terminology, 271; taxation, 40, 92-93, 95, 102, 140-41, 156, 159, 164, 272, 274, 276, 290; *zu'ar,* 154-63, 174-77. *See also* Aleppo; Cairo; Damascus
al-Qubaybāt, 28, 86-88, 93, 154, 156, 160, 259, 272
Quraysh, 155
Quṣayr, 28
Quṭr, 271
Quṭṭā' al-Ṭarīq, 270

Ra'ā', 264
Ragusans, 41
al-Raḥba, 12, 247, 251
Rahn, 282
Ra'īs: of corporations, 96; of Jews, 288; of *kārimī* merchants, 125-26, 211, 274; of *khawājās,* 214-15, 285; of Koran readers, 111; of law schools, 112, 280; of merchants, 96, 212-13; of religious functionaries, 111, 279-80; of village, 273
al-Ra'iyya (plural, *ra'āyā*), 80, 264
Ramaḍān, 21, 32
Ramla, 39, 58, 87, 136, 245-46, 251, 253, 271-72, 287
Ra's, 171, 274. *See also Ra'īs*
Rasūlids, 211
Raṭl, 53, 57-58
Rebellion, 36, 39, 89, 93-94, 141, 150-53, 156-57, 159, 162, 166-67, 248, 255, 289. *See also* Mob violence; Protests
Red Sea, 125, 255
Refugees, 13-14, 84, 86-87, 90-91, 128, 132-33, 244, 271
Religious leaders, *see* Ulama
Rhodes, 27, 32, 34, 134, 164
Ribāṭ, 105, 199-201, 207
Rimāya, 56, 92-93, 258. *See also* Forced purchases; Taxation
Roman Empire, 2-4, 256, 269, 277
Rosetta, 35
Russia, 44, 122-23

al-Ṣa'ālīk, 271. *See also* Beggars
Ṣābūn, 273
al-Ṣābūniyya Madrasa, 272
Ṣadīq al-Sulṭān, 216
Ṣadr, 211-12, 285
Safad, 12, 71, 245, 253, 271-73
Safavid, 93
Ṣāḥib al-Sulṭān, 216
Ṣaḥnāyā, 91
Ṣahyūn, 28
al-Ṣa'īd, 251
al-Sā'il, 271. *See also* Beggars
Sājūr River, 70
Saladin, 9, 11
al-Ṣalībiyya, 174, 176, 293
al-Ṣāliḥiyya, 13, 79, 85-86, 88, 91, 93, 112, 132, 140, 151, 154-56, 160, 165-66, 262
Salt, 272
Samaritans, 271
Samarkand, 27, 213
Samkarī, 155
Sanqar al-Ashqar, 243
Sanitation, 48, 66, 72-73, 93, 270
Sarmīn, 17, 28, 253, 276
Sassanians, 5, 266
Sayf al-dīn Arghūn, 70
Sayf al-dīn Baydamur, 247
Sayf al-dīn Sallār, 51
Ṣayrifī, 83, 120-21, 281-82
al-Sayyid Ibrāhīm, 155
al-Sayyid Quraysh, 155
Scribes, *see* Mamluk Empire, administration
Selim, Sultan, 133
Shādd, 72, 255, 261, 275-76
Shāfi'ī, 24, 62, 86, 112, 137, 166, 213-14, 280
al-Shāghūr, 88, 93, 151, 154-61, 251
Shāh-bandar, 215, 284
Shāh Buḍa', 38
Shāh Ismā'īl, 93
Shāh Suwār, 38, 255, 283
al-Shahāb ibn al-Muḥawjib, 155
Shalāq, 89, 176-77, 272
al-Shāmiyya al-Juwāniyya Madrasa, 75
al-Sharāb-khānā, 262
Shari'a, 7, 112, 185
Sharīf, 155, 158
Shaykh, *see* Sheikh
Shaykh al-Mashāyikh, 274
Shaykh al-Shuyūkh, 105-06, 287
Shayzar, 90
Sheikh: of bedouins, 180-82; of *ḥarāfīsh,* 180-82; of Islam, 134-35, 156; of markets, 96, 99; of quarters (*ḥāra*), 73, 86, 92-93, 133, 135, 141, 152, 155-56, 273; of religious functionaries, 111-12, 135, 279-80; of Sufis, 73, 105-06, 111, 135, 137, 171, 181-82, 277; as Ulama, 37, 71, 80, 84, 88, 103-04, 109, 113, 138-39, 161, 164, 173, 213, 215, 265, 278-79; of village, 151, 273

Shi'ites, 13, 133, 171, 243
Shipbuilding, 35, 65, 249, 260
Shopkeepers, 66, 72, 82, 99, 103, 144, 154, 159, 163-64, 179, 244, 267
al-Shurṭa, 270
Shuṭṭār, 272, 290
al-Shuwayka, 165, 290
Sidon, 12, 16, 18, 249-50
Sikak, 271
Silk, 14, 18, 34, 60, 83, 102, 153, 244, 246-47, 252, 276, 284. *See also* Textiles
Silver, 30-31, 51, 83, 122, 247. *See also* Coinage; Dirhems
al-Simsār, 52, 212, 280-81. *See also* Brokers
Sinjar al-Ḥalabī, 243
Sinjar al-Jāwalī, 73
Slave: gangs, 105, 170-72, 292; labor, 65; as lumpenproletarians, 84, 169, 177, 190, 270; merchant-owned, 119; riots, 94-95, 171-72, 292-93; trade, 23, 35, 41, 44, 71, 82, 122-23, 125, 127, 254-55, 282, 284. *See also* Mamluk emirs
Soap, 17, 19, 33, 41, 57-58, 70, 245-46
Spice trade, 23, 30, 36, 41, 125-27, 254-55, 280-84. *See also* International trade; *Kārimī*
Street repairs, *see* Public works
Sufi: beggars, 55, 84, 110, 139, 178, 181-82, 271; chief sheikh, 105-06, 135, 137, 287; convents, *see Khānaqā, Ribāṭ, Zāwiya*; enforce Muslim norms, 106; fraternities, 102-03, 105-06, 181-82, 276-77; *ḥarāfīsh,* 181-82; in holy war, 164; labor on canals, 64; in Mamluk families, 69, 117; notables, 75; protests, 151; sheikhs, 73, 105-06, 111, 135, 137, 171, 181-82, 277; ulama, relations with, 104, 107, 109-10, 112, 186, 265, 279
Sugar, 19, 56-58, 100, 127, 147, 212, 247, 258, 284
Sultan: ceremonials, 99, 269; control of real estate, 63, 140, 260; economic influence, 14, 58-60, 97, 244, 256, 261; forced purchases, 40, 53, 56-58; gifts received, 178, 256; grain holding, 52-55, 147; *ḥarāfīsh,* relations, 178, 180-82; household, 44, 65-66, 84, 122, 189, 269, 281; loans, 121-22, 216, 282; mass support in civil wars, 167-68, 174; merchants, relation to, 124, 211-12, 214, 216; merchants in bureaucracy, 122, 128, 282, 284-85; monopolies, 36, 52-53, 56-58, 66-67, 126-27, 275, 283-84; officials, 46, 53, 96, 105-06, 117, 129-30, 136-37, 266-67, 276, 284; pleas and petitions, 101, 141, 145, 147, 181; property owner, 36, 46, 51, 58-60, 63, 67-68, 119, 127, 261; public works, 70-71, 246; slave trade, 123; spice monopoly, 125-27, 215, 284; suppresses rebellions, 152; taxation, 16, 35, 100, 172-73; ulama recognition, 132, 134; waqf endowments, 59, 73, 195, 197-99, 203-07; waqf property acquisitions, 61, 135; waqf regulation, 75-76; work shops, 65-67; *zu'ar,* relations with, 177. *See also* Barqūq; Barsbāy; *etc.*
Sultan Ḥasan Madrasa, 148
Sultan of *ḥarāfīsh,* 180-82
Sunni, 171
Suq, 95-96, 100, 163-64
Sūq al-Qaṣb, 262
Sūq Jaqmaq, 151
Sūq al-Ṭawāqiyyīn, 151
al-Sūqa, 82, 179, 267, 270
al-Surrāq, 270
al-Suwayqa, 154, 290. *See also* al-Shuwayka
Synagogues, 86, 169, 292
Syndics of Prophet's descendants, *see Naqīb al-Ashrāf*
Syria: agricultural decline, 90, 251; bedouins, 21, 28, 36, 39, 60, 88, 90, 92, 164, 251, 254; communal feuds, 36, 43, 90-91, 154; constructions, 65, 246, 260-61; invasions and wars, 11-12, 15, 27, 32, 35, 38, 132, 164, 183, 250-51; Mamluk civil wars, 21, 42, 166, 174, 251; postal routes, 12; refugees, 84, 128, 150, 176, 244, 271; resources, 35-36, 67; trade, 17-19, 23-24, 30, 33-34, 39, 41, 52, 67, 246-47, 253-55, 283; urban militias, 154, 159; urban quarters, 94, 150; urban rebellions, 152-53, 273. *See also individual cities*

Taghrī Birdī, Emir, 256
Taghrīwirmish, 167-69
Taḥkīr, 60, 100, 275
Ṭā'ifa (plural, *ṭawā'if*), 112, 166, 180, 272, 280
Tāj al-dīn al-Arminī, 121
Tamerlane, 9, 22, 27, 30, 64, 71, 132-33, 167, 249, 251-52

Tanam, 151
al-Ṭanbudī, 96
Tankiz, Governor, 22, 50, 59, 62, 70, 72, 75, 118, 259, 262-63
Taqy al-dīn ibn Qāḍī Ajlūn, 93
Taqy al-dīn Qāḍī Zar', 155
Ṭarḥ, 56, 258. *See also* Forced purchases
al-Ṭarḥī, 84, 270-71
Ṭarīq, 181
Tarsus, 32, 38, 159
Tatars, 9, 26-27, 30, 34, 75, 123, 132, 178, 249-50. *See also* Mongols; Tamerlane
Taxation: abolition of taxes, 167, 252, 254, 282, 288, 291, 293; abuses, 29, 35-36, 40, 53, 56-59, 77, 92-94, 99-100, 102, 126, 152, 166, 172, 252, 254, 283; collected by bedouins, 39, brokers, 36, 149, 281, 284, Mamluks and officials, 35, 40, 48, 55-56, 93, 95-96, 99-100, 125, 135, 148, 172, 188, 213, 244, 254, 275-76, 283, 285, 290, 293, *Muḥtasib,* 35, 40, 97, 99-100, 135, 156, 254, Mongols, 13, 26; collected from Christians, 288, crafts, 29, 35, 56, 267, customs, 18, 30, 39, 121, *ḥarāfīsh,* 183, Jewish community, 288, markets and trade, 35, 41, 58, 60, 92-93, 96, 98, 100-01, 120, 123, 275, merchants, 56, 97, 101, 125, 140, 244, 275, nomads, 52, quarters, 40, 92-93, 95, 102, 140-41, 156, 159, 164, 272, 274, 276, 290, vice, 60, 172-73, waqfs, 40, 77, 93, 140, 274; resistance to, 37, 93, 102, 144, 149, 153, 156-57, 162, 175, 278, 289-90; revenues, 16, 31, 59; *zu'ar* and, 156, 158, 162. *See also* Forced purchases
Templars, 65
Textiles, 14, 17-19, 29, 31, 33-34, 41-42, 51, 60, 70, 83, 102, 119, 153, 244-47, 250, 252-53, 276, 284
Thenaud, 118
Tiberias, 253
al-Ṭībī, 96
Ṭīna, 35, 255
Toreh, 272
Tortosa, 249
Trade, *see* Aleppo; Cairo; Damascus; Egypt; International trade; Spice trade; Syria
Tripoli: bedouin fighting, 90; construction, 16, 25, 73, 245; defense, 35; forced purchases, 40, 53, 57-58; governor, 134, 150-51; grain trade, 52; international trade, 41, 283; Jews, 271; monetary abuse, 150; mosques, 16, 73; *qayṣariyyas,* 196-97; quarters, 150; pirate attacks, 27, 250, 255; products, 19, 33, 247, 252-53; rebellions, 150-52; taxation, 172, 267; villages, 39
al-Tujjār, see Merchant
Turkey, 119, 172, 255. *See also* Anatolia; Ottoman Empire
Turkomans, 12, 21-22, 25-28, 32, 34, 36, 52, 87, 92, 123, 164, 169, 174, 248-49, 251, 272
Turks, 6, 44, 159-61, 175, 187. *See also* Mamluk emirs
al-Ṭuruqiyya, 267
Ṭushṭu, Emir, 180
Tyre, 16, 73, 123, 249, 282

Ulama, 107-15, 130-41; assist in taxation, 93, 135; attitude to associations, 104; banking, 120; clienteles, 111, 113, 140; defense of property rights, 62-63, 140, 288; employment in state bureaucracy, 46, 98, 108, 134-35, 137-38, 279, 287; families, 110, 117; forced purchases, 56-57; income, 138-39; instructions in religion, 103; law schools, 112-13; Mamluk regime and, 109-110, 115, 131-35, 141-42, 164, 286-87; preach holy war, 134, 164; in quarter disputes, 92, 101-02; in rebellions and protests, 13, 140-41, 150-53, 172, 191, 266; relation to artisans, 109, 278-79, bureaucrats, 108, 279, *ḥarāfīsh,* 181-82, Mamluks, 168, 187, 288, merchants, 108-09, 120, 211-16, 279, Sufis, 106, *zu'ar,* 155; status, 6-7, 80-81, 264-66, 278; syndics, chiefs, etc., 279-80; treat with invaders, 129-30, 132-33, 286; waqf administration, 74-75, 77; waqf endowments, 37, 59-60, 73, 195, 198-210
Umayyad Caliphate, 5, 88
Umayyad Mosque, *see* Damascus
'Uqayba, 13
Ustādār, 255
'Uthmān ibn Musāfir, 282

Venice, Venetians, 23-24, 27, 32, 41-42, 120, 264, 271, 273, 285
Viziers, 52, 121, 137, 211, 285-86

Wakīls, 122, 137, 149, 215, 255, 279, 285-86
Wālīs, 285. *See also* Governors
Waqf, 18, 195-98; administration, 40, 74-77, 108-09, 136, 278, 286; beneficiaries and stipendiaries, 39, 72, 75, 124, 138-39, 178, 195-98, 256, 262, 275, 287; confiscation, 60-62, 135, 140, 168; endowed by governors, 73, 195-203, 205-10, *kārimī,* 211-13, *khawājās,* 197-98, 202-05 209-10, 214, 216, Mamluk emirs, 22, 48, 59-60, 195-210, merchants, 22, 37, 59-60, 196-206, 208-10, 288, officials, 59-60, 117, 195, 197, 199, 201-02, 204, 210, qadis, 37, 59, 74, 196, 198, 200-01, 203-07, 209-10, Sultan, 59-60, 73, 195, 197-99, 203-07, ulama, 37, 59-60, 73, 195, 198-210; family interests, 74, 263; location, *see* Aleppo, Cairo, Damascus; taxation of, 40, 77, 93, 140, 149, 274
Water works, 15, 19, 22, 27, 38, 62, 64, 68-72, 178-79, 189, 249, 259-60, 262
Waẓā'if dīniyya, 279
Wazīr, see Viziers
Weapons, 19, 33, 42, 50-51, 83
Wheat, *see* Grain
Wine, 65, 82-84, 93, 106, 120, 149, 170, 173, 181
Witnesses: bureaucratic posts, 108; *kārimī* as, 211, 213; law school affiliation, 112; organized by qadis, 111, 137, 141, 287; property transfers, 61, 77, 119; status, 109, 265, 267, 287; taxation of, 36, 100
Wood, 23, 42, 56, 58, 66-67, 127, 249
Working people, 82-83, 267-68; *'arīf* of crafts, 98-99, 275; guilds, 97-105, 275-77; mobility, 109, 129-30, 153; religious practices, 103-04, 277; shopkeepers, 66, 72, 82, 99, 103, 154, 159, 163-64, 179, 244, 267; status, 82, 268-69; wages, 50, 64, 256, 261; weavers, 83, 102, 147-48, 153, 276

Yalbughā Mosque, 285
Yalbughā al-Nāṣirī, 165, 174
Yemen, 23, 120-21, 123-26, 211-13, 215, 282
Yemen (tribe), 88-90

al-Ẓāhiriyya Madrasa, 14, 62
Zakāt, 101, 211. *See also* Taxation
Zāwiya, 73, 105, 161, 197-206, 212, 278
Zu'ar, 42, 88, 143, 153-64, 173-77

PUBLICATIONS OF THE JOINT CENTER FOR URBAN STUDIES

The Joint Center for Urban Studies, a cooperative venture of the Massachusetts Institute of Technology and Harvard University, was founded in 1959 to organize and encourage research on urban and regional problems. Participants have included scholars from the fields of anthropology, architecture, business, city planning, economics, education, engineering, history, law, philosophy, political science, and sociology.

The findings and conclusions of this book are, as with all Joint Center publications, solely the responsibility of the author.

PUBLISHED BY HARVARD UNIVERSITY PRESS

The Intellectual versus the City: From Thomas Jefferson to Frank Lloyd Wright, by Morton and Lucia White, 1962
Streetcar Suburbs: The Process of Growth in Boston, 1870–1900, by Sam B. Warner, Jr., 1962
City Politics, by Edward C. Banfield and James Q. Wilson, 1963
Law and Land: Anglo-American Planning Practice, edited by Charles M. Haar, 1964
Location and Land Use: Toward a General Theory of Land Rent, by William Alonso, 1964
Poverty and Progress: Social Mobility in a Nineteenth Century City, by Stephan Thernstrom, 1964
Boston: The Job Ahead, by Martin Meyerson and Edward C. Banfield, 1966
The Myth and Reality of Our Urban Problems, by Raymond Vernon, 1966
Muslim Cities in the Later Middle Ages, by Ira Marvin Lapidus, 1967

PUBLISHED BY THE M.I.T. PRESS

The Image of the City, by Kevin Lynch, 1960
Housing and Economic Progress: A Study of the Housing Experiences of Boston's Middle-Income Families, by Lloyd Rodwin, 1961
Beyond the Melting Pot: The Negroes, Puerto Ricans, Jews, Italians, and Irish of New York City, by Nathan Glazer and Daniel Patrick Moynihan, 1963
The Historian and the City, edited by Oscar Handlin and John Burchard, 1963
The Federal Bulldozer: A Critical Analysis of Urban Renewal, 1949–1962, by Martin Anderson, 1964
The Future of Old Neighborhoods: Rebuilding for a Changing Population, by Bernard J. Frieden, 1964
Man's Struggle for Shelter in an Urbanizing World, by Charles Abrams, 1964
The View from the Road, by Donald Appleyard, Kevin Lynch, and John R. Myer, 1964
The Public Library and the City, edited by Ralph W. Conant, 1965

LIST OF PUBLICATIONS

Regional Development Policy: A Case Study of Venezuela, by John Friedmann, 1966

Urban Renewal: The Record and the Controversy, edited by James Q. Wilson, 1966

Transport Technology for Developing Regions, by Richard M. Soberman, 1966

The Joint Center also publishes monographs and reports.

HARVARD MIDDLE EASTERN STUDIES

1. *Desert Enterprise: The Middle East Oil Industry in Its Local Environment,* by David H. Finnie, 1958
2. *Middle Eastern Capitalism: Nine Essays,* by A. J. Meyer, 1959
3. *The Idea of the Jewish State,* by Ben Halpern, 1961
4. *The Agricultural Policy of Muhammad 'Alī in Egypt,* by Helen Anne B. Rivlin, 1961
5. *Egypt in Search of Political Community: An Analysis of the Intellectual and Political Evolution of Egypt, 1804–1952,* by Nadav Safran, 1961 (also a Harvard Political Study)
6. *The Economy of Cyprus,* by A. J. Meyer, with Simos Vassiliou, 1962*
7. *Entrepreneurs of Lebanon: The Role of the Business Leader in a Developing Economy,* by Yusif A. Sayigh, 1962*
8. *The Opening of South Lebanon, 1788–1840: A Study of the Impact of the West on the Middle East,* by William R. Polk, 1963
9. *The First Turkish Republic: A Case Study in National Development,* by Richard D. Robinson, 1963
10. *The Armenian Communities in Syria under Ottoman Dominion,* by Avedis K. Sanjian, 1965
11. *Muslim Cities in the Later Middle Ages,* by Ira Marvin Lapidus, 1967

* Published jointly by the Center for International Affairs and the Center for Middle Eastern Studies.